Auditing and Assurance

Auditing and Assurance

Published in 2009 by
Chartered Accountants Ireland
Chartered Accountants House
47-49 Pearse Street
Dublin 2

ISBN 978-0-903854-89-4

Copyright of publication rests in entirety with Chartered Accountants Ireland. All rights reserved. No part of this text may be reproduced or transmitted in any form or by any means, including photocopying, Internet or e-mail dissemination, without the written permission of Chartered Accountants Ireland. Such written permission must also be obtained before any part of this document is stored in a retrieval system of any nature.

This publication is designed to provide accurate and authoritative information in regard to the subject matter covered. It is provided on the understanding that Chartered Accountants Ireland is not engaged in rendering professional services. If professional advice or other expert assistance is required, the services of a competent professional should be sought.

© Chartered Accountants Ireland, 2009

Designed by Datapage, Dublin, Ireland
Printed by ColourBooks, Dublin, Ireland

CONTENTS

Preface   *xi*

PART I   THE AUDITING AND ASSURANCE ENVIRONMENT

Chapter 1   Corporate Governance and Statutory Audit   3
1.1   Defining the Term "Audit"   3
1.2   The Need for Audit and Historic Development of Auditing and Assurance   4
1.3   Types of Audit and Assurance Engagement   5
1.4   Statutory Framework   7
1.5   Regulatory Framework   10
1.6   Ethical Framework   10
1.7   Corporate Governance   11
Questions   12

Chapter 2   The Audit Process   14
2.1   Acceptance of the Audit   15
2.2   Communication with those Charged with Governance   17
2.3   Planning the Audit   18
2.4   Developing an Audit Plan   25
2.5   Timing of Audit Procedures   30
2.6   Extent of Testing   31
2.7   Documentation of Audit Plan and Strategy   32
2.8   Performing the Audit   32
2.9   Completion of the Audit   34
Appendix 2.1 – Example of an Audit Engagement Letter – Extracted from Appendix to ISA 210   39
Appendix 2.2 – The Systems-based Audit Approach   40
Questions   41

vi CONTENTS

PART II THE AUDIT AND ASSURANCE PROCESS AND EVIDENCE

Chapter 3 The Risk Assessment Process — 45
3.1 Introduction — 45
3.2 Business Risk — 46
3.3 Audit Risk — 46
3.4 Components of Audit Risk — 48
3.5 The Auditor's Approach to Assessing the Risk of Material Misstatement — 49
3.6 Risk Assessment Procedures used by the Auditor to Obtain an Understanding of the Entity — 50
3.7 Understanding the Entity and its Environment, including its Internal Control — 52
3.8 Assessing the Risks of Material Misstatement — 57
3.9 Communicating with those Charged with Governance and Management — 61
3.10 The Auditor's Response to Assessed Risks — 62
3.11 Types of Audit Procedures to be Performed — 64
3.12 Adequacy of Presentation and Disclosure — 68
3.13 Evaluating the Sufficiency and Appropriateness of Audit Evidence Obtained — 68
3.14 Documentation — 69
3.15 The Relationship between Materiality and Audit Risk — 69
Questions — 70

Chapter 4 Fraud and Compliance with Laws and Regulations (FAE Core) — 74
4.1 Introduction — 74
4.2 The Audit Approach to Fraud and Error — 76
4.3 Aggressive Earnings Management — 80
4.4 Responsibilities for Fraud and Error — 80
4.5 Discussion Among the Engagement Team — 81
4.6 Detection of Fraud – Policies and Procedures — 82
4.7 Limitations on Audit Procedures in Detecting Fraud and Error — 84
4.8 Fraud and CAATs — 85
4.9 Management Representations — 85
4.10 Duty and Right of Auditors to Report to Management and Third Parties — 86
4.11 Required Documentation Related to Detecting and Preventing Fraud — 87
4.12 The Current Environment and Fraud — 88
4.13 Steps to Prevent Corporate Fraud — 90
Questions — 90

Chapter 5 Gathering Audit Evidence — 91

- 5.1 The Concept of Audit Evidence and its Relevance to the Audit Process (ISA 500 Audit Evidence) — 91
- 5.2 What is Sufficient and Appropriate Evidence? — 92
- 5.3 What is Reliable Audit Evidence? — 92
- 5.4 Audit Assertions and Obtaining Audit Evidence — 94
- 5.5 Methods of Obtaining Audit Evidence — 96
- 5.6 Evaluating Audit Evidence — 100
- 5.7 Tests of Controls and Substantive Testing — 100
- 5.8 Substantive Testing — 103
- 5.9 Tests of Details — 104
- 5.10 Audit Sampling — 108
- 5.11 Selection of Work and Appraisal of Work of Experts — 113
- 5.12 Substantive Analytical Procedures — 116
- Questions — 120

Margin notes:
- ISA 200 – Gen Principles
- ISA 300 – Planning
- ISA 330 – Response to risks
- ISA 500 – Audit evidence
- ISA 510 – Opening balances
- ISA 520 – Analytical Proc
- ISA 530 – Sampling / Testing
- ISA 540 – Acc estimates
- ISA 620 – Experts

Chapter 6 Auditing in a Computer Environment and E-Commerce — 122

- 6.1 Introduction — 122
- 6.2 The Auditor's Approach — 123
- 6.3 Controls in a Computerised Environment — 124
- 6.4 Computer Assisted Audit Techniques (CAATs) — 128
- 6.5 E-Commerce — 131
- Questions — 132

Margin notes:
- ISA 315 – Understanding entity
- ISA 330 – Response to risks
- ISA 402 – Entities using service orgs

PART III AUDIT PROCEDURES

Chapter 7 The Audit of Tangible Fixed Assets — 141

- 7.1 What is a Tangible Fixed Asset? — 141
- 7.2 Risks Associated with Tangible Fixed Assets — 142
- 7.3 Audit Objectives and the Audit of Tangible Fixed Assets — 142
- 7.4 Developing the Audit Plan — 144
- 7.5 Substantive Procedures for the Audit of Tangible Fixed Assets — 145
- 7.6 Impairment Review — 150
- 7.7 Revaluation of Fixed Assets — 151
- 7.8 Examining Documentary Evidence — 151
- 7.9 Safeguarding Tangible Fixed Assets – The "Fixed Asset Register" — 152
- 7.10 Disclosure Requirements — 152
- Questions — 157
- Appendix 7.1 — 160

Margin notes:
- ISA 510 – Opening balances
- ISA 540 – Acc estimates
- ISA 600 – Work of another auditor
- ISA 610 – Internal audit
- ISA 620 – Experts

viii CONTENTS

Chapter 8	**The Audit of Stock and Work in Progress**	**164**
8.1	Introduction	165
8.2	Risk of Material Misstatement	166
8.3	Understanding of Controls Over Inventory	166
8.4	Design Substantive Audit Procedures in Response to the Audit Risks Identified	168
8.5	Goods Purchased Subject to "Retention/Reservation of Title"	172
8.6	Audit Procedures that Address the Assertions for Transactions and Account Balances	172
8.7	Use of CAATs in Auditing of Inventory	181
8.8	Audit Procedure Performed at Interim Dates	182
8.9	Completion of the Audit of Inventory	182
	Questions	183
	Appendix 8.1 – Extracts from Audited Financial Statements	186
Chapter 9	**The Audit of Sales and Debtors**	**187**
9.1	Background to Sales and Debtors	187
9.2	Financial Statement Assertions Surrounding the Audit of Sales and Debtors	188
9.3	The Sales System	190
9.4	Typical Components of an Efficient Sales and Debtors Cycle	195
9.5	Controls Testing Over the Sales and Accounts Receivable Cycle and Related Assertions	197
9.6	Substantive Testing	199
9.7	Substantive Analytical Procedures	200
9.8	Substantive Tests of Details	205
9.9	Comfort Obtained from Controls Testing, Substantive Analytical Review and Substantive Tests of Details	214
9.10	Loans	216
	Questions	216
	Appendix 9.1 – Extracts from Audited Financial Statements	222
Chapter 10	**The Audit of Bank and Cash**	**225**
10.1	Assess the Risk of Material Misstatement	226
10.2	Audit Procedures that Address the Assertions Above	228
10.3	Bank Accounts	231
10.4	Cash	234
	Questions	235
	Appendix 10.1 – Extracts from Audited Financial Statements	236

CONTENTS ix

Chapter 11 The Audit of Investments — 237
ISA 500 – Audit evidence
ISA 505 – External confirmations
ISA 501 – Evidence-specific items-valuation

11.1 Assess the Risk of Material Misstatement — 238
Questions — 244
Appendix 11.1 – Extracts from Audited Financial Statements — 246

Chapter 12 The Audit of Purchases and Creditors — 247
ISA 500 – Audit evidence
ISA 501 – Evidence-specific items
ISA 505 – External confirmations
ISA 520 – Analytical procedures
ISA 540 – Acc estimates

12.1 Audit of Internal Controls over Purchases and Creditors — 249
12.2 Audit of Internal Controls over Payroll — 255
12.3 Audit Work to be Performed — 258
12.4 Substantive Audit Procedures over Purchases and Creditors — 258
12.5 Search for Unrecorded Liabilities (Completeness) — 261
Questions — 264
Appendix 12.1 – Extracts from Audited Financial Statements — 268

Chapter 13 The Audit of Share Capital and Reserves — 272
ISA 500 – Audit evidence
ISA 501 – Evidence-specific items
ISA 505 – External confirmations
ISA 520 – Analytical procedures
ISA 540 – Acc estimates

13.1 What is Share Capital? — 272
13.2 What are Reserves? — 272
13.3 Audit Objectives and the Audit of Share Capital and Reserves — 273
13.4 Substantive Procedures for the Audit of Share Capital and Reserves — 273
Questions — 278
Appendix 13.1 – Extracts from Audited Financial Statements — 279

Chapter 14 Audit Work Conclusions — 282
ISA 220 – Quality controls
ISA 260 – Communication with client
ISA 320 – Materiality
ISA 501 – Evidence-specific items
ISA 520 – Analytical procedures
ISA 560 – Subsequent events
ISA 570 – Going concern
ISA 580 – Mgmt responsibilities

14.1 Final Analytical Procedures (ISA 520) — 283
14.2 Audit Differences — 284
14.3 Subsequent Events Review (ISA 560) — 286
14.4 Types of Events — 287
14.5 Provisions, Contingent Liabilities and Contingent Assets — 290
14.6 Going Concern — 292
14.7 Management Representations (ISA 580) — 296
14.8 Management Letter/Letter of Weakness — 298
14.9 Audit Conclusion — 299
Questions — 303

PART IV AUDIT REPORTING

Chapter 15 Audit Reports — 309
ISA 570 – Going concern
ISA 700 – Auditors report
ISA 701 – Modifications report
ISA 710 – Comparatives
ISA 720 – Other info in documents

15.1 Introduction — 309
15.2 Basic Aspects of the Audit Report — 311
15.3 Forming the Audit Opinion — 315
15.4 Unqualified Audit Opinion — 315

	15.5	Qualified Audit Opinion	319
	15.6	Adverse Opinion and Disclaimer	323
	15.7	Matters That Do Not Affect the Auditor's Opinion – Emphasis of Matter	327
	15.8	Qualified Audit Reports and Dividends	328
	15.9	Further Disclosures within the Auditor's Report	328
	15.10	Listed Companies – Special Provisions	329
	15.11	Other Reporting Considerations	330
	Questions		334
	Appendix 15.1 – Example of Unqualified Audit Report – Republic of Ireland Company		338
	Appendix 15.2 – Example of Unqualified Audit Report – Northern Ireland Company		340
	Appendix 15.3 – Extracts from Audited Financial Statements – Independent Auditor's Report to the Shareholders of Large Company Limited		342

Appendices

A	Past Exam Questions Reference List	345
B	Large Company Limited: *Directors' Report and Financial Statements* Year Ended 31 December 20X8	351

Solutions

	Suggested Solutions to Review Questions	413
Index		489

PREFACE

Auditing and Assurance was first published in 2008. In this Second Edition, 2009, the contents have been enhanced and expanded to include, not only the requirements of the CAP 2 Auditing and Assurance syllabus, but also that of the Final Admitting Exam (FAE) Core Auditing and Assurance syllabus Chartered Accountants Ireland. (Copies of those syllabi are available from www.charteredaccountants.ie)

A number of new content features have been introduced as follows:

- At the beginning of each chapter a checklist of relevant Professional Statements is given to help guide you towards further technical study of the topics contained in the chapter.
- At the end of each chapter a series of short self-test questions is included. This provides an opportunity for you to focus on the key topics arising in the chapter and to help you to determine whether you have fully understood the material in the text.

The text also attempts to overcome a perennial difficulty that students of auditing experience, i.e. putting the audit process into an intelligible context. As far as we can determine, none of the currently available textbooks on auditing seek to relate the audit process specifically to an organisation's financial statements. The audit process in this text is treated as a continuous discussion related directly to the final outcome (end product), i.e. the auditor's report and the attached financial statements.

This text includes a full set of financial statements (prepared using IFRS) for illustrative purposes only in **Appendix B. These financial statements are not intended as the basis for studying financial reporting.** You can in your own way relate the audit process to these financial statements upon which the external auditor has expressed an opinion. Furthermore, at the end of each chapter (where relevant), extracts are included from the financial statements to help you to focus on the typical assertions and disclosures that need to be addressed as part of your audit process.

Students in general study financial accounting and reporting under the International Financial Reporting Standards (IFRS) regime. However, while IFRS is mandatory for

PLCs, the FRS (UK–Irish GAAP) regime applies to the vast majority of companies (private) at present. For this reason, the terms used in the text are still as per FRS. As accounting students are aware of the interchangeable terms, there should be no difficulty arising from this approach.

For any student of auditing the sheer volume of knowledge required can be daunting. However, the fundamental challenge in auditing is about making sound judgements based on all the available information in a given set of circumstances. Such skill is acquired over time and through practical experience. In exam situations students are often required to make judgements as if they were experienced auditors. This textbook seeks to narrow the gap between theoretical knowledge and practical experience as much as possible.

Recommended Further Reading

Wide reading is essential to gain the fullest understanding of auditing. Accordingly, the following sources are recommended:

Journals
- *Accountancy Ireland* (published by ICAI)
- *Accountancy* (published by ICAEW)
- *Accountancy Age*
- A good daily and Sunday newspaper

Texts (latest editions)
- *Principles of External Auditing,*
  Brenda Porter, Jon Simon and David Hatherley
  3rd edition, 2008.
- *Auditing,*
  Alan Millichamp and John Taylor
  9th edition, 2008.

- *The Audit Process: Principles, Practice and Cases,*
  Iain Gray and Stuart Manson
  4th edition, 2008.

- *Modern Auditing,*
  Graham W. Cosserat
  3rd edition, 2008.

Part I

THE AUDITING AND ASSURANCE ENVIRONMENT

Chapter 1

CORPORATE GOVERNANCE AND STATUTORY AUDIT

Learning Objectives

Acquire a knowledge of how auditing developed and of the regulatory framework for ensuring quality audit and assurance services.

Chapter 1 addresses the statutory and regulatory environment in which auditors work. This topic forms the basis of Part 1 of the *CAP 2 Auditing and Assurance Proficiency Statement* and meets its learning outcomes. (The chapter should be studied in conjunction with Section 1 of your Audit and Assurance Toolkit.)

Checklist of Relevant Professional Statements

IAASB – International Framework for Assurance Engagements
ISA 200 – Objective and General Principles Governing an Audit of Financial Statements

The chapter is structured as follows:

- Defining the Term Audit
- The Need for Audit and the Historical Development of Auditing
- Types of Audit Engagement
- Statutory Framework
- Regulatory Framework
- Ethical Framework
- Corporate Governance
- Questions

1.1 Defining the Term "Audit"

Auditing is one of the key accounting disciplines and forms the backbone of many accounting practices. As trainee accountants, you will spend at least part of your training contract engaged in this discipline, as it is Chartered Accountants Ireland requirement that all trainees have a minimum level of auditing experience before they can gain their Chartered Accountancy qualification. In very simple terms, an audit involves an independent accounting firm examining financial information prepared by a client in order to verify its authenticity and accuracy.

ISA 200 (Objectives and general principles governing an audit of financial statements – ISAs discussed later in this chapter) defines the objective of a financial statement audit as follows:

> The objective of an audit of financial statements is to enable the auditor to express an opinion whether the financial statements are prepared, in all material respects, in accordance with an applicable financial reporting framework.

The term "audit" itself refers to the process undertaken by the auditor to gather and assess a range of audit evidence which will enable such an opinion to be formed and expressed by the auditor. Evidence is gathered in a number of forms and using a wide variety of methods, and these will be discussed in more detail in **Chapters 5 to 13** of this text. The topics of forming and expressing an audit opinion will be covered in **Chapters 14 and 15** respectively. In **Chapters 1 to 4** the legal and regulatory environment which impacts on auditing will be covered along with a number of key concepts which are fundamental to the entire audit process.

1.2 The Need for Audit and Historic Development of Auditing and Assurance

The need for audit has essentially been driven by the increasing separation of ownership from the management of businesses. Although it is said that some form of auditing and accounting existed in Greece as long ago as 500 BC, it was only with the industrial revolution and the growth of publicly owned companies in the 19th Century that the need for auditing really developed. The premise of a publicly owned company is that it is funded by capital raised from the selling of shares to the public. The shareholders together own the company but are not responsible for its day to day management, which is performed by a team of managers/directors employed by the company. As such the managers act as the agents of the shareholders (principals), and are responsible for the stewardship of the company. The managers should run the company with the aim of maximizing the return for the shareholders. However there may exist a conflict of interests between the personal interests of management and the interests of the shareholders (e.g. management may extract resources from the company for personal gain). As a result shareholders seek to monitor management by requiring them to prepare accounts detailing how they have used the company's resources, and shareholders gain assurance over the accuracy and legitimacy of these accounts through having them checked by an independent source – i.e. through the annual financial statement audit.

Over the years the need for audit services has increased as the numbers of users of financial statements (and other information produced by companies) have increased. Users of financial statements would commonly include the following groups: financial institutions, suppliers, customers, employees, government and the general public. All of these groups now look for the audit report as a means of gaining assurance over the financial statements. As the number of users of financial statements has increased, so too has debate over the issue of whether or not the auditor is liable for negligence to any of these users of financial statements in cases where the audit opinion is found to have been incorrect as a result of negligence on the part of the auditor. This debate continues to evolve on a case by case basis, and this area is not examinable under the CAP 2 Auditing and Assurance syllabus. In essence auditors are generally not liable to any parties other than the direct client, unless there are very specific circumstances whereby the auditor was expressly aware of the intentions of another user to place reliance on the audit report.

The last decade has seen a number of very high-profile accounting frauds including, most famously, Enron, along with World-Com, Xerox and Parmalat. These cases have resulted in a considerably increased focus on the need for a robust audit of financial statements, and there has been a number of changes in statutory and regulatory guidance over the past number of years (see further discussion below). However, it must be remembered by students that the role of the financial statement auditor does not extend to providing any assurance over the absence of fraud from financial statements. Any such assurance would have to be provided under the terms of a separate assurance engagement. The old adage of the British judge Lord Justice Lopez remains true today:

> ". . . the role of the auditor is that of a watchdog, not that of a bloodhound".

1.3 Types of Audit and Assurance Engagement

Auditing and assurance

Auditing is a specific discipline which exists within the wider discipline of assurance reporting. Assurance reporting is defined within the IFAC International Framework for Assurance Engagements:

> An "Assurance engagement" means an engagement in which a practitioner expresses a conclusion designed to enhance the degree of confidence of the intended users other than the responsible party about the outcome of the evaluation or measurement of a subject matter against criteria . . . .

The above definition is broader and less specific than the definition of an audit in 1.1. The subject matter is not confined to financial statements, and in practice can be any number of different things including both financial and non-financial information. However, a common theme to all assurance engagements, including financial statement audits, is that they all contain the following three core elements:

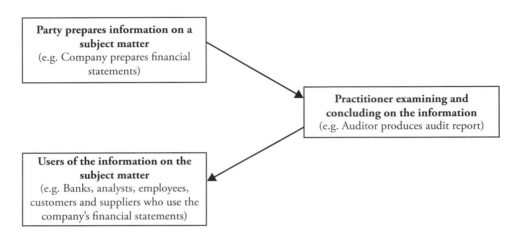

When most people think of the discipline of auditing, they most commonly associate it with the annual statutory audit of a company's financial statements (statutory requirements are discussed in more detail below). In this case, the auditor gathers evidence on the items included within the company's financial statements and then expresses an opinion on how these statements were prepared. This is the most common form of auditing in practice, and as such it is the most closely regulated, with guidance and requirements to be found in auditing standards issued by accounting bodies (e.g. International Standards on Auditing (ISAs)) and within government legislation. This regulation adds a degree of uniformity to procedures applied and reports produced in the financial statement audit. Such regulations will be discussed in more detail below.

> The CAP 2 Competency Statement outlines that the CAP 2 Auditing and Assurance paper will focus on the financial statement audit specifically, and accordingly the remainder of this text focuses on the financial statement audit process. It is, however, important for students to be aware of the existence of other types of audit and assurance engagements.

Other Types of Audit and Assurance Engagements

There is a wide range of other types of audit and assurance engagements. Each of these attracts their own specific regulatory requirements and guidance which influence the type of procedures undertaken by the auditor and the format of the reports issued. Examples of the other main types of audit and assurance engagements include the following:

- Audit of Pension Schemes
- Audit of claims for funding from grant awarding bodies
- Forensic audits to uncover frauds
- Audit of returns to industry specific regulatory bodies, e.g:
    - Banking – FSA returns
    - Travel – ATOL/ABTA returns

1.4 Statutory Framework

Generally under companies' legislation in both the Republic of Ireland and Northern Ireland all companies are required to have their annual financial statements audited. However, there are some exemptions afforded under companies' legislation which remove the requirement for audit for the annual accounts of small companies meeting certain defined criteria.

Northern Ireland

For companies registered in Northern Ireland, Paragraph 475 of the Companies Act 2006 requires all companies to have their annual accounts audited. However, Paragraph 477 states that companies which meet each of the following three criteria are exempt from this requirement:

(a) Not more than 50 employees
(b) Turnover not more than £5.6 million
(c) Balance Sheet Total not more than £2.8 million

This exemption from audit *does not apply to public companies.*

Republic of Ireland

For companies registered in the Republic of Ireland, paragraph 160 of the Companies Act 1963 requires all companies to appoint an auditor. However, Paragraph 32 of the Companies (Amendment) (No. 2) Act 1999 states that companies meeting each of three criteria are exempt from this requirement. The three criteria were subsequently updated in the Companies (Auditing and Accounting) Act 2003 and most recently in section 9 of the Investment Funds, Companies and Miscellaneous Provisions Act 2006. The current criteria are:

(a) Average number of employees not greater than 50
(b) Turnover does not exceed €7.3 million
(c) Balance Sheet Total does not exceed €3.65 million

This exemption from audit *does not apply to public companies or to companies limited by guarantee.*

Statutory responsibilities of auditors

Companies' legislation in the Republic of Ireland and Northern Ireland also sets out a number of responsibilities and duties of auditors. A key statutory responsibility for directors under both Republic of Ireland and Northern Ireland companies' legislation is the requirement to produce accounts which give a true and fair view of the state of affairs of the company. Under companies' legislation the key responsibility of the auditor is to report whether in his opinion the directors have fulfilled this requirement (Northern Ireland: Companies Act 2006 Paragraph 495 (3), Republic of Ireland: section 193 Companies Act 1990).

These areas are examined in **Chapter 15**, which looks at auditors' reports.

Statutory responsibilities of directors

Companies' legislation also sets out the responsibilities of company directors. Again the responsibilities vary somewhat between the legislation in the Republic of Ireland and in Northern Ireland. These responsibilities are set out in a statement included in the annual financial statements. Directors' responsibilities in relation to maintaining adequate standards of corporate governance are dealt with separately below.

Included are examples of directors' responsibilities in a Northern Ireland and Republic of Ireland registered company:

Northern Ireland Company – Statement of Directors' Responsibilities

The directors are responsible for preparing the directors' report and the financial statements in accordance with applicable law and regulations.

Company law requires the directors to prepare financial statements for each financial year. Under that law the directors have elected to prepare the financial statements in accordance with UK Accounting Standards.

The group and parent company financial statements are required by law to **give a true and fair view of the state of affairs of the group** and the parent company and of the profit or loss for that period.

In preparing these financial statements, the directors are required to:

- select suitable accounting policies and then apply them consistently;
- make judgments and estimates that are reasonable and prudent;
- state whether applicable UK Accounting Standards have been followed, subject to any material departures disclosed and explained in the financial statements; and
- prepare the financial statements on the going concern basis unless it is inappropriate to presume that the company will continue in business.

The directors are responsible for keeping proper accounting records that disclose with reasonable accuracy at any time the financial position of the parent company and enable them to ensure that its financial statements comply with the Companies (Northern Ireland) Order 1986. They have general responsibility for taking such steps as are reasonably open to them to safeguard the assets of the group and to prevent and detect fraud and other irregularities.

Under applicable law the directors are also responsible for preparing a directors' report that complies with that law.

Republic of Ireland Company – Statement of Directors' Responsibilities

The directors are responsible for preparing the Annual Report and company's financial statements, in accordance with applicable law and regulations.

Company law requires the Directors to prepare financial statements for each financial year. Under that law the directors have elected to prepare the financial statements in accordance with Generally Accepted Accounting Practice in Ireland, comprising applicable law and the accounting standards issued by the Accounting Standards Board and promulgated by the Institute of Chartered Accountants in Ireland.

The Company's financial statements are required by law to **give a true and fair view of the state of affairs of the Company** and of the profit or loss for that period.

In preparing those financial statements, the Directors are required to:

- select suitable accounting policies and then apply them consistently;
- make judgments and estimates that are reasonable and prudent; and
- prepare the financial statements on the going concern basis unless it is inappropriate to presume that the Company will continue in business.

The Directors are responsible for keeping proper books of account which disclose with reasonable accuracy at any time the financial position of the Company and enable them to ensure that the financial statements comply with the Companies Acts, 1963 to 2009 and with the European Communities (Undertakings for Collective Investment in Transferable Securities) Regulations, 2003. They are also responsible for safeguarding the assets of the Company. In this regard they have entrusted the assets of the Company to a trustee for safe-keeping. They have general responsibility for taking such steps as are reasonably open to them to prevent and detect fraud and other irregularities.

The directors are also responsible for preparing a Directors' Report that complies with the requirements of the Companies Acts.

1.5 Regulatory Framework

The Auditing Practices Board (APB) is responsible for issuing guidance on financial statement auditing in the UK and Ireland. The APB does this through issuing International Standards on Auditing (ISAs) on behalf of the International Federation of Accountants (IFAC).

International Standards on Auditing (ISAs) (UK and Ireland) contain basic principles and essential procedures together with related guidance in the form of explanatory and other material, including appendices. **They apply to all audits of financial statements for periods commencing on or after 15 December 2004.**

ISAs are accepted as best practice by accounting professional bodies and any auditor that does not apply these standards to an audit engagement leaves themselves open to regulatory action. ISA 200 states:

> In determining the audit procedures to be performed in conducting an audit in accordance with International Standards on Auditing, the auditor should comply with each of the International Standards on Auditing relevant to the audit.

In addition, failure to apply these standards in practice could leave the auditor open to accusations of negligence should the audit opinion they express subsequently prove to be incorrect. Reference to the fact that the audit has been carried out in accordance with ISAs is generally included within the audit report (see **Chapter 15**).

In all there are 32 ISAs, of which 14 are examinable under the CAP 2 Competency statement. The majority of these standards are covered in the remaining chapters of this textbook within the context of the various stages of the audit process. In each chapter references have been made to the applicable ISAs where relevant. Students should, however, ensure that they are familiar with the contents of each of the 14 ISAs referred to in the CAP 2 Competency statement.

1.6 Ethical Framework

In addition to issuing ISAs which govern procedures and practices to be employed during the financial statement audit process, the APB has also issued a number of Ethical Standards. Ethical Standards (ESs) contain basic principles and essential procedures to be applied by auditors in order to help protect and maintain auditors' **integrity, objectivity and independence**. These three attributes are essential to an effective audit service.

The current Ethical Standards were issued in response to growing concern over what were seen to be increasing threats to the integrity, objectivity and independence of financial statement auditors. In particular, the accounting scandal which emerged in the US energy firm Enron raised many questions in relation to the perceived lack of independence of Enron's auditors, Arthur Andersen. It was alleged that due to the level of fees earned by

Arthur Andersen from Enron (in respect of both audit and non-audit services) they were unable to remain truly independent, and this may have impacted upon their audit opinions. The scandal led to the collapse of the worldwide Arthur Andersen firm.

In total there are six Ethical Standards. Each standard is structured in a way whereby threats to integrity, objectivity and independence are identified and appropriate actions for auditors to take in response to these threats are laid out.

The six Ethical Standards are:

ES 1 (Revised) – Integrity, objectivity and independence
ES 2 (Revised) – Financial, business, employment and personal relationships
ES 3 (Revised) – Long association with the audit engagement
ES 4 (Revised) – Fees, remuneration and evaluation policies, litigation, gifts and hospitality
ES 5 (Revised) – Non-audit services provided to audit clients
ES (Revised) – Provisions Available for Small Entities

Only ES 1 – Integrity, Objectivity and Independence is examinable on the CAP 2 Competency Statement. Students should familiarize themselves with the material contained in this standard, the main topics are outlined below:

- Definition of Integrity, Objectivity and Independence
- Requirement for audit firms to establish policies and procedures to ensure maintenance of Integrity, Objectivity and Independence
- Requirement for firms to designate Ethics Partners
- Outline and definition of main types of threat to integrity, objectivity and independence:
    - Self-interest threat
    - Self-review threat
    - Management threat
    - Advocacy threat
    - Familiarity threat
    - Intimidation threat
- Engagement Quality Control Reviews

1.7 Corporate Governance

An increasingly important theme within auditing and assurance is that of corporate governance. Corporate governance is defined as:

> the system or process by which companies are directed and controlled. It is based on the principle that companies are accountable for their actions and therefore broad-based systems of accountability need to be built into the governance structures of companies.

In simple terms, Corporate governance is the means by which directors ensure that a company is adequately managed in order to protect the interests of shareholders.

Over the years a range of guidance and directives has been issued outlining best practice for company directors to ensure adequate corporate governance structures are in place. This guidance was collated into a single document – "The Combined Code on Corporate Governance", which was issued in June 2006. The Combined Code on Corporate Governance sets out standards of good practice in relation to issues such as board composition and development, remuneration, accountability and audit and relations with shareholders. **All listed companies** are required to report on their compliance with the combined code in their financial statements.

Auditors are required to review companies' statements of compliance with the combined code and report any inconsistencies they are aware of in relation to 9 specific provisions of the combined code only. The nine specific provisions which auditors must review and report on are:

- C1.1   The directors should explain their responsibility for preparing the accounts
- C2.1   The directors should, at least annually, conduct a review of the effectiveness of systems and controls and should report to shareholders that they have done so
- C3.1   The board should establish an audit committee
- C3.2   The main roles and responsibilities of the audit committee should be set out in written terms of reference
- C3.3   The terms of reference of the audit committee should be made available
- C3.4   The audit committee should review arrangements by which staff in the company can raise concerns about possible improprieties in matters of financial reporting or other matters
- C3.5   The audit committee should monitor and review the effectiveness of internal audit
- C3.6   The audit committee should have primary responsibility for appointment, re-appointment and removal of external auditors
- C3.7   The annual report should explain to shareholders how auditor objectivity and independence is maintained if the auditor provides non-audit services to the company.

Although only listed companies are required to comply with the Combined Code's principles, the principles are seen as best practice which directors of all companies should seek to follow where practicable. Auditors' requirements to review statements of compliance with the Combined Code extend only to listed companies, however.

QUESTIONS

Self-test Questions

1. What is the primary objective of an audit?

2. What is the advantage of the existence of ISAs?
3. Comment on the effect of high-profile audit failures on the reputation of the auditing profession.

Review Questions

(See Solutions to Review Questions at the end of this textbook.)

Question 1.1

Read the following passage regarding an audit client of your firm. Identify four threats to your firm's integrity, objectivity and independence and suggest what action your firm should take prior to commencing the next annual financial statement audit for this client, quoting relevant guidance.

> Your firm has been the auditor of Trafford Ltd since the company's formation 10 years ago. The company's owner and Managing Director, Arnold Ferguson, is an old school friend of an audit partner in your firm, who has also acted as the partner on the audit of Trafford Limited throughout the client's relationship with your firm. Arnold Ferguson has a reputation for being a very hands-on Managing Director, and is involved in many aspects of the business. He does not suffer fools gladly; indeed he has been known on occasion to be vocal in his castigation of underperforming staff. He has also been quite curt in the past in response to questioning from members of the audit team and does not respond well to questioning of his judgements. This approach has, however, served him well over the years, and under his leadership Trafford Limited has grown to be one of the largest manufacturers of fertiliser in Ireland. As a result of this growth, the scope of the Trafford Limited audit has grown significantly, with the audit fee growing over the years. The fee for last year's audit was some £65,000. Your firm's total fee income from audits last year was approximately £250,000. As a result of Trafford Limited's growth, Arnold Ferguson is keen to keep a close watch on internal controls. He has recently contacted your audit partner to enquire about the possibility of your firm providing internal audit services to Trafford Limited.

Question 1.2

An audit client of your firm, Istanbul Ltd, has informed you that they are considering raising funds through a stock-market flotation. You have had a meeting with the Finance Director, Rick Parry, who has explained that he is aware that Istanbul Ltd will have to look closely at improving their Corporate Governance arrangements prior to listing. Rick has asked you for some advice on the types of structures and arrangements that he needs to introduce within Istanbul Ltd.

Requirement Draft a memo to Rick explaining the types of corporate governance arrangements required of a listed company, including relevant guidance.

Chapter 2

THE AUDIT PROCESS

Learning Objectives

- To develop an overview of the stages involved in the audit process and the roles of the staff auditors at each of these stages.

Checklist of Relevant Professional Statements

ISQC	Quality Control for Firms that Perform Audits and Reviews of Historical Information and Other Assurance and Related Services Engagements
ISA 200	Objectives and General Principles Governing an Audit of Financial Statements
ISA 210	Terms of Audit Engagements
ISA 220	Quality Control for Audits of Historical Financial Information
ISA 300	Planning an Audit of Financial Statements
ISA 315	Obtaining an Understanding of the Entity and its Environment and Assessing the Risks of Material Misstatement
ISA 320	Audit Materiality
ISA 330	The Auditor's Procedures in Response to Assessed Risks
ISA 500	Audit Evidence

The Audit Process

When an audit team is engaged with a client to undertake the audit of the financial statements there are a number of phases which the audit team will move through in order to reach the end goal which is to issue an opinion on the financial statements. The audit process can be compared to a route map which gives directions and guidance for the audit team to follow throughout the audit in order to help them reach the correct final conclusion i.e. whether the financial statements reflect a true and fair view of the position of the company at the period end. The four phases involved in the performance of an audit are as follows:

1. Acceptance of the audit
2. Planning the audit
3. Performing the audit and gathering audit evidence
4. Completing the audit and issuing an audit opinion on the financial statements

For each audit undertaken the approach to phases 1, 2 and 4 will be quite similar and involve the same procedures, however, phase 3 will vary from audit to audit as the methods of gathering audit evidence are dependent on the nature of the entity's business, the internal control function and the transactions and balances included within the financial statements. Keeping this in mind, phase 2 is critical to phases 3 and 4 as, if not adequately planned, the approach to performing the audit and gathering evidence may not be suitable resulting in sufficient appropriate audit evidence not being obtained by the audit team and an incorrect audit opinion being issued. It should be remembered that the phases of the audit cycle are not stand alone, they are intricately interlinked and each phase is necessary to ensure that the audit opinion reached by the audit engagement leader is correct. The four phases are discussed below in further detail.

2.1 Acceptance of the Audit

When approached by a new client who is trying to engage the audit team for performance of an audit of the financial statements, the auditor is required to consider whether the audit firm should accept the engagement. Similarly each year in relation to existing audit clients, the auditor must consider whether the firm should continue the engagement with the client. This process for new and existing clients is known as acceptance and continuance.

As stated in ISQC 1, audit firms should establish policies and procedures for the acceptance and continuance of client relationships and specific engagements. These should be designed to provide the firm with reasonable assurance that it will only undertake or continue relationships and engagements where it:

(a) has considered the integrity of the client and does not have information that would lead it to conclude that the client lacks integrity;
(b) is competent to perform the engagement and has the capabilities, time and resources to do so, and
(c) is in compliance with ethical requirements.

These thoughts are reiterated in ISA 220 Quality Control for Audits of Historical Financial information.

The overriding theme is that an audit firm does not want to engage with a client who brings with it unacceptable levels of risk, therefore it is essential that a thorough assessment is made of the prospective engagement prior to the firm becoming engaged with the client.

Integrity of the client

With regard to the integrity of a client, the auditor should consider the following:

– the identity and business reputation of the client's principal owners, key management, related parties and those charged with its governance;

- the nature of the client's operations, including its business practices;
- information concerning the attitude of the client's principal owners, key management and those charged with its governance towards such matters as aggressive interpretation of accounting standards and the internal control environment;
- whether the client is aggressively concerned with maintaining the firm's fees as low as possible;
- indications of an inappropriate limitation in the scope of work;
- indications that the client might be involved in money laundering or other criminal activities;
- the reasons for the proposed appointment of the firm and non-reappointment of the previous firm (in the case of an initial engagement).

Information on the above areas may come from the following sources:

- Previous auditors; under ISA 300 the Auditor should communicate with the previous auditor, where there has been a change of auditors, in compliance with relevant ethical requirements;
- Bankers and legal representatives; and
- Background searches of relevant databases.

Competency of the audit firm to perform the engagement

With regard to the competency of the firm to perform the engagement, the auditor should consider whether:

- the firm's personnel have knowledge of the relevant industry or subject matters;
- the firm's personnel have experience with relevant regulatory or reporting requirements, or the ability to gain the necessary skills and knowledge effectively;
- the firm has sufficient personnel with the necessary capabilities and competences;
- experts e.g. actuaries for valuation of a pension fund, tax specialists for computation of corporation tax are available if needed;
- individuals meeting the criteria and eligibility requirements to perform engagement quality control review are available, where applicable; and
- the firm is able to complete the engagement within the reporting deadline.

Ethical considerations

With regard to ethical considerations the auditor should consider whether:

- the audit firm is independent of the client; and
- acceptance of the audit does not create an actual or perceived conflict of interest with an existing audit client.

Where issues arise out of any of the above considerations, the firm must conduct appropriate consultations with the client or third parties and, should the firm decide to engage with the client, the resolution to the issues should be documented clearly in the audit file.

Final decision

The final decision as to whether to engage with a new client or continue engaging with an existing client is the responsibility of the audit engagement leader, as outlined in ISA 200:

> The engagement partner should be satisfied that appropriate procedures regarding the acceptance and continuance of client relationships and specific audit engagements have been followed, and that conclusions reached in this regard are appropriate and have been documented (Para 14).

Where the engagement leader determines that the firm can engage successfully with the client the next stage in the initial phase of the audit process is the issuance of an engagement letter.

2.2 Communication with those Charged with Governance

Engagement letters

When an audit is accepted an engagement letter must be issued by the firm to the client. As stated in ISA 210, Terms of Audit Engagements, the auditor and the client should agree on the terms of the engagement and the terms should be recorded in writing. Issuance of an engagement letter is in the interest of the firm and the client as it helps avoid any misunderstandings with respect to the engagement. The client and the auditor should agree on all the terms of the engagement and this agreement should be recognised through the signing of the engagement letter.

Contents of the engagement letter

As outlined in ISA 210, in the UK and Ireland, the auditor should ensure that the engagement letter documents and confirms the auditor's acceptance of the appointment and includes a summary of the responsibilities of those charged with governance and of the auditor, the scope of the engagement and the form of any reports to be issued by the auditor.

The following are the main points of reference included in an engagement letter:

- The objective of the audit of financial statements;
- Management's responsibility for the financial statements;
- The scope of the audit, including reference to applicable legislation, regulations, or pronouncements of professional bodies to which the auditor adheres;
- The form of any reports or other communications of results of the engagement;
- The fact that, because of the test nature and other inherent limitations of an audit, together with the inherent limitations of internal control, there is an unavoidable risk that even some material misstatement may remain undiscovered; and
- Unrestricted access to whatever records, documentation and other information requested in connection with the audit.

See **Appendix 2.1** at the end of this chapter for a sample engagement letter.

Recurring audits

A new engagement letter may not be required each year of a continuing engagement. However, each year the auditor should consider whether circumstances require the terms of the engagement to be revised and whether there is a need to remind the client of the existing terms of the engagement (ISA 210).

Factors which could trigger the need for a new letter may include the following:

- any indication that the client misunderstands the objective and scope of the audit;
- any revised or special terms of the engagement;
- a recent change of senior management or those charged with governance;
- a significant change in ownership;
- a significant change in nature or size of the client's business; and
- legal or regulatory requirements.

In some cases the client may request a change to the terms of the engagement. Should this arise the auditor and the client should agree on the new terms, as outlined in ISA 210, provided that the auditor feels that there is reasonable justification for changing the terms. Where the auditor is unable to agree to a change of the engagement and is not permitted to continue the original engagement, the auditor should withdraw and consider whether there is any obligation, either contractual or otherwise, to report to other parties, such as those charged with governance or shareholders, the circumstances necessitating the withdrawal.

2.3 Planning the Audit

ISA 300, Planning an Audit of Financial Statements, states that the auditor should plan an audit so that the engagement will be performed in an effective manner and reduce audit risk to an acceptably low level. In order to achieve this planning an audit at two levels is necessary, with ISA 300 requiring the auditor to:

1. establish an overall audit strategy; and
2. develop an audit plan.

Engagement leaders and key audit team members should be involved in the planning phase of the audit in order to share knowledge and experience with junior team members and alert the team to areas where the assessed risk of misstatement could be high. It also helps to ensure that audit work is assigned to team members with the appropriate level of skill and experience. The nature and extent of planning activities will not be the same on all engagements and will depend on the size and complexity of the client, the auditor's previous involvement with the client and changes in circumstances that occur during the audit engagement.

It is important for the audit team to realise that planning is not a discrete activity, while it is initially completed at the commencement of the audit, planning does not cease at this point. It is a dynamic process which should continue during the entire audit cycle, being amended and adapted when new information becomes available or issues arise during the course of audit testing.

The overall audit strategy

Before the auditor can develop a detailed audit plan which outlines the testing which the audit team must perform in order to gain sufficient appropriate audit evidence, the auditor must consider a number of key factors at the outset in order to ensure that the detailed plan is the most efficient approach to the completion of the audit. This process leads to the development of the overall audit strategy which guides the detailed audit plan. Outlined below are the key areas which the auditor must consider when developing the overall audit strategy:

- the characteristics of the engagement that define its scope, such as the financial reporting framework used, industry-specific reporting requirements, the locations of the divisions within the entity
- the reporting obligations for the entity in order to determine the timing of the audit, e.g. in the UK a limited company must file company accounts with the Companies Registry within 10 months of the period end date
- key dates for communication with management and those charged with governance and the form of communications, e.g. written or oral communication
- assignment of roles and responsibilities within the audit team and consideration of whether the audit team possess suitable skills and experience to carry out the audit
- assessment of the need for the involvement of an expert e.g. where inventory is highly specialised and material to the financial statements, independent valuation by an expert may be necessary
- the determination of appropriate materiality levels to be applied when carrying out audit testing
- consideration of the risk of fraud and management override within the entity
- consideration of high risk areas within the entity i.e. areas which could be materially misstated
- identification of material balances within the financial statements
- discussion of areas where issues arose in prior year audits in order for the audit team to be alert to these areas of difficulty during the current audit
- consideration and evaluation of internal control within the entity
- consideration of experience gained during other engagements performed for the entity or during the acceptance and continuance phase
- performance of a preliminary analytical review of the financial statements
- consideration of laws and regulations which apply to the entity e.g. VAT regulations, PAYE/NIC regulations, corporation tax law, planning law, building regulations, bank and loan covenants

- identification of related parties and transactions with related parties requiring disclosure
- consideration of the entity's ability to continue as a going concern.

Information sources when developing the overall audit strategy

The auditor has a number of sources of information which can be used when developing the overall strategy for the audit, these are discussed below.

(a) **Communication with those charged with governance** A meeting is often held with management during the planning stages of the audit. The meeting provides an opportunity for the auditors to gain an understanding of the main developments in the client's business since the previous audit where the engagement is continuing or to gain an initial understanding of the business environment, internal control and corporate governance procedures if the audit is a new engagement.

(b) **Observation and Inspection** This can involve reviewing prior year working papers, inspecting legal documents, minutes of shareholder/director meetings, significant contracts or visiting the client's premises. Prior year working papers provide a vital planning tool in a recurring audit. They provide an insight into any weaknesses found in prior year audits and indicate areas of risk which should be concentrated on in the forthcoming audit. Inspecting legal documents and minutes of meetings may highlight significant events during the year e.g. the allotment of shares, acquisition of new investments or appointment of directors. They usually act as supplementary information to that gained in the preliminary planning meeting held with the client. A tour of the client's premises can help the auditor gain an understanding of the manufacturing process and the overall operations of the company.

(c) **Analytical Procedures** Preliminary analytical procedures can be used to gain an overall understanding of the financial statements of the client and to identify areas of higher risk which require special attention. Preliminary analytical procedures allow the auditor to assess the movement between current and prior period results or to compare actual results for the current period to budgeted results for the same period. Where unusual or unexpected movements are identified by the audit team during the planning phase, this alerts the team to the need to investigate and gain explanations for such movements further during the audit testing phase of the audit.

Key areas to consider when developing the overall audit strategy

Some of the key areas in the development of the overall audit strategy are the assessment of the internal control function within the entity, the determination of materiality, the concept of risk, assessment of the risks of material misstatement, developing responses to risks at financial statement and assertion levels and assigning roles and responsibilities to the audit team. These important areas are discussed in further detail below.

Assessment of the internal control function within the entity, risk assessment process and developing responses to assessed risks

ISA 315 states that the auditor must develop an understanding of the internal control function within the entity. In order to do this s/he must become aware of the controls operating within the entity and how the design and implementation of the controls prevent material misstatements from occurring or detect and correct material misstatements should they arise. The audit team should consider the following when doing this:

- Participation by those charged with governance
- Management's philosophy and operating style
- Communication and enforcement of integrity and ethical values
- Organisational structure
- Assignment of authority and responsibility
- Human resource policies and practices
- Commitment to competence.

Should the audit team have doubts surrounding the integrity of management or those charged with governance and their attitude to internal control, the potential impact on the audit should be considered as this raises the risk of management misrepresentation and fraud. Further, if doubt arises over the reliability and condition of the entity's records the audit team should consider the huge impact this could have on the audit opinion i.e. a qualified audit opinion could be the end result. At this point in determining the overall strategy the audit engagement leader should consider if it is necessary to withdraw from the engagement.

The auditor's understanding of internal control includes:

- Evaluating internal control design — are the internal control procedures, individually or in combination with other internal control procedures, capable of effectively preventing, or detecting and correcting, material misstatements?
- Determining internal control implementation — does the internal control exist and is the entity using it?

Inquiry alone is not sufficient to gain the information required by the auditor when assessing the design and implementation of the internal control function.

Risk assessment procedures are used to perform this work which include:

- Inquiring of entity personnel;
- Observing the application of specific controls and inspecting documents and reports; and
- Tracing transactions through the information system relevant to financial reporting.

If an internal control is improperly designed, determining its implementation is not necessary. Instead, the auditor should consider if it represents a material weakness in the entity's internal control. If so, it should be communicated to management and those charged with governance.

After the evaluation of internal control is performed the auditor must consider the risk of material misstatement at the financial statement and assertion levels and, where identified, develop responses to the risks. Assessment of the risks of material misstatement is directly linked to the evaluation of the internal control function within the entity. As a general assessment:

- where the internal control function is assessed to be weak, the risk of material misstatement is higher; and
- where the internal control function is assessed to be strong the misstatement will be significantly lower.

The internal control function and risk assessment process are discussed in detail in **Chapter 3**.

Determination of audit materiality levels (ISA 320)

During the planning phase the auditor must consider and determine what level of misstatement would result in the financial statements being materially misstated given that all errors identified if undisclosed will not materially change the user's view of the position of the entity at the period end. Consider the following scenarios which address simply the concept of materiality:

1. The auditor has discovered during the performance of audit testing that inventory has been understated by €/£2,500,000. The inventory balance included in the financial statements is the highest balance on the balance sheet.
2. The auditor has discovered during the performance of audit testing that the debtor's balance is overstated by €/£300. Total debtors balance at the period end is €/£2,500.

In scenario 1, if the error identified is not adjusted, the financial statements will be materially misstated due to the size of the error in relation to the financial statements taken as a whole.

In scenario 2, if the error identified is not adjusted the financial statements will not be materially misstated due to the size of the error in relation to the financial statements taken as a whole.

Misstatements are considered to be material if they, individually or in the aggregate, could reasonably be expected to influence the economic decisions of users, e.g. if the error in scenario 1 is not adjusted the economic decisions of the users will be impacted.

When a misstatement (or the aggregate of all misstatements) is significant enough to change or influence the decision of an informed person, a material misstatement has occurred.

Below this threshold, the misstatement is regarded as immaterial. For example where a misstatement of £/€200,000 is deemed to materially misstate the financial statements and affect the decisions of users, then the materiality level is deemed to be £/€200,000 and audit testing should be planned to identify errors greater than this amount individually or in aggregate.

Materiality is always a matter of professional judgement and is determined by the auditor after consideration of the needs of the user.

Materiality levels should be determined during the planning phase of the audit. The auditor should develop firstly an overall materiality level for the financial statements as a whole and secondly a materiality level for particular classes of transactions, account balances or disclosures where appropriate. This materiality level should be lower than the overall materiality level to allow for the possible existence of undetected and immaterial misstatements aggregating to a material amount. Consider the following:

- Overall materiality is defined as £/€100,000
- Total fixed asset balance is £/€85,000 and is misstated by £/€90,000
- Total prepayments balance is £/€35,000 and is misstated by £/€30,000

If overall materiality level is used neither the fixed asset balance nor the prepayments balance will be tested and a material unidentified error of £/€120,000 will not be detected. Therefore to avoid this, a lower materiality level will be established. In this scenario a suitable materiality level may be 75% of overall materiality i.e. £/€75,000. Using this lower level of materiality the fixed asset balance will be tested and will result in the misstatement of £/€90,000 being identified. The prepayment balance will still not be tested, however, the unidentified misstatement will now be £/€30,000 and will not be material to the financial statements i.e. it is lower than the overall materiality level.

There is no definite formula for calculating materiality, however, the auditor can base the materiality level on any of the following depending on the nature of the business and the key drivers within the business:

- profits – where an entity is profit orientated, e.g. 5% of profits
- net assets – where an entity is asset driven, e.g. 0.5% of net asset position
- revenues – where an entity is not for profit, e.g. 0.5% of total revenue

The materiality level should be updated for any new information gained during the audit.

During the performance of the audit, the auditor's attention will be directed towards material balances and transactions and detailed testing will be focused on these areas in order to provide evidence that the financial statements are not materially misstated.

At the conclusion of the audit, both the overall materiality and the lower amounts established for particular transactions, account balances, or disclosures will be used for evaluating the effect of identified misstatements on the financial statements and the opinion in the auditor's report. Where the total effect of identified misstatements is greater than overall materiality then, if not adjusted in the financial statements, the audit opinion may be qualified as a result of the errors arising. In contrast, where the total effect of identified misstatements is lower than overall materiality then non-adjustment for the errors in the financial statements will not impact on the overall reasonableness of the financial statements or the audit opinion.

Resourcing the audit – roles and responsibilities of audit team

As part of the planning stages of the audit the resourcing of the engagement must be considered. ISA 300 states: "The auditor should plan the nature, timing and extent of direction and supervision of engagement team members and review of their work."

An audit team usually consists of a partner, manager, audit senior and junior. The following are factors to be considered when selecting the audit team.

- Does the proposed audit team have the necessary skill levels and resources?
- Has the correct level of staff been assigned to the job i.e. manager, audit senior and audit junior(s)
- Are all staff members independent of the client?
- Is continuity of staff required? (For example, continuity of staff brings efficiencies and knowledge to the audit.)
- Has an engagement quality control reviewer been assigned?
- Is each member of the team aware of their role and responsibility within the audit team
- Have dates for audit team meetings been set to discuss:
  – Detailed audit plans and sharing information about the entity?
  – Identifying the possibility of fraud? (See Paragraph 27 of ISA 240.)
  – Engagement deadlines and timing of file reviews?
- Have dates been agreed with the client for the commencement of the audit, performance of stocktake etc.?
- If the work of experts or other auditors is to be relied on have these parties been contacted and dates agreed by which their fieldwork to is to be completed (ISA 620)?
- Has a budget been set for the audit engagement?

Role of team members

The following is a brief description of the typical role of the various team members in the audit process. Please remember that this list is not exhaustive and differences in responsibilities assigned may occur between auditing firms.

Partner:
- Acceptance and Continuance Procedures
- Primarily involved in the planning and completion stages of the audit
- Reviewing critical areas of the file

- Reviewing the financial statements prior to being issued
- Signing of audit report on financial statements

Manager:
- Review of audit file – both audit senior and juniors audit work
- Responsible for the planning of the audit – timing, nature and extent of testing
- Review of financials prior to partner review
- Review of critical matters prior to partner review
- Review of client deliverables prepared by audit senior

Audit Senior:
- Liaise with manager with regard to audit planning
- Review work of audit junior
- Notify manager of any contentious issues
- Perform audit work
- Provide on the job training for audit junior
- Prepare client deliverables and/or reports to other auditors

Audit Junior:
- Perform audit work
- Notify senior of any issues

Once the auditor has determined the overall strategy, the next step is to develop the detailed audit plan. The plan should be developed in response to various issues identified within the overall audit strategy. The detailed audit plan is discussed below.

2.4 Developing an Audit Plan

ISA 330 states that the auditor should develop an audit plan in order to reduce audit risk to an acceptably low level. The audit plan is more detailed than the overall strategy and determines the nature, timing and extent of audit procedures to be performed by the audit team in order to gain sufficient appropriate audit evidence over account balances and transactions and allow the audit firm to issue an opinion on the financial statements.

The audit plan includes the following elements:

(a) a description of the nature, timing and extent of planned risk assessment procedures sufficient to assess the risks of material misstatement
(b) a description of the nature, timing and extent of planned further audit procedures at the assertion level for each material class of transactions, accounts balance and disclosure; and
(c) other audit procedures required to be carried out for the engagement to comply with auditing and accounting standards.

The nature, timing and extent of further audit procedures should:

- Respond to the assessed risks (identified during the risk assessment process);
- Reduce audit risk to an acceptable level; and
- Respond to assessed risks of material misstatements for each material class of transactions, account balance, and disclosure.

When considering the nature of further audit procedures the audit team should take into account the areas below which will impact on the audit plan.

Nature of assessed risks

The questions below should be addressed when assessing the nature of risks:

- How significant is the assessed risk?
- How likely is the assessed risk to occur?
- What is the combined assessment of impact and likelihood?
- What assertions are affected?
- Is it a "significant risk"?
- What is management's response?
- Are there any unique characteristics?

Use of tests of controls

The auditor must decide whether it is appropriate to test the operating effectiveness of the internal control function in response to assessed risks. When doing this the following should be considered:

- Is it efficient to test internal control? The auditor should consider whether the testing of internal control would address the assessed risk for a particular assertion adequately and what substantive testing could be reduced by performing tests of controls. Where it is considered that it would not be efficient to test controls, a substantive approach should then be taken to address the risks assessed at the assertion level.
- Are there assertions that can only be addressed appropriately by tests of controls? In some cases the use of substantive procedures will not be sufficient to address the assessed risk at the assertion level. In this instance tests of controls will be necessary.

Need for unpredictability

Based on the nature of the assessed risks the auditor should consider if some of the planned procedures should be performed unannounced, changed from prior years or performed at unpredictable times.

Other basic or required audit procedures

A number of specific further audit procedures may be required (regardless of the assessed risks) to comply with the ISAs and local requirements. Examples might include attending the inventory count, external confirmations, and subsequent events' review.

Designing audit procedures to address risks

When the auditor has determined risks at the assertion level the next stage in the planning phase is to develop audit procedures in order to reduce the risk of material misstatement to an acceptably low level.

When risks are assessed the auditor must consider which financial statement assertions the risks impact on and, following on from this, the auditor must develop audit procedures which will specifically address the risk and the associated assertion.

Consider the following examples:

Assessed Risk	Assertion	Audit Procedures Designed to Address Risk at Assertion Level	Comment
All sales invoices raised may not be posted to sales ledger	Completeness	Where sales invoices are in sequential order select an invoice number and confirm that the next 100 invoices are posted to the sales ledger e.g. choose invoice number 5 and confirm that invoice numbers 6 – 105 are posted to the ledger	The audit procedure described addresses the risk that total sales per financial statements may not be complete
Debtor balances on the debtors ledger may not exist	Existence/ Occurrence	Perform a debtors circularisation to confirm existence of debtor balances	The audit procedure described addresses the risk that debtor balances on the debtors ledger may not exist

ISA 500 states that the auditor should use assertions for classes of transactions, account balances, and presentation and disclosures in sufficient detail to form a basis for the assessment of risks of material misstatement and the design and performance of further audit procedures. Therefore it is essential that the audit team considers the financial statement assertions on which identified risks impact.

The audit assertions applicable for transactions, balances and presentation and disclosure of the financial statements are shown below.

Classes of transactions

Assertion	Description
Occurrence	Transactions and events that have been recorded, have occurred, and pertain to the entity.
Completeness	All transactions and events that should be recorded, have been recorded
Accuracy	Amounts and other data relating to recorded transactions and events have been recorded appropriately.
Cut-off	Transactions and events have been recorded in the correct accounting period.

Balances

Assertion	Description
Completeness	Everything that should be recorded or disclosed in the financial statements has been included. There are no unrecorded or undisclosed assets or liabilities.
Existence	Everything that is recorded or disclosed in the financial statements exists at the appropriate date and should be included. Assets and liabilities exist, have occurred and pertain to the entity.
Rights and obligations	The entity has sufficient rights to assets included on the balance sheet and the entity has sufficient obligations to settle liabilities included on the balance sheet.
Valuation and allocation	Assets, liabilities, and equity interests are recorded in the financial statements at the appropriate amount (value). Any valuation or allocation adjustments required by their nature or applicable accounting principles have been appropriately recorded.

Presentation and disclosure

Occurrence, rights and obligations	Disclosed events, transactions, and other matters have occurred and pertain to the entity.
Completeness	All disclosures that should have been included in the financial statements have been included.

Classification and understandability	Financial information is appropriately presented and described, and disclosures are clearly expressed.
Accuracy and valuation	Financial (and other) information is disclosed fairly and at appropriate amounts.

Nature of testing

As noted above the auditor must develop and perform audit procedures to address identified risks at the assertion level. The two types of testing which can be used are as follows:

− Substantive testing
− Tests of controls.

An appropriate approach might include a combination of tests of controls and substantive testing. The auditor should consider which type of testing will address the assessed risk in the most efficient and effective manner and reduce the risk of material misstatements to an acceptably low level. When determining which combination of controls and substantive testing should be used, the auditor should give consideration to a number of factors. These are outlined below.

Nature of assertions	Certain audit procedures might: • be more appropriate for addressing some assertions than others. Evidence for completeness of sales may best be obtained through a test of controls, whereas evidence to support the valuation of inventory will probably be obtained with substantive procedures; and • provide more reliable evidence for an assertion. A confirmation of receivables to determine existence may provide better evidence than simply examining invoices or performing some analytical procedures.
Assessed level of risk	The higher the risk of misstatement, the more reliable and relevant is the audit evidence required. This can affect both the types and the combination of different types of audit procedures to be performed. For example, to ensure the existence of high value inventory, a physical inspection may be performed in addition to examining the supporting documents.
The Reasons for Risk	The underlying reasons for the risk should be considered in the design of both tests of controls and substantive procedures. This will include the characteristics of the financial statement area (inherent risks) and the internal control in place (control risk). If the assessed risk is low because of good internal control, tests of controls may reduce the need for or extent of substantive procedures.

Source of Information	If non-financial information produced by the entity's information system is used in performing audit procedures, evidence should be obtained about its accuracy and completeness. For example, the number of rental units in a high-rise apartment could be multiplied by the monthly apartment rental to compare with the total revenues recorded.
Dual Purpose Tests	Where efficient, a test of internal control could be performed concurrently with a test of details on the same transaction. An invoice could be examined for approval (test of controls) and to substantiate the transaction (test of details). If the test of details reveals a misstatement not caught by the internal control system, it might be indicative of a material weakness in internal control. Such weaknesses should be communicated to management and to those charged with governance, and the need for additional audit procedures considered. This will include updating the risk assessment and developing an appropriate audit response.

Guide to using international standards on auditing in the audits of small- and medium-sized entities (IFAC)

When these factors are considered, the auditor can then develop a testing plan which will combine the use of substantive testing and tests of controls. Both forms of testing are discussed in further detail in **Chapter 5**.

2.5 Timing of Audit Procedures

When the auditor has decided upon the audit procedures to be performed, consideration must then be given to the timing of the procedures i.e. when will the audit team carry out the testing?

Audit procedures can be performed at an interim date or at the period end. Some audit testing can only be performed at the period end e.g. attendance at period end physical inventory count, post-period end collection of debtor balances, post-period end payment of accrued expenses. However, where testing can be performed at an interim date there are some advantages:

- performing testing unannounced or at unpredictable times
- balancing the workload of the audit team
- helping to identify issues at an early stage and giving the audit team time to respond to issues.

If audit procedures are to be performed before the period end the following factors should be taken into account:

- How good is the overall control environment? Performing a roll forward between an interim date and the period end is unlikely to be effective if the general control environment is poor.
- How good are the specific controls over the account balance or class of transactions being considered?
- Is the required evidence available to perform the test? Electronic files may subsequently be overwritten or procedures to be observed may occur only at certain times.
- Would a procedure before the period end address the nature and substance of the risk involved?
- Would the interim procedure address the period or date to which the audit evidence relates?
- How much additional evidence will be required for the remaining period between the date of procedure and period end?

2.6 Extent of Testing

Extent of testing refers to the quantity (sample size) of a specific audit test to be performed. As a general rule, where the assessed risk is deemed to be high the extent of testing to be performed will be greater. The objective of the audit team is to obtain audit evidence which is sufficient and appropriate to gain comfort over the assertions surrounding the transactions, balances or disclosures which are being tested.

Sufficient appropriate audit evidence can be obtained by:

- Selecting all items (100% examination)

This is appropriate when:

- the population constitutes a small number of large value items;
- there is a significant risk and other means do not provide sufficient appropriate audit evidence; and
- CAATs can be used in a larger population to electronically test a repetitive calculation or other process.

- Selecting specific items

This is appropriate for:

- High value or key items;
- All items over a certain amount;
- Items to obtain information about matters, such as the nature of the entity, the nature of transactions, and internal control; and
- Items to test control activities.

- Selecting a representative sample of items from the population

This can be performed using judgment or statistical methods.

The decision as to how to determine sample sizes will depend on the specific circumstances of the balances and transactions being tested.

2.7 Documentation of Audit Plan and Strategy

It is important for the audit team to document each step involved in developing the overall audit strategy and the detailed audit plan, this is specified in ISA 300:

> The auditor should document the overall audit strategy and the audit plan, including any significant changes made during the audit engagement.

The auditor should document the details of the strategy and audit plan as evidence that it was completed and to record the key decisions considered necessary to properly plan the audit and to communicate significant matters to the audit team.

It is important for the audit team to realise that audit planning is a continuous process which does not cease when the overall strategy and the detailed plan are developed. Both should be updated and changed as necessary throughout the audit cycle in response to risks identified and results of audit testing performed. Reasons for significant changes should be documented along with the auditor's response to the events, conditions or results of audit procedures that resulted in such changes.

The usual means of documenting the detailed audit plan is to outline the following:

− nature of testing to be performed
− extent of testing to be performed
− assertions which testing addresses
− details of who is performing the testing
− results of testing.

Communication of the Audit Plan

It can be helpful for the audit team to communicate elements of the detailed audit plan to management or those charged with governance. This allows management to gain a greater insight into the audit process and to identify the information which the audit team will request from the entity's personnel.

2.8 Performing the Audit

After the auditor has accepted the audit engagement, developed the overall strategy and the detailed audit plan, the audit team will then be in a suitable position to carry out the audit procedures necessary to gain sufficient comfort over the financial statements. Performing the audit involves collecting and analysing quantitative (financial) and qualitative data and documenting the results.

Performing audit procedures

Audit procedures are performed in order to gain sufficient appropriate audit evidence over account balances and transactions. This is necessary in order to gain evidence over the assertions surrounding each balance and class of transaction and issue an opinion on the financial statements as a whole.

The performance of audit procedures on the financial statement areas below are discussed in the following chapters:

> Tangible Fixed Assets – Chapter 7
> Inventory – Chapter 8
> Sales and Debtors – Chapter 9
> Bank and Cash – Chapter 10
> Investments – Chapter 11
> Purchases and Creditors – Chapter 12
> Share Capital and Reserves – Chapter 13

Documentation of work performed The results of all tests completed and conclusions drawn should be documented in the audit working papers. ISA 230 gives the following guidance for documentation of all work performed:

- Documentation should be sufficiently complete and detailed to provide an overall understanding of the audit
- Information on planning the audit, the nature, timing and extent of the audit procedures performed and the results thereof, and the conclusions drawn from the audit evidence performed should each be documented
- The auditor should record in the working papers the auditor's reasoning on all significant matters which require the exercise of judgement and the auditor's conclusions
- Documentation should enable an experienced auditor, having no previous connection with the audit, to understand the following:
  (a) The nature, timing, and extent of the audit procedures performed to comply with ISAs and applicable legal and regulatory requirements;
  (b) The results of the audit procedures and the audit evidence obtained; and
  (c) Significant matters arising during the audit and the conclusions reached thereon.

The documentation of work should include the tests carried out, how the sample was chosen for testing, the results of the tests and conclusions drawn. It also should note the risks and assertions addressed and the details of by whom, and when the work was completed and reviewed.

The auditors should ensure that the documentation is stored confidentially, securely and in a place where it is easily retrievable. The confidentiality and safety of the records may be protected through the use of passwords, back-up copies of electronic files or restricted access to hard copy files.

Audit documentation may be stored electronically or through hard copy files. For ease of use and for efficiency, hard copy files can be scanned and held on electronic files.

2.9 Completion of the Audit

When the audit team has performed the audit testing as laid down in the detailed audit plan, the final stage of the audit cycle is the completion phase.

The following are the main steps involved in completing the audit:

1. Evaluate whether sufficient audit information has been obtained
2. Evaluate misstatements noted during the audit
3. Perform final analytical procedures (ISA 520)
4. Perform subsequent events review (ISA 560)
5. Consider the ability of the entity to continue as a going concern (ISA 570)
6. Report to those charged with governance
7. Form an opinion and issue a suitable audit opinion on the financial statements (ISA 700).

Evaluate whether sufficient audit information has been obtained

During the completion phase of the audit, it is essential that the auditor assesses whether adequate audit information has been obtained. According to ISA 220 before the auditor's report is issued, the engagement partner, through review of the audit documentation and discussion with the engagement team, should be satisfied that sufficient appropriate audit evidence has been obtained to support the conclusions reached and for the auditor's report to be issued.

If sufficient information has not been obtained the auditor should assess whether additional information can be obtained or whether the audit opinion may require modification. As noted in ISA 330, where the auditor has not obtained sufficient appropriate audit evidence as to a material financial statement assertion, the auditor should attempt to obtain further audit evidence. If the auditor is unable to obtain sufficient appropriate audit evidence, the auditor should express a qualified opinion or a disclaimer of opinion in the audit report.

The following factors will impact on whether the level of audit work performed is assessed as adequate:

- What is the level of misstatements noted in the audit testing completed—if there is a low level of misstatements noted then there may be a low risk that the untested balance contains misstatements.
- What are management's responses to misstatements noted? This may give an insight into the corporate governance in place in the company.
- Prior year knowledge gained – has there been a high level of misstatements noted in the past?

- Have any indications of fraud or error been noted?
- Has information obtained to date been deemed reliable?

Evaluate misstatements noted during the audit

The auditor must evaluate the impact of unadjusted misstatements identified during the audit in order to determine if the financial statements are materially misstated as a result of the errors not being adjusted in the final accounts. As stated in ISA 320:

> In evaluating whether the financial statements are prepared, in all material respects, in accordance with an applicable financial reporting framework, the auditor should assess whether the aggregate of uncorrected misstatements that have been identified during the audit is material.

The auditor must consider the overall materiality level and the total impact of the adjusted differences together. Where the total unadjusted difference is greater than the overall materiality level then it can be concluded that, as a result of errors not being adjusted in the final accounts, that the financial statements are materially misstated. In contrast, where the total unadjusted difference is below the overall materiality level then it can be concluded that the financial statements are not materially misstated as a result of errors not being adjusted in the final accounts.

Consider the following:

During the audit of company X with a year end of 31 December 2008 it was noted that rent for December 2008 of £/€100,000 was not paid until January 2009. Accrued rent had not been provided for at the year end by the client. The following correcting journal has been noted on the summary of unadjusted differences:

Dr	Rental Expenses	P&L	£/€ 100,000
Cr	Accruals	BS	£/€ 100,000

Being adjustment for rent accrual for December 2008.

Overall materiality level assessed for the audit during the planning phase was £/€50,000.

The auditor must review the summary of unadjusted differences and determine which adjustments should be made to the financial statements. In the example above, if unadjusted, the financial statements will be materially misstated, therefore it will be necessary for the adjustment to be made to the financial statements. As outlined in ISA 230, if management refuses to adjust the financial statements and the results of extended audit procedures do not enable the auditor to conclude that the aggregate of uncorrected misstatements is not material, the auditor should consider the appropriate modification to the auditor's report in accordance with ISA 700.

Perform final analytical procedures

ISA 520 states: 'The auditor should apply analytical procedures at, or near the end, of the audit when forming an overall conclusion as to whether the financial statements as a whole are consistent with the auditor's understanding of the entity.'

Final audit procedures are performed in order to check if the financial statements are consistent with the overall knowledge gained during the audit.

The following questions should be kept in mind:

1. Are the financial statements consistent with the knowledge gained during the audit?
2. Is the presentation and disclosure of items in the financial statements correct?
3. Is the impact of uncorrected misstatements on the financial statements material?

See **Chapter 14** for further details.

Perform a subsequent events review

Subsequent events refer to:

- Events occurring between period end and the date of the auditor's report - the auditor should perform audit procedures designed to obtain sufficient appropriate evidence that all events up to the date of the auditor's report that may require adjustment of, or disclosure in, the financial statements have been identified (ISA 560);
- Facts discovered after the date of the auditor's report but before the financial statements are issued – when, after the date of the auditor's report but before the financial statements are issued, the auditor becomes aware of a fact which may materially affect the financial statements, the auditor should consider whether the financial statements need amendment, should discuss the matter with management, and should take the action appropriate in the circumstances (ISA 560); and
- Facts discovered after financial statements have been issued but before the laying of the financial statements before the members or equivalent – when, after the financial statements have been issued, the auditor becomes aware of a fact which existed at the date of the auditor's report, and which, if known at that date, might have caused the auditor to modify the auditor's report, the auditor should consider whether the financial statements need revision, should discuss the matter with management, and should take the action appropriate in the circumstances (ISA 560).

In the UK and Ireland the auditor has responsibility for identifying such events and facts when considering subsequent events (ISA 560). The purpose of considering subsequent events is to determine if the impact of such events should be reflected in the financial statements and/or the audit opinion issued.

The following procedures will enable the auditor to make this assessment:

- Read the most recent minutes of shareholder meetings
- Obtain the latest set of management accounts and review for any large movements
- Inquiries with management
- Inquiries with legal counsel concerning litigation and claims.

If a matter is noted which may require the financial statements to be modified it should be discussed with management and appropriate action taken. If the matter is noted after the date of the auditor's report a new auditor's report must be issued dated not earlier than the date of the revised financial statements.

Consider the ability of the entity to continue as a going concern (ISA 570) When planning and performing audit procedures and in evaluating the results thereof, the auditor should consider the appropriateness of management's use of the going concern assumption in the preparation of the financial statements (ISA 570). The going concern assumption is a fundamental principle in the preparation of financial statements and, where an entity is assessed at the date of the signing of the audit report as a going concern, it is viewed as continuing in business for the foreseeable future. It is the responsibility of management to determine whether the entity is a going concern and the responsibility of the auditor to assess the appropriateness of management's use of the going concern assumption in the preparation of the financial statements and whether there are material uncertainties about the entity's ability to continue as a going concern that need to be disclosed in the financial statements.

Report to those charged with governance

ISA 260 states that the auditor should relate audit matters of governance interest arising from the audit of financial statements to those charged with governance of an entity.

This can take the form of written communication or face to face communication with those charged with governance of the entity.

Communication will include discussion of key findings from audit procedures performed. This could include:

- significant control issues noted during the audit;
- non-compliance with rules and regulations;
- uncorrected misstatements aggregated by the auditor during the audit that were determined by management to be immaterial, both individually and in aggregate to the financial statements as a whole;
- reasons for modification to audit report if applicable;
- any other matters which the auditor believes are of significance.

An agenda and a detailed file note should be kept on file as evidence of items discussed and the conclusions drawn.

Form an opinion and issue audit report

An audit opinion is the primary deliverable at the end of the audit. If no issues are noted an unqualified audit opinion is issued. However, in the case where sufficient audit evidence has not been obtained or it is deemed that the financial statements are not true and fair a modified opinion is issued.

ISA 320 states: "If management refuses to adjust the financial statements and the results of extended audit procedures do not enable the auditor to conclude that the aggregate of uncorrected misstatements is not material, the auditor should consider the appropriate modification to the auditor's report in accordance with ISA 701, 'Modifications to the Independent Auditor's Report'."

File completion

When the audit report is issued it indicates that the audit work is completed.

The auditor has a 60-day period after the date the audit opinion is signed to ensure that the work is documented in full on the audit file. After the 60-day period has expired information should not be deleted from the file. All audit files must be retained for a minimum of 5 years by the audit firm.

The following is a summary checklist which outlines procedures to be performed during the completion stage of the audit:

- Perform a subsequent events review
- Perform final analytical procedures
- Finalise and obtain management representations
- Finalise the management letter
- Communicate with those charged with governance
- Obtain further audit evidence for specific items from fieldwork e.g. legal case
- Complete disclosure checklist on financial statements
- Ensure file has been reviewed in accordance with audit firm policies
- Agree trial balance/management accounts to the financial statements
- Confirm wording of audit opinion
- Finalise the schedule of unadjusted differences
- Consider whether proper books of account have been kept
- Assess the findings of the audit and the impact on the audit report.

Appendix 2.1 – Example of an Audit Engagement Letter – Extracted from Appendix to ISA 210

The following letter is for use as a guide in conjunction with the considerations laid down in this ISA and will need to be adapted to individual requirements and circumstances.

To the Board of Directors or the appropriate representative of senior management:

You have requested that we audit the balance sheet of .... as of ...., and the related statements of income and cash flows for the year then ending. We are pleased to confirm our acceptance and our understanding of this engagement by means of this letter. Our audit will be made with the objective of our expressing an opinion on the financial statements.

We will conduct our audit in accordance with International Standards on Auditing (or refer to relevant national standards or practices). Those Standards require that we plan and perform the audit to obtain reasonable assurance about whether the financial statements are free of material misstatements. An audit includes examining, on a test basis, evidence supporting the amounts and disclosures in the financial statements. An audit also includes assessing the accounting principles used and significant estimates made by management, as well as evaluating the overall financial statement presentation.

Because of the test nature and other inherent limitations of an audit, together with the inherent limitations of any accounting and internal control system, there is an unavoidable risk that even some material misstatements may remain undiscovered. In addition to our report on the financial statements, we expect to provide you with a separate letter concerning any material weaknesses in accounting and internal control systems which come to our notice.

We remind you that the responsibility for the preparation of financial statements including adequate disclosure is that of the management of the company. This includes the maintenance of adequate accounting records and internal controls, the selection and application of accounting policies, and the safeguarding of the assets of the company. As part of our audit process, we will request from management written confirmation concerning representations made to us in connection with the audit.

We look forward to full cooperation with your staff and we trust that they will make available to us whatever records, documentation and other information are requested in connection with our audit. Our fees, which will be billed as work progresses, are based on the time required by the individuals assigned to the engagement plus out-of-pocket expenses. Individual hourly rates vary according to the degree of responsibility involved and the experience and skill required.

This letter will be effective for future years unless it is terminated, amended or superceded.

Please sign and return the attached copy of this letter to indicate that it is in accordance with your understanding of the arrangements for our audit of the financial statements.

XYZ & Co.

Acknowledged on behalf of ABC Company by

(signed)

....

Name and Title

Date

Appendix 2.2 – The Systems-based Audit Approach

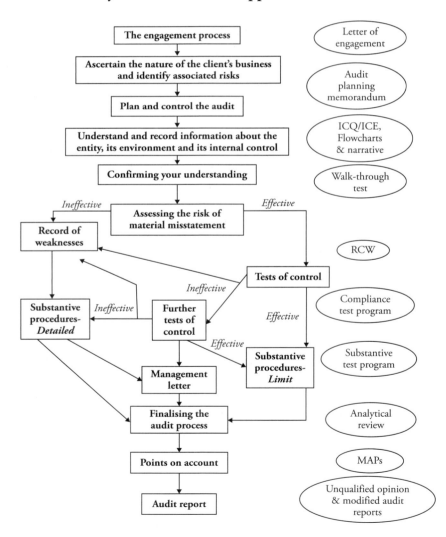

QUESTIONS

Self-test Questions

1. Why is it advisable for an auditor to investigate the integrity of the management of a proposed new audit client?
2. List 10 key areas which the auditor must consider when developing the overall audit strategy.
3. Define materiality.

Review Questions

(See Solutions to Review Questions at the end of this textbook.)

Question 2.1

Your audit firm has been asked to accept the position of auditor to CAT Ltd, as the incumbent auditor is retiring. CAT Ltd is a long established and successful large company manufacturing medicines. Your firm's first audit of the company will be for its year ended 31 December 2007 and you have been asked by the audit partner to draft an engagement letter for the audit and to begin initial planning.

Requirement

(a) Explain the procedures that an auditor should adopt before accepting an appointment.
(b) Identify the matters which should be included in a letter of engagement.

Question 2.2

You are employed by a practising firm, one of whose clients is LEOVILLE Ltd. ("LEOVILLE"), a family owned company in the textile industry. LEOVILLE has recently reached agreement with a rival company, POYFERRE Ltd ("POYFERRE"), to jointly develop and manufacture a new range of children's clothing for sale through multiple retailers. A new company, LAS CASES Ltd, will be formed for this purpose with LEOVILLE and POYFERRE each owning 50% of the share capital.

Several days ago, you accompanied the audit partner to a meeting with LEOVILLE shareholders/management at which they explained that the company would need to raise an amount of €4 million to fund its investment in LAS CASES Ltd. They propose that this will be funded entirely from debt and have already held a preliminary meeting with their bankers.

LEOVILLE has agreed with its bankers that it will make a formal presentation to them in four weeks' time in relation to this application for finance. The principal elements of the presentation will be:

- a business plan for the new venture; and
- LEOVILLE's management accounts for the six months ended 30 June, 2006.

At your meeting with LEOVILLE's management, they indicated that they required assistance from your firm in relation to both of these matters. This assistance is to include the following:

- Drafting the business plan and preparation of trading projections for the new venture for the period from 1 January, 2007 to 31 December, 2008. It is apparent that management from both LEOVILLE and POYFERRE will have significant input into drafting the plan and, in addition, you are aware that they intend to retain specialist textile industry consultants to advise on particular aspects of the venture. In essence, it seems that your firm will be involved in "project managing" the preparation of the business plan.
- As LEOVILLE's bankers have requested that the management accounts for the six months to 30 June, 2006 should be reviewed by LEOVILLE's auditors, your firm has been requested to undertake such a review as soon as possible. You understand that the bank merely wishes your firm to confirm that the management accounts have been "properly prepared".

Your firm's procedure requires that an engagement letter should be issued for all assignments, which it is asked to undertake. The audit partner has asked that you prepare a draft of this letter for his review at a meeting to be held in two days' time.

Requirement Prepare a draft engagement letter for the work which LEOVILLE Ltd has asked your firm to undertake.

Question 2.3

You are a senior working for a firm of Chartered Accountants. The partner responsible for staff training has asked you to prepare some training material on the firm's audit approach for the trainees about to join. In particular, the partner has asked you to prepare the material on your firm's approach to planning, controlling and recording of an audit in order to ensure that the trainees are aware of the high standards expected of an auditor in this area.

Requirement Prepare a memorandum to new trainees, highlighting the key points they should be aware of in:

(a) planning an audit;
(b) controlling an audit;
(c) documenting audit work.

Part II

THE AUDIT AND ASSURANCE PROCESS AND EVIDENCE

CHAPTER 3

THE RISK ASSESSMENT PROCESS

Learning Objectives

- Be familiar with the risk assessment process used at specific points in the audit process
- Develop the skill to respond to such risks to include
  - Understanding the business and related business risk
  - Understanding the system of internal control (to include evaluating the design of the controls and determining whether they have been implemented)
  - Assessing the risks of material misstatement
  - Developing overall responses to risks
  - Developing responses to risks at the assertion level.

Checklist of Relevant Professional Statements

ISA 200 – Objectives and General Principles Governing an Audit of Financial Statements
ISA 315 – Understanding the Entity and its Environment and Assessing the Risks of Material Misstatement
ISA 320 – Audit Materiality
ISA 330 – The Auditor's Procedures in Response to Assessed Risks
ISA 500 – Audit Evidence

3.1 Introduction

As discussed above, the objective of an audit of financial statements is to enable the auditor to express an opinion as to whether the financial statements give a true and fair view, in accordance with generally accepted accounting policies, of the state of the company's affairs at the reporting date. The auditor should plan and perform an audit with an attitude of professional scepticism recognizing that circumstances could exist that cause the financial statements to be materially misstated (ISA 315). In order to mitigate material misstatement the auditor must consider the risks of material misstatement arising at the assertion level and plan the audit in a manner which will reduce such risks to an acceptable level. In order to reach this stage the auditor must:

- Identify business risks affecting the entity;
- Consider the control environment within the entity including the internal control function;

- Make an assessment of the risks of material misstatement arising;
- Identify the level of audit risk arising as a result of the risk assessment process;
- Determine materiality in view of audit risk; and
- Plan the nature, timing and extent of audit procedures to be performed in order to reduce the risk of material misstatement to an acceptably low level.

3.2 Business Risk

All entities are exposed to business risks; the types of business risk will depend on the nature of the entities' trading activities and the industry which they operate in, how they are regulated, the size of the entity and complexity of operations. It is management's responsibility to consider the business risks facing the entity and respond appropriately to these risks. It is important to remember that not all business risks will translate into risks associated with the preparation of the financial statements. Ultimately the auditor is concerned only with risks that could affect the financial statements and lead to them being materially misstated.

3.3 Audit Risk

With every audit that is conducted an audit opinion is expressed on the truth and fairness of the financial statements. This opinion is issued only after the auditor has obtained sufficient appropriate audit evidence over the account balances and classes of transactions in the financial statements which provides reasonable assurance about the truth and fairness of the financial statements. The concept of reasonable assurance acknowledges that there is a risk that the audit opinion may not be appropriate. The risk that the auditor will fail to reach a proper conclusion about the company and the accounting information on which the auditor is reporting is known as "audit risk".

As stated in ISA 315, the auditor should plan and perform the audit to reduce audit risk to an acceptably low level that is consistent with the objective of an audit. In order to do this the auditor must design and carry out a detailed audit plan which provides sufficient appropriate audit evidence to allow the auditor to draw reasonable conclusions on which to base an audit opinion. When audit risk is reduced to a reasonably low level, reasonable assurance has been obtained.

Audit risk comprises:

- The risk that the financial statements are materially misstated i.e. "the risk of material misstatement"; and
- The risk that the auditor will not detect the misstatements i.e. "detection risk".

In order to respond to audit risk the auditor:

- Assesses the risk that the financial statements are materially misstated; and
- Performs audit procedures which reduce the risk of misstatements not being detected to an acceptably low level.

The overriding concern for the auditor is:

- What could possibly go wrong and what is the best way to plan the audit to reduce the risk of things going wrong to an acceptably low level?

Material misstatements

The auditor is only concerned with misstatements which ***materially*** misstate the financial statements (the concept of materiality is also discussed in this text).

In order to assess whether there are misstatements which materially impact on the financial statements taken as a whole, the auditor must consider the risk at two levels:

- The overall financial statement level; and
- The classes of transactions, account balances, and disclosures and the related assertions.

Risk of material misstatement at the overall financial statement level

The level of risk is described as follows in ISA 200:

- The risk of material misstatement that relates pervasively to the financial statements as a whole and potentially affects many assertions;
- Risks of this nature often relate to the entity's control environment;
- Risks are not necessarily identifiable with specific assertions at the class of transactions, account balance or disclosure level;
- Risks represent circumstances that increase the possibility that there could be material misstatements in any number of different assertions;
- Examples include fraud risk and the risk of management override of controls;
- The auditor's response to the assessed risk of material misstatement at this level includes consideration of the knowledge, skill and ability of personnel assigned to significant engagement responsibilities, including whether to involve experts; the appropriate levels of supervision; and whether there are any events or conditions that could cast significant doubt on the entity's ability to continue as a going concern.

The risk of material misstatement at the class of transactions, account balances, and disclosure level

This level of risk is described as follows in ISA 200:

- Risk at this level is considered in order to assist the auditor in determining the nature, timing and extent of further audit procedures at the assertion level;
- The auditor seeks to obtain sufficient appropriate audit evidence at the class of transactions, account balances, and disclosure level in such a way that enables the auditor, at the completion of the audit, to express an opinion on the financial statements taken as a whole at an acceptably low level of audit risk.

3.4 Components of Audit Risk

While audit risk is twofold as discussed above, the concept can also be broken down into the following components:

- Inherent risk
- Control risk
- Detection Risk

Inherent risk

This is the susceptibility of an assertion to a misstatement that could be material, either individually or when aggregated with other misstatements, assuming that there are no related controls (ISA 200) for example:

- Complex calculations are more likely to be misstated than simple calculations; and
- Accounting estimates, e.g. accruals, bad debt provision, inventory provision subject to significant measurement uncertainty have greater risk surrounding them than balances based on factual, routine data, e.g. bank and cash balances.

Control risk

This is the risk that a misstatement could occur in an assertion that could be material, either individually or when aggregated with other misstatements, and will not be prevented, or detected and corrected, on a timely basis by the entity's internal control (ISA 200). This risk is directly linked to the design and implementation of the entities' internal control function.

Detection risk

This is the risk that the auditor will not detect a misstatement that exists in an assertion that could be material, either individually or when aggregated with other misstatements.

Detection risk is a function of an audit procedure and of its application by the auditor (ISA 200). Detection risk cannot be reduced to zero because of the following:

- the auditor usually does not examine all of a class of transactions, account balance, or disclosure; and
- other factors including the possibility that the auditor may choose an inappropriate auditing procedure to gain assurance over an assertion, choose an appropriate procedure but use it incorrectly or interpret the results incorrectly. Such mistakes can be avoided through proper audit planning (discussed later in this chapter).

The relationship between the three components of audit risk can be summarised as follows:

- the greater the risk of material misstatement (i.e. due to inherent and control risk) the lower the level of detection risk that can be accepted i.e. as the chance of material misstatement is high, the risk that the auditor will not detect the material misstatement must be low; and
- the lower the risk of material misstatement (i.e. due to inherent and control risk) the greater the level of detection risk that can be accepted i.e. as the chance of material misstatement is low, the risk that the auditor will not detect the material misstatement can be higher.

3.5 The Auditor's Approach to Assessing the Risk of Material Misstatement

Only after the risk of material misstatement is assessed can a meaningful audit plan be developed which will provide the auditor with sufficient appropriate audit evidence to express an opinion on the financial statements. In order to do this the auditor understands the entity and the environment within which it operates:

> The auditor should obtain an understanding of the entity and its environment, including its internal control, sufficient to identify and assess the risks of material misstatement of the financial statements whether due to fraud or error and sufficient to design and perform further audit procedures. (ISA 315)

This will allow the auditor to assess the risks of material misstatement and develop an audit plan in response to these risks, for example, the findings will be used when considering the following:

- Setting an appropriate materiality level (the more risks associated with an entity the lower the level of materiality should be);
- The ability of the entity to continue as a going concern;

- Significant risk areas which need special audit consideration; and
- The appropriateness of management's oral and written representations.

The auditor should use professional judgement when assessing the level of understanding that is required of the entity and its environment with the overriding consideration being whether:

> ... the understanding that has been obtained is sufficient to assess the risks of material misstatement of the financial statements and to design and perform further audit procedures. (ISA 315)

It is important to note that the understanding that is required by the auditor is less than the understanding held by the entity's management board.

3.6 Risk Assessment Procedures used by the Auditor to Obtain an Understanding of the Entity

Obtaining an understanding of the entity is a continuous process during the audit.

The three key ways of obtaining the desired understanding are:

- Inquiries of management and others within the entity;
- Analytical Procedures; and
- Observation and inspection.

In addition to these the auditor could decide to perform other auditing procedures to help in the identification of material misstatements such as contacting external independent parties, e.g. the entity's legal representative or valuation experts used by the entity.

Inquiries of management and others within the entity

The audit team should carry out preliminary information-gathering meetings with management and other entity employees in order to gain an understanding, for example, of the following:

- the control processes in place within the entity such as the revenue and receivables, purchases and payables and treasury cycle;
- the management structure;
- instances of fraud taking place during the reporting period;
- changes in key personnel taking place during the reporting period;
- application of accounting policies within the entity;
- related parties and related party transactions taking place during the reporting period.

Inquiries of personnel other than management is also important to allow corroboration of information obtained from management and to provide the auditor with a different perspective in identifying risks of material misstatements.

Analytical procedures

The performance of analytical procedures at the beginning, during and at the end of the audit may identify unusual transactions, incorrect treatment of transactions/balances and omissions from the financial statements. When using analytical procedures as risk assessment tools the auditor develops expectations for classes of transactions and account balances based on factors such as the economic climate, changes in the entity's trading operations during the reporting period or information obtained from management. Where actual results differ significantly from expected results this may alert the auditor to areas where material misstatement might exist at the early stages of the audit for further investigation during substantive testing. Analytical procedures are discussed elsewhere in this text.

Observation and inspection

These tools of risk assessment can be used to corroborate information obtained from management and personnel. Such audit procedures include the following (ISA 315):

- observation of entity's activities and operations;
- inspection of documents and entity records, e.g. business plans, internal control manuals;
- reading reports prepared by management and those charged with governance, e.g. quarterly management accounts, monthly/annual budgets, minutes of directors'/management meetings;
- tracing transactions through the information system relevant to financial reporting–walk through testing (used often for the purpose of controls testing).

Cumulative audit knowledge and experience

For continuing audit engagements, i.e. audits which are performed annually by the auditor, information which has been obtained in prior years in relation to the entity and the environment which it operates within can be used provided that the auditor determines whether changes have occurred during the reporting period which may affect the relevance of such information in the current period audit.

Discussion among the engagement team

Prior to the commencement of the audit it is worthwhile for the audit team to discuss the potential for the entity's financial statements to be materially misstated. This discussion will allow more experienced team members such as the engagement leader and the team manager to share their knowledge of the entity, including significant risk areas and past instances of fraud or misstatement, with the rest of the team.

3.7 Understanding the Entity and its Environment, including its Internal Control

As stated in ISA 315, the auditor's understanding of the entity and its environment consists of a familiarity with:

(a) Industry, regulatory, and other external factors, including the applicable financial reporting framework.
(b) Nature of the entity, including the entity's selection and application of accounting policies.
(c) Objectives and strategies and the related business risks that could result in a material misstatement of the financial statements.
(d) Measurement and review of the entity's financial performance.
(e) Internal Control.

Focusing on each component above will provide the auditor with a detailed knowledge and understanding of the entity before assessing the risk of material misstatements and developing the audit plan.

The auditor can obtain the information necessary to gain an understanding of the entity from external and internal sources. Tables 3.1 and 3.2 below offer examples of where information can be obtained.

Table 3.1 Financial Information

Internal Sources	External Sources
• Budgets	• Industry information
• Management accounts	• Competitive intelligence
• Financial reports	• Credit rating agencies
• Financial Statements	• Creditors
• Minutes of director meetings	• Government agencies
• Income tax returns	• Franchisors
• Decisions made on accounting policies	• The media and other external parties
• Judgements and estimates	

Table 3.2 Non-Financial Information

Internal Sources	External Sources
• Vision	• Trade association data
• Mission	• Industry forecasts
• Objectives	• Government agency reports
• Strategies	• Newspaper/magazine articles
• Organisation structure	• Information on the Internet
• Minutes	
• Job descriptions	
• Operating performance	
• Business drivers	
• Capabilities	
• Policy and procedure manuals	
• Non-financial performance measures/metrics	

Guide to using International Standards on Auditing in the Audits of Small- and Medium-Sized Entities (IFAC)

In order to gain a suitable understanding of areas (a) to (d) above there are certain things which the auditor should consider. Tables 3.3 to 3.6 below consider each area in turn.

Table 3.3

(a) Industry, regulatory, and other external factors, including the applicable financial reporting framework

- Industry conditions, such as the competitive environment, supplier and customer relationships, and technological developments.
- The regulatory environment, including the applicable financial reporting framework.
- Specific risks arising from the nature of the business or the degree of regulation.
- The legal and political environment and environmental requirements affecting the industry and the entity.
- Laws or regulations that, if violated, could reasonably be expected to result in a material misstatement in the financial statements.
- Other external factors, such as general economic conditions.

Table 3.4

(b) Nature of the entity, including the entity's selection and application of accounting policies

- Entity's operations.
- Ownership and governance, including owners, family members, those charged with governance and relationships between owners and other people or entities.
- Types of investments (acquisitions, equipment, people, new products, locations, R&D, etc.) that the entity is making and plans to make.
- Entity structure (locations, subsidiaries, etc.) Complex structures may give rise to risks of material misstatement such as:
  - Allocation of goodwill and its impairment; and
  - Accounting for investments.
- How related party transactions are identified and accounted for.
- How the entity is financed.
- Are the accounting policies appropriate for the business?
- Are the accounting policies used in the relevant industry?
- Are the accounting policies consistent with the applicable financial reporting framework?
- What methods are used to account for significant and unusual transactions?
- Are there significant accounting policies in controversial or emerging areas for which there is a lack of authoritative guidance or consensus? If so, consider the effect of using such policies.
- Are there any changes in the entity's accounting policies during the period? (This includes new financial reporting standards/regulations.) If so:
  - Document the reasons and consider appropriateness; and
  - Consider consistency with requirements of the applicable financial reporting framework.
- Is there adequate disclosure of material matters in the financial statements? Consider form, arrangement and content of the financial statements and footnotes

Table 3.5

(c) Objectives and strategies and the related business risks that could result in a material misstatement of the financial statements

- Obtain a copy of any mission, vision or values statement produced by the entity (such as in promotional or web-based materials) and consider its consistency with

Table 3.5 (*Continued*)

the entity's strategy and objectives. In smaller entities, this information will not often be documented but could possibly be obtained through discussions with management and observation of how they respond to such matters.

- Identify and document the entity's strategies (that is, operational approaches by which management intends to achieve its objectives).
- Identify and document the entity's current objectives (that is, its overall plans for the entity both short-term and long-term). In smaller entities, this information will likely be obtained through inquiry of management and observation of how they respond to such matters.
- Based on the understanding obtained about mission, vision, business strategies and objectives, identify and document the related business risks.
- Business risks result from significant conditions, events, circumstances, actions or inactions that could adversely affect the entity's ability to achieve its objectives and strategies.

Table 3.6

(d) Measurement and review of the entity's financial performance

- Identify the key measures used by management to assess the entity's performance and achievement of objectives.
- Are there external parties that measure and review the entity's financial performance (regulators, franchisors, lending institutions, and so forth)? If so, consider whether copies of such reports should be obtained from the entity (for example, credit rating agency reports).
- Did the performance measures motivate management to take action to:
  - Improve the business performance?
  - Heighten risk by taking aggressive actions to achieve objectives?
  - Meet personal goals such as achieving a bonus threshold?
- Do the performance measures:
  - Highlight any unexpected results or trends?
  - Indicate trends or results consistent with the industry as a whole?
- Are the performance measures based on reliable information and precise enough to be used as a basis for analytical procedures?

Guide to using International Standards on Auditing in the Audits of Small- and Medium-Sized Entities (IFAC)

Internal control

In terms of part (e), the auditor must gain an understanding of internal control within an entity which is relevant to the audit, as directed by ISA 315. This understanding is then used to identify potential areas where misstatements could occur, consider factors that affect the risk of material misstatement and design the nature, timing and extent of further audit procedures.

As described in ISA 315:

> Internal control is the process designed and effected by those charged with governance, management, and other personnel to provide reasonable assurance about the achievement of the entity's objectives with regard to reliability of financial reporting, effectiveness and efficiency of operations and compliance with laws and regulations.

Internal control has the following components:

- The control environment;
- The entity's risk assessment process;
- The information system, including the related business processes, relevant to financial reporting, and communication;
- Control activities; and
- Monitoring of controls.

At this stage of the process the auditor must consider how the design and implementation of internal controls prevent material misstatements from occurring and if they did occur how the system would detect and correct these material misstatements. It must also be noted that this consideration by the auditor could also identify weaknesses in the internal control function. Where weaknesses are detected the risks of material misstatement will be increased. Internal Control weaknesses are discussed later in this chapter.

Internal control limitations

No matter how well internal controls are designed and implemented by the entity, they can only provide reasonable assurance over the achievement of financial reporting objectives. Possible limitations to internal control include the following:

- Human error/mistake;
- Human decision-making – the correct decision is not always made;
- Controls can be circumvented as a result of collusion by two or more people;
- Controls can be circumvented as a result of management override of control; or
- Segregation of duties is often not possible within smaller entities resulting in the reality that internal control functions may not operate in an ideal manner.

3.8 Assessing the Risks of Material Misstatement

When the auditor has obtained an understanding of the entity and its environment, including the internal control function, an assessment must be made as to the risk of material misstatement occurring at the financial statement level, and at the assertion level for classes of transactions, account balances, and disclosures. In order to make this assessment the auditor:

- Identifies risks throughout the process of obtaining an understanding of the entity and its environment, including relevant controls that relate to the risks, and by considering the classes of transaction, account balances, and disclosures in the financial statements;
- Relates the identified risks to what can go wrong at the assertion level;
- Considers whether the risks are of a magnitude that could result in a material misstatement of the financial statements; and
- Considers the likelihood that the risks could result in a material misstatement of the financial statements (ISA 315).

This assessment will dictate the nature, timing and extent of further audit procedures to be performed which will be in response to the assessed risks.

The risk assessment process should be adequately documented by the audit team and include information such as:

- Engagement team discussions on the entity's control environment;
- How the understanding has been obtained;
- Key points of the understanding obtained;
- The identified and assessed risks of material misstatement;
- Identification of significant risks which need to be specifically addressed; and
- Risks for which substantive procedures alone will not provide sufficient appropriate audit evidence.

Factors to be considered when making a risk assessment

Some of the factors which should be considered by the auditor when making a risk assessment are outlined in Table 3.7 below.

Table 3.7

What Risks have been identified?	
Financial Statement Level	• Risks resulting from poor entity level internal controls or general IT internal controls. • Significant risks.

Table 3.7 (*Continued*)

	• Risk factors relating to management override and fraud. • Risks that management has chosen to accept, such as a lack of segregation of duties in a smaller entity.

Assertion Level	• Specific risks relating to the completeness, accuracy, existence or valuation of:
	   – Revenues, expenditures, and other transactions;
	   – Account balances; and
	   – Financial statement disclosures.
	• Risks that could give rise to multiple misstatements.

Related Internal Control Procedures	• Significant risks. • The appropriately designed and implemented internal control procedures that help to prevent, detect or mitigate the risks identified. • Risks that can only be addressed by performing tests of controls.
What magnitude of misstatement (monetary impact) could possibly occur?	
Financial Statement Level	• What events, if they occurred, would result in a material misstatement in the financial statements? Consider management override, fraud, unexpected events, and past experience.
Assertion Level	Consider: • The inherent nature of the transactions, account balance or disclosure; • Routine and non-routine events; and • Past experience.
How likely is the event (risk) to occur?	
Financial Statement Level	Consider: • "Tone at the top"; • Management's approach to risk management; • Policies and procedures in place; and • Past experience.
Assertion Level	Consider: • Relevant internal control activities; and • Past experience.
Related Internal Control Procedures	Identify the elements of management's risk response that are crucial in reducing the likelihood of an event from occurring.

Guide to using International Standards on Auditing in the Audits of Small- and Medium-Sized Entities (IFAC)

Significant risks

As part of the risk assessment process within an entity, the auditor must consider each risk individually and how pervasive it could be to the financial statements. Not all risks will be of equal significance and therefore not all risks will have the potential to lead to a material misstatement in the financial statements. Risks that have the potential to impact significantly on the financial statements and which need special audit consideration as a result in order to mitigate the risk are known as "significant risks" (ISA 315).

When determining significant risks, which will arise on most audits, the auditor must use professional judgement and assess the following:

- the nature of the risk;
- the likely magnitude of the potential misstatement; and
- the likelihood of the risk occurring (ISA 315).

When considering the above points the auditor must ignore the controls in place within the entity to mitigate the risk and make an assessment which does not consider the safeguards in place against the risk.

Significant risks often relate to:

- significant transactions that are not usual for the nature of the business; and
- matters which require significant judgement.

Significant transactions that are outside the normal routine transactions of the entity give rise to the risk of incorrect processing, classification and disclosure in the financial statements.

Matters requiring significant judgement are inherently risky given that they are often very subjective in nature, represent the views of a small number of individuals e.g. the directors, and cannot be substantiated by third-party evidence.

Significant non-routine transactions and judgemental matters are often the basis of significant risks particularly in smaller entities; this is considered in the Table 3.8.

Table 3.8 Risks Relating to Non-Routine and Judgemental Matters

Subject Matter/Information	Characteristics
Significant Non-routine Transactions	• High inherent risk (likelihood and impact). • Occur infrequently. • Not subject to systematic processing.

Table 3.8 (*Continued*)

Subject Matter/Information	Characteristics

	• Unusual due to their size or nature (such as the acquisition of another entity).
	• Require management intervention:
	  – To specify accounting treatment; and
	  – For data collection and processing.
	• Involve complex calculations or accounting principles.
	• Nature of transactions makes it difficult for entity to implement effective internal controls over the risks.

Significant Judgmental Matters	• High inherent risk. • Involve significant measurement uncertainty (such as the development of accounting estimates). • Accounting principles involved may be subject to differing interpretation (such as preparation of accounting estimates or application of revenue recognition). • Required judgment may be subjective, complex, or require assumptions about the effects of future events (such as judgments about fair value, valuation of inventory subject to rapid change.

Guide to using International Standards on Auditing in the Audits of Small- and Medium-Sized Entities (IFAC)

The auditor's response to significant risks

The auditor must gain an understanding, if this has not already been obtained, of the controls designed and implemented around any significant risks identified:

> For significant risks, to the extent the auditor has not already done so, the auditor should evaluate the design of the entity's related controls, including relevant control activities, and determine whether they have been implemented (ISA 315).

Assessment of the robustness of the controls surrounding significant risks is necessary in order for the auditor to have all the information needed to develop an appropriate audit approach. As a general rule:

- Where the controls identified around significant risk areas are weak or where no controls exist, the auditor must perform appropriate substantive testing in order to mitigate the risk of material misstatement; or

- Where the controls identified around significant risk areas are strong, the level of substantive testing performed can be reduced as is deemed appropriate by the auditor.

Where it is concluded by the auditor that management have not responded appropriately to a significant risk through the design and implementation of appropriate controls, this is noted as an internal control weakness and should be communicated to those charged with governance. Communicating internal control weaknesses is discussed later in this chapter. However, at this point it is appropriate to explain that, where the control environment is weak or does not exist, and the auditor does not believe that substantive procedures alone can reduce the risk of material misstatement to an acceptably low level, then the impact of this on the audit opinion must be considered.

It is important to note also that, where controls exist around significant risks, these controls must be tested during each audit engagement by the audit team. Reliance on evidence attained in previous audits is not permitted (ISA 330).

For all significant risks identified it is essential that the auditor documents the following:

- The nature of the significant risk identified;
- Management's response to the significant risk; and
- Audit response to the significant risk i.e. audit testing to be performed to mitigate the risk of material misstatement arising as a direct result of the significant risk identified.

Examples of significant risks

Some examples of key risks which arise often on audit engagements are the following:

- fraud risk;
- management override of controls;
- revenue recognition; and
- personal expenditure of directors being included in the expenses of the company.

3.9 Communicating with those Charged with Governance and Management

The auditor should make those charged with governance or the management team aware, as soon as practicable, and at an appropriate level of responsibility, of material weaknesses in the design or implementation of internal control which have come to the auditor's attention (ISA315). This can take the form of verbal communication and/or written communication in the form of an internal control weaknesses document which outlines the following:

- the weakness identified;
- the level of risk associated with the weakness, i.e. low, moderate or high;
- suggestions as to how the control environment can be improved in order to remove the weakness.

It should be noted that the risk assessment process does not end after the initial assessment is made and communication is made to management of control weaknesses; rather the auditor must remain alert throughout the audit for additional risk areas which are identified and for evidence of internal controls not operating as intended. When this occurs the original risk assessment must be updated to reflect the new information along with the audit plan, which should be amended if necessary in response to the new risks identified.

3.10 The Auditor's Response to Assessed Risks

When the auditor has assessed the risks of material misstatement at the financial statement level, further audit procedures should be designed whose nature, timing and extent are in response to the assessed risks (ISA 330). There should be a clear link between the risks identified and the audit procedures performed to mitigate these risks. The overall aim of the auditor's response to assessed risks is to reduce audit risk to an acceptably low level.

ISA 330 states that the auditor should consider the following when designing further audit procedures:

- The significance of the risk;
- The likelihood that a material misstatement will occur;
- The characteristics of the class of transactions, account balance or disclosure involved;
- The nature of the specific controls used by the entity and in particular whether they are manual or automated;
- Whether the auditor expects to obtain audit evidence to determine if the entity's controls are effective in preventing, or detecting and correcting, material misstatements.

The nature of audit procedures used in response to assessed risks is critical in order to reduce audit risk to an acceptably low level.

Considering the nature, timing and extent of further audit procedures

Nature The nature of audit procedures refers to their purpose and their type:

Purpose:

- controls testing; and
- substantive testing.

Type:

- inspection;
- observation;

- enquiry;
- confirmation;
- recalculation;
- reperformance; or
- analytical procedures.

It is important to realise that some forms of testing are more appropriate for some assertions than for others. For example:

- controls testing is not appropriate for gaining comfort over the cut-off assertion, whereas substantive testing is appropriate;
- substantive testing is usually more appropriate than controls testing for gaining comfort over the completeness and accuracy assertions for accounting estimates such as prepayments, accruals or provisions e.g. bad debt, inventory; and
- controls testing is most responsive to the assessed risk of misstatement of the completeness assertion in relation to revenue, whereas substantive procedures are most responsive to the assessed risk of misstatement of the occurrence assertion.

When considering the nature of the testing to be performed the auditor must remain firmly focused on the risk assessment made i.e. the higher the assessed risk the more reliable and relevant the audit evidence obtained by the auditor from substantive testing must be.

Timing This simply refers to when the audit procedures are performed. Audit procedures can be performed at an interim date or at the period end and later. As a general guide the higher the assessed risk, the more likely it is that the auditor will consider it more effective to perform audit procedures nearer to and after the period end. In some circumstances, in order to introduce an element of predictability into audit testing, it is worthwhile to perform some audit procedures at an unpredictable time or unannounced. In other instances performing audit procedures before the period end can alert the auditor to significant matters at any early stage of the audit. Table 3.9 below summarises key points to consider when deciding whether to perform audit procedures at an interim date.

Table 3.9 Interim Audit Procedures

Factors to Consider	
Should Audit Procedures be Performed Before the Period End?	How good is the overall control environment? Performing a roll forward between an interim date and the period end is unlikely to be effective if the general control environment is poor.

Table 3.9 (*Continued*)

Factors to Consider
• How good are the specific controls over the account balance or class of transactions being considered? • Is the required evidence available to perform the test? Electronic files could subsequently be overwritten or procedures to be observed could occur only at certain times. • Would a procedure before the period end address the nature and substance of the risk involved? • Would the interim procedure address the period or date to which the audit evidence relates? • How much additional evidence will be required for the remaining period between the date of procedure and period end?

Guide to using International Standards on Auditing in the Audits of Small- and Medium-Sized Entities (IFAC)

It is important to remember that certain procedures can only be performed at or after the period end such as cut-off testing, unrecorded liabilities testing and post-balance sheets events testing.

Extent Extent relates to the quantity of a specific audit procedure to be performed e.g. the sample size to be used when testing client cut-off procedures, the number and value of debtor balances to be circularised or the number of observations of a control activity to be performed. The extent of the testing to be performed is determined by the judgement of the auditor after considering the following:

- materiality;
- assessed risk; and
- the degree of assurance necessary (ISA 330).

Where the assessed risk is greater, the extent of testing to be performed will be increased as appropriate. As a general rule:

- where the risk is assessed as high, the greater the extent of testing to be performed; and
- where the risk is assessed as low, the extent of testing to be performed is less.

3.11 Types of Audit Procedures to be Performed

The auditor can use tests of controls and substantive testing to reduce the assessed risk of misstatement to an acceptably low level. These types of testing are considered below.

Controls testing

When the auditor's assessment of risks of material misstatement at the assertion level includes an expectation that controls are operating effectively, the auditor should perform tests of controls to obtain sufficient appropriate audit evidence that the controls were operating effectively at relevant times during the period under audit (ISA 330).

It is not enough for the auditor to understand the entity and the control environment, the auditor must validate the information that has been obtained from management and personnel in relation to the controls operating within the entity throughout the entire period under review.

Nature of tests of controls

The auditor must obtain an understanding of the controls within the environment and then validate the controls through testing, which can include inspection, reperformance or walk through testing. Tests of controls are discussed in detail in **Chapter 5**. Some examples of tests of controls are outlined in Table 3.10 below.

Table 3.10 Examples of Tests of Controls

Internal Control Cycle	Validation
Treasury	
Bank reconciliations are performed on a monthly basis by accounts assistant and are reviewed by accounts manager.	• Inspect monthly bank reconciliations and confirm that they are being correctly prepared • Inspect reconciliations for evidence of review by the accounts manager
Accounts Receivable	
Aged debtor listings are reviewed on a monthly basis by the accounts manager and old debts are followed up.	• Inspect monthly aged debtor listings for evidence of review by the accounts manager • Obtain evidence that old debts are being chased
Sales	
(a) Sales orders are raised for each order received	• Inspect sales orders and agree details to relevant GDN and sales invoice including items delivered and quantity

Table 3.10 (*Continued*)

Internal Control Cycle	Validation
(b) Goods delivery notes are produced in duplicate when an order is filled, one copy is kept by the customer on delivery and one copy is filed at head office. GDNs are signed on receipt by the customer and the delivery person.	• Inspect GDNs for sign off by customer and delivery person
(c) When signed GDNs are returned to head office a sales invoice is raised.	• Inspect final invoice and verify that it has been posted to the sales ledger in the correct period and at the correct amount

The basic principal of controls testing is to validate the controls that are said to be in place within an entity and to confirm that they have been operating effectively throughout the entire period under review.

Timing of tests of controls

Key guidance from ISA 330 regarding the timing of tests of controls is as follows:

- When the auditor obtains audit evidence about the operating effectiveness of controls during an interim period, the auditor should determine what additional audit evidence should be obtained for the remaining period;
- If the auditor plans to use audit evidence about the operating effectiveness of controls obtained in prior audits, the auditor should obtain audit evidence about whether changes in those specific controls have occurred subsequent to the prior audit. The auditor should obtain audit evidence about whether such changes have occurred by performing inquiry in combination with observation or inspection to confirm the understanding of those specific controls;
- If the auditor plans to rely on controls that have changed since they were last tested, the auditor should test the operating effectiveness of such controls in the current audit;
- If the auditor plans to rely on controls that have not changed since they were last tested, the auditor should test the operating effectiveness of such controls at least once in every third audit;
- When there are a number of controls for which the auditor determines that it is appropriate to use audit evidence obtained in prior audits, the auditor should test the operating effectiveness of some controls at each audit;
- When, in accordance with paragraph 108 of ISA 315, the auditor has determined that an assessed risk of material misstatement at the assertion level is a significant risk and the auditor plans to rely on the operating effectiveness of controls intended to mitigate

the significant risk, the auditor should obtain audit evidence about the operating effectiveness of those controls from tests of controls performed in the current period.

Extent of tests of controls

The auditor must consider to what extent controls testing should be performed. This will depend on the following:

- The nature of the control i.e. if it is a manual or an automated control;
- The frequency with which the control is performed, for example, monthly bank reconciliations, daily posting of purchase invoices to the purchase ledger, quarterly preparation of management accounts, annual input of NIC/PAYE rates on the payroll system;
- The relevance and reliability of the audit evidence to be obtained in supporting that the control prevents, or detects and corrects, material misstatements at the assertion level;
- The extent to which the audit evidence is obtained from tests of other controls related to the assertion being tested;
- The extent to which the auditor plans to rely on the operating effectiveness of the control in the assessment of risk; and
- The expected deviation from the control.

As a general rule, the more the auditor intends to rely on tests of controls to reduce the risk of material misstatement to an appropriately low level, the greater the extent of the controls testing to be performed will be.

Testing of computer automated controls is discussed in detail in **Chapter 6**, Auditing in a Computer Environment & E-Commerce.

Substantive testing

Substantive tests of details are those tests which are carried out in all audits regardless of the identified risk of material misstatement as discussed elsewhere in this text. As a minimum the following should be performed:

- Agreeing the financial statements to the underlying accounting records; and
- Examining material journal entries and other adjustments made during the course of preparing the financial statements.

Where the risk of material misstatement is deemed low the above procedures will be sufficient for a specific area or assertion, however, where the risk is not deemed low, the procedures to be performed should be extended in order to respond to the assessed risks.

Where the auditor has determined that an assessed risk is a significant risk at the assertion level, it is necessary for suitable substantive procedures to be performed which address this risk. For example, where the existence of customers with significantly high debtor balances at the year end is questionable, a debtors' circularisation targeting such customers can be performed under the control of the auditor to confirm existence.

Nature Substantive procedures take the form of substantive analytical procedures and substantive tests of details. Both types of testing are discussed in detail in other chapters.

Timing Usually substantive testing is performed after the period end date e.g. cut-off testing, the circularisation of debtors, unrecorded liability testing, testing of key period end reconciliations. There are some instances where testing is performed at the period end date e.g. attendance at the physical inventory count on the final day of the reporting period. In addition, in some circumstances, substantive procedures may be performed at an interim date, when this happens the auditor should perform further substantive procedures combined with tests of controls to cover the remaining period that provide a reasonable basis for extending the audit conclusions from the interim date to the period end (ISA 330).

Extent The greater the risk of material misstatement at the assertion level, the greater the extent of substantive testing to be performed. As the risk of material misstatement takes into consideration the operating effectiveness of key controls, where control weaknesses are identified during the performance of tests of controls, it follows that the extent of substantive testing must be increased in response to such weaknesses.

3.12 Adequacy of Presentation and Disclosure

After controls testing and substantive procedures have been performed, the auditor must consider the appropriateness of the presentation and disclosure of the trading results of the entity and all assets and liabilities of the entity. The auditor must ensure that the presentation and disclosure in the financial statements of such items is in accordance with the applicable financial reporting framework. The auditor should consider the form, nature and arrangement of the financial statements including the related notes, focusing on the terminology used, the amount of detail given, the classification of items in the financial statements and the circumstances surrounding matters which have not been disclosed by management, for example, pending litigation or a significant change in the borrowing structure of the entity (ISA 330).

3.13 Evaluating the Sufficiency and Appropriateness of Audit Evidence Obtained

After audit procedures have been performed and audit evidence obtained, the auditor should consider the initial risk assessment at the assertion level and conclude if the risks identified still remain appropriate. Overall the auditor should then make an assessment as to whether the audit evidence obtained is sufficient and appropriate to reduce the risk of material misstatement in the financial statements to an acceptably low level (ISA 330). Whether audit evidence is sufficient and appropriate is a matter of professional judgement for the auditor.

Where the auditor concludes that sufficient appropriate audit evidence has not been obtained, attempts should be made to obtain such evidence. Where it is not possible to obtain such evidence the auditor must consider the impact on the audit opinion issued.

3.14 Documentation

It is essential that the auditor documents the nature, timing and extent of audit procedures which have been performed in response to assessed risks of material misstatement at the assertion level. Equally the auditor must document the results of the testing performed (ISA 330).

3.15 The Relationship between Materiality and Audit Risk

When planning the audit, the auditor considers what would make the financial statements materially misstated. The auditor's understanding of the entity and its environment establishes a frame of reference within which the auditor plans the audit and exercises professional judgement about assessing the risks of material misstatement in the financial statements and responding to those risks throughout the audit. It also assists the auditor to establish materiality and in evaluating whether the judgement about materiality remains appropriate as the audit progresses. For instance, where significant risks of material misstatement are identified, audit materiality should be adjusted to reflect the new information obtained. Where this is the case, the auditor must consider the impact on the audit approach and may consider it necessary to alter the nature, timing and extent of the audit plan. An example of this in reality would be as follows:

(a) Auditor has established preliminary materiality level as €/£35,000
(b) Total trade debtors balance at the period end is €/£275,000
(c) Trade debtor balances equalling €/£240,000 have been circularised, resulting in the untested balance being immaterial for further testing
(d) Factors are identified during the preliminary assessment of materiality which result in the auditor exercising judgment and reducing materiality to €/£21,000 due to further risk assessment
(e) The impact on the audit testing performed on trade debtors balance is that the balance which has not been tested through circularisation is no longer immaterial to the financial statements. The result is that further testing to the extent of €/£14,000 must

now be performed in order to reduce the untested balance to below the amended materiality level.

The key point to remember is that there is an inverse relation between materiality and audit risk i.e.:

- the greater the audit risk the lower the level of materiality; and
- the lower the audit risk the greater the level of materiality.

Conclusion

Assessing the risk of material misstatements occurring in the financial statements is critical for the auditor in order to determine an appropriate audit plan which will reduce the risk of misstatement to an acceptably low level. This is a complex process and the auditor must develop the skills necessary in order to achieve the following:

- Understand the business and related business risk;
- Obtain an understanding of the system of internal control (to include evaluating the design of the controls and determining whether they have been implemented);
- Assess the risks of material misstatement;
- Develop overall responses to risks; and
- Develop responses to risks at the assertion level.

If a suitable risk assessment process is not carried out and appropriate responses in the form of auditing procedures performed to reduce the risk to an appropriate level, then the validity of the audit opinion on the state of affairs of the financial statements will be questionable.

QUESTIONS

Self-test Questions

1. Explain the relationship between materiality, audit risk and audit planning.
2. Distinguish between inherent risk, control risk and detection risk.
3. What is the overall aim of the auditor's response to assessed risks?

Review Questions

(See Solutions to Review Questions at the end of this textbook.)

Question 3.1

You are the audit senior on the audit of Oh So Chic Ltd which is a retailer of cutting-edge designer fashion clothing. The audit is scheduled to commence in 2 weeks. The audit partner has drawn the following information to your attention and would like to know your thoughts:

Significant Risk

After a recent meeting with the company financial director, she explained that sales have slowed down during the year under review. Normally the company experiences a very quick turnaround time for stock, given that their retail cutting-edge designer fashion of the moment has been extremely in demand in the past. As fashion trends are moving away from designer to high street, the financial director is concerned about the appropriateness of the year-end stock valuation. The value of stock held at the year end is £2.75m which is material to the financial statements.

Internal Control

The financial director also revealed at the meeting that a key member of the accounts team had been absent from work through sickness for the final 5 months of the accounting period under review. His responsibility included preparation of the following key reconciliations:

- Daily till reconciliations; and
- Monthly supplier statement reconciliations.

In his absence, the above reconciliations were not prepared.

Other Information

The company is considering commencing a supplying contract with Gorgeous Shoes Ltd, a company which is owned by a director of Oh So Chic Ltd, in an attempt to improve company sales.

Requirements

(a) Outline the approach you would adopt to address the significant risk identified above in relation to stock.
(b) Discuss the impact of the absence of the key member of the accounts team noted above on the audit plan and approach, including a discussion of the financial statement areas and assertions which may be affected.
(c) Document briefly the audit considerations if a contract is to be agreed with Oh So Chic Ltd.

Question 3.2

You are currently auditing County Builders Ltd, a long established building company whose principal activity is building residential housing developments. You are performing the audit for the year to May 2008. As a result of a recent contraction in the housing market the company's trading results have been significantly affected. See financial information below:

	2008	**2007**	**2006**
Turnover	€2.2m	€4.6m	€6.2m
Net profit/Loss	(€750k)	(€300k)	€750k
Reserves	€150k	€900k	€1.2m
Gearing	75%	60%	50%

The company is coming under increasing pressure to fulfil interest payments on significant loans held by the company.

The company has not secured any significant contracts for the coming year and 35 houses remain unsold out of a total of 50 houses built on the previous significant contract secured by the company.

You are required to discuss the risk that the above presents to the current year's audit. Outline how the auditor should respond to any risks identified.

Question 3.3

The following is a description of the payroll function in a company you are auditing:

- Employees record hours worked each day on a manual time sheet.
- Each week time sheets for each employee are reviewed for accuracy by line managers.
- Reviewed time sheets are passed to the payroll assistant for processing onto the payroll system.
- Hourly wage rates, PAYE rates and NIC rates are maintained as standing data on the payroll system.
- Wages are paid via BACS each week.
- The payroll manager reviews the BACS payment listing for all employees prior to authoring the BACS payment.
- Authorisation codes are required from the payroll manager and the accounts manager in order to process the BACS payment.

Describe the testing which the auditor should perform in order to obtain assurance that the total wages figure recorded in the financial statements is accurate.

Question 3.4

As audit senior you are involved for the first time on the audit of a long-standing client of your auditing firm. The engagement leader has alerted you to the fact that the company has a board consisting of 3 directors, with 2 of these directors being perceived to exert dominant influence over the operations of the company.

Discuss the risks this may create for the audit and how the audit plan should be tailored to respond to these risks.

Chapter 4

FRAUD AND COMPLIANCE WITH LAWS AND REGULATIONS (FAE CORE)

Learning Objectives

Identify:

- Fraud in the context of audit
- Where fraud typically occurs
- Risk factors associated with fraud
- Procedures when fraud occurs and
- Be cognisant of the duty and right of auditors to report to third parties

Checklist of Relevant Professional Statements

- ISA 200 – Objective and General Principles Governing an Audit of Financial Statements
- ISA 210 – Terms of Audit Engagements
- ISA 240 – The Auditor's Responsibility to Consider Fraud in an Audit of Financial Statements
- ISA 250 – Section A: Consideration of Laws and Regulations in an Audit of Financial Statements
- ISA 315 – Understanding the Entity and its Environment and Assessing the Risks of a Material Misstatement
- ISA 330 – The Auditor's Procedures in Response to the Assessed Risks
- APB: The Audit Agenda: Next Steps
- APB: Aggressive Earnings Management

4.1 Introduction

There is a "perception gap" between the public and the auditing profession in relation to the auditor's duty in respect of fraud and error. The auditors place their emphasis on ensuring that, subsequent to their independent examination, the financial statements show a true and fair view. In order to do this, they must determine, with reasonable certainty, whether or not the financial statements are materially misstated as a result of fraud or non-compliance with laws and regulations. The public believe that it is the duty of the auditor to detect and prevent fraud and error. Clearly it is the responsibility of management, not the auditor, to ensure that the operation of the entity is conducted in accordance with relevant laws and regulations and that steps are taken to prevent and detect the occurrence of fraud.

In planning and performing the audit to reduce audit risk to an acceptably low level, the auditor should consider the risks of material misstatements in the financial statements due to fraud or error. The auditor is concerned with both fraud and error since either may cause a material misstatement in the financial statements on which the auditor is giving an opinion.

The following factors can increase the risk of fraud and error occurring:

- Lack of segregation of duties amongst the various functions
- Unnecessary complex corporate structure
- Understaffed accounting department
- Inadequate working capital
- Significant transactions with related parties
- Volatile business environment

Based on their risk assessment, the auditor should design audit procedures so as to have a reasonable expectation of detecting misstatements arising from fraud or error which are material to the financial statements. The auditor must gather sufficient appropriate audit evidence to determine whether the financial statements give a true and fair view. Therefore, the auditor should aim to identify all material fraud and error as these directly affect the view on the financial statements.

Case Law

Kingston Cotton Mill Co (No. 2) (1896)

This case held that it was not the auditors' duty to count stock and that they were not negligent in accepting a certificate signed by the company officials as long as they had no suspicion of fraud. Lopes L.J. concluded that "auditors must not be made liable for not tracing out ingenious and carefully laid out schemes of fraud where there is nothing to arouse their suspicion, and when those frauds are perpetrated by tried servants of the company and are undetected for years by the directors".

Auditors are expected to exercise reasonable skill, care and caution appropriate to the circumstances at hand, and are not expected to "ferret out" every occurrence of fraud. (The auditor is "a watch-dog not a bloodhound" – Lopes L.J.)

Irish Woollen Co Ltd v. Tyson and Others (1900)

The auditors were found to be negligent for failing to detect fraud owing to lack of reasonable care and skill. It was noted that the audit was conducted in a rather mechanical manner and entries raised after the end of the period but dated prior to the end of the period were not questioned.

Error Versus Fraud

An error is considered a simple "unintentional" mathematical or clerical mistake in the financial statements. Examples include the unintentional misapplication of an accounting policy, incorrect accounting estimate arising from oversight or misinterpretation of facts or a mistake in the gathering of the initial data. The auditor must design and implement procedures to prevent, detect and disclose errors in the financial statements. At the completion stage of the audit, the auditor assesses the total level of errors and misstatements detected and forms an opinion as to the adequacy of the records kept and their impact on the "true and fair" view of the financial statements. Depending on conclusions reached, a qualified report may have to be issued.

ISA 240.6 defines fraud as "an intentional act by one or more individuals among management, those charged with governance, employees, or third parties, involving the use of deception to obtain an unjust or illegal advantage". The standard also explains that the auditor is concerned with fraud that causes a material misstatement in the financial statements. "Two types of intentional misstatements are relevant to the auditor, that is, misstatements resulting from fraudulent financial reporting and misstatements resulting from misappropriation of assets" (ISA 240.7).

4.2 The Audit Approach to Fraud and Error

At the initial stages of the audit, before the audit commences, the risk of material misstatements occurring as a result of fraud or error must be evaluated as this may affect the entire audit process. The assessment of risks occurring is an ongoing process, which requires continual review.

For new and existing clients the auditor must consider:

- The nature of the business, its services and products which may be liable to misappropriation e.g. cash, stock etc.
- The laws and regulations regarding the entity and industry and whether procedures are in place to ensure compliance.
- Whether a "Money Laundering Reporting Officer" (MLRO) has been appointed. Employees should be informed to report any breaches to MLRO.
- The internal controls implemented in the entity and whether they are sufficient to identify and assess the risks of material misstatements due to fraud or error.
- Circumstances favourable to management overrides and misappropriations.
- The existence of related party transactions.
- The materiality and complexity of transactions and areas considered the most vulnerable.

Where Fraud Generally Occurs

Generally, there are three conditions present when fraud occurs. This is also known as the "fraud triangle" (See Table 4.1 below.)

Table 4.1 Fraud Triangle

Stage 1: Incentive/Pressure to Create Fraud

Employee

- Individual is living beyond their means
- Personal debt and/or unforeseen expenses
- Pressure to meet expectations/targets which may be unrealistic
- Performance-related bonus/pay incentives
- Impossible targets set

Company Directors/Management

- Company has performed badly and is making a loss
- Market is expecting a certain level of profit from the company
- Company does not wish to make shareholders and the market aware of its liquidity problems
- Continual growth trends wish to be sustained

Stage 2: Opportunity for Fraud to Occur

Employee

- Opportunity may be perceived or actual and there is a belief that no-one will notice
- Individual is in a position of trust
- Ineffective or absent controls
- Knowledge of specific weakness in an area of internal control
- The ability of management to override control
- No internal audit function

Company Directors/Management

- Complex overseas transactions allow opportunities for fraudulent transactions and reporting

Stage 3: Rationalisation of the Individual/Company

- Prevailing rationalisations of action/culture of the entity
- Acceptable competitive behaviour either internal to the entity or external with third parties
- No visible harm – "other people are doing it"
- No alternative employment opportunity
- Previous fraudulent activities have occurred in the company

Appendix 1 to ISA 240, The Auditor's Responsibility to Consider Fraud in an Audit of Financial Statements, gives further examples of fraud risk factors for both misstatements arising from fraudulent financial reporting and from the misappropriation of assets.

Fraud Risk Factors

The auditor must identify situations where there is a higher than usual risk of fraud or error occurring. There are various factors that hamper detecting the occurrence of fraud. These include:

- The nature of evidence available to the auditor. Often "sufficient appropriate" audit evidence is not available to resolve the auditor's suspicions of fraud occurring.
- Management and directors overriding internal controls.
- The focus on providing a "true and fair view" of the financial statements rather than on the incidence of fraud.
- Time constraints imposed on the auditor to have the financial statements published by a specific date.

ISA 240 "The Auditor's Responsibility to Consider Fraud in an Audit of Financial Statements", stresses a number of key factors:

- The auditor must discuss with management and those charged with governance the procedures they follow when fulfilling their responsibilities for detecting fraud. Discussions should include management's assessment of fraud occurring, procedures to minimise fraud occurring and the ethical attitudes communicated to the organisation.
- The auditor should ascertain if management and those charged with governance are aware of any fraud that has occurred or is occurring.
- The auditor should determine the procedures implemented by the internal audit team aimed at detecting fraud and what conclusions they have reached.
- Those charged with governance should be approached to determine what processes and procedures have been used by management to identify the risks of fraud occurring and how management responded to these risks.
- The auditor should consider what fraud risk factors, if any, already exist.
- Analytical review techniques should be used by the auditor to identify any unexpected relationships which might suggest the possibility of material misstatement due to fraud.

Characteristics of Fraud

As previously mentioned material misstatements may arise from fraudulent financial reporting or from the misappropriation of assets. Fraudulent financial reporting involves intentional misstatements. The intention is to result in financial statements which give a misleading impression of the financial affairs of the entity. These may include omissions of amounts or disclosures in financial statements to deceive financial statement users. Management are the general perpetrators of this type of fraud, motivated by what they consider to be in their own best interests in terms of reporting of the financial position and performance of the entity.

Characteristics include (ISA 240.8-10):

- Manipulation, falsification (including forgery), or alteration of accounting records or supporting documentation from which the financial statements are prepared
- Misrepresentation in, or intentional omission from, the financial statements of events, transactions or other significant information
- Intentional misapplication of accounting principles relating to amounts, classification, manner of presentation, or disclosure
- Management override of controls, for example, the recording of fictitious journal entries particularly close to the period end

Misappropriation of assets involves the theft of an entity's assets and is often perpetrated by employees in relatively small and immaterial amounts. It may also involve management who are usually better able to disguise or conceal misappropriations in ways that are difficult to detect. Often false or misleading records are created in order to conceal the fact that assets are missing or have been pledged without authorisation. Unlike fraudulent financial reporting, misappropriation of assets usually occurs for one's personal gain. Characteristics include (ISA 240 11-12):

- Embezzling receipts (e.g. misappropriating collections on accounts receivable or diverting receipts in respect of written-off accounts to personal bank accounts)
- Stealing physical assets or intellectual property (for example, stealing inventory for personal use or for sale, stealing scrap for resale, colluding with a competitor by disclosing technological data in return for payment)
- Causing the business to pay for goods not actually received (for example fictitious suppliers)
- Using an entity's assets for personal use (for example, using the entity's assets as collateral for a personal loan or a loan to a related party)

Research has shown that perpetrators of fraud are generally those who come to auditors for explanations and assurance of information. The auditor should maintain a professional scepticism when conducting his duties in light of his knowledge of the entity and evidence he has obtained. Other general characteristics of fraud that the auditor should be aware of are as follows:

- Unusual behaviour, for example, defensiveness or failure to re-assign work when overloaded
- Stale items in the bank reconciliation, missing lodgements or missing cheques. With each reconciliation performed, the reconciling items may be on the increase

- Excessive journals posted or credit notes issued
- Missing documents and lack of explanations and procedures to locate the document
- Absence of original invoices which are substituted by copies
- Common names, addresses etc., identified of employee or family and friends of employee
- Excessive purchases relative to the nature of the entity
- Duplication of payments
- Fictitious employees noted on wages records
- Inventory shortfalls relative to the nature of the entity
- Large and often round-sum payments made with little or no backup documentation
- Post office boxes used as shipping addresses

4.3 Aggressive Earnings Management

In 2001, the APB issued a Consultation Paper entitled "Aggressive Earnings Management". The APB defines aggressive earnings management, as "accounting practices including the selection of inappropriate accounting policies and/or unduly stretching judgements as to what is acceptable when forming accounting estimates. These practices, while presenting the financial performance of the companies in a favourable light, do not necessarily reflect the underlying reality."

Auditors should be alert and responsive to the existence of aggressive earnings management. The auditor should:

- Recognise the pressures on directors or management to report a specific level of earnings
- Act with a greater professional scepticism when alerted to circumstances indicative of aggressive earnings management
- Take a strong stance with directors when requesting adjustments for misstatements identified during the audit
- Communicate openly and frankly with the entity, in particular the directors and the audit committee.

The audit policies and procedures described later in the chapter incorporate the steps required to identify aggressive earnings management.

4.4 Responsibilities for Fraud and Error

The primary responsibility for the prevention and detection of fraud rests with the directors (in particular the finance director), management and those charged with governance. This is highlighted in ISA 210 Terms of audit engagements, where the standard indicates that it is the responsibility of directors to maintain adequate internal controls and safeguard the assets of the company. The auditor is not required to assist in this function but he/she should inform directors and relevant management of their responsibilities through the engagement letter issued at the start of the audit and through other relevant communications. The fact that an audit is carried out may, however, act as a deterrent to potential fraudsters. The auditor should advise management on how to set "the tone at the top" for the running of their business. Communication is key. They can do this through:

- Developing an accepted Code of Conduct for all employees
- Promoting a culture of honesty and integrity within a positive work environment
- Implementing an ethics programme based on a strong set of core values to be communicated to the entire organisation
- Establishing penalties and procedures for dealing with prosecutors
- Implementing e-banking for payroll and other recurring outgoings
- Establishing an appropriate control environment and maintaining strong internal controls which provide reasonable assurance with regard to reliability of financial reporting, effectiveness and the efficiency of operations and compliance with applicable laws and regulations
- Establishing an internal audit function, an audit committee and an independent compliance function to which the auditor can report any incidence of suspected fraud
- Taking action in response to actual, suspected and alleged fraud

The auditor is required to provide reasonable assurance that the financial statements are free from material misstatement, whether caused by fraud or error. There is the unavoidable risk that some material misstatements may, however, go undetected. The auditor's responsibility is to obtain sufficient appropriate audit evidence to support their opinion on the financial statements. This can be done by:

- Identifying the risk of material misstatement due to fraud
- Identifying the risks that may result in material misstatement due to fraud
- Evaluating the client's programmes and controls that address the identified risks
- Responding to the risks identified in the assessment
- Communicating to management, the audit committee, those charged with governance etc.

4.5 Discussion Among the Engagement Team

ISA 240.27–32 requires the members of the audit engagement team to discuss the susceptibility of the entity's financial statements to material misstatements due to fraud and how it might occur. This discussion should occur with a questioning mind and professional scepticism. Any belief that management and those charged with governance act with honesty and integrity should be set aside. Items to be discussed include:

- How and where the financial statements may be susceptible to material misstatement due to fraud, how management could perpetrate and conceal fraudulent financial reporting, and how assets of the entity could be misappropriated

- The circumstances that might indicate earnings management and the practices that might be followed by management to manage earnings that could lead to fraudulent financial reporting
- How external and internal factors affecting the entity could create an incentive or pressure for management or others to commit fraud, provide the opportunity for fraud to be perpetrated, and indicate a culture or environment that enables management or others to rationalise committing fraud
- Management's involvement in overseeing employees with access to cash or other assets susceptible to misappropriation
- Any unusual or unexplained changes in behaviour or lifestyle of management or employees which have come to the attention of the engagement team
- The importance of maintaining professional scepticism and a proper state of mind throughout the entire audit process regarding the potential for material misstatement due to fraud
- Circumstances that could indicate the possibility of fraud, the risk of management override of controls, how an element of unpredictability must be incorporated into the nature, timing and extent of procedures performed and how the audit procedures are selected relative to the likelihood of material misstatement
- Allegations of fraud that have already come to light.

4.6 Detection of Fraud – Policies and Procedures

Auditors are concerned with evaluating controls for the efficient and effective use of company resources. The auditor must be alert to the fact that controls may be poorly enforced or otherwise irrelevant. They must be actively alert to the likelihood of fraud occurring. Auditing standards require the auditor to assess the risk of material misstatement in the financial statements resulting from fraud and to consider this assessment when planning and performing their audit.

There are a number of conditions to consider when assessing the likelihood of fraud:

1. Consider whether risk factors indicate the existence of fraud. Review the operating and control environment of the entity, including the external, legal, regulatory environment etc.
2. Assess the potential and/or actual risks and exposures, for example, monetary loss, theft of assets etc.
3. Enquire of management to obtain their understanding and assessment of the likelihood of fraud occurring.
4. Review the risks and exposures from the perspective of the fraudster.
5. Gain an understanding of the symptoms of fraud, for example, what can go wrong, how it can go wrong and who might be involved.

6. Be alert to the symptoms of fraud, for example, volume of activity, significant changes from the prior period, complexity and variability of transactions.
7. Document the conclusions of their fraud risk assessment, the specific risk factors identified and their responses to those factors. At the final stages of the audit, these will be reassessed.

ISA 240 details specific procedures to be undertaken by the auditor when considering the possibility of fraud:

- Make enquiries of management, those charged with governance and others as appropriate to obtain an understanding of how those charged with governance exercise oversight of management processes for identifying and responding to the risks of fraud and the internal control that management has established to mitigate these risks.
- Perform audit procedures so as to identify the risk of material misstatements due to fraud. This will include evaluating the integrity of management and the inherent risks relating to the client's business. Evaluate any unusual or unexpected relationships.
- Walkthrough tests should be performed to confirm the adequacy of the system and related documentation and whether the control objectives are met.
- At both the individual transaction level and the financial statements as a whole, identify and assess the risk of fraud occurring. This will include evaluating the efficiency of the internal control procedures relevant to the assessed risks.
- Use audit software/CAATs to test controls, for example, searching for journal entries over a certain limit.
- Determine audit responses to the assessed risks. This will include the assignment and supervision of personnel, the accounting policies used and the unpredictability when selecting the audit procedures.
- Design and perform audit procedures responsive to management override of controls. This will include testing the appropriateness of journal entries and other adjustments recorded, reviewing the appropriateness of accounting estimates used and obtaining an understanding of the business rationale of significant transactions outside the normal course of business.
- Consider whether any identified misstatements or error indicate the possibility of fraud occurring.

When the auditor becomes aware that a fraud or error may have occurred, they should obtain an understanding of the nature of the event and the circumstances in which it has occurred, and other relevant information to evaluate the possible effect on the financial statements. If the auditor determines that the potential fraud or error could have a material effect on the financial statements, she/he should perform appropriate modified or additional procedures.

This should include:

- Increasing the scope and variety of tests performed.
- Ensuring that suitably qualified staff are assigned to the audit team.
- Incorporating an element of unpredictability into their audit tests, for example, the timing or nature of audit tests performed.
- Concentrating their testing on areas which are subjective, involve management judgement or where management have considerable influence.

In assessing the potential materiality of the fraud or error, the auditor should consider:

- The potential financial consequence. If the matter is material, appropriate audit procedures will need to be performed. Management should also be informed.
- Whether the potential financial consequence requires disclosure. If an error or other irregularity has occurred, the auditor must ensure the financial statements have been prepared taking these into consideration. Management must be notified of the error or irregularity.
- Whether the potential financial consequences are so serious that the view of the financial statements must be called into question.

4.7 Limitations on Audit Procedures in Detecting Fraud and Error

There are unavoidable limitations where, even though the audit will be properly planned and performed, fraud or error may not be detected. ISA 200.2, Objective and General Principles Governing an Audit of Financial Statements, states that the objective of an audit of financial statements is to enable the auditor to express an opinion as to whether the financial statements are prepared, in all material respects, in accordance with an applicable financial reporting framework. Thus the primary responsibility is not to detect fraud. In addition, the auditor is only required to give an opinion on the financial statements, not a guarantee. Therefore the evidence gathered in terms of persuasiveness is limited to that required to arrive at their opinion.

Due to the volume of transactions going through an entity's general ledger and bank account, including all journals and other adjustments, the auditor uses sampling methods when performing audit tests. It is inevitable that every error or misstatement is not going to be detected. Management could also have concealed fraud from the auditors, deliberately manipulated the books and records of the entity, made intentional misrepresentations or deliberately not recorded transactions. Where judgement has been exercised it may be difficult to ascertain whether misrepresentations were caused by fraud or error. Unless 100% of transactions are tested, the auditor must accept the possibility that the fraud may simply go undetected in the financial statements.

4.8 Fraud and CAATs

Computer-assisted audit techniques (CAATs) are a very important tool for the auditor in their detection of fraud. In order to work effectively, CAATs must be strategically adapted to the situation and the various audit objectives and procedures of the entity under review. There are many benefits to utilising CAATs when searching for indications of fraudulent activity.

CAATs can be used to:

- Search for duplicate payments
- Match vendor address to employee address
- Search for duplicate employee and supplier details
- Search for duplicate addresses e.g. payroll, payables, receivables
- Analyse overridden transactions
- Identify large round-sum payments
- Identify scrapped inventory followed by re-orders
- List missing items e.g. items on cheque payments summary to bank reconciliation
- Identify any employee or directors' accounts with a large volume of transactions for large amounts
- Search for classes of transactions known to have high exposure e.g. loans, health claims
- Search for patterns, for example, customers changing their payment methods, sales returns following a disputed account

4.9 Management Representations

"Written representations" are routinely obtained from management in which management confirms, in writing, significant representations made to the auditor. ISA 240.90 details specific representations required from management that it:

- Acknowledges its responsibility for designing, implementing and maintaining internal controls to prevent and detect fraud
- Has disclosed to the auditor:
  - the results of its assessments of the risk that the financial statements may be materially misstated as a result of fraud
  - its knowledge of fraud or suspected fraud affecting the entity involving management, employees who have significant roles in internal controls and others where the fraud could have a material affect on the financial statements.
  - its knowledge of any allegations of fraud, or suspected fraud, affecting the entity's financial statements communicated by employees, former employees, analysts, regulators or others.

4.10 Duty and Right of Auditors to Report to Management and Third Parties

If the auditor suspects fraud or discovers a material error, having obtained all the necessary evidence, he should report his findings to an appropriate level of management, the directors or those charged with governance. The auditor must make sure he is fully informed on the situation, the nature of the fraud and the magnitude of the situation. The situation must be fully documented in the working papers.

If a material fraud is discovered which affects the financial statements, directors and/or those charged with governance should be asked to consider amending the financial statements to reflect the impact of the fraud. The impact on other audit work must also be considered. Management can be asked to carry out additional procedures to determine if the auditor has uncovered the full extent of the fraud. If management, other than the directors, are suspected of committing a fraud, the directors should be informed.

Even if fraud or suspected fraud has not been encountered, the auditor should discuss with the directors the concerns they have relating to fraud. For example:

- Concerns about the nature, extent and frequency of management's assessments of the controls in place to prevent and detect fraud and of the risk that the financial statements may be misstated
- A failure of management to appropriately address identified material weaknesses in internal control, or to appropriately respond to an identified fraud
- The auditor's evaluation of the entity's control environment, including questions regarding the competence and integrity of management
- Actions by management that may be indicative of fraudulent financial reporting such as management's selection and application of accounting policies that could be indicative of management's effort to manage earnings in order to deceive financial statements users by influencing their perceptions as to the entity's performance and profitability
- Concerns about the adequacy and completeness of the authorisation of transactions that appear to be outside the normal course of business.

Once the auditor reports his suspicions, it is expected that those charged with governance take action. If management and directors are indifferent to investigating the fraud, the auditor will need to reassess their integrity and the control environment and will need to consider the impact on the audit report.

If the auditor believes that the published financial statements are materially affected by a fraud or error, an explanatory paragraph should be added to the audit report to qualify his report, depending on the circumstances.

Party	Obligation
Shareholders	Shareholders/members must be informed if the auditor concludes that the financial statements do not give a true and fair view, comply with applicable accounting framework, or proper books and records have not been kept. Errors and irregularities need not be reported.
Management	*Top management/those charged with governance:* If lower level management are suspected of being involved in fraudulent activities, top management and/or the audit committee must be informed. *Lower level management:* Lower level management should be informed of all errors and irregularities noted by the auditor. This can be done through the management letter.
Third parties	When reporting to third parties, confidentiality is key. The auditor should consider obtaining legal advice to determine the appropriate course of action. Where breaches of the law have occurred, there is a public duty to disclose the breach and the relevant authority must be notified (e.g. money laundering).

If a misstatement resulting from fraud or a suspected fraud is discovered, which brings into question the auditor's ability to continue performing the audit, the auditor should:

- Consider the professional and legal responsibilities applicable in the circumstances, including whether there is a requirement for the auditor to report to the person or persons who made the audit appointment or, in some cases, to regulatory authorities;
- Consider the possibility of withdrawing from the engagement; and
- If the auditor withdraws from the engagement the auditor must discuss with the appropriate level of management and those charged with governance the reason for the withdrawal. The auditor must also consider whether there is a professional or legal requirement to report to the person or persons who made the audit appointment or, in some cases, to regulatory authorities, the auditor's withdrawal from the engagement and the reasons for the withdrawal.

4.11 Required Documentation Related to Detecting and Preventing Fraud

There has been an increase in regulatory requirements relating to the documentation of audit procedures performed to detect fraud and the steps taken to report detected and/or suspected fraud. Matters that must be documented include: (ISA 240.107–111)

- Significant decisions reached during the engagement team discussions regarding the susceptibility of the entity's financial statements to material misstatements due to fraud
- Identified and assessed risks of material misstatements due to fraud at financial statement and assertion level
- Overall responses to the assessed risks of material misstatements due to fraud at financial statement level and the nature, timing and extent of audit procedures performed in response to assessed risks of material misstatement at the assertion level
- Results of audit procedures performed, including those designed to address the risk of management override of controls
- Communications about fraud made to management, those charged with governance, regulators or others
- If the auditor has concluded that improper revenue recognition does not present a risk of material misstatement due to fraud, the reasons supporting that conclusion

4.12 The Current Environment and Fraud

In times of recession and financial difficulty, the occurrence of fraud becomes more and more prevalent as motivation and opportunity increase. In such times, where individuals and companies suffer financially, behaviour can change and the line of legality can be crossed, and activities undertaken in order to maintain the lifestyles, financial performance etc., previously accustomed to.

Recent studies have shown that the cost of fraud to the Irish economy over recent years was in the region of €900 million. Total reported fraud in the UK stood at £1.19bn for 2008, up 14% from 2007, according to BDO Stoy Hayward's annual FraudTrack report. In the US whistleblower hotlines operated by The Network, a US compliance group, reported that 21% of their calls in the first quarter of 2009 related to reports of fraudulent activity, compared to 16.5% in 2008 and 11% in 2007. In a survey of 507 fraud examiners, over 50% have seen a rise in fraud in the past year.

Major companies report some type of fraud every two to three years. Costs to the company include investigations, prosecution, management time loss and damage to the entity's reputation. This can cost in the region of up to €500 million. US organisations lost 7% of their revenue, on average, to fraud in 2008, according to the association of Certified Fraud Examiners. Fraud not only relates to fraudulent financial reporting and the misappropriation of assets, as previously discussed, but also to lesser-known frauds. Recessionary times bring out types of fraud that may or may not be easy to identify. The key to detecting fraud is to understand how the opportunity can arise in the company and assess the risk of the fraud actually occurring.

Examples of lesser-known frauds include:

The fictitious firm

In this case the fraudster sets up a fictitious supplier, which may even be registered with the Companies Registration Office. Invoices are submitted and payments are made to this company. The key to concealing this type of fraud is keeping the payments small. The auditor should review any new suppliers detected. The company address should be checked to ensure the company is not assigned to a PO Box number. The address of the individual authorising the payments to such company should also be investigated.

Inventory theft

Inventory is the balance sheet item most susceptible to theft. Inventory may be written off as a loss, scrap stolen to sell as scrap or simply not entered onto the balance sheet. The auditor should investigate inventory shortfalls relative to the nature of the entity, investigate journal entries relating to write offs and stock write-downs and perform variance analysis procedures.

Tampering with employee records

This is especially prevalent in large companies where not everyone knows everyone's name. When an employee leaves the firm, the fraudster, who generally is associated with the payroll department, instead of removing the employee from their records, alters their bank account details to that of their own. The auditor should identify employees who have ceased employment with the firm and ascertain whether payments were made to that individual and their bank account after their leaving date.

Identity theft

Identity theft is the misuse of personal information to impersonate someone for financial gain. Identity theft can take the form of identity cloning (assuming someone else's identity), financial (theft from existing accounts or the setting up of a new account) and benefit theft (impersonating an individual to obtain benefits). The most common method of obtaining your personal information is by way of a "phishing attack", where you receive an email requesting your personal information from an individual or organisation you trust. This information is then used to steal your identity. The auditor and, indeed, management have a duty to protect their client and employees respectively. The auditor has a legal duty to protect their client's personal and financial information and thus they must be protected from the risk of identity theft. The auditor must ensure that management are alert to the occurrence of identity theft and protect their staff from this vicious crime. Personal records should be safeguarded, passwords changed regularly, memory sticks encrypted, anti-virus and anti-spyware programmes installed, only reputable suppliers dealt with and clear policies and procedures implemented and reviewed regularly.

4.13 Steps to Prevent Corporate Fraud

To counteract the motivation for and occurrence of fraud, there are a number of simple steps which can be enforced by the directors (in particular the finance director), management, the audit committee and those charged with governance.

1. Apply proper and consistent procedures when taking on all new employees. These procedures can include performing background checks and contacting references listed on their CV.
2. Communicate your corporate and ethical policy throughout the entire organisation. Encourage tip-offs and formal whistle-blowing facilities. Procedures must be enforced to allow employees come forward in confidence to voice their concerns; otherwise the potential incidence of fraud may go undetected.
3. Segregate the duties of those controlling the cash and those accounting for the cash. A cash trail should be maintained. Profits should be transformed into cash. Suspense accounts should also be highlighted.
4. Make expenses procedures as transparent as possible as expenses are one of the easiest things to abuse.
5. Encourage holiday leave. Fraudsters do not like to take holidays as this means that someone else will be running their side of the operation and may discover irregularities.
6. Implement and maintain proper procurement policies, for example, procedures for taking on and changing suppliers. Independent reviews should also be performed. Other internal procedures and controls should also be enforced.
7. Implement access to both physical and financial assets and information. Develop and implement policies to determine how financial transactions are initiated, authorised, recorded and reviewed.
8. Prosecute aggressively all instances of fraud. Fraud cannot be seen to be taken lightly and quick and decisive action will hopefully deter any future cases of fraud in the organisation.

QUESTIONS

Self-test Questions

1. Distinguish between errors and fraud.
2. How should an auditor take into account error or fraud at the audit planning stage?
3. Outline six procedures to be undertaken by an auditor when considering the possibility of fraud.
4. How can CAATs assist in the search for fraud?

CHAPTER 5

GATHERING AUDIT EVIDENCE

Learning Objectives

To become familiar with evidence-gathering principles and procedures in order to:

- Apply evidence-gathering principles and procedures
- Explain the distinction between the testing of controls and substantive testing, including analytical procedures
- Identify circumstances where control tests vs tests of details vs analytical procedures are appropriate
- Describe the factors which influence judgements on the extent of testing
- Audit sampling techniques
- Enable selection of work and appraisal of work of experts

Checklist of Relevant Professional Statements

- ISA 200 Objective and General Principles Governing an Audit of Financial Statements
- ISA 300 Planning an Audit of Financial Statements
- ISA 330 The Auditor's Procedures in Response to Assessed Risks
- ISA 500 Audit Evidence
- ISA 510 Initial Engagements – Opening Balances and Continuing Engagements – Opening Balances
- ISA 520 Analytical Procedures
- ISA 530 Audit Sampling and Other Means of Testing
- ISA 540 Audit of Accounting Estimates
- ISA 620 Using the Work of an Expert

5.1 The Concept of Audit Evidence and its Relevance to the Audit Process (ISA 500 Audit Evidence)

The primary purpose of an audit is for the auditor to issue an audit opinion on the financial statements. In order to do this the auditor must gain evidence which supports the balances, transactions and disclosures in the financial statements, an audit opinion cannot be issued where sufficient appropriate audit evidence has not been obtained.

ISA 500, Audit Evidence, describes audit evidence as all the information used by the auditor in arriving at the conclusions on which the audit opinion is based, and includes the information contained in the accounting records underlying the financial statements and other information.

In summary, audit evidence is what the auditor requires in order to support and conclude whether or not the financial statements give a true and fair view.

Examples of audit evidence include the following:

- Sales/purchase/sundry invoices
- Supplier statements
- Contracts for work to be performed
- Client spreadsheets e.g. budgets
- Entity control manuals
- Valuation reports e.g. from surveyors or inventory valuation experts
- Minutes from shareholder/director meetings
- Third-party confirmations e.g. bank confirmations, legal confirmations or debtor confirmations.

5.2 What is Sufficient and Appropriate Evidence?

ISA 500 outlines that the auditor must obtain evidence that is sufficient and appropriate. Sufficiency is the measure of the quantity of audit evidence while appropriateness is the measure of the quality of the evidence, that is its relevance and reliability in providing support for or detecting misstatements in account balances, classes of transactions and disclosures. The quantity of audit evidence is directly linked to the risk of material misstatement which has been identified at the assertion level. For example where the auditor has assessed the risk of the period-debtors balance being understated as high, then the level of audit evidence required around this balance will be significantly higher than when the risk of the period-end debtors balance being understated is assessed as low. As a general rule the higher the level of risk the more audit evidence is required. The quantity of audit evidence is also directly linked to the quality of the evidence, as a general rule the better the quality of the evidence the less evidence may be required. Hence the sufficiency and appropriateness of audit evidence are interrelated, however, simply obtaining a greater quantity of audit evidence may not compensate for poor quality.

5.3 What is Reliable Audit Evidence?

Reliability of audit evidence varies and often the auditor needs to use professional judgement in deciding whether the audit evidence received is sufficient to be relied upon.

ISA 500, paragraph 9 states that audit evidence is more reliable when:

- It is obtained from an independent source e.g. bank confirmation letter
- When entity controls are effective if generated internally. However, if the controls operating within the entity are not deemed to be effective then the quality of the evidence produced by the entity will most likely not be reliable e.g. reports generated from an accounting system which has been found to be unreliable and susceptible to errors should not be assessed as reliable
- Obtained directly by the auditor e.g. debtor confirmation letters where responses are sent directly to the audit firm removing the opportunity for entity management to manipulate responses
- It is in documentary form rather then verbal e.g. verbal evidence can often be denied whereas if obtained in documentary form the facts are held on record by the auditor
- It is provided from original documents e.g. copies of sales contracts can be easily manipulated to present future contracts won by the client more favourably.

In general, reliability of evidence depends upon the circumstances surrounding its origin and source. Consider the following practical examples which highlight how the degree of reliability may vary depending on the nature of the audit evidence obtained.

Reliable	Less Reliable
Confirmation of debtor balance received directly from customer	Debtor balance per year end ledger
Year-end debtors aged listing if tests of controls have concluded that system can be relied upon	Year-end debtors aged listing if tests of controls have concluded that the system has material weaknesses and cannot be relied upon
Observation of the application of a control by the auditor e.g. the need for two people to authorise a BACS payment via entry of passwords on the computer system	Documentation of the control by client and given to auditor
Letter from solicitor confirming that there are no claims against the client at the period end	Oral representation from client stating there are no claims against the client at the period end
Original bank statement	Fax of period-end bank statement from client
Attendance by auditor at period-end inventory count	Inspection of period-end inventory listing supplied by client

In all instances the auditor should endeavour to gain the most reliable evidence available.

5.4 Audit Assertions and Obtaining Audit Evidence

Management prepare and present the financial statements to the auditors with the expectation that they:

- Give a true and fair view
- Meet the assertions regarding recognition, measurement, presentation and disclosure.

ISA 500 states that the auditor should use assertions for classes of transactions, account balances, and presentation and disclosures in sufficient detail to form a basis for the further assessment of risks and material misstatement and the design and performance of further audit procedures.

In line with this, the auditor designs audit tests to ensure that the financial statements comply with the assertions, therefore the auditor must consider which types of audit tests and audit evidence will provide assurance over the financial statement assertions. At the end of the audit, the auditor must be sure that sufficient audit testing has been performed around each of the assertions relating to each item in the financial statements.

Audit evidence is used to test each of the assertions as follows:

Transactions and Events During the Period

Assertion	Objective of Audit Evidence
Occurrence	To ensure transactions and events have been recorded and pertain to the entity
Completeness	To ensure that all transactions that should have been recorded, have been recorded
Accuracy	To ensure that all transactions have been recorded correctly
Cut-Off	To ensure transactions and events have been recorded in correct period
Classification	To ensure that transactions and events have been recorded in the correct accounts

Account Balances at Year End

Assertion	Objective of Audit Evidence
Existence	To ensure that all assets and liabilities in year-end balance sheet exist
Rights and obligations	To ensure the entity holds the rights to the assets and has obligations

Assertion	Objective of Audit Evidence
Completeness	To ensure that all assets and liabilities that should have been recorded, have been recorded
Valuation and allocation	To ensure that all assets and liabilities are included in financial statements at correct valuation and in correct account in the correct period

Presentation and Disclosure

Assertion	Objective of Audit Evidence
Occurrence and rights and obligations	To ensure that all events and transactions recorded have occurred and pertain to the entity
Completeness	To ensure that all disclosures that should have been included, have been included
Classification and understandability	To ensure that financial information is appropriately presented and described and disclosures are clearly expressed
Accuracy and Valuation	To ensure that financial and other information is disclosed fairly and at appropriate amounts

The auditor will seek appropriate audit evidence to satisfy all of the objectives above. Different types of testing will be necessary in order to address each assertion at the financial statement level and in some instances a combination of tests will be used. The detailed audit testing plan will be developed during the planning phase of the audit and will be updated as necessary throughout the audit cycle.

Consider the following practical examples which identify how audit tests are developed to cover assertions relating to classes of transactions and balances in the financial statements.

Financial Statement Area	Audit Test	Nature of Audit Test	Assertions Addressed
Fixed Assets	Agreeing fixed asset additions to supporting documentation	Substantive	Accuracy, existence/occurrence, cut-off
Sales	Invoices are system generated and are issued in sequential number order, choose	Controls	Completeness

Financial Statement Area	Audit Test	Nature of Audit Test	Assertions Addressed
	an invoice number and confirm that the following 50 invoices have been posted to the sales ledger		
Accounts Payable	Reconciliation of balance per creditors ledger to supplier statements	Substantive	Completeness, accuracy, existence/occurrence
Inventory	Attendance at period-end physical inventory count	Substantive	Completeness, accuracy, existence/occurrence, valuation

5.5 Methods of Obtaining Audit Evidence

There are a number of methods by which the auditor can obtain audit evidence. The method used will depend on the nature of the testing being performed.

Some of the key methods are discussed below.

The auditor obtains evidence using one or more of the following procedures (ISA 500):

- Inquiry
- Inspection
- Observation
- Confirmation
- Recalculation
- Re-performance
- Analytical

Inquiry

Inquiry is the most utilised audit technique for gathering audit evidence. It consists of seeking information from knowledgeable persons inside or outside the entity. It is seldom used alone to provide sufficient audit evidence – it is used in conjunction with other corroborating evidence.

Inquiries may consist of oral or written requests for information from persons inside the entity or from third-party sources. The response to these enquires will either necessitate the auditor getting corroborative evidence to substantiate the inquiry, or the auditor may receive information which differs significantly from other information that the auditor has received and will therefore provide a basis for the auditor to modify, or perform additional, audit procedures.

Examples of inquiry are as follows:

- The auditor inquires from management about the control process around the sales process – in order to rely on the information the client provides, the auditor must back this up with further corroborative evidence, for example, observing the process
- The auditor inquires why motor expenses have increased significantly. Management may state that this is because of rising fuel prices throughout the year – in order to rely on this information, the auditor must corroborate this information by reviewing invoices or looking at industry trend
- The auditor inquires as to the presence of "other debtors" on the balance sheet – when an explanation is received from management, the auditor must obtain sufficient audit evidence to substantiate the existence of this asset.

Inspection

Inspection involves examining, reviewing, vouching, tracing or verifying records or other documents, processes, conditions or transactions. Inspection also relates to the inspection of physical assets for existence, however, further documents must be inspected to verify rights and obligations to the asset.

Inspection of documents provides the auditors with varying degrees of reliability, for example:

- Are the documents generated internally or externally?
- Have they been received directly by the auditors?
- Is the source reliable?

Examples of the use of inspection when gathering audit evidence are as follows:

- The auditor inspects the solicitor's letter for the existence of any legal liabilities [reliable third-party confirmation]
- The auditor vouches the debtors confirmation to the debtors balance per the listing [reliable third-party confirmation]
- The auditor vouches bank balance per the client to bank confirmation letters [reliable third-party confirmation].

Observation

Observation consists of looking at a process or procedure being performed by others. Observation allows the auditor to obtain audit evidence on how adequately the process or procedure is performed. Observation will seldom gain adequate audit evidence on its own but may identify areas where further audit evidence is required.

Examples of observation are as follows:

- Observation of inventory count – further audit procedures required could comprise recounting a sample of stock and tracing to final stock listing at time of the audit fieldwork
- Observation of processes surrounding the sales system – inquiry from management would have indicated that there are processes; observation would then be used to verify that the systems are in place. If the observation concludes that the systems are strong, reduced substantive testing would be required on the debtors listing; however, if observation indicated weak controls, increased substantive tests would need to be designed around the existence and completeness of the debtors listing.

Confirmation

Confirmation is the process of receiving direct representation from a third party to verify information included in the financial statements. The auditor usually contacts the third party directly, or through the client, and requests the confirmation to be sent directly to the auditor.

Since confirmations are written representations from independent third parties received directly by the auditor, they are highly persuasive evidence.

Examples of confirmations are as follows:

- Confirmation from banks of period-end balances
- Confirmation from customers of period-end debtor balances
- Confirmation from public warehouse which holds stock for the client.

Recalculation

Recalculation consists of verifying the mathematical accuracy of documents and accounting records and recomputing financial statement amounts or supporting details, including client schedules.

Examples of recalculations are as follows:

- Rechecking totals in stock, creditors and debtors listing
- Extending stock values by quantities and checking calculations

- Recalculating balances denominated in a foreign currency to ensure that they are carried in the financial statements at the correct amount, this will be done using a suitable exchange rate obtained from a suitable third party
- Recalculating depreciation charge for the period under review, comparing to the charge per the client and assessing for reasonableness.

Re-performance

Reperformance is the auditor's independent execution of procedures or controls that were originally performed as part of the entity's internal control, either manually or through the use of CAATs.

Examples of re-performance are as follows:

- Re-performing the ageing of accounts receivable balances by obtaining invoices making up the balance and assessing the aging of these invoices.

Analytical procedures

Analytical procedures involve evaluating financial and non-financial information and comparing actual results to expectations. It also involves identifying significant fluctuations and relationships that deviate from expectations. Expectations should be developed based on the auditor's knowledge of the operation of the business during the period under review and information obtained through performance of other audit tests.

Where deviations from expectation are significant the auditor will use enquiry to discuss with management the reasons for these movements. Reasons for deviations should be corroborated through inspection of documentation which will underpin the reasons disclosed by management. This approach is outlined in ISA 520:

> When analytical procedures identify significant fluctuations or relationships that are inconsistent with other relevant information or that deviate from predicted amounts, the auditor should investigate and obtain adequate explanation and appropriate corroborative audit evidence.

Examples of analytical procedures are as follows:

- Comparing profit and loss expenses year on year and investigating any unexpected fluctuations.
- Comparison of period-end accruals and prepayments to prior period balances and investigating any unexpected fluctuations.

Summary of audit procedures

The audit procedures discussed above, or combinations thereof, may be used as risk assessment procedures, tests of controls or substantive procedures, depending on the context in which they are applied by the auditor.

5.6 Evaluating Audit Evidence

The goals in evaluating audit evidence are to decide, after considering all relevant data obtained, whether:

- The assessments of the risks of material misstatement at the assertion level are appropriate; and
- Sufficient evidence has been obtained to reduce the risks of material misstatement in the financial statements to an acceptably low level.

When misstatements or deviations are found when performing audit testing, consideration should be given to the following:

- Reason for the misstatement or deviation
  - Are there indicators or warning signals of possible fraud?
- Do the misstatements/deviations
  - Indicate a previously unidentified risk or weakness in internal control that could be material?
  - Impact on risk assessments and other planned procedures?
  - Head to the need to modify or perform further audit procedures?

The auditor should remember that an audit is a cumulative process of gathering and evaluating audit evidence. All evidence obtained should be evaluated together and the auditor should ensure that evidence is corroborative and not contradictory.

5.7 Tests of Controls and Substantive Testing

Two types of audit testing can be used by the auditor to gain sufficient appropriate audit evidence, these being tests of controls and substantive testing. The auditor uses the methods of obtaining evidence which are described above when performing both types of testing.

Tests of controls

Tests of controls are used in two instances:

- To reduce substantive testing should the results of the tests of control conclude that the systems can be relied upon as described in ISA 330, paragraph 23:

"When the auditor's assessment of risks or material misstatement at the assertion level includes an expectation that controls are operating effectively, the auditor should perform tests of controls to obtain sufficient appropriate audit evidence that the controls were operating effectively at relevant times during the period under audit."
- When substantive testing alone does not provide sufficient audit evidence at the assertion level, as described in ISA 330:
"When….. the auditor has determined that it is not possible or practicable to reduce the risks of material misstatement at the assertion level to an acceptably low level with audit evidence obtained only from substantive procedures, the auditor should perform tests of relevant controls to obtain audit evidence about their operating effectiveness."

As discussed in detail in **Chapter 3**, tests of control should be designed to obtain audit evidence about:

- How internal controls were applied at relevant times during the period under review. If substantially different controls were used at different times during the period, each control system should be considered separately.
- The consistency with which internal controls were applied.
- By whom or by what means controls were applied.

Procedures used to test controls are as follows:

- Inquiries with appropriate personnel
- Inspection of relevant documentation
- Observation of the company's operations
- Re-performance of the application of the control e.g. a walkthrough of the process.

Inquiry alone is not sufficient evidence to support a conclusion about the effectiveness of a control. A combination of the above audit procedures is required. It is the nature of the control to be tested that influences the type of audit procedure required.

For example, to test the operating effectiveness of internal control over cash receipts, the auditor might observe the procedures for opening the mail and processing cash receipts. Because an observation is pertinent only at the point in time at which it is made, the auditor would supplement the observation with inquiries from the entity personnel and inspection of the documentation about the operation of such internal control at other times.

Tests of control at the entity level tend to be more subjective e.g. commitment to competence within the entity. They can also be more difficult to document than internal control at the business process level, such as checking to see if a payment was authorised, which can be documented with a simple yes/no response. As a result, the evaluation of entity level and IT general controls is often documented with memoranda to the file and supporting evidence.

For example, to test whether management communicates the need for integrity and ethical values to all personnel, a sample of employees could be selected for interviews. The employees could be asked about communications they have received from management, what relevant policies and procedures exist, and what values they see demonstrated on a day-to-day basis by management. If the common response among the employees is that management has indeed communicated the need for integrity and ethical values, then the test would be a success. Details of each employee interview and supporting documentation such as the entity's policies or communications would then be recorded in a memo with conclusions reached.

Although most entity level and IT general controls will be tested through the exercise of professional judgement objectively applied to the circumstances, there are some situations where the application of a statistically-based formula may be applicable. ISA 530 sets out examples of factors influencing sample size for tests of controls:

Factor	Effect on Sample Size	Explanation
An increase in the extent to which the risk of material misstatement is reduced by the operating effectiveness of controls	Increase	If further tests of controls are carried out, more reliance can be placed on the control system therefore reducing the level of substantive testing required
An increase in the rate of deviation from the prescribed control activity that the auditor is willing to accept	Decrease	If tolerable error increases, the smaller the sample size required
An increase in the rate of deviation from the prescribed control activity that the auditor expects to find in the population	Increase	The higher the rate of deviation the auditor expects, the greater the sample size
An increase in the auditor's required confidence level	Increase	The greater level of confidence the auditor requires to conclude that the sample is indicative of population, the greater the sample size

All these factors are considered by the auditor during the planning stage when designing the tests of controls.

Design of controls testing

There are a number of factors to consider when designing the tests of controls. As a general rule, it is not worth testing controls that are unreliable. These are controls where there is a strong likelihood that exceptions may be found. This is because the sample sizes commonly used for testing controls are based on no exceptions being found. Otherwise, the sample sizes required would be much larger.

Reliability of controls

Some of the factors to consider in assessing the reliability of controls are as follows:

- Is it possible that management can override the established procedures?
- Is there a significant manual element involved in the control that could be prone to error?
- Does the small number of staff involved in the control operation make meaningful segregation of duties impractical?
- Is there a weak IT control environment?
- Are general IT controls poor?
- Is the ongoing monitoring of internal control poor?
- Have personnel changes occurred during the period that significantly affect the application of the control?
- Have changing circumstances necessitated the need for changes in the operation of the control?

Once tests of controls are carried out, the auditor is then able to plan substantive procedures given that the level of substantive testing to be performed and the nature of the control environment are directly linked. If the auditor concluded from the tests of controls that the control environment is very strong, substantive testing will be minimal since the auditor can rely on the information produced by the system. However, if the tests of controls indicated that the control environment is very weak, the level of substantive testing will be increased.

5.8 Substantive Testing

As stated above a combination of controls testing and substantive testing can be used to gain assurance over the financial statement assertions and reduce the risk of material misstatement to an acceptably low level. It has been noted that, where the control environment is identified as strong, the level of substantive testing to be performed will be reduced compared to the level of substantive testing which would need to be performed if the control environment was assessed as weak. However, the auditor must realise that

ISA 330 states that the following substantive procedures should be performed at a minimum for each material class of transactions, account balance, and disclosure, irrespective of the assessed risk of material misstatement:

- Agreeing the financial statements to the underlying accounting records, and
- Examining material journal entries and other adjustments made during the course of preparing the financial statements.

Further to this, ISA 315 outlines that substantive testing should be performed over:

- areas which have been identified as significant risk areas; and
- material classes of transactions, account balances and disclosures.

Substantive procedures are used to gather evidence - that is substantiate - in respect to all material classes of transactions, account balances, and disclosures. They are designed to be responsive to the assessed risks of material misstatement at the assertion level. There are two types of substantive procedures which can be used by the auditor to achieve this evidence:

1. tests of details
2. substantive analytical procedures.

Designing substantive testing

In some situations where a significant risk has not been identified, performance of substantive analytical procedures alone, where the control environment is assessed as strong, will be enough to gain sufficient audit evidence. In other cases a combination of tests of details and substantive analytical procedures may be necessary where the control environment is assessed as weak or where a significant risk has been identified. In the case of a significant risk, substantive tests must be designed so as to respond directly to the risk identified. In other cases, tests of details along with control testing will be sufficient and an analytical review (non-substantive) will be sufficient to gain assurance over the material balance or class of transaction being tested. The key principle is that the combination of tests will depend on the nature of the balances and the specific circumstances applicable to the entity being audited.

5.9 Tests of Details

These procedures are used to obtain audit evidence that will substantiate a financial statement amount. They are used to obtain audit evidence regarding certain assertions such as existence, accuracy and valuation.

When designing a procedure, the auditor needs to consider carefully the nature of the assertion for which evidence is required. This will determine the type of evidence to be examined, the nature of the procedure, and the population from which to select the sample.

For example, evidence for the existence assertion would be obtained by selecting items that are already contained in a financial statement amount. Selecting receivable balances for confirmation will provide evidence that the receivable balance exists. However, selecting items that are already contained in a financial statement amount would not provide any evidence in respect of the completeness assertion. For completeness, items would be selected from evidence indicating that an item should be included in the relevant financial statement amount. To determine whether the sales are complete - that is, no unrecorded sales - the selection of shipping orders and matching them to sales invoices posted to the sales ledger would provide evidence for any omitted sales.

Consider the practical examples of substantive tests of details and the assertions which they address discussed below.

Financial Statement Area	Test of Detail	Assertion Addressed
Sales and accounts receivable	Testing sales cut-off	Cut-Off
Accounts receivable	Assessing adequacy of allowance for doubtful debts	Valuation
Accounts payable	Reconciling balances per accounts payable listing to supplier statements	Completeness, accuracy, existence/occurrence and rights and obligations
Accounts payable	Testing for unrecorded liabilities	Completeness and cut-off
Tangible Fixed Assets	Verification of ownership of fixed assets	Existence/occurrence and rights and obligations
Tangible Fixed Assets	Recomputation of depreciation expense	Accuracy
Bank	Testing bank reconciliations	Accuracy, existence/occurrence and completeness

Financial Statement Area	Test of Detail	Assertion Addressed
Bank	Confirmation of bank accounts	Accuracy, existence/occurrence, rights and obligations and cut-off
Prepayments	Testing prepaid expenses	Accuracy, existence/occurrence, cut-off and completeness
Other tax and social security	Testing compliance with VAT regulations	Accuracy

Through the performance of substantive testing and controls testing the auditor must ensure that financial statement assertions surrounding each transaction, balance and presentation and disclosure are covered adequately by the testing performed. For example, considering the detailed tests above surrounding fixed assets, the assertions of valuation and completeness have not been addressed. The following testing would address these assertions:

Valuation

1. Evaluating the accounting policy for fixed assets including the depreciation policy; and
2. Reviewing valuations performed in relation to fixed assets held, for example, by the directors or independent valuation experts

Completeness Review of repairs and maintenance accounts for items incorrectly treated as revenue expenditure rather than capital expenditure

At the end of the audit the auditor must consider if sufficient, appropriate audit evidence has been obtained over all financial statements areas and the relevant assertions.

Extent of testing when performing tests of details

The auditor uses sample sizes when determining the extent of testing to be performed when using tests of details. The sample size will, for example, depend on the total size of the population, the level of assurance required from the test, other testing performed during the audit on the balance or transaction and the level of risk associated with the balance or transaction.

ISA 530 discusses the factors influencing sample sizes for tests of details:

Factor	Effect on Sample Size	Explanation
An increase in the auditor's assessment of the risk of material misstatement	Increase	If the auditor feels the risk of material misstatement increased, the sample size will be increased in order to test an adequate sample that indicates the whole of the population
An increase in the use of other substantive procedures directed at the same assertion	Decrease	The more the auditor is relying on other substantive procedures to reduce detection risk, the lower the sample required
An increase in the auditor's required confidence level	Increase	The greater level of confidence the auditor requires to conclude that the sample is indicative of population, the greater the sample size
An increase in level of error the auditor is willing to accept	Decrease	The greater the tolerable error (which is driven by materiality), the less the sample is required
An increase in amount of error the auditor expects to find in the population	Increase	The greater the amount of error the auditor expects, the greater the sample size in order to make a reasonable estimate of the actual amount of error in the population

Practical example of substantive tests of details procedure using sampling:

The auditor has decided that tests of detail will be used to verify the year-end accounts payable balance.

The accounts payable balance at the year end is £/€2,500,000 and is made up of 450 suppliers.

> The balance is material to the financial statements.
>
> The sample size chosen will depend on the assessed risk surrounding the balance and results of tests of control performed by the audit team.
>
> If the auditor concludes that the tests of controls around the purchases and payables cycle are weak and that she/he cannot rely on the internal control system, the auditor may decide to verify 100% of the year-end balance by agreeing each supplier balance to the relevant supplier statement. This test would verify the completeness, accuracy, existence/occurrence and rights and obligations of the entity to the balance at the year end.
>
> If the auditor concludes that the tests of controls around the purchases and payables cycle are strong, a reduced sample may be selected given that the auditor can place reliance on, and gain assurance from, the tests of controls performed. In this instance the auditor may decide to verify 50% of the year-end balance by agreeing supplier balances to the relevant supplier statement. In order to achieve this level of coverage (i.e. 50%) the auditor will need to select supplier balances which in total will test 50% of the year-end balance. The auditor may decide to select all balances greater than £/€50,000 on the year-end ledger in order to achieve the coverage required.
>
> As a further test, the auditor may look at invoices and payments after the year end to ensure that all relevant liabilities have been recorded in the correct period – this would verify the completeness of the balance at the year end.

5.10 Audit Sampling

International Standard on Auditing (ISA) 530: *Audit sampling and other means of testing* defines audit sampling as: "The application of audit procedures to less than 100% of items within a population of audit relevance such that all sampling units have a chance of selection" (Para 3a).

The objective of the auditor when using audit sampling is to provide an appropriate basis for the auditor to draw conclusions about the population from which the sample is selected. Audit sampling can use either a statistical or non-statistical approach.

In general terms, sampling is the examination of a few items (or sampling units) drawn from a defined mass of data (or population), with a view to inferring characteristics about the mass of data as a whole.

Sampling has been an accepted auditing technique since the early part of the 20th Century and today is recognized as an essential feature of most audits. Three main reasons account for its importance, namely:

- In the modern business environment it is not economically feasible to examine the details of every transaction and account balance;
- Testing a sample of transactions is faster and less costly than testing the whole population;
- Auditors are required to form an opinion about the truth and fairness of the financial statements. They are not required to reach a position of certainty or to be concerned about the statements' absolute accuracy. The task can usually be accomplished by testing samples of evidence; there is no need to test the whole population.

Sampling may *not* be appropriate in certain circumstances. These are primarily:

- When the auditor has already been advised of a high level of errors or systems' failures or a possible fraud.
- Where populations are too small for a valid conclusion – it may be more effective to check them all.
- Where all the transactions in a population are material, e.g. a manufacturer of aeroplanes – they may only sell a few in a year but each contract is worth several hundred million pounds.
- Where data is required by law to be fully disclosed in the financial statements, e.g. directors' emoluments.
- Where the population is not homogeneous.

Non-statistical judgmental sampling vs statistical sampling

When discussing audit sampling, it is important to distinguish between judgmental and statistical sampling.

1. **Judgmental Sampling** Judgmental sampling refers to the use of sampling techniques in circumstances where the auditor relies on his or her own judgment to decide:
   - How large the sample should be;
   - Which items from the population should be selected;
   - Whether to accept or not accept the population as reliable based on the results obtained from the sample units examined.

This sampling method has advantages over statistical sampling in that it is generally faster, and therefore less costly, to apply. However, unlike statistical sampling, the method provides no measure of sampling risk and, should the auditor's judgment be challenged (particularly in a court of law), the conclusions reached with respect to the sample may be difficult to defend. Further, when using judgmental sampling it is difficult not to introduce sample bias – whether it be in relation to sample size, the items selected or the conclusions reached with respect to the population.

2. **Statistical Sampling** Statistical sampling refers to the use of sampling techniques which rely on probability theory to help determine:
   - how large the sample should be
   - whether to accept or not accept the population as reliable based on the results obtained from the sample units examined.

We should note that, when statistical sampling is used, sample units *must* be selected at random (ISA 530 para. 43).

This sampling method has certain important advantages over judgmental sampling:

- it is unbiased;
- should aspects of the sampling be challenged, because it is based on probability theory and, therefore, considered to be objective (rather than based on the auditor's subjective judgment), it is readily defensible;
- it permits quantification of sampling risk. For example, if a sample is selected on the basis of a 5% sampling risk, there is a 5% chance that the sample is not representative of the population and, as a result, an inappropriate conclusion may be reached about the population.

However, statistical sampling is viewed as more complex and costly to apply than judgmental sampling.

Designing the sample

Auditors need to consider:

- **Population**
  As already stated the population (classes of transactions or account balances) is the data set from which the sample will be chosen. The essential feature of the population is that it be homogeneous.
- **Level of confidence**
  Auditors work to levels of confidence which can be expressed precisely. For example, a 5% confidence level means that there are 19 chances out of 20 that the sample is representative of the population as a whole. The converse view is that there is one chance in 20 that the sample, on which the auditor draws conclusions, is non-representative of the population as a whole.
- **Precision**
  From a sample it is not possible to say that the auditors are 95% certain that, for example, the error rate in a population of stock calculations is 5%, but only that the error rate is x%± y% where ± y% is the precision interval, Clearly the level of confidence and the precision interval are related, in that for a given sample size higher confidence can be expressed in a wider precision interval and vice versa.

- **Tolerable error**
  Tolerable error is the maximum error in the population that auditors are willing to accept (ISA 530 para. 12) and still conclude that audit objectives have been achieved. The tolerable error in a population is usually determined in the planning stage, It is related to and affected by:
  - Materiality considerations;
  - Assessment of control risk;
  - Results of other audit procedures.

  The essential procedure is to set a tolerable error rate then to project the error rate in the population implied by the sampling results and to compare the two. If the projected error is larger than the tolerable error then further auditing procedures will be necessary in the area.

- **Expected error**
  This is the level of error the auditors might expect to find in the population. Sample sizes need to be larger in populations where a high level of error is expected than if the population is expected to be error free. This is because it is necessary to prove that the actual level of error is greater than the expected error.

- **Materiality**
  This is really a subset of risk. Materiality is fundamental to auditing and with all populations being sampled, materiality should be considered in fixing the sample size because populations that are material to the overall audit opinion (e.g. stock, debtors, creditors) must be sampled with smaller precision intervals and higher confidence levels.

Sampling methods (ISA 530 Appendix 3)

In auditing, a sample should be

- Random – a random sample is one where each item of the population has an equal (or specified) chance of being selected. Statistical inferences may not be valid unless the sample is truly random.
- Representative – the sample should be representative of the items in the whole population. For example, it should contain a similar proportion of high- and low-value items to the population.

Random Sampling This is simply choosing items subjectively but trying to avoid bias. Bias might come in by tendency to favour items in a particular location or in an accessible file or conversely in picking items because they appear unusual, This method is acceptable for non-statistical judgmental sampling but is insufficiently rigorous for statistical sampling.

Simple Random All items in the population have (or are given) a number. Numbers are selected by a means which gives every number an equal chance of being selected. This is done using random number tables or computer- or calculator-generated random numbers.

Stratified Sampling Auditing efficiency may be improved if the audition stratifies a population (ISA 530 para. 36). This means dividing the population into discrete subpopulations (strata = layers) and is useful when parts of the population have higher than normal risk (e.g. high-value items, overseas debtors). Frequently high-value items form a small part of the population and are 100% checked and the remainder are sampled. The information can be produced by a report generator from the management information system and used by the auditor to design the test.

Systematic Selection This method involves making a random start and then taking every nth item thereafter. The sampling interval is decided by dividing the population size by the sample size, i.e. if the population is 1000 and the number to be sampled is 10 the sampling interval will be every tenth transaction. The starting point can be determined randomly.

Multi-Stage Sampling This method is appropriate when data is stored in two or more levels. For example, stock in a retail chain of shops. The first stage is to randomly select a sample of shops and the second stage is to randomly select stock items from the chosen shops.

Block Sampling Choosing at random one block of items, e.g. all March invoices. This common sampling method has none of the desired characteristics and is not recommended. Analogous to this is *cluster sampling* where data is maintained in clusters (groups or bunches), as wage records are kept in weeks or purchase invoices in months. The idea is to select a cluster randomly and then to examine all the items in the cluster chosen. The problem with this method is that the sample may not be representative as the month or cluster chosen may have unique characteristics.

Value Weighted Selection This method (ISA 530 para. 3a) uses the currency unit value rather than the items as the sampling population and is sometimes called *Monetary Unit Sampling* (MUS).

- Its application is appropriate with large variance populations. Large variance populations are those like debtors or stocks where the individual units of the population are of widely different sizes.
- The method is suited to populations where errors are not expected.
- It implicitly takes into account the auditor's concept of materiality.

Attribute Sampling This provides results based on two possible attributes, i.e. correct/not correct and is used primarily in connection with the testing of internal controls, i.e. non-monetary testing. It is generally used in compliance testing where the extent of application of a control is to be determined, i.e. the test is "complies/does not comply". Each deviation from a control procedure is given an equal weight in the final evaluation of results. MUS is an attribute sampling technique as it measures monetary deviations.

5. GATHERING AUDIT EVIDENCE

Projecting the error into the population

For tests of detail, the auditor should project monetary errors found in the sample to the population and should consider the effect of the projected error on the particular audit objective and on other areas of the audit (ISA 530 para. 51). Once errors have been identified they should be projected into the population. Suppose that out of a population of €/£100 000 errors of €/£600 are discovered based on a sample size of transactions totalling €/£20,000. The error in the population would then be expected to be (within the confidence levels):

$$\frac{€/£600 \times €/£100\ 000}{€/£20,000} = €/£3,000$$

The auditor would have to take a view as to whether this was material if it exceeds the level of tolerable error. If it does the auditors may well perform additional tests to ensure that the level of error they have discovered is constant. This may, of course, only serve to demonstrate that the population is materially incorrect, which would result in a degree of substantive testing if the figures were material to the financial statements.

5.11 Selection of Work and Appraisal of Work of Experts

IAS 620 *Using the Work of an Expert* states:

> When using work performed by an expert, the auditor should obtain sufficient appropriate audit evidence that such work is adequate for the purposes of the audit (para 2).

In other words it is up to the auditors to confirm whether or not the work performed by the expert is "adequate" for the audit – the responsibility remains, as always, with them.

In general the auditor's programme of work will provide them with sufficient reliable relevant evidence to enable them to substantiate their opinion. However, there can be circumstances where the auditor's knowledge is insufficient and they may then need to rely on the opinions of experts or specialists to help them form an opinion.

What is meant by an expert?

IAS 620 defines an expert as:

> A person or firm possessing special skill, knowledge and experience in a particular field other than accounting or auditing.

Examples of specialists whose work may be relied upon by auditors include (ISA 620 para. 6):

- Valuers – on the value of fixed assets such as freehold and leasehold property or more rarely plant and machinery and on the value of specialist stock in trade such as beers, wines and spirits or specialist stock such as jewellery, precious stones and works of art.
- Quantity surveyors – on the value of work done on long-term contracts.
- Actuaries – on the liability to be included for pension scheme liabilities.
- Geologists – on the quantity and quality of mineral and petroleum reserves.
- Stockbrokers – on the value of stock exchanges securities.
- Lawyers – on the legal interpretation of contracts and agreements, statutes and regulations or the outcome of disputes and litigation.

Points to consider

In general, in deciding whether the auditors need to have specialist opinions they will consider:

- The knowledge and abilities and previous experience of the audit team – does it have the expertise to deal with the issue itself? If not an expert may have to be called.
- The risk of a material misstatement based on the nature, complexity and materiality of the matter being considered.
- The quantity and quality of other audit evidence which can be obtained.

The expert can be hired either by the auditor or the client – either way the client is likely to end up paying – so cost considerations are important. The auditor should involve experts *only* when no other sufficient appropriate evidence is available.

Factors that may influence the auditor to rely upon or not to rely upon the work of an expert include:

- *The professional competence of the expert* – This may be indicated by technical qualifications, certification and licensing or membership of professional bodies. The expert also should have some level of reputation or standing in the area of their expertise.
- *The experience of the expert* – The expert should have the appropriate experience to carry out the work. For example, if the matter involves a valuation of commercial property it would not be appropriate to engage an expert whose experience was only that of valuing domestic property.
- *The objectivity of the expert* – the degree of relationship with the client may be the key factor. Any expert who is related to the directors or employees of the client or who has financial interest (other than his fee) with the client is clearly less than wholly independent.

Scope of the expert's work

If it is the intention of the auditor to place reliance on the work of an expert, it is important to hold a consultation between auditor, client and expert, at the time the expert is appointed, to reach agreement on the work to be performed. The agreement should cover:

- Objectives and scope of the expert's work.
    - Assumptions upon which the expert's report depends and their compatibility with the accounts, for example, are going concern or market values to be taken into account?
- A statement of the bases used in previous years and any change to be made.
- The use to be made of the expert's findings.
- The form and content of the expert's report or opinion.
- The sources of information to be provided to the expert.
- The identification of any relationship which may affect the expert's objectivity.
- Confidentiality of the entity's information.

Evaluation of the expert evidence

As we have seen the sufficiency and appropriateness of such evidence will depend upon:

- The nature of the evidence required;
- The materiality of the items being evidenced;
- The auditor's assessment of the competence of the expert;
- Their independence from the client.

The auditors have to review the findings of the experts and draw their own conclusions. In particular they will consider:

- The source data used i.e. what has the expert based their opinion on?
- The assumptions and methods used – and their consistency with previous periods.
- When the expert's work was carried out.
- An overall evaluation of the expert's work in the light of the auditors' overall knowledge of the business and the industry and the results of other audit procedures (ISA 620 para. 12).

The auditors may well want to:

- Review the sources themselves to ascertain whether or not they source data is relevant and reliable;
- Review the specialists procedures; and
- Review or test the data used by the expert for themselves

in order to satisfy themselves that the work the expert has done can be relied on. Clearly the auditor does not have the same level of expertise and experience as an expert and the expert's assumptions and methods can be difficult to challenge.

The key points are:

- The expert's opinion is their responsibility – they have to carry out the work they do to the best of their ability;
- Whether that work provides sufficient appropriate evidence for the auditor is the *auditors'* responsibility – and that is what they alone can decide.

If the auditors are not happy with the expert's work they have certain options:

- Employ another expert – cost considerations are important and there is no guarantee the outcome will be any different.
- Discuss the situation with the client and the expert together to see if difficulties can be resolved.
- Apply additional audit procedures.
- As a last resort it may be necessary to modify (qualify) the auditors' report.

5.12 Substantive Analytical Procedures

Substantive analytical procedures involve a comparison of amounts or relationships in the financial statements with a precise expectation developed from information obtained from understanding the entity and other audit evidence gained during the engagement.

To use an analytical procedure as a substantive procedure, the auditor should design the procedure to reduce the risk of not detecting a material misstatement in the relevant assertion to an acceptably low level. This means that the expectation of what the recorded amount should be must be precise enough to indicate the possibility of a material misstatement, either individually or in aggregate, in the balance or class of transaction being tested.

There are a number of techniques that can be used to perform substantive analytical procedures. The objective is to select the most appropriate technique to provide the intended levels of assurance and precision.

These techniques include:

- ratio analysis
- trend analysis
- break-even analysis
- pattern analysis.

In designing substantive analytical procedures, the following factors should be considered:

- suitability of testing given the nature of the assertions
- reliability of the data (internal or external) from which the expectation of recorded amounts or ratios are developed. This will require tests on the accuracy, existence and completeness of the underlying information such as tests of controls or performing other specific audit procedures, possibly including the use of CAATs
- whether the expectation is sufficiently precise to identify a material misstatement at the desired level of assurance
- amount of any difference in recorded amounts from expected values that would be acceptable.

See **Chapter 9** for a worked example of the performance of substantive analytical procedures for sales and debtors.

In establishing meaningful relationships between information, the following questions should be addressed:

- are the relationships developed from a stable environment? Reliable and precise expectations may not be possible in a dynamic or unstable environment
- are the relationships considered at a detailed level? Disaggregation of amounts can provide more reliable and precise expectations than an aggregated level
- are there offsetting factors or complexity among highly summarised components that could obscure a material misstatement?
- Do the relationships involve items subject to management discretion? If so, they may provide less reliable or precise expectations.

The degree of reliability of the data used to develop expectations needs to be consistent with the levels of assurance and precision intended to be derived from the analytical procedure. Other substantive procedures may also be required to determine whether the underlying data is sufficiently reliable. Tests of controls may also be considered to address other assertions such as data's completeness, existence and accuracy. Internal control over non-financial information can often be tested in conjunction with other tests of controls.

In considering whether the data is sufficiently reliable for achieving the audit objective, the following questions should be addressed:

- Is the data obtained from sources within the entity or from independent sources outside the entity?
- Is data from sources within the entity developed by persons not directly responsible for its accuracy?
- Was the data developed under a reliable system with adequate internal controls?
- Is broad industry data comparable for use within the entity?
- How relevant is the data?

- Was the data subject to audit testing in the current or prior periods?
- Were the auditors' expectations regarding recorded amounts developed from a variety of sources?

To avoid unwarranted reliance on a source of data used, the auditor should perform substantive tests of the underlying data to determine whether it is sufficiently reliable or test whether internal control over the data's completeness, existence and accuracy is operating effectively.

Examples of highly substantive analytical procedures:

Financial Statement Amount	Relationship and Procedure
Sales	Selling price applied to volume information about shipments
Amortisation expenses	Amortisation rate applied to capital asset balances allowing for effect of additions and disposals
Overhead element of inventory	Relating actual overheads to actual direct labour or production volumes
Payroll expense	Pay rates applied to number of employees
Commission expense	Commission rate applied to sales

Other analytical procedures can take the form of:

- Detailed comparisons of current financial statements or financial data with that of prior periods or with current operating budgets e.g. an increase in accounts receivable with no corresponding increase in sales could indicate that a problem exists in the accounts receivable collectability and an increase in the number of employees in a professional organisation would lead the auditor to expect an increase in salary expenses and a corresponding increase in the professional fee revenue.
- Comparative data on the various types of products sold or types of customers – this could help explain month-to-month or year-to-year sales fluctuations.
- Ratio analysis – ratios can provide support to the current financial statements (for example, comparable to industry norms or prior year results) or raise points for discussion. Certain institutions, such as banks and trade associations, produce financial statistics on an industry-wide basis. Such statistics can be useful when compared to those of an entity's operation and inquiries made where differences from industry trends occur.

Detailed discussion of the performance of tests of controls and substantive testing in practice in relation to specific financial statement areas are discussed in the chapters noted below:

Inventory – **Chapter 8**
Sales and Debtors – **Chapter 9**
Tangible Fixed Assets – **Chapter 7**
Bank and Cash – **Chapter 10**
Investments – **Chapter 11**
Purchases and Creditors – **Chapter 12**
Share Capital and Reserves – **Chapter 13**

Audit Evidence Conclusions and Summary

- Audit evidence is what an auditor requires in order to conclude whether or not the financial statements give a true and fair view
- Professional judgement is utilised by auditors when assessing the reliability of audit evidence
- All audit assertions should be satisfied by the use of audit evidence
- Tests of controls are used to conclude as to the operating effectiveness of the internal control function within an entity
- If tests of control conclude that there is a strong control environment, the level of substantive testing necessary will be reduced; if tests of control conclude that there is a weak control environment, the level of substantive testing necessary will be greater
- Substantive testing encompasses both tests of detail and substantive analytical testing
- When designing substantive procedures, the auditor needs to consider the nature of the assertion for which evidence is required – this will determine the evidence to be examined, the nature of the procedure to be performed and the population from which to select a sample for testing
- The auditor obtains audit evidence using one or more of the following procedures:
  - Inquiry
  - Inspection
  - Observation
  - Confirmation
  - Recalculation
  - Reperformance
  - Analytical

QUESTIONS

Self-test Questions

1. What is the difference between a test of control (compliance test) and a substantive test?
2. Define analytical procedures
3. Explain the meaning of the term "assertion" and list four assertions relating to account balances.
4. Distinguish between judgemental sampling and statistical sampling.
5. What is tolerable error?
6. Explain monetary unit sampling (MUS).
7. When should an auditor be concerned about the need for the help of an expert?

Review Questions

(See Solutions to Review Questions at the end of this textbook.)

Question 5.1

(a) Identify and explain 3 substantive tests of detail and for each one outline the following:
   i) the financial statement area that it addresses
   ii) the financial statement assertions that it addresses.
(b) Identify and discuss the work an auditor will usually perform to gain sufficient appropriate audit evidence over obsolete and unsaleable stock.

Question 5.2

Big Match Ltd is an audit client of your firm. The annual audit for the year ended 31 March 2008 has just been completed, however, the audit senior has taken unexpected leave and has left the following list of issues to be followed up with the client:
 (i) A liability of £/€350,000 has been included in the results of the company in relation to shareholder dividends.
 (ii) Company land and buildings were revalued during the year and have been included in the financial statements at the revalued amount.
(iii) A significant customer of Big Match Ltd went into liquidation in November 2007. The company manufactured a specialized product for this company which was exclusively sold to them and manufactured to meet their specific needs. At the year end the company has £/€500,000 stock in its books which was manufactured solely for this company. The company has not sold any of this stock since the customer went into liquidation. The client is currently attempting to win a contract with a new customer who uses the same product.
(iv) On review of invoices for legal fees a pending case against the company was identified.

In order to finalise the audit what further information/audit evidence would you require from management in respect of these items?

Question 5.3

State four audit procedures you would undertake to ensure the completeness of sales and debtor balances.

Question 5.4

Fresh Food Ltd is a supplier of food and drink to supermarkets. You, as audit senior, have been asked to review the work performed by the audit junior on creditors and purchases for the year end 31 December 2007 audit. Total purchases were £/€38m in the last year and the company has 175 suppliers on its records.

You have received the following summary information on the work performed by the assistant on supplier statement reconciliations.

Supplier Name	Balance Per Aged Creditor Listing £/€000	Balance Per Supplier £/€000	Assistant's Comments
A	34	80	Appears to be cut-off issue as supplier has recorded £/€45,200 in invoices in December not recorded by client
D	89	55	Credit note on statement but not on the client ledger
R	120	122	Difference is not material for further work
W	61	70	Difference is due to £/€3,000 cash payment from October not yet received by the supplier and claim by Fresh Food Ltd for discount of £/€4,000 which has not been granted on supplier statement

(i) Explain the purpose of the audit procedures carried out on in respect of supplier statement reconciliations.
(ii) What follow up work would you request of the assistant?

Chapter 6

AUDITING IN A COMPUTER ENVIRONMENT AND E-COMMERCE

Checklist of Relevant Professional Statements

- ISA 315 – Understanding the Entity and its Environment and Assessing the Risks of a Material Misstatement
- ISA 330 – The Auditor's Procedures in Response to Assessed Risks
- ISA 402 – Audit Considerations Relating to Entities using Service Organisations

6.1 Introduction

Today, the computer has become a basic necessity in our lives. Whether the auditor is auditing a small company or a large multinational, the computer will be used in processing financial information.

Small companies usually use readily available general accounting software which fulfils their requirements.

Larger companies usually will have tailor-made software to suit their needs. In many cases these software solutions are full Enterprise Resource Planning (ERP) solutions. ERP systems are designed to cover all or the majority of the core functions of an enterprise, no matter what the organisation's business is.

Regardless of the computer systems used the audit objectives and approach will remain largely unchanged.

1. Audit objective – The audit objective will not change as the auditor must *obtain sufficient appropriate audit evidence to draw reasonable conclusions on which to base the audit opinion.*
2. Audit approach – The audit approach will not change as the auditor must continue to plan, ascertain, record, and evaluate.
3. Overall control will not change as the normal elements of internal control present in a manual system will still exist in a computer system.

The normal elements of internal control, such as personnel, authorisation, physical, organisational, arithmetic and accounting, are just as important in a computer system as they are in a manual system.

6.2 The Auditor's Approach

In the earlier days, the auditor was interested to verify that data was being correctly input and processed by the computer.

This approach was called auditing "around the computer". Audit activity was primarily focused on ensuring that the source documentation was processed correctly and the auditor would verify by checking source documentation to the output documentation.

What actually happened in the computer itself was largely ignored.

Computers today are more complex. A number of computer systems are "real time" and hence there might be only a limited amount of paper work. This would make the auditing "around the computer" far more difficult, at best, or impossible, as there would be no paper trail.

Under these circumstances where there is a lack of paper trail, the auditor will use an approach which is called auditing "through the computer system". This involves the auditor performing tests on the controls to evaluate if they are effective.

After performing these tests, if the auditor finds that the controls are effective, then the auditor can go on to perform a reduced amount of substantive testing.

When considering whether or not to rely on computer controls a first step for the auditor is to assess the company's use of computer systems. In order to make this assessment the auditor could consider the use of computers under three headings similar to those set out below:

- Extent of Use;
- Importance to the Business; and
- Complexity.

In general, the greater the extent of use, importance and complexity, the greater the need to assess computer controls.

When the auditor decides that there is a need to assess computer controls his key focus will be to identify and evaluate the controls in place which ensure the Integrity, Availability and Confidentiality of the data processed and stored by the computer systems.

Typically the auditor will ask – what controls are in place to prevent unauthorized changes to the data – integrity; what measures are in place to ensure that the data is available when required – availability; and what controls are available to ensure that only authorised personnel can access the data – confidentiality?

In a computerised accounting system, there are differences that the auditor needs to consider and take into account when planning his audit approach.

Some of these differences include the following:

1. The processing can be centralised, which means systems like wages, sales and purchases are all processed in the same computerised environment in one location.
2. Invisibility of processing can lead to a lack of audit trail.
3. You can have potentially better internal controls.
4. The computer system will ensure speed, accuracy and consistency of processing.
5. Staff will need to be trained, and be technically competent.

6.3 Controls in a Computerised Environment

There are two major classifications of controls in a computerised environment:

1. **General controls** – these are general controls, which cover the environment in which the computer system is operating. Broadly speaking, this category covers organisational controls, systems development and maintenance controls, access controls and other general controls.
2. **Application Controls** – these are controls which seek to ensure the accuracy and completeness of input processing, processing controls and output controls. These application controls are designed to detect errors before, during and after processing.

Typically, an auditor would evaluate general controls and assess their effectiveness.

General Controls can be divided into three categories to allow for ease of testing:

- IT Operations;
- IT Security; and
- IT System Change Controls.

When reviewing the controls in these areas the focus is also to ensure the integrity, availability and confidentiality of the data.

If the auditor considers general controls to be weak then it is unlikely that he would look at the effectiveness of the application controls instead he would then consider taking a wholly substantive approach.

Computer controls as with all internal controls are of three different categories - preventative controls, detection controls and correction controls.

Preventative controls are considered to be the strongest type of controls which would prevent the error from occurring in the first place.

In a real life situation, take the example of a passenger who wants to travel by train from Dublin to Cork.

The ticket examiner on the platform checks that all passengers possess a valid ticket before he allows you board the train. This is an example of a preventative control.

Once you're on the train, the ticket collector comes around and examines your ticket to ensure that it's a valid ticket for travel. If he finds that you do not have a valid ticket for travel, then you will be required to pay a fine and buy a proper ticket. This is an example of a detection and corrective control.

General Controls

As set out above the key audit objectives when reviewing general controls is to ensure that the integrity, availability and confidentiality of the data is appropriately controlled.

In order to meet these objectives the auditor will look to identify and test relevant control activities under each of the general control categories which satisfy these objectives.

Examples of control activities for each of the main general control areas include:

IT operations

1. Interface Controls – as part of this control, measures should be in place to monitor data flows between systems to ensure that interfaces have operated as intended. The auditor should also look to review any procedures which the company has in place to identify and remediate data flows which fail to operate correctly.
2. Operator controls – under this category, responsibility for scheduling and monitoring operational tasks should be divided between operators and adequate operators should be scheduled to address the work load as required.
3. Standby facilities – in case of a catastrophic event occurring, the company or the business should make appropriate arrangements, either with other businesses who operate a similar system or with specialist service providers, so that processing can continue with minimum interruption.

IT security

1. Logical Access Controls – computer systems should be secured by the use of passwords and other suitable security parameters. These measures should be regularly reviewed to ensure that they remain effective.
2. User Access Management – businesses should ensure that appropriate controls are in place to govern access to their computer systems. In particular a process should be established to ensure that sufficient User Access Management controls are in place i.e. that the granting of user access is appropriately approved and that accounts are removed when staff leave employment or change roles.
3. System Security – this control deals with making sure that antivirus software is up-to-date, and that there is adequate protection for the system via firewalls etc. Employers

should ensure that all employees who use their systems are provided with guidance and policies in relation to the use of e-mails, Internet and other business tools.
4. Physical Security – In addition to good logical security settings organisations should also ensure that physical access to their computer systems is appropriately restricted.

IT system change controls

1. Systems Development Approvals – these controls relate to the development of the system. There should be controls to ensure that users' needs are addressed and that all system changes are approved. Typically, this will involve coordination between the users and management and the experts who will be implementing and developing the computer system. All changes to the computer system or requirements should be authorised by management.
2. System Change Documentation – There should be adequate documentation of the system. Typically systems' documentation consists of either flowcharts or narrative descriptions or a combination of both. It would also have documentation and examples of input documentation and output documentation. It will have details on organisation charts and job descriptions for personnel and details of the system hardware and the location of equipment on the premises.
3. System Change Testing – There should also be adequate testing and training. This involves testing of individual programs to ensure that they are working properly. Typically this will involve the use of test data. This also involves the testing of the actual hardware in the system to ensure that it is functioning properly. All staff should also be properly trained in their jobs to carry out the tasks that will be allocated to them.
4. Segregation of duties – this is a very basic internal control and should ensure that there is adequate segregation between systems' maintenance, operators, data preparation and the user department. Segregation of duties is particularly important in ensuring that those who are responsible for making changes to IT systems and developing IT systems do not have access to the production or live systems.
5. File controls – these controls will ensure that only correct files are taken for processing, that files are maintained in a library and only given to authorised persons. Files should also be properly labelled, and logged in and out from the library.

Application Controls

Under this category, there are three groups of controls, namely input controls, processing controls and output controls.

These controls exist to provide reasonable assurance to the auditor that the recording, processing and the reports by the computer system are being properly performed for specific applications. Auditors will consider these three categories separately for each system. For example, the internal controls surrounding the payroll function will be considered separately from the purchasing system or the sales system.

Input Controls

Input controls are exceptionally important as a lot of errors could occur at the input stage. These controls are designed to ensure that the input data has been correctly authorised, is complete, and is in a machine readable form. If input errors are detected, these need to be reviewed, corrected and resubmitted for inputting into the system again.

Authorisation

Each transaction should be properly authorised in accordance with management's instructions and general rules. Authorisation can occur in a number of ways, for example, a password could be input into the system or a document could be stamped or there could be manual signature as proof of authorisation.

Conversion of Data to be Input

These controls are designed to ensure that data has been correctly converted into a machine readable form. These controls also ensure that the converted data is valid.
Specific controls include some of the following:

- **Control Totals**: these are also known as batch check totals. These controls include document or record counts, which are the number of documents or records to be processed;
- **Hash Totals,** which are computed by adding together values, that would not be typically added together, for example employee numbers, stock code numbers etc. These hash totals are only used for the purpose of control and for no other purpose.
- **Editing Checks:** these controls are intended to detect incorrect or unreasonable or incomplete data. They include the following:
- **Key Verification** – this involves the data being keyed in twice by two separate operators and unless the data matches it will be rejected.
- **Missing data check:** this ensures that all the data has been correctly filled in, and that no files are missing. For example, if you are processing invoices, it should have complete customer account codes, stock quotes, quantities, etc.
  If any of these fields are missing the computer will reject it for further review and follow up.
- **Check digit verification:** this ensures that a detailed account number is proved using a predetermined mathematical calculation and matched to the check digit. If it matches the check digit the account number will be accepted as being a valid entry.
- **Sequence check:** the computer ensures that there are no missing sequence numbers or duplicate sequence numbers.
- **Control totals:** these totals are based on document counts of hash totals or batch totals as discussed earlier.
- **Manual visual scanning:** this involves the manual scanning of individual input documents against a listing of items that have been processed by the computer.

Processing Controls

These controls are designed to provide reasonable assurance that the computer processes have been performed as intended. They ensure that the transactions are not duplicated or lost or improperly changed in any way and errors are identified and corrected on a timely basis.

These controls include the following:

- **Reasonableness checks** – this will ensure that the item is reasonable; for example, if typically customers order no more than six to eight items of a typical stock item, and if the item input is greater than eight the computer will flag it for further follow up to make sure it is a genuine and valid quantity.
- **Find identification labels** – all files should be manually labelled so that only the correct files are used in processing. These files would also have an internal label in a machine readable form, which will be matched to the operator's instructions before processing can start.
- **Before and after report** – this report will show the number of entries that should be updated and actual number of accounts that were updated. For example, if despatches were made to a hundred customers, the report will also show that a hundred customer accounts were updated with invoices.
- **Control totals** – this involves the computer checking the totals of the input documents for that run to the processed amounts in that run to ensure that they match.

Output Controls

These controls are designed to ensure that the processing has been correctly carried out, and the output reports are then distributed to authorised personnel only.

These controls include the following:

- **Visual scanning** – this involves manual scanning to see if the output looks reasonable, and could involve comparing actual results with estimated results. This could also involve source documents being matched to output reports on a sample basis.
- **Reconciliation** – this involves the output totals being matched to input totals and processing totals by various departments within the organisation, for example, the user department and the computer department.

6.4 Computer Assisted Audit Techniques (CAATs)

Cost and other considerations

In considering the use of CAATs, the auditor will not need to consider the benefit of using it versus the actual cost of implementing it.

However, he will need to consider whether it will constitute sufficient and appropriate audit evidence.

Typically, CAATs are expensive to set up in the first year of the audit but are far more cost effective in the long run as they can be used with minor modifications if required in future years.

Further, in using CAATs the auditor can test for more transactions. In some instances, certain tests can only be performed using CAATs. For example, in a company having about 500 employees, it would be practically impossible for the auditor to search for duplicate PPS numbers. However, the CAATs' program could do this for the auditor fairly quickly.

Some of the benefits associated with the use of CAATs include:

- The ability to test the entire population or a much greater part of the population than using a sample approach;
- Common tests can be designed and programmed so that they can be repeated several times and thus increase audit efficiency;
- Using most data analysis tools so that data once imported to the system cannot be changed thus reducing the risk of accidental change or deletion of the data.

However, when using CAATs the auditor would also need to consider the level of expertise needed among audit staff in performing the audit in a computerised environment and the availability of the necessary information in a useable format.

Tests of control

This typically involves the auditor using test data. This data is not a genuine transaction data, but a data that is generated by the auditor. Test data is sometimes referred to as dummy data. This test data consists of both valid and invalid data. The auditor knows in advance what the results of the processing should be. For instance, if he was processing dispatch notes, he would put in both valid and invalid transactions in various combinations.

For example, he might miss out a customer code on one dispatch note (which should be rejected by the computer) or he might put in an incorrect customer code, which also should be rejected by the computer. On another transaction, he might put in an incorrect stock code number.

In testing a payroll system, the auditor might input an invalid employee number expecting it to be rejected. He might input excessive hours to see if the system will flag it as excessive hours, for further review.

In this manner, the auditor will have calculated in advance the expected results of the processing. If the computer processing matches his expected results, then the auditor can conclude that the controls are functioning.

Test data can be processed as part of a regular processing run ("live" run) or it could be processed separately on its own ("dead" run).

There are certain other factors the auditor needs to consider.

In a dead run, the conditions in which this test data are being processed may be artificial.

In a live run, there is a possibility that the test data might actually corrupt genuine client data. In rare circumstances, it might even cause the system to crash.

Substantive testing

Audit software is used to interrogate and extract and analyse data in files.

In substantive testing, the auditor is trying to verify the truth and fairness of transactions and balances (completeness, accuracy, etc) in the financial statements.

The amount of substantive testing that the auditor will perform will depend upon the results of his tests of controls.

In this section, we will look at various types of substantive procedures that an auditor can perform using CAATs.

For instance, in the audit of debtors the auditor can extract a sample to be circularised and get the program to print out the confirmation letters with the addresses and balances to be confirmed. He could use CAATs to print out a list of large and unusual balances, including credit balances in debtors' balances. Other tests will include totalling the accounts receivable ledger and comparing it to the general ledger total.

In the audit of payroll, the program could be used to recalculate the payroll cost for the year which could be agreed to the General Ledger. It could identify employees that might have worked excessive hours for further follow-up by the auditor.

Here are some further examples:

Stocks

- Testing overhead allocations.
- Checking the mathematical accuracy of the stock records by multiplying the cost by the quantity.
- Adding the total values of stock items to come up with a total value of stock included in the financial statements.
- Identifying slow-moving items by comparing two sales records.

Tangible fixed assets

- Analysing assets by different classes
- Reperforming depreciation calculations to ensure that they have been correctly calculated.

- Verifying the mathematical accuracy of different asset classes and agree to the financial statements.
- Selecting a sample of additions during the year for further testing.
- Selecting a sample from the repairs and maintenance account for further testing to ensure that those items should not have been capitalised.

6.5 E-Commerce

E-Commerce has been one of the significant business growth areas in recent years and it continues to expand and be an important source of business for many organizations. When auditing a company which is involved in E-Commerce there are a number of important factors that the auditor should consider. These include:

Complexity – in an online environment it is very likely that transactions will be much more complex than in an historical business. The auditor will need to ensure that he is fully aware of the transaction flows in order to identify relevant risks and controls.

Volume – for the majority of online businesses the volume of transactions is going to be very high. This can pose several difficulties for the auditor and may demand the use of CAATs or some such automated techniques in order to ensure appropriate coverage of the population.

Transaction Speed – in addition to the high volume of transactions, in the online environment transactions tend to be automated and completed at high speed. This usually means that there are limited manual controls to govern the process and the auditor must rely on automated controls in order to obtain sufficient assurance.

Security – in an online environment the need for appropriate security is vitally important. The E-Commerce business will typically be responsible for collecting sensitive information such as credit card numbers and person details and will need to ensure that these are not lost. The Internet is also fundamentally insecure and in addition to its responsibilities to its customers the auditor will also need to ensure that the business has also protected its own information assets.

Third Parties – in the E-commerce environment there is increased use of third parties as outsourced partners to support the business. In addition to considering the controls and practices at the auditee the auditor may also need to understand and review the controls in place at relevant third-party organisations.

Summary

From this chapter, you should have learnt that auditing in a computer environment is very similar to that of auditing in a manual environment that the auditor still needs to obtain sufficient and appropriate audit evidence to support his opinion. The basic approach is very similar.

However, the auditor will have to ensure that staff are properly trained and have the knowledge to be able to audit in a computer environment.

The nature of the tests, i.e. tests of control and substantive tests, are also similar to performing an audit in a non-computerised environment. The major difference here is that the auditor has to use the computer in performing his tests, in both tests of control and substantive tests.

QUESTIONS

Self-test Questions

1. Distinguish between general controls and application controls.
2. What are the benefits associated with using CAATs?
3. What important factors does the auditor need to consider when auditing a company which is involved in E-Commerce?

Review Questions

(See Solutions to Review Questions at end of this text book.)

Question 6.1

The incumbent auditor of DRUID Ltd ("DRUID") has reached retirement age and the directors are planning to appoint a new auditor to take over the appointment. The directors of DRUID have decided to put the audit out to tender and your firm is interested in being considered.

The directors have told you that they require an auditor who can demonstrate clear, jargon-free knowledge of the most modern auditing techniques. In particular, one of the non-executive directors has told the Board how the auditor of his own company uses Computer-Assisted Audit Techniques (CAATs). The directors of DRUID have requested you to give them an authoritative definition of CAATs and a jargon-tree explanation of how you, as a potential auditor, might use CAATs specifically in relation to the substantiation of DRUID's year-end debtor balance.

The directors have provided you with the following details regarding debtors:

1. The directors regard trade debtors as their most important asset. Accounting for debtors is carried out through a bespoke software package that is three years old. The package has been trouble-free and the directors are very happy with it. The package is fully integrated with the general ledger.

2. DRUID analyses its debtors' accounts as follows:

Type	No of Accounts	Definition
Active	50,000	Account having more than one transaction per week
Semi-Active	75,000	Account having more than one transaction per month
Semi-Dormant	135,000	All other accounts on the system

3. At anyone time DRUID has approximately 50 large debtor balances. Each of these large balances can fluctuate between £50k to £500k. At the year end, the average large balance is £l50k. The remaining accounts have, on average, balances between £0.5k and £10.5k.
4. The directors regard any amount greater than £250k as material.

Requirement On the assumption that your firm has been appointed auditors, draft a letter to the Board of Directors of DRUID explaining how you would apply CAATs to the debtors' ledger of the company.

Your letter should deal with each of the following issues:

(a) The general application of CAATs.
(b) The application of CAATs in the specific circumstances of DRUID Ltd.

Question 6.2

Controls in a computer system may be classed as either "input", "processing" or "output" controls. Such controls, together with security controls, help ensure the completeness, integrity and accuracy of information in a computer system.

Requirement

(a) Define the terms input controls, processing controls and output controls and give one example of each.
(b) State the computer security controls specific to situations where the national telephone system is used for transmitting data between computers, using modems or similar electronic equipment.

Question 6.3

In most organisations a significant amount of accounting information is held on computers in various electronic formats, including spreadsheets and databases. Poor controls may lead to sensitive commercial information ending up in the hands of unauthorised personnel.

Requirement

(a) Explain what is meant by
   (i) physical access controls; and
   (ii) logical or programmed access controls in relation to computer systems.
(b) Set out examples of controls that might be used within a computer system program to restrict access to authorised personnel where the system is based on –
   (i) a standalone PC;
   (ii) a local area network;
   (iii) a network of PCs communicating via the public telephone network.
(c) Give THREE examples of controls that might be deployed in a computer system to detect any unauthorised access.

Question 6.4

Auditors use Computer Assisted Auditing Techniques (CAATs) as an economical way of carrying out substantive tests for large audit clients.

Requirement Give TWO different examples of CAATs that could be used to make substantive testing more efficient and effective in respect of the audit of each of the following areas for a large audit client:

(a) Sales and trade debtors
(b) Stocks
(c) Purchases and trade creditors
(d) Wages and salaries
(e) Fixed assets.

Question 6.5

You are a senior in the Computer Audit Department in DAVIS & Co., Chartered Accountants & Registered Auditors. You have been assigned to review the general computer controls for BETA Ltd ("BETA"), a client company.

BETA has a separate Data Processing Department which is headed up by the DP manager, Ms Nicola Prendergast. The Data Processing Department staff consists of ML Floyd Gibson, who is a trained systems analyst and programmer, two assistant programmers and three computer operators. All software in use was originally supplied by NEW DOLPHIN, a well respected software house. Changes have been made to the systems in use but only after consultation with the end user and with NEW DOLPHIN. Only members of the Data Processing Department have access to the computer room.

Requirement

(a) Define what is meant by "general computer controls".
(b) Set out the typical controls that you would expect to see in operation in BETA under each of the following headings:
   (i) Development controls.
   (ii) Organisational controls.

Question 6.6

You are the senior engaged on the audit of the Silver Birch Hotel, a client of your firm of Chartered Accountants & Registered Auditors.

The Silver Birch Hotel is owned by a partnership of individuals who have employed a general manager to operate the hotel on their behalf. The partnership meets on a quarterly basis to review the hotel's performance. It is a four-star hotel which opened for the first time in April 1999, and comprises 60 bedrooms, a leisure centre, a function room, a lounge, a bar and a restaurant. The accounting system is a state of the art integrated point of sale system with electronic recording of reservations, food and drink sales, bedroom sales, telephone, laundry charges etc. Manual credits can be input on to the system by the Bar/Restaurant Manager or the Head Receptionist. Cash is banked twice weekly on Monday and Friday. The hotel has a full-time Accountant, Mary Hamilton, who appears competent although she is not fully qualified.

Extracts from the management accounts for the year ended 30 April 2001, with comparatives from the year ended 30 April 2000, are presented below. The General Manager has informed you that, despite the significant impact on operations arising from the Foot and Mouth crisis and the slowdown in tourist traffic, the hotel's performance was satisfactory and he is confident about current and future trading prospects.

You are provided with the following information:

	Year Ended 30 April 2001 €/£ '000	Year Ended 30 April 2000 €/£ '000
Revenue		
Rooms	220	120
Bar	380	400
Restaurant	510	550
Other	75	80
	1,185	1,150
Gross profit (gross margin %)	408 (34%)	318 (28%)
Depreciation	560	500
Marketing expenditure	120	250

Payroll costs – management	120	150
Security and other building-related costs	40	50
Other costs	65	80
	905	1,030
Net loss	(497)	(712)

Requirement

(a) With regard to the Silver Birch Hotel, set out the risks and benefits associated with the use of a computerised system for the recording and processing of the following transactions:
   (i) Bedroom revenue
   (ii) Bar and restaurant revenue.
(b) Set out FIVE Computer Assisted Audit Techniques (CAATs) that could be used on the audit of the Silver Birch Hotel and explain clearly the benefits of using each of the techniques you have outlined.

Question 6.7

IT systems require continuous upgrade and improvement. Most companies have spent significant funds on IT and now rely heavily on IT to support all aspects of their businesses, including the financial systems. The maintenance of these business systems is a key function of any IT department. Furthermore, as software and hardware products are upgraded and improved to later and newer versions, the process of change needs to be carefully managed.

ELEGANT Ltd is a client of the firm of Chartered Accountants and Registered Auditors in which you work. You have just had a phone call from the Managing Director informing you that he lost all of the information which was held on his hard drive (which he had not backed up) when one of his young children dropped his laptop on to a hard floor. As a result of this mishap, he has decided to initiate a review of IT maintenance and security and is seeking your advice.

Requirement

(a) Advise the Managing Director on each of the following matters:
   (i) The procedures that should be put in place for the maintenance of computer systems.
   (ii) The steps which you as auditor would take in order to carry out a review of the security of an IT environment.
(b) You have been asked by the audit partner to review the installation of the new accounting system in the company. What are the main headings under which you would report?

Question 6.8

UGARS Ltd ("UGARS") has been a client of your firm since its establishment two years ago. The audit approach is primarily to perform substantive testing of detail, as the company has an unsophisticated computer system.

1. The Finance Director has recently informed you that, given the company's BONZA growth, a new computer system has been acquired and implemented. He has asked you to review the remote and local security within the new computer system. In your discussion with the Finance Director, you noted the following with regard to stock (inventory) functionality within the new system:
   - The stock system is fully integrated with the nominal ledger
   - Stock can be 100% tracked from receipt to delivery to customer
   - Ageing of stock is recorded within the system
   - Enhanced cycle count functionality exists.
2. The Finance Director has delegated the preparation of the statutory financial statements to the Financial Controller for the forthcoming year for the first time. The Financial Controller has just phoned you and he has indicated that he will have the financial statements ready within a week of the audit fieldwork commencing and a number of the disclosures will be "ballpark" correct and not materially misstated.

Requirement

(a) Write a letter to the Financial Director of UGARS describing the various security settings that an auditor would want to consider in reviewing remote and local security controls within the new system.
(b) What factors should an auditor consider in determining materiality, and is there any issue arising from the statement that disclosures will be "ballpark" correct?
(c) Give an example of how the implementation of the new computer system could impact positively on the audit approach adopted.

Part III

AUDIT PROCEDURES

CHAPTER 7

THE AUDIT OF TANGIBLE FIXED ASSETS

Learning Objectives

- To identify the audit objectives applicable to tangible fixed assets
- To determine the audit strategy for tangible fixed assets
- To identify substantive tests to audit tangible fixed assets

Checklist of Relevant Professional Statements:

ISA 510 – Initial Engagements – Opening Balances and Continuing Engagements – Opening Balances
ISA 540 – Audit of Accounting Estimates
ISA 600 – Using the Work of Another Auditor
ISA 610 – Considering the Work of Internal Audit
ISA 620 – Using the Work of an Expert
IAS 16 – Property, Plant and Equipment
IAS 17 – Leases
IAS 36 – Impairment of Assets
IAS 40 – Investment Property

7.1 What is a Tangible Fixed Asset?

On the balance sheet, it includes land and buildings (freehold or leasehold), plant and equipment (including those held under finance lease) and the related accumulated depreciation. In terms of the income statement, these include depreciation charges, repairs and maintenance costs, finance charges on finance leases and rent on operating leases.

IAS 16 states "the cost of an item of property, plant and equipment shall be recognised as an asset if and only if: (a) it is probable that future economic benefits associated with the item will flow to the entity; and (b) the cost of the item can be measured reliably." (Paragraph 7, IAS 16)

Tangible assets are those assets that are retained for use in the company's operations. These include land and buildings, plant and equipment, fixtures and fittings and motor vehicles.

7.2 Risks Associated with Tangible Fixed Assets

Before developing the audit plan, the auditor needs to consider a number of risks that may arise whilst verifying tangible fixed assets:

- The company may not actually own the tangible assets included in the financial statements
- The tangible assets included in the financial statements might not actually exist
- Tangible assets are overstated in the financial statements e.g. the value of the tangible asset may have fallen to less than its current net book value
- The depreciation rate may be too low
- Tangible assets may have become obsolete
- The client may have failed to record disposals of tangible assets
- Revenue items may have been charged in error to capital expenditure
- Control over tangible assets may be poor and fixed asset registers may not have been kept up to date
- Changes in technology may render the assets obsolete
- A revaluation may have previously occurred with consequent subjectivity in valuation
- A significant number of idle assets and assets under construction are held with uncertainty as to future use.

7.3 Audit Objectives and the Audit of Tangible Fixed Assets

As discussed in **Chapter 5** on Gathering Audit Evidence, it is necessary for the auditor to seek appropriate audit evidence to satisfy all of the audit objectives and to eliminate the possibility of any of the aforementioned risks occurring.

In addition to the specific audit objectives listed below, the following are control objectives the auditor should seek to satisfy when auditing tangible assets:

- Ensure all tangible assets actually exist and are owned by the company.
- Ensure all tangible fixed assets are correctly recorded by the client and are maintained via the fixed asset register.
- Ensure all additions and disposals are properly authorised by management, directors etc.
- Ensure the depreciation policy of the client is adequate and properly applied to each class of asset.

The following represents the specific audit objectives for tangible fixed assets:

Transactions and Events During the Period

Assertion	Objective of Audit Evidence
Occurrence	To ensure recorded additions represent fixed assets acquired during the period under review.
	To ensure recorded disposals represent fixed assets sold, transferred or scrapped during the period under review.
Completeness	To ensure that all additions and disposals which occurred during the period under review have been recorded.
Accuracy	To ensure that all additions and disposals have been correctly posted.
Cut-off	To ensure all additions and disposals have been recorded in the correct period.
Rights and obligations	To ensure the entity holds the rights to all fixed assets resulting from recorded purchase transactions.
Classification	To ensure all additions and disposals have been recorded in the correct accounts and adequately support their classification in the financial statements.

Account Balances at Year End

Assertion	Objective of Audit Evidence
Existence	To ensure that recorded fixed assets represent productive assets that are in use at the balance sheet date (i.e. to ensure the fixed assets exist at balance sheet date).
Rights and obligations	To ensure the entity holds the rights to all recorded fixed assets at the balance sheet date.
Completeness	To ensure that all fixed assets which should have been recorded, have been recorded at the balance sheet date.
Valuation and allocation	To ensure that fixed assets are included in financial statements at appropriate figures for cost or valuation *less* accumulated depreciation at the balance sheet date.

Assertion	Objective of Audit Evidence
Presentation and disclosure	To ensure fixed assets are correctly disclosed in the financial statements at the balance sheet date. This includes disclosing: • Cost/Revaluation, accumulated depreciation and net carrying amount. • Disposals and the related profit or loss on disposal. • Depreciation, including the total depreciation charged, the depreciation method and useful economic life or depreciation rate. Where assets are held under finance lease and/or hire purchase contracts ensure separate disclosure is made of the depreciation charged in the period on these assets. • The pledging of collateral.

7.4 Developing the Audit Plan

Inherent risk, control risk and detection risk

Before the audit of tangible fixed assets is undertaken an assessment of audit risk must be completed. (Audit Risk = Inherent Risk + Control Risk + Detection Risk - see **Chapter 3** on The Risk Assessment Process for detailed explanations of the terms.)

Inherent Risk Inherent risk can vary depending on the different fixed asset account. Inherent risk for the existence assertion of a manufacturing company may be high as there is a risk that scrapped or old machinery may not be taken off the fixed asset register or small tools or equipment used in production may be stolen.

Inherent risk for the existence assertion of a sole trader (e.g. a dentist) may be low as plant and equipment are not normally vulnerable to theft.

Control Risk and Detection Risk Control risk varies depending on the type of asset class. Fixtures and fittings may have a lower assessed level of control risk as these are processed as routine purchase transactions.

On the other hand, land and buildings will be subject to separate controls, such as capital budgeting and specific authorisation by the board of directors.

Because fixed asset transactions are infrequent and high in monetary value, a predominantly substantive audit approach is adopted for fixed assets and as a result the planned level of detection risk is low.

In summary, because transactions involving fixed assets are infrequent and usually are for material amounts, auditors rarely test controls over fixed asset transactions but instead adopt a substantive audit approach. This approach is discussed in detail below.

7.5 Substantive Procedures for the Audit of Tangible Fixed Assets

Substantive procedures for the audit of tangible fixed assets must be designed so as to achieve the desired low level of detection risk.

Opening balances

Initially, evidence must be obtained as to the accuracy of the opening balances and the ownership of the assets comprising the balances. This can be completed as follows:

- Agree opening balances to prior year working papers and signed financial statements. This will highlight any adjustments booked in the prior-year financial statements that need to be carried forward into the current year opening balances
- Inspect the permanent audit file for details of title deeds and registered charges such as mortgages
- If this is the first year of engagement, a copy of the previous auditors' working papers are obtained and opening balances are agreed to these working papers along with the prior-year signed financial statements.

Analytical procedures

The client provides schedules of additions and disposals during the year and with details of any depreciation charge calculated. The mathematical accuracy of these schedules is tested. These schedules are also traced to the related general ledger accounts to ensure the accuracy of the schedules provided by the client.

Analytical procedures can include:

- Re-performing calculations and reconciling to the nominal ledger balances.
- A review of the current year depreciation charge vs the prior year depreciation charge.
- A review of the current year repairs and maintenance charge vs the prior year charge.
- Calculating ratios and analysing results against industry information, prior year results, budgets etc.

Tests of details

Tests of details on transactions are performed on additions, disposals, depreciation and repairs and maintenance.

Additions

As stated in IAS 16 Property, Plant and Equipment,

"The costs of an item of property, plant and equipment comprises:

a) its purchase price, including import duties and non-refundable purchase tax, after deducting trade discounts and rebates.
b) any costs directly attributable to bringing the asset to the location and condition necessary for it to be capable of operating in the manner intended by management.
c) the initial estimate of the costs of dismantling and removing the item and restoring the site on which it is located."

Paragraph 17 of IAS 16 outlines examples of directly attributable costs (which can be capitalised) and these include the following:

1. Costs of employee benefits arising from the construction or acquisition of the item of property, plant and equipment;
2. Costs of site preparation;
3. Initial delivery and handling costs;
4. Installation and assembly cost;
5. Costs of testing whether the asset is functioning properly; and
6. Professional fees.

Paragraph 19 of IAS 16 gives examples of costs which cannot be capitalised and these include the following:

1. Costs of opening a new facility;
2. Costs of introducing a new product or service;
3. Costs of conducting business in a new location or with a new class of customer; and
4. Administration and other general overhead costs.

Additionally, it should be noted that as stated in IAS 23, Borrowing Costs:

"Borrowing costs that are directly attributable to the acquisition, construction or production of a qualifying asset shall be capitalised as part of the cost of that asset."

IAS 16 Property, Plant and Equipment requires the capitalisation of borrowing costs attributable to tangible non-current assets.

The auditor should:

- Obtain a schedule of borrowing costs as prepared by the client and recompute the income statement charge (average liability multiplied by the interest rate)
- Verify the interest rate utilised to relevant loan documentation
- Agree all payments made to loan agreements, bank statements, nominal ledger postings etc.
- Confirm that the difference between the borrowing cost charged and the interest paid has been included in the carrying value of the related liability.

The following procedures should be performed in relation to tangible fixed asset additions:

- The auditor should obtain a copy of the fixed asset budget of the entity. This document not only confirms authority to purchase but will also highlight any significant variances between actual and budgeted purchases. In addition, a review of budgeted expenditure not yet incurred will indicate if the entity has adequate funds and working capital to finance such projections. Budget approval should be verified through a review of the board approving minutes.
- An understanding of the client's capitalisation policy must be obtained. This is an understanding of the client's policy for deciding whether a purchase is a capital item or whether it should be expensed to the profit and loss account. Broadly speaking, most companies set a monetary value below which, regardless of their nature, purchases are expensed. The auditor must ensure that this policy is consistent year on year.

> *Example*
>
> The client's capitalisation policy is to capitalise all items greater than £/€1,000 which are of a capital nature.
>
> Included in the fixed asset additions are the following:
>
> | Description | Cost |
> |---|---|
> | Laptop | £/€1,200 |
> | Memory keys | £/€400 |
>
> The client has correctly capitalised the laptop in line with its capitalisation policy, as the asset is of a capital nature and it cost more than €/£ 1,000. However, the client has incorrectly capitalised the memory keys as capitalisation of these items is not in line with its policy (cost is less than £/€ 1,000).

The cost of additions must be verified. This can be completed on a test basis if there are a large number of additions. This is done by tracing the amount capitalised as per the additions schedule to the supporting purchase invoice. A number of items on the invoice must be agreed:

1. The date of the invoice must be within the accounting period under review.
2. The invoice must be addressed to the client being audited.
3. The cost per the invoice must be agreed to the amount capitalised as stated in the additions schedule.

4. Ensure that VAT has been properly accounted for (i.e. if the client is registered for VAT and reclaimable, the assets must be capitalised at cost less the VAT element, if the client is not registered for VAT assets are capitalised at cost including the VAT element).
5. Ensure all costs capitalised are allowable under IAS16, Property, Plant and Equipment (as noted above)
    - For major additions, the assets should be physically inspected. It is important on physical inspection to ensure that details of the asset are agreed to the invoice and to the capitalised amount (i.e. serial number, description).
    - Leases may be classified as either finance leases or operating leases. For fixed assets held under lease agreements it is important that the auditor obtains a copy of the lease agreements and ensures they are correctly classified in line with IAS 17, Accounting for Leases. For assets held under finance leases, these assets should be included in the client's fixed asset register. The cost of assets held under finance leases should be agreed to purchase invoices. This cost should also be agreed to the cost as stated in the finance lease agreement. IAS 17 states that, at the commencement of the lease term, finance leases should be recorded as an asset and a liability at the lower of the fair value of the asset and the present value of the minimum lease payments (discounted at the interest rate implicit in the lease, if practicable, or else at the enterprise's incremental borrowing rate) [IAS 17.20].
    - When a client internally manufactures its fixed assets, the auditor should verify that all costs have been properly classified as such, including cost of materials, labour, interest costs and overhead, if applicable. There is potential for inherent risk in this area and the auditor needs to evaluate company controls and perform substantive procedures, as necessary, to ensure costs are genuine, accurate and complete.

Repairs and maintenance

- As stated in IAS 16, Property, Plant and Equipment "an entity does not recognise in the carrying amount of an item of property, plant and equipment the costs of day-to-day servicing of an item. Rather, these costs are recognised in the profit and loss as incurred" (Paragraph 12). Therefore, repairs and maintenance costs are not capitalised but instead expensed to the profit and loss account as they are incurred. It is important to look out for this when auditing the costs capitalised.
- The auditor must also scan the repairs and maintenance accounts to ensure items of a capital nature have not been incorrectly expensed to the profit and loss account.

Disposals

- A list of disposals during the period under review is obtained from the client.
- To ensure that all disposals have been accounted for, the auditor must confirm all such disposals with management, re-analyse any miscellaneous income that may relate to the

sale of a tangible fixed asset and reconcile the results of a physical inventory count of relevant fixed assets to the general ledger as this may highlight any possible omissions.
- Supporting documentation should be obtained and inspected for sales and trade-ins of fixed assets. This documentation should include cash remittance advices and/or sales agreements. This documentation is examined to determine the accuracy of the accounting records, including the recognition of any related gain or loss. The gain or loss on disposal of a fixed asset is recomputed by the auditor to ensure its accuracy. Proceeds received should be traced to bank statements.

Depreciation

- As previously mentioned, at the initial procedures stage, an analytical review of the depreciation charge is completed.
- The client's depreciation methods must be reviewed to ensure they are reasonable and consistent with the prior year. It is also important to ensure the depreciation policy used by the client is in agreement with the depreciation policy as outlined in the financial statements.
- The auditor verifies the accuracy of the depreciation charge by recalculation. This can be completed on a test or sample basis by recomputing certain depreciation charges and agreeing the charges calculated by the auditor to the client's charges.
- Following the revaluation of a tangible fixed asset, the current and future depreciation charge should be based on this revalued amount.
- The auditor should check that all properties have been properly classified as investment properties and that appropriate treatment and disclosures have been made. According to IAS 40, investment properties do not need to be depreciated provided they are carried at fair value.
- A reasonableness test is also performed on depreciation, this involves computing the depreciation by class on an overall basis. The following example illustrates how to test depreciation on a reasonableness test:

Rate of Depreciation	Freehold Property 2%	Motor Vehicles 20%	Total	Additional information re Motor Vehicles
Cost	€	€	€	
Opening cost at 1/1/07	100,000	30,000	130,000	
Additions	–	15,000	15,000	Acquired June 2007
Disposals	–	(10,000)	(10,000)	Disposed of September 2007
Closing cost at 31/12/07	100,000	35,000	135,000	

Freehold property has a closing cost of €100,000, if the rate of depreciation is 2% per annum, then the expected depreciation charge for 2007 is €2,000 (€100k × 2%).

Similarly, motor vehicles' depreciation charge for the year can be calculated as follows:

		£/€000
Opening cost	£/€30,000 × 20%	£/€6
Additions	£/€15,000 × 20% × 6/12 months	£/€1.5
Disposals	£/€10,000 × 20% × 9/12 months	£/€1.5
Expected depreciation charge		£/€9

If the client's calculation of depreciation is similar to the above calculation then the auditor can be satisfied the depreciation charge is reasonably stated at the period end provided the motor vehicles are not more than 5 years old.

Tests of details of balances

Tests of details of balances relate to valuation and disclosure. These tests include considering the need for the provision for impairment, determining the appropriateness of a revaluation and examining documentary evidence of title.

7.6 Impairment Review

An impairment review is required at the end of the first financial year following their acquisition, and annually where their useful lives exceed 20 years or are indefinite. IAS 36 recognises that an impairment review should be carried out when there is some indication that impairment has occurred. Impairments generally arise when there has been an event or change in circumstances. It may be that something has happened to the asset themselves (e.g. physical damage), or there has been a change in the economic environment in which they are used (e.g. new regulations).

As stated in IAS 36, Impairment of Assets, the auditor must ensure that the carrying value of fixed assets does not exceed the greater of their net realisable value (i.e. sale value) or value in use. This can be tested by completing the following:

- Reviewing the client's workings on the impairment.
- Reviewing the reasonableness of the assumptions used in the calculation of the impairment. Enquire of management of any potentially overvalued assets. Obsolete and damaged units should be physically inspected and compared to values included in financial statements.
- Determine if any units are held that relate to discontinued activities.

7.7 Revaluation of Fixed Assets

The client may decide to revalue fixed assets so as to reflect a more accurate value in the Balance Sheet. A revaluation of a tangible asset should reflect the "real" conditions of the company based on actual market conditions. According to IAS 16 "If an item of property, plant and equipment is revalued, the entire class of property plant and equipment to which that asset belongs shall be revalued" (Paragraph 36, IAS 16).

If assets are revalued during the period under review the auditor must obtain a copy of the valuer's report. As stated in ISA 620, Using the Work of An Expert, "The auditors should

- Evaluate the appropriateness of the expert's work as audit evidence regarding the assertion being considered.
- Review the source data used, the assumptions and methods of valuation used and their consistency with prior periods when the work was carried out, and the results of the expert's work in light of the auditor's overall knowledge of the business and of the results of other audit procedures.
- Evaluate the professional competence of the expert who performed the revaluation. As stated in ISA 620, this includes "considering the expert's: (a) Professional certification or licensing by, or membership of, an appropriate professional body; and (b) Experience and reputation in the field in which the auditor is seeking audit evidence".

As stated in IAS 16, Property, Plant and Equipment

"Revaluations shall be made with sufficient regularity to ensure that the carrying amount does not differ materially from that which would be determined using fair value at the balance sheet date" (Paragraph 31).

Additionally,

> the frequency of revaluations depends upon the changes in fair values of the items of property, plant and equipment being revalued. Some items of property plant and equipment experience significant and volatile changes in fair value, thus necessitating annual revaluation. Such frequent revaluations are unnecessary for items of property, plant and equipment with only insignificant changes in fair value. Instead, it may be necessary to revalue the item only every three or five years (Paragraph 34).

7.8 Examining Documentary Evidence

Ownership of fixed assets can be verified by documentary evidence.

The following are the various types of documentary evidence an auditor may seek to confirm ownership and existence of tangible fixed assets:

- Freehold Property – Review title deeds and insurance policies. Public records may also be viewed (e.g. Land Registry Offices)
- Motor Vehicles – Review vehicle registration certificates and insurance policies
- Fixtures and Fittings – Review physical purchase invoice, preferably showing "paid" on the invoice.

7.9 Safeguarding Tangible Fixed Assets – The "Fixed Asset Register"

The main safeguard over tangible fixed assets is the preparation of a fixed asset register. The fixed asset register should be maintained by an individual independent of those actually using the assets. In order for this register to be relied on the auditor should perform the following procedures:

- Sample select a number of assets listed on the register and physically inspect the items
- Reconcile the fixed asset register to the various nominal ledger accounts associated with tangible fixed assets e.g. additions, disposals, depreciation, and investigate any differences arising
- Ascertain the cover on each class of asset and compare to cost or net book value of the asset.

If this register is not maintained or is subject to error, control risk will increase and the auditor may need to extend his substantive tests.

7.10 Disclosure Requirements

The following fixed asset items require disclosure in the financial statements (Paragraphs 73–79, IAS 16):

- The measurement bases used for determining the gross carrying amount;
- The depreciation methods used;
- The useful lives or the depreciation rates used;
- The gross carrying amount and the accumulated depreciation;
- A reconciliation of the carrying amount at the beginning and end of the period showing
  - Additions
  - Disposals
  - Acquisitions through business combinations
  - Impairment losses/impairment losses recognised in the P&L
  - Depreciation
  - Net exchange differences arising on the translation of the financial statements from the functional currency into a different presentation currency;
- The existence and amounts of restrictions on title, along with details of property, plant and equipment pledged as security for liabilities;

- The amounts of expenditures recognised in the carrying amount of an item of property, plant and equipment in the course of its construction;
- The amount of contractual commitments for the acquisition of property, plant and equipment;
- The amount of compensation from third parties for items of property, plant and equipment that were impaired, lost or given up that is included in the profit and loss. Any assets charged as security for loans;
- Future capital commitments.

If revaluations have been performed during the period the following require disclosure:

- The effective date of the revaluation;
- Whether an independent value was involved;
- The methods and significant assumptions applied in estimating the items' fair values;
- The extent to which the items' fair values were determined directly by reference to observable prices in the active market or recent market transactions on arm's length terms or were estimated using other valuation techniques;
- For each revalued class of asset, the carrying amount that would have been recognised had the assets been carried under the cost model;
- The revaluation surplus.

If any finance leases were held during the period the following must be disclosed by the lessee:

- The carrying amount of the asset;
- A reconciliation between total minimum lease payments and their present value;
- Amounts of minimum lease payments at balance sheet date and the present value thereof, for:
  – the next year;
  – years 2 through 5 combined;
  – beyond five years;
- Any contingent rent recognised as an expense;
- Total future minimum sublease income under non-cancellable subleases;
- A general description of significant leasing arrangements, including contingent rent provisions, renewal or purchase options, and restrictions imposed on dividends, borrowings, or further leasing.

and by the lessor:

- A reconciliation between gross investment in the lease and the present value of minimum lease payments;

- Details of gross investment and present value of minimum lease payments receivable for:
  - the next year;
  - years 2 through 5 combined;
  - beyond five years;
- Any unearned finance income;
- Any un-guaranteed residual values;
- Accumulated allowance for uncollectible lease payments receivable;
- Any contingent rent recognised in income; and
- A general description of significant leasing arrangements.

Summary of Audit Tests

Audit Assertion	Audit Test
Existence	1) Summarise the fixed asset capitalisation policy and review for appropriateness and consistency of the accounting method with the prior year. 2) Verify ownership of significant freehold land and buildings by inspecting documents of title. 3) Physically verify fixed assets as described in the fixed asset register.
Completeness	1) Agree the total on the fixed asset register to the nominal ledger. 2) Review invoices for additions to fixed assets and ensure they have been correctly analysed and included in the accounts. 3) Scan the repairs and maintenance account items for reasonableness, noting any large or unusual items. 4) Cast the fixed asset subsidiary ledgers and agree the total with the general ledger accounts and the permanent file schedules. 5) Enquire whether there have been any fixed asset transfers between related companies, locations, or account classifications and determine whether such items have been accounted for properly.
Accuracy	1) For all material additions, verify asset details to documents of title, ensure arithmetical accuracy of the document and check the addition was properly authorised by management.

	2) Check the addition is correctly classified as capital expenditure and it has been posted to the correct nominal ledger account. Verify postings to the fixed asset register. 3) For all disposals, ensure such transactions are properly authorised. Ensure the full cost and depreciation have been removed from the financial statements and check the profit or loss on disposal has been correctly calculated. 4) Ensure depreciation has been calculated on all tangible assets, by reference to the fixed asset register. 5) Ensure the depreciation policy applied is in accordance with IAS 16 and is consistent with the prior year. Ensure fully depreciated assets have not been depreciated.
Valuation	1) Identify significant fixed asset additions — Examine appropriate supporting documentation; — Determine whether such additions were appropriately authorised; — Ensure VAT has been correctly accounted for. 2) Determine whether depreciation or amortisation charged to profit and loss account is calculated on a consistent and reasonable basis. 3) Compare the depreciation and amortisation provision to prior periods and to expectations. 4) Ensure that the depreciation of the asset takes into account the current residual value of the asset's expected condition at the end of its useful life. 5) Ensure that any fixed assets that have suffered a permanent diminution in value have been written down appropriately. 6) Consider performing an impairment review on obsolete and damaged items. 7) For assets that have been revalued during the year, ensure the valuer is appropriately qualified and independent of the client.
Cut Off	1) Ensure additions have been accounted for in the correct financial period. 2) Ensure disposals have been accounted for in the correct financial period.

Rights and Obligations/ Ownership	1) Inspect documentary evidence e.g. contract agreement, title deeds, for a sample of fixed assets. 2) Review board approving minutes, statutory books and records and perform a company search to ensure the property is owned by the client and whether any charges exist over such assets. 3) Vouch payments in relation to property upkeep. 4) Enquire whether any fixed assets have been pledged as security by reviewing loan agreements, contracts etc. 5) Enquire as to any plans or commitments to acquire fixed assets. 6) Confirm that there is adequate insurance cover in place in respect of all fixed assets.
Presentation/Disclosure	1) If revaluations are not performed or are not incorporated in the financial statements consider whether the differences between the market value and the book value of interests in land and buildings held as fixed assets are of such significance as to require disclosure in the directors' report. 2) Ensure proper disclosure of the movement in the cost/revaluation, accumulated depreciation and net carrying amounts. 3) Ensure that appropriate disclosure is made of all additions to fixed assets, including grants, and disclosure within the cash flow statement. 4) Ensure that appropriate disclosure is made of all disposals of fixed assets, including disclosure within the cash flow statement. Ensure that profits and losses on disposals are disclosed after operating profit where appropriate, as required by IAS 1. 5) Ensure that appropriate disclosure is made of depreciation, including the total depreciation charged, the depreciation method and useful economic life or depreciation rate. Where assets are held under finance lease and/or hire purchase contracts ensure separate disclosure is made of the depreciation charged in the period on these assets.

QUESTIONS

Self-test Questions

1. What are the key audit risks associated with tangible fixed assets?
2. Give four examples of suitable analytical procedures in relation to tangible fixed assets.
3. Set out suitable audit procedures to establish the ownership and existence of freehold property.

Review Questions

(See Solutions to Review Questions at the end of this textbook.)

Question 7.1

Outline the audit procedure which is most likely to detect the incorrect capitalisation of an expense to fixed assets.

Question 7.2

When auditing fixed assets, why might the auditor decide to assess control risk as high and therefore perform predominantly substantive testing?

Question 7.3

Builder Limited (Builder) is a new client of your firm. Builder is an engineering company. You are the audit senior. The accounts clerk in Builder has provided you with the draft accounts which show the following tangible fixed assets for the year ended 31 March 2005.

	Freehold Land and Buildings €000	Plant and Machinery €000	Motor Vehicles €000	Total €000
Cost				
At 1 April 2004	1,231	679	423	2,333
Additions	122	242	147	511
Disposals	–	(125)	(162)	(287)
At 31 March 2005	**1,353**	**796**	**408**	**2,557**

	Freehold Land and Buildings €000	Plant and Machinery €000	Motor Vehicles €000	Total €000
Depreciation				
At 1 April 2004	674	333	267	1,274
Charge for year	54	80	82	216
Disposals	–	(99)	(138)	(237)
At 31 March 2005	**728**	**314**	**211**	**1,253**

The manager on the engagement has asked you to prepare a memorandum for the assistant assigned to the job, setting out the work programme that the assistant should carry out in the audit of the tangible fixed assets in Builder.

Question 7.4

Handitel Limited (Handitel) manufactures a range of mobile phones and operates a cellular phone network. You are audit senior on Handitel and have been provided with the following reconciliation of Handitel's fixed assets for year ended 31 December 2007.

Reconciliation of Fixed Asset Register to the Nominal Ledger

	Notes	€000
Balance as per fixed asset register at 31 December 2007		14,802
Less		
Plant held on operating lease	1	(357)
Repairs posted to fixed asset register	2	(174)
Assets purchased 5 January 2008	3	(1,400)
Add		
Assets excluded from fixed asset register	4	589
Adjustment for capitalisation of interest	5	73
Asset constructed internally	6	3,061
		16,594

1) This piece of plant was leased in August 2007 for a six-month term.
2) The clerk responsible for maintaining the fixed asset register was on maternity leave for six months from March to September 2007. A placement student was taken on to carry out her duties while on leave. On review of the fixed asset register the accountant uncovered two revenue expense items which were posted to the register in April 2007.
3) This vehicle was ordered in November 2007 and delivered on site on 15 December 2007. A 20% deposit was paid at the time of the order with the balance paid on 5 January 2008.
4) Assets received in September 2007 but not posted to the fixed asset register until January 2008.
5) Handitel decided to change its accounting policy on capitalisation of interest and now opts to capitalise all interest payments.
6) This asset was brought into use in October 2007 with the most significant construction cost being own labour.

Prepare the audit programme in respect of the fixed asset reconciliation above, detailing the specific audit tests you would perform on each reconciling item.

Appendix 7.1

LARGE COMPANY LIMITED
EXTRACTS FROM AUDITED FINANCIAL STATEMENTS

Statement of accounting policies

(for the year ended 31 December 20X8)

Tangible Fixed Assets

All tangible fixed assets are initially recorded at historic cost. Freehold land and buildings (all non-specialised properties) are revalued on the basis of existing use value, adjusted for the addition of notional directly attributable acquisition costs where material. The revaluation surplus/(deficit) is taken to/(from) the revaluation reserve.

Revaluation gains are recognised in the profit and loss account (after adjustment for subsequent depreciation) to the extent that they reverse revaluation losses on the same assets that were previously recognised in the profit and loss account. All other revaluation gains are recognised in the statement of total recognised gains and losses.

Revaluation losses caused by a clear consumption of economic benefits are recognised in the profit and loss account. Other revaluation losses are recognised in the statement of total recognised gains and losses until the carrying amount reaches its depreciated historical cost. Beyond this the loss is recognised in the profit and loss account, except where the recoverable amount of the asset is greater than its revalued amount. Then the loss is recognised in the statement of total recognised gains and losses to the extent that the recoverable amount is greater than its revalued amount.

Finance costs directly attributable to the construction of freehold buildings are capitalised as part of the cost of these assets. The capitalisation rate used is the weighted average rate of general borrowing outstanding during the period.

Depreciation

Depreciation is provided on all tangible fixed assets, other than freehold land and investment properties, at rates calculated to write off the cost or valuation, less estimated residual value, of each asset systematically over its expected useful life, as follows:

Freehold buildings	–	straight-line over 50 years
Leasehold land and buildings	–	straight-line over the term of the lease
Plant and machinery	–	reducing balance over 5 to 15 years
Motor vehicles	–	reducing balance over 5 years

An amount equal to the excess of the annual depreciation charge on revalued assets over the notional historical cost depreciation charge on those assets is transferred annually from the revaluation reserve to the profit and loss reserve.

The carrying values of tangible fixed assets are reviewed annually for impairment in periods if events or changes in circumstances indicate the carrying value may not be recoverable.

LARGE COMPANY LIMITED

EXTRACTS FROM AUDITED FINANCIAL STATEMENTS

Statement of Financial Position as at 31 December 20X8

	Notes	20X8 €'000	20X8 €'000	20X7 €'000	20X7 €'000
Fixed assets					
Intangible assets	12		1,150		1,140
Tangible assets	**13**		**130,050**		**140,500**
Financial assets	14		112,200		110,200
Derivative financial instruments	25		1,900		1,460
			245,300		253,300

LARGE COMPANY LIMITED

EXTRACTS FROM AUDITED FINANCIAL STATEMENTS

Notes *(forming part of the financial statements)*

13. Tangible Fixed Assets/Property, Plant & Equipment

	Freehold land & buildings €'000	Plant & machinery €'000	Motor vehicles €'000	Total €'000
Cost:				
At 1 January 20X8	400,000	113,625	28,800	542,425
Additions	-	82,250	35,000	117,250
Deficit on revaluation	(355,000)	-	-	(355,000)
Disposals	-	(49,000)	(14,655)	(63,655)
At 31 December 20X8	45,000	146,875	49,145	241,020
Depreciation				
At 1 January 20X8	319,800	61,725	20,400	401,925
Charge for year	18,000	48,705	14,500	81,205
Elimination on revaluation	(337,800)	-	-	(337,800)
Disposals	-	(29,000)	(5,360)	(34,360)
At 31 December 20X8	-	81,430	29,540	110,970
Net book value				
At 31 December 20X8	**45,000**	**65,445**	**19,605**	**130,050**
At 1 January 20X8	80,200	51,900	8,400	140,500

Freehold land and buildings

Freehold land (€15,000,000) which is not depreciated is included in land and buildings. On 31 December the land was valued at its original cost by the external surveyors (details in next paragraph).

The freehold buildings were valued at €30,000,000 being their value in use, in accordance with the Appraisal and Valuation Manual of the Royal Institution of Chartered Surveyors, on 31 December 20X8 by external professional surveyors, Big Value Valuers & Co., Chartered

Surveyors. The property had been revalued to €385,000,000 but by 31 December 20X8 was depreciated to €47,200,000. The sudden decline in value of the freehold buildings was caused by the upsurge of political trouble and the exit of commercial businesses in the local area. The total reduction in the net book value is €17,200,000. The year-end valuation (€30,000,000) is not materially different to the open market value.

Chapter 8

THE AUDIT OF STOCK AND WORK IN PROGRESS

Learning Objectives

- Gain an appreciation of the audit of inventory
- Identify risks associated with inventory
- Assess the risk of material misstatement in each area
- Gain an understanding of the controls that may surround inventory
- Gain an understanding of the inter-relationship between the testing of controls and substantive testing in respect of accruals and inventory
- Identify circumstances where control tests vs tests of details vs analytical procedures are appropriate in the areas
- Assess how to audit a standard costing system
- Determine the audit strategy for stock and work in progress
- Identify substantive tests to audit stock and work in progress

Checklist of Relevant Professional Statements

ISA 315 – Obtaining an Understanding of the Entity and its Environment and Assessing the Risks of Material Misstatement
ISA 320 – Audit Materiality
ISA 500 – Audit Evidence
ISA 501 – Audit Evidence – Additional Considerations for Specific items
ISA 520 – Analytical Review
ISA 540 – Audit of Accounting Estimates
ISA 620 – Using the Work of an Expert
ISA 700 – The Auditor's Report on Financial Statements
IAS 2 – Inventories
IAS 11 – Construction Contracts
Practice Note 25: Attendance at Stocktaking
L405: Attendance at Stocktaking
K1-U11: Stock in trade and work in progress

8.1 Introduction

Inventory is commonly referred to as stock. In a manufacturing company stock consists of three elements: raw materials, work in progress and finished goods. For example, in the car manufacturing business raw material relates to the steel, work in progress to the chassis and finished goods to the finished car which will be the final product for sale. However in a retail company there will only be goods for sale.

Stocks may be verified by a physical count, most commonly at the year end or recorded on a continuous "rolling" system. In either case, extensive tests of control must be performed over both the recording of inventory and the maintenance of inventory records in order to "obtain sufficient appropriate audit evidence regarding its existence and condition"(ISA 501). ISA 501 paragraph 6 states that, if unable to attend the physical inventory count on the date planned due to unforeseen circumstances, the auditor should take or observe some physical counts on an alternative date and, when necessary, perform audit procedures on intervening transactions.

It is interesting to note the following historical cases when studying the topic of stock and work in progress:

1. *Kingston Cotton Mill Co Ltd (1896)*

The auditor relied on information provided by management detailing the amount of stock held at the year end date. This information was only agreed to the stock journal and a summary detailing number of units in stock and their value. As these agreed, no further testing was performed. It was subsequently found that stock was largely overstated. The judge popularised the phrase "he is a watchdog, not a bloodhound" meaning all suspicious circumstances should be investigated. In this case, the auditors were exonerated on the basis that they were entitled to rely on other parties for the details of stock in trade. In today's environment, auditors should be particularly careful to investigate all aspects of an entity's operation!

2. *McKesson and Robbins Inc., USA (1939)*

Fictitious records were created by the company directors of sales, purchases, bank accounts held, debtors and stock, so that assets were overstated by over $20m. Auditors did not detect this as they did not attend the stocktake.

3. *Allied Crude Vegetable Oil Refining Corporation of New Jersey (1963)*

When auditors arrived to perform the stock count, various methods were used by the entity to trick the auditors into thinking more stock actually existed e.g. oil tanks were filled with water and a thin film of oil was poured on top and then the contents of an oil tank once counted were transferred into a second tank for counting. The entity had fraudulently used such stocks as collateral for millions of dollars worth of loans.

8.2 Risk of Material Misstatement

The first step the auditor must make is to assess the risk of material misstatement. According to ISA 315 the auditor should use professional judgement to assess the risk of material misstatement. Risk factors relating to inventory include:

- Reliability of the inventory recording system – see details of cycle counting below.
- Volume of transactions that have occurred during the year i.e. sales, purchases and transfers. If these are high then there is a greater chance of misstatements occurring.
- The saleability of products is constantly affected by demand and competition.
- Valuation allocations relating to materials, labour and overheads, accounting for scrap and obsolescence, joint product costs etc.
- Timing of inventory counts and reliability of roll forward procedures in place if the inventory count not held at year end. Roll forward procedures include tracking movements in and out of stock between the count and the period end. The assessment of controls surrounding the movements of stock is critical in determining whether a count can be performed pre-year end.
- Location of inventory as often stock may be stored in multiple locations.
- Physical controls over inventory and its susceptibility to theft.
- Degree of fluctuations in inventory levels.
- Nature of the inventory and the requirement of specialist knowledge.
- Susceptibility of inventory to obsolescence. This is more prevalent in some industries than others i.e. pharmaceuticals, where the goods may go out of date compared to a textiles factory where this is not an issue.
- Risks due to fraud. These include false sales, movement of inventory between different entities with stock counts on different days (increase inventory in both locations) application of inappropriate estimation techniques, altered inventory count sheets, additional inventory count records being added to those prepared during the count.

The auditor will place less focus on those risk factors which he determines will not have a material impact on the financial statements. These controls are not relevant; an example of risk in the inventory cycle could be obsolescence in long-term durable goods.

The auditor must also consider whether other transactional risks exist that could result in a material misstatement if not mitigated.

8.3 Understanding of Controls Over Inventory

After the risks have been identified the auditor should gain an understanding of the controls over inventory. ISA 315 paragraph 41 states that "The auditor should obtain an understanding of internal control relevant to the audit". The auditor uses the understanding of internal control to identify types of potential misstatements, consider factors that affect the risks of material misstatement, and design the nature, timing, and extent of further audit procedures.

The purpose of the step is to identify the existence of internal controls that mitigates the risk factors listed above.

The most efficient way to get an overview of the controls in place is to perform a walk-through of the process. There are various forms of documenting the controls in place. These include flowcharts, narratives and notes.

The extent of documentation required will vary depending on the size, nature, and complexity of the entity and is a matter of professional judgment.

The following is a sample of the main controls over the inventory process.

(**Purchasing:** See **Chapter 12** for controls over the purchasing of inventory items.)

Below are examples of how control risk can be minimized over the acquisition, disposal, safeguarding, valuation, condition, existence and ownership of stock.

- Issues to and from inventories are made only on properly authorized requisition orders. Disposals of stock should be based on informed decisions and evidenced in writing. Only when this is done should an adjustment to the stock records be made. Title to stock must be known at all times, especially if consignment stock is held or stock subject to retention of title.
- All receipts and issues of inventory should be recorded on inventory cards and cross-referenced to appropriate GRN/Requisition documents.
- Reviews of damaged, obsolete and slow-moving inventories are carried out during the year. Write-offs from inventory are authorised by a responsible official.
- Review of standard costs is carried out to ensure they relate to actual costs being incurred.
- Reconciliation of inventory records to the general ledger is completed and discrepancies are investigated. Reconciliation should be reviewed by an appropriate person.
- Inventory levels should be checked against records by a person independent of store personnel and differences investigated.
- Standard costs should be reviewed to ensure they are reliable and that costing is made on a consistent basis year on year. Variances should be investigated.
- A full inventory count should be held once a year.
- Re-order quantities should be set and reviewed regularly.
- Stock should be held in an environment which prevents deterioration and is easily accessible. Separate centres should be identified at which goods are held.
- Deliveries of goods should pass through a goods in section and recorded and checked when received.
- Access to stores should be restricted i.e. Swipe badges.

Only when it has been established that the internal controls relevant to the audit have been properly designed and implemented is it worth considering the following:

- What tests of the operating effectiveness of controls (if any) will reduce the need for other substantive testing?
- What controls require testing because they cannot be tested substantively?

Tests of controls

After the auditor has answered these questions, he/she should perform tests of operating effectiveness on relevant controls, these may include

- Test procedures for movement of goods.
- Test authorisation limits for adjustments to inventory.
- Test authorisation of write-off of goods.
- Inspect reconciliation between count records and inventory records.
- Check sequence of despatch and GRN for completeness.
- Observe physical security of storage facilities.

8.4 Design Substantive Audit Procedures in Response to the Audit Risks Identified

Use of assertions in obtaining audit evidence

> "The auditor should use assertions for classes of transactions, account balances and presentation and disclosure in sufficient detail to form a basis for the assessment of risks of material misstatement and the design and performance of further audit procedures" (ISA 500).

The specific audit objectives in relation to stocks are as follows:

Transactions and Events during the Period

Assertion	Audit Objective
Existence	To ensure all purchase and sales transactions represent inventories acquired and sold during the year
	To ensure that all transfers between locations and categories are correctly recorded
Completeness	To ensure all purchases, sales and transfers of inventory above have been recorded

Assertion	Audit Objective
Accuracy/valuation	To ensure all materials, labour and overheads have been accurately calculated for each class of inventory
Cut off	To ensure that all purchases, sales and transfers of inventory have been recorded in the correct accounting period
Ownership	To ensure that all inventory held during the period is the property of the entity
Presentation and Disclosure	To ensure that all inventory transactions have been properly classified in the financial statements in accordance with applicable accounting standards
Account Balances at Year End	
Existence	The stock amounts in the balance sheet exist at the balance sheet date
Completeness	All stocks have been recorded in the financial statements at the balance sheet date
Accuracy	Stock items have been accurately identified, measured and recorded at the lower of cost and net realisable value
Valuation	Stocks are properly valued, making provisions for damaged, slow-moving or obsolete stock
Cut-off	All transactions relating to the movements of stock have been recorded in the correct accounting period
Ownership	All stock items in the balance sheet are owned by the client
Disclosure	Stocks have been properly classified and disclosed in the financial statements

Initial procedures

Initially, evidence must be obtained as to the accuracy of the opening balances. This can be completed as follows:

- Agree opening balances to prior year working papers and signed financial statements. This will highlight any adjustments booked in the prior-year financial statements that need to be carried forward into the current year opening balances
- If this is the first year of engagement, a copy of the previous auditors' working papers are obtained and opening balances are agreed to these working papers along with the prior-year signed financial statements

- In instances where perpetual records are kept, scan the general ledger for any unusual items. Where these records will form the basis of the stock valuation at the period end date, check the listing to and from the records, re-perform tots and agree to the control account.

Analytical review (ISA 520)

Standard analytical review procedures for the audit of stocks include:
- Reconcile changes in inventory quantities from the start to the end of the year to purchase, sales and production records
- Compare quantities and amounts of inventories in their various categories to those at the prior-year balance sheet date and to current sales and purchases
- Compare gross profit, inventory turnover ratios year on year
- Examine standard costing records
- Obtain industry comparisons and trends.

In performing analytical procedures the auditor should develop an expectation/define a variance and compare actual results to the expectation and investigate any differences greater than the defined variance.

Analytical procedures can be applied effectively in the testing of inventory. Analytical procedures should be performed prior to the substantive tests of detail in order to get an overview in the movement of inventory balances.

When performing analytical procedures on inventory an expectation of the inventory balance can be developed by using the following comparison:

- To prior year
- To budgets (should test the controls over preparation of budgets and their reliability)
- Apply last year's days stock on hand to this year's sales to create an expectation.

The expectation should be then compared with the actual balance and any material differences investigated further through substantive tests of details and inquiry with management.

Example
Company A

	2008	**2007**
Cost of Sales	€100,000	€50,000
Inventory	€7,000	€3,000

> 1. Create an expectation of 2008 inventory levels
>   Stock days 2007 = Inventory/Cost of Sales * 365
>   = (3,000/50,000)365 = 22 days
> 2. Apply last year's stock days to 2008 sales
>   (x/100,000) 365 = 22 => 6,027
> 3. Compare expectation to actual i.e. 7,000 v 6,027 and discuss reasons for differences with management and substantiate the reasons if possible.

Tests of detail of transactions

Tests of detail of transactions are only performed where perpetual inventory records determine the closing valuation to be included in the financial statements.

- Perform two-way testing on inventory records to supporting documentation.
- Test cut-off information provided during the stock count in relation to sales, purchases and transfers in and out of stock.

Tests of detail of balances

- Observe the entity's stock count. It is the responsibility of management to supervise the actual counting of the stock, not the auditors. The auditor attends to ensure that reliance can be placed on the outcome of the count and to ensure that internal control procedures are operating efficiently. Under ISA 620, Using the Work of an Expert, if an external specialist is used by the entity to count the goods the auditor must still be present.
- Test the clerical accuracy of stock listings. This can be done by comparing records made during the count to final listings, performing two-way testing on rough and final listings and re-performing tots and calculations on extensions.
- Movements in inventory between the date of the count and the balance sheet date should be investigated and verified.
- Test valuation methods used. As already noted, IAS 2 requires that inventory be valued at the lower of cost and net realisable value. Component costs of a sample of items must be vouched to supporting documentation e.g. supplier invoices.
- Stock may have been written down to net realisable based on estimates. In such cases ISA 540, Audit of Accounting Estimates, may need to be followed. The auditor must examine the assumptions used in formulating such estimates, re-perform calculations and ensure management has properly approved the write down by examining board-approving minutes.
- Confirm stock held at various locations outside the entity through direct communications with the custodian. Where material, the auditor should arrange to physically inspect the stock and request confirmation of title to the goods.

- Examine contracts and agreements relating to goods held on consignment. A consignment sale is one which is made on a sale or return basis where payment is generally required on subsequent sale to a third party. Often consignment stock can be pledged as security for loans. Auditors should inquire of management as to such arrangements and ensure this is properly disclosed in the financial statements.

8.5 Goods Purchased Subject to "Retention/Reservation of Title"

In may cases, goods may be acquired subject to the condition that title to the goods does not pass to the purchaser until they have been fully paid for. Despite legal ownership thus remaining with the supplier, these goods must be included in the financial statements of the purchasing entity.

The following terms indicate the transaction is one subject to "retention of title"

- the goods are clearly defined and their usage specified
- the goods are stored in a different location to other goods
- full title remains with the supplier until fully paid for.

The auditor should perform the following:

- Identify the creditors who supplied the goods subject to the reservation of title clause.
- Quantify the amounts due to such suppliers at the year end date.
- Ensure that financial statements disclose adequate information in relation to the goods sold subject to reservation of title. Where an amount is material, the additional security required to safeguard such goods should also be disclosed, where possible.

8.6 Audit Procedures that Address the Assertions for Transactions and Account Balances

The auditor must design and perform audit procedures that address the relevant assertions for transactions and account balances relating to stock and work in progress.

Existence

The existence of inventory can be verified through either attendance at the year-end stocktake or through attending a cycle count. The auditor should ensure that the overall responsibility for the count should be an individual who is independent to the custody of inventory or the maintenance of inventory records.

(a) **Attend the physical stock count at year end** This enables the auditor to inspect the inventory, observe compliance with the operation of management's procedures for recording and controlling the results of the count and provide audit evidence as to the reliability of management's procedures (ISA 501 para 6). There are three steps involved: planning, performing and completing the stock count. The responsibilities of the auditor are detailed below:

1. Planning the count
   - Review prior-year inventory records and enquire of management if there are any significant changes to the current year
   - Ensure the stock is sub-divided into manageable areas and all inventory to be counted is properly identified
   - Identify any high value and obsolete stock early on in the process
   - Consider risk of material misstatement
   - Ensure pre-numbered stock sheets are provided to all involved
   - Nature of internal controls related to inventory specific to stock-take i.e. collection of used stock sheets, accounting for unused stock sheets and count and recount procedures
   - Consider timing of the count
   - Communicate instructions to all involved to ensure that sock is only counted once
   - Obtain details of the locations of where the inventory is held. If stock is held in a number of locations the auditor may decide only to count items based on materiality, inherent and internal control risk
   - Is an expert required i.e. if the auditor cannot identify the value themselves e.g. antiques
   - Are proper instructions in place for the stock counters?

Items that should be included in the instructions include

- Details of where and when the stocktake is taking place
- Has enough time been allocated for the count to be successfully completed?
- Details of how premises should be arranged i.e. obsolete stock put to one side of the warehouse
- Identify personnel and method of counting
- Procedures for movement of stock
- Pre-numbered stock sheets
- Details of how counted items are identified i.e. marked by a 'C'
- Instruct that the counting should be done in pairs and where possible one team member is an independent counter
- Count sheets should be initialled by both team members once each location is counted
  - Consider quantities held
  - Discuss inventory counts with management
  - Consider internal audit involvement
  - Establish if any stock within stores is held on behalf of third parties and how client ensures that these items are excluded from the count.

2. Performing the count
    - Observe the counters to ensure they are following the instructions provided
    - Ensure there is no movement in and out of stock while the count is being performed
    - Count a sample of items from the stock count sheets to the inventory on the floor. This covers the assertion "existence" as the auditor will determine if the stock listed on the count sheets actually exist
    - Count a sample from the floor to the stock count sheet to ensure that items that may be omitted from the sheets are included. This covers the assertion completeness as the auditor will determine whether all inventory on the floor is listed on the stock sheets
    - Obtain cut-off information i.e. last 6 GRN and last 6 dispatch dockets before the stocktake. This will help in performing cut-off testing later
    - If inventory is held by a third party obtain direct confirmation of the amount of inventory held from the third party.
3. After the stock count
    - Review the listing for reasonableness
    - Take photocopies of all rough stock sheets utilised and ensure all sheets are in order. Follow up on missing sheets. Ensure that final stock sheets are properly prepared from the rough sheets
    - Ensure final stock sheets are properly authorised and re-perform tots and calculations
    - Record details of the count in the external working papers. If any areas proved unsatisfactory, inform management and request a recount
    - Agree the counts performed to the final inventory listing
    - Check cut-off details provided during the count to actual inventory records
    - If the count was performed at a date other than year end roll forward to the final listing by accounting for all movements between the year end date and the date of the count i.e. sales, purchases
    - Inform management of any issues noted during the count.

(b) **Continuous Stocktaking** Some companies do not carry out a full stock count at year end but perform ongoing counts of their inventory throughout the year. These ongoing counts are commonly known as cycle counts. This proves less disruptive to the operations of the business and also ensures that any discrepancies noted in the stock quantities held can be identified and investigated on an ongoing basis. Cycle counts also ensure that companies can meet tight year-end reporting deadlines.

When cycle counting is in place the auditor will not have a full stocktake report to rely on to cover the existence assertion. The book quantities held at year end must be relied on. Therefore they must be confident that the stock system is reliable. The following are factors that the auditor can assess:

1. Reliable internal controls over stock - see above for details of controls which may be in place
2. Properly planned programme of continuous counting
   - Clear responsibility for the count
   - Detailed count plans to ensure all items are counted at least once with high value items on a more regular basis
   - Segregation of duties i.e. independence of counter from storekeepers.

(c) **Where the physical count is before or after the year-end** The counting of stock may occur before or after the year-end for various reasons. For audit purposes, this is deemed acceptable provided records of stock movements in the intervening periods are maintained such that the movements can be examined and substantiated. Difficulties in performing this calculation should be lessened provided a well-developed system of internal control exists and satisfactory stock records are kept. The physical count should ideally occur no more than 3 months before or after the year-end so as to allow for any investigation of differences, the assessment of slow-moving or obsolete stock and the timely completion of the financial statements.
   - Investigation of differences noted
   - Review of stock-counts performed by an appropriate official.

The auditor should obtain supporting documentation of cycle counts held throughout the year and ensure that the above apply i.e. the counts are reviewed and discrepancies followed up. A cycle counting summary should also be obtained which details how often each item of inventory has been counted during the year. A cycle count should also be attended by the auditor to assess whether the cycle count is performed correctly.

Completeness

The auditor should ensure that any stocks held by third parties on behalf of the client are included within the stock records. If stock is held by third parties on behalf of the client a direct confirmation should be obtained by the auditors of the quantities of stock held.

Accuracy

The auditor should

- Determine the client's policy for the valuation of stocks and work in progress and ensure it is in accordance with applicable accounting standards
- Ensure that all stocks are recorded at the lower of cost and net realisable value
- Where production overheads are allocated to stocks, ensure that the overheads reflect the client's normal level of activity

- Obtain a copy of the reconciliation between the stock control account in the nominal ledger and the stock listing, and any differences should be investigated
- Also the stock figure per the control account should be agreed to the stock figure in the financial statements.

Valuation

The auditor should determine the client's policy for the valuation of stock and ensure it is in line with IAS 2. IAS 2 states that inventory must be valued at the lower of cost and net realisable value.

Net realisable value is the sales price less the cost to completion, less selling, marketing and distribution costs. It may also be defined as the value the stock would achieve in the open market based on its present condition. An example of how to test that the inventory is costed correctly would be to obtain a sample of invoices to support the cost of a sample of inventory and obtain a copy of the most recent sales invoice to support the sale price. Compare the sale price to the cost and ensure it is valued at the lower of both.

Examples of when NRV is likely to be less than costs include when there has been:

- an increase in costs and a decrease in selling price
- physical deterioration of stock or obsolescence
- a marketing decision to sell below cost
- errors in production or purchasing.

IAS 2 defines cost as "all costs of purchase, costs of conversion and other costs incurred in bringing the inventories to their present location and condition". The cost of inventory may be stated at actual cost (conventional method) or at a standard cost (standard costing method). Cost should be calculated for each category of stock and not for stock as a whole. A standard costing system involves the company setting a budget/standard cost for inventory items at the beginning of the year. The standard is then used to price the inventory as it passes through the company's costing system. Any difference from the standard results in variances i.e. when the cost of purchasing the goods is more/less than the standard. These purchase price variances are then allocated to COS/Inventory as appropriate.

Closing stock should be valued using FIFO (first in first out), unit cost or weighted average. LIFO (last in first out) and replacement cost approaches are not acceptable. When examining the value at which stock is recorded, the auditor should ascertain the prices at which finished goods have been sold post-year-end as this will highlight any items which may need to be reduced to below cost. The auditor should ensure that the selling price takes into account any trade discounts allowed and whether such selling price has been reduced by disposal costs. This adjusted selling price should then be compared to the carrying value of the finished goods.

The auditor should also review post year-end sales of stock to establish whether or not it will be realised. A provision may be required for slow-moving or obsolete stock based on this review.

Substantive audit tests that should be performed are as follows:

- Determine the policy of the entity for valuing stock and ensure it has been accurately and consistently applied
- Test the inclusion of overheads in a sample of items
- For items valued at net realisable value examine the basis for this
- Re-perform tots and calculations
- Determine if any profits or losses have been included in the valuation
- Review the reasonableness of the stock provision when determining if stock has been correctly valued
- Ensure calculations and disclosures are in line with accounting policies adopted by the entity.

Valuation of raw material

Conventional costing system The auditor needs to determine that the inventory is stated at the lower of cost or NRV. This can be tested through verifying the cost to a purchase invoice and the sales price to a related sales invoice close to the year end for a sample of inventory items and ensuring that the inventory is held at the lower of the cost or the sales price.

Standard Costing System The auditors must satisfy themselves that the standard cost approximates the actual cost. This can be verified through agreeing the standard to a supporting purchase invoice for a sample of raw materials. Also the purchase price variances which arise should be reviewed as they indicate the attainability of the standard. The standard should also be compared to the NRV as detailed above to ensure that no NRV issues occur. Also the auditor should first gain a good understanding of the standard costing system and the process for developing standards. The auditor should assess how often the standards are revised and who sets them i.e. are the standards set annually/quarterly and how attainable are they. If standards are attainable the level of variances should be low. Also the procedures for setting standards should be reviewed.

Valuation of work in progress/finished goods

Conventional costing system Work in progress (WIP) includes both short-term WIP and long-term WIP. Long-term WIP often relates to construction contracts and can cover many accounting periods and often proves to be a problematic area for auditors to review. The auditor may have to exercise judgement and involve an expert valuer. The auditor should:

- Examine contracts to determine timescales and penalty clauses
- Ascertain which costing system was used and determine whether it can be relied on given the nature of the contract
- Ensure that costs incurred are accurate, genuine and complete
- Assess the stage of completion and ensure that costs are properly charged to the item based on the stage reached
- Enquire into the qualifications etc., of the valuer certifying the completed work
- Ensure that all profits realised are eliminated from work in progress. IAS 2 does allow elements of profit to be included and should be consulted
- Identify any losses on contracts as these have to be recognised in the valuation
- Ensure that any self-constructed assets of the entity are not included in both work in progress and tangible fixed assets.

WIP and FG will also contain an element of labour and overheads that have brought the raw materials to the WIP/finished goods stage.

Raw material element Cost accounting records should be cross-checked to accounting records and vice versa. In order to test the material component a bill of materials should be obtained and the raw materials input should be tested as described above. The price of materials bought in and the material content of WIP and finished goods should be compared to supplier invoices. All documentation should be properly authorised and any variances investigated.

Labour element The labour element should be tested by comparing the labour content to job sheets/time sheets and compare the labour rate to payroll records. The auditor should:

- Reconcile financial and cost accounting records
- Ensure the wage rate indicated on the job sheet agrees to wage rates determined by social security documentation etc., and that the total time indicated on the job sheet is the actual labour cost allocated to the job
- Ensure that idle time has not been charged to the job, and is instead charged to overhead expenses.

Overhead element An understanding should be gained of how the overheads are allocated to inventory items i.e. machine hours or labour hours. The basis for allocating overheads should be broadly in line with the prior year and based on normal production levels in the company. All overheads relating to abnormal activity levels should be written off the income statement i.e. idle time when machinery is being repaired. The overhead absorption calculation should then be reperformed through agreeing the relative factors to underlying documentation i.e. machine hours to production schedule/labour hours to time sheets. All related supporting documentation should be examined.

Valuation of work in progress/finished goods

Standard Costing System The standard for WIP and FG also includes an element for labour and overheads. The allocation will be based on a standard labour rate and standard machine hours. The basis for setting these standards should be reviewed by the auditor to ensure they are attainable standards. The standards should then be recalculated to ensure that the correct proportions of labour and overhead have been applied. A review should be completed of all labour and overhead variances along with Purchase Price Variances (PPV). If standards are not set realistically large variances will occur during the year.

Standard costing – treatment of variances

As previously mentioned, the auditor should compare actual and standard costs of items included in the year-end valuation. Due to the nature of standard costing differences will always arise between the standard set and the actual cost of production. These variances may be as a result of differences relating to the price of raw materials, differences in the cost of labour or differences in the cost of overheads related to the product. During the audit the level of variances should be analysed. This will provide an indication of the reliability of the standards set. Attainable standards will not give rise to large variances as the standard will approximate cost. As a rule variances which relate to inefficiencies and are not as a result of a poorly set standard should be expensed to the profit and loss account. However, if the standards are not set accurately the variances which arise should be apportioned between Cost of Sales and Inventory appropriately. For example, if there are 30 days stock on hand at year end there should be 30 days variances capitalised. The auditor should ascertain the last time the standards were reviewed and determine whether the current standards are still relevant in light of changes in general prices, production methods and product specification. Any changes in standards set should be properly authorised.

Inventory provisions

The auditor should ensure slow moving, damaged and obsolete inventory is provided for in the accounts and review the reasonableness of the stock provision.

Stock held at the current year-end should be compared to that held at the prior year-end to identify any non-moving items. Records of the physical stock count should be reviewed for items noted of an unsaleable condition.

In relation to work in progress, review records for any items which have no expenses charged to time of late as this will highlight items which have no work being done on them or where the work in progress has been cancelled. This may also be completed through reviewing the ageing of the stock provision. The auditor may also test the ageing through agreeing a sample of inventory to their related goods received notes to determine how old the inventory is and agreeing the age of the inventory to the aged inventory listing. In reviewing the stock provision the auditor may also review the stocktake report for details of obsolete inventory and testing the controls over identification of obsolete stock. Some companies may perform monthly/quarterly review of obsolete inventory which will determine amounts to be written off and amounts to be provided for.

Cut-off

Cut-off testing ensures that all movements of stock are recorded in the correct period. In order to test this assertion a review should be made of GRNs and despatch dockets around the period end to ensure they are sequential and any missing numbers should be investigated. Also a sample of goods in/out on either side of year end should be selected for testing to ensure they are recorded in the correct period. The GRNs (goods received noted) and despatch dockets should have been obtained during the attendance at the year end stock count and these should be used as evidence of the last goods in and the first goods out.

In order to guarantee accurate cut-off, the auditor should ensure that management:

- Allocate the responsibility to a certain individual for ensuring cut-off details are accurate
- Ensure there is no movement in and out of stock while the stock count is being performed
- Ensure that, if movements are occurring, records are being kept of all movements and goods inward are being held in a separate location until the count has ceased.

Ownership

Stock items belonging to third parties should be identified and excluded from the final stock summary. Also one must ensure that stocks awaiting dispatch which have been included in sales are excluded from stock figures. The following situations often pose problems for auditors when reviewing stock and work in progress:

1. The ownership of goods bought near the year end
   This relates to goods purchased, but not yet delivered to the entity at the balance sheet date. The auditor must ascertain whether legal title has passed based on the terms of the individual contract. The auditor must also determine whether the goods in question have been either correctly or incorrectly included in the financial statements at the balance sheet date. An adjustment may be required based on his findings.
2. The ownership of goods sold near the year end
   This relates to goods sold, but are still on the client's premises at the balance sheet date. The auditor must ensure that these goods are not included in the financial statements.
3. Consignment stock
   This relates to goods that are not owned by the client, but are held on consignment or under a franchise agreement, until a specified condition is met. These items should not

form part of the stock figure at the balance sheet date. The auditor should also ensure that the opposite is also the case, where stock owned by the client which is held on consignment or under a franchise agreement by a third party is included in the closing stock figure at the balance sheet date. In this case the auditor should physically inspect the stock where possible. If this is not permitted, they should request confirmation from the third party as to the quantities and condition of items held or perform other audit procedures which will provide sufficient appropriate audit evidence as to the existence and condition of the stock.

Presentation and disclosure

IAS 2 details the disclosures required for inventory. These include

- Accounting policies used to value stock including the cost formula used
- Carrying amount of inventories at fair value less costs to sell
- Ensuring the correct classification of stocks between finished goods, raw materials and WIP
- Ascertaining the value of stock sold under retention of title clauses and ensure adequate disclosure. Retention of title otherwise known as reservation of title, relates to where the supplier retains title of the goods sold until he has been paid
- Ensuring correct disclosure of stock pledged as security for liabilities of the client or third parties
- Details of the write-down of inventories expensed during the year
- If a reversal of a write-down occurred, a description of the circumstances which caused this to happen
- Details of any inventory pledged as security.

8.7 Use of CAATs in Auditing of Inventory

Computer assisted audit techniques may be used in the audit of inventory. The substantive audit procedures that CAATS may be used to assist are as follows:

- Report negative balances
- Stratify and analyse stock balances
- Re-perform ageing of stock
- Re-tot ledger
- Identify missequencing of invoice numbers
- Report slow-moving obsolete stock
- Report unusual slow moving/obsolete stock
- Identify round sum amounts
- Select items below re-order level

- Compare stock cost to purchase ledger records
- Compare finished goods stock data to sales records.

8.8 Audit Procedure Performed at Interim Dates

ISA 315 states that tests of controls or substantive testing may be performed at an interim date.

Inventory counts are an example of an audit procedure sometimes performed at an interim date. Attending an inventory count before year end may facilitate a company with short reporting deadlines

When considering whether to test inventory balances at an interim date the auditor must assess the following:

- Control environment
- Risks over inventory
- When relevant information is available i.e. when the client's stocktaking takes place
- Reliability of stock control system
- Length of period between stock count and year end
- Materiality of stock figures.

If the stocktake is performed at an interim date roll forward procedures must be completed in order to agree the quantities counted to the stock listing at year end. The following are examples of roll forward procedures:

- Test completeness of raw material receipts between the stocktake and the year end. This may be tested through testing the sequence of Goods Received Notes (GRNs) and tracing a sample of the GRNs to the raw material sub ledger.
- Test the completeness of the transfer in to WIP from raw materials and the transfer out of WIP to finished goods. This may be completed by testing a sample of journals for transfers of WIP to FG and WIP to raw material.
- Check completeness of despatches of FG. This should be tested by checking the sequence of despatch notes and tracing a sample of items in Sales/COS reports to the FG sub ledger.

Other audit procedures can only be performed at the year end i.e. cut-off as the risk only occurs at the year end.

8.9 Completion of the Audit of Inventory

When the audit of inventory has been completed the audit information should be reviewed. All audit evidence should be documented in the working papers. The evidence should be assessed for its impact on the audit report and all misstatements documented and concluded upon.

ISA 320 "if the auditor has identified a material misstatement resulting from error, the auditor should communicate the misstatement to an appropriate level of management."

ISA 700 "The auditor should review and assess the conclusions drawn from the audit evidence obtained as the basis for expression of an opinion on the financial statements."

QUESTIONS

Self-test Questions

1. Many errors and fraud take place in relation to inventories. Explain why this happens.
2. Analytical review procedures can be very useful in the audit of inventories. Give four examples of such procedures.
3. Explain why auditors attend stockcounts.

Review Questions

(See Solutions to Review Questions at the end of this textbook.)

Question 8.1

CASTELYONS Ltd ("CASTELYONS") is a long-established audit client of your firm. The company has had moderate success over the years, but in recent years trading has deteriorated. CASTELYONS sells assembled components to mechanical manufacturers. It can also sell some of the unassembled components separately.

The audit for the year ended 30 June 2007 is to commence in two weeks. In advance of the audit, the audit file has been delivered. You are reviewing the client's inventory schedule, which is in the same format as for the last number of years.

Product No.	Cost per Item €/£	Quantity €/£	Total
Z110	2,100	25	52,500
Z111*	3,200	40	128,000
Z112	1,110	30	33,300
Z114	4,333	8	34,664
Z115	2,000	9	18,000
Z116*	5,100	21	107,100

Product No.	Cost per Item €/£	Quantity €/£	Total
Z117*	5,420	40	216,800
Z118	1,000	52	52,000
Z120	900	54	48,600
Z121*	3,450	34	117,300
			808,264

* = *components can be sold separately.*

Management have asserted that the inventory amount of €/£ 808,264 will be included in current assets in the financial statements.

Requirement:

(a) Assuming the quantities of the components are correct, outline what further audit work you would perform on the inventory schedule provided.
(b) As the audit commences, the Financial Controller informs you that there was an error in the inventory count.
    Outline the audit procedures you would perform to handle this situation.
(c) Outline the implicit and explicit assertions of management reporting the inventory figure of €/£ 808,264 in current assets in the financial statements.

Question 8.2

Your firm is the auditor of Tulla Wholesalers limited. Each month a stocktake is undertaken when all high-value stock is counted. Other stock is counted at least every 4 months to ensure that all stock is counted at least 3 times in the year. You are to attend a stock-count on the 15 December. The year end is the 31 December. No stock-count is being performed at this date. The stock quantities per the system are being relied on at year end by management.

Requirement:

(a) Detail the procedures you should perform when you attend the stock-count on the 15 December.
(b) Detail the checks you will perform over cut-off at the date of the stock-take and at the year end.
(c) Detail how you will verify that stock quantities used in the valuation of stock at year end are correct.

Appendix 8.1 – Extracts from Audited Financial Statements

LARGE COMPANY LIMITED
STATEMENT OF ACCOUNTING POLICIES
(for the year ended 31 December 20X8)

Stocks and Work in Progress

Stocks are stated at the lower of cost and net realisable value. In the case of finished goods and work in progress, cost is defined as the aggregate cost of raw material, direct labour and the attributable proportion of direct production overheads based on a normal level of activity. Net realisable value is based on normal selling price, less further costs expected to be incurred to completion and disposal.

Statement of Financial Position

as at 31 December 20X8

	Notes	20X8 €000	20X8 €000	20X7 €000	20X7 €000
Current assets					
Stocks/Inventories	15		49,774		35,020
Debtors:					
amounts falling due after one year	16	8,700		10,250	
amounts falling due within one year	17	6,500		7,250	
			15,200		17,500

Notes

(forming part of the financial statements)

15. Stocks/Inventories

	20X8 €000	20X7 €000
Raw materials and consumables	9,320	7,770
Work in progress	12,530	10,750
Finished goods and goods in transit	27,924	16,500
	49,774	35,020

There are no material differences between the replacement cost of stock and the balance sheet amounts.

Chapter 9

THE AUDIT OF SALES AND DEBTORS

Learning Objectives

To be able to

- Select and apply appropriate audit procedures to typical income statement and balance sheet captions.
- Develop the ability to select and apply audit procedures to typical accounting estimates
  - Obtain an understanding of typical systems of internal control
  - Identify the critical risks and related controls within those systems
  - Select and apply appropriate tests to identified controls
  - Select and apply appropriate substantive audit tests to typical financial captions which address identified risks at the assertions level
  - Describe the types of audit evidence available to support accounting estimates
  - Select and apply audit procedures to typical/simple accounting estimates.

Checklist of Relevant Professional Statements:

ISA 500 Audit evidence
ISA 501 Audit Evidence – Additional Considerations for Specific Items
ISA 505 External Confirmations
ISA 520 Analytical Procedures
ISA 540 Audit of Accounting Estimates

9.1 Background to Sales and Debtors

In the financial statements the sales figure represents the income received by a business in return for the passing of title on goods or services. The debtors balance arises as a result of sales made and represents money due to the business from customers for sales made.

The value of total sales generated in the period under review and the value of period end debtors is material to the financial statements in most businesses which is why the testing to be performed on the area by the auditor is so important.

As discussed in **Chapter 5**, ISA 500 states the need for the auditor to obtain sufficient appropriate audit evidence over classes of transactions (sales) and accounts balances (debtors).

188 AUDITING AND ASSURANCE

To perform the appropriate audit procedures and obtain the level of evidence necessary to provide comfort over the transactions and balances the auditor must consider the following:

- the control process surrounding the sales and debtors cycle (**Chapter 3** ISA 315)
- the existence of any significant risks surrounding the sales and debtors cycle (**Chapter 3** ISA 315)
- the materiality of the sales figure and debtors balance to the financial statements as a whole (ISA 320)
- the financial statement assertions which must be covered by the testing performed (ISA 500).

Based on this assessment the type of testing to be performed will be decided on, which may include all or a combination of the following:

- controls-based testing (ISA 330)
- substantive analytical procedures (ISA 330)
- substantive tests of detail (ISA 330).

9.2 Financial Statement Assertions Surrounding the Audit of Sales and Debtors

In **Chapter 5** financial statement assertions were discussed, explaining how the auditor must design and perform audit testing which will provide comfort over the assertions associated with a particular account balance or class of transaction. The relevant financial statement assertions surrounding the audit of sales and debtors are outlined below:

Sales	
Assertion	**Objective of audit evidence**
Completeness	To ensure that all transactions that should have been recorded, have been recorded
Occurrence	To ensure all transactions and events have been recorded and pertain to the entity
Accuracy	To ensure that all transactions have been recorded correctly
Cut-off	To ensure transactions and events have been recorded in the correct period
Presentation and disclosure	To ensure that all amounts are properly disclosed and presented in the financial statements

Debtors	
Assertion	**Objective of audit evidence**
Existence	To ensure that all assets and liabilities in year end balance sheet exist
Completeness	To ensure that all assets and liabilities that should have been recorded, have been recorded
Rights and Obligations	To ensure the entity holds the rights to the assets and has obligations
Valuation and allocation	To ensure that all assets and liabilities are included in financial statements at correct valuation and in the correct account
Cut-off	To ensure transactions and events have been recorded in the correct period
Presentation and disclosure	To ensure that all amounts are properly disclosed and presented in the financial statements

When designing tests of controls, substantive analytical review and tests of details, the auditor must ensure that sufficient comfort has been obtained over all assertions noted above. This is usually achieved through designing an audit testing plan which includes all three types of testing above or a combination of testing (this has been discussed further in **Chapters 3** and **5**).

General rules:

- Where the sales figure and debtors balance are not material to the financial statements limited controls and substantive testing will be performed
- Where a significant risk has been identified in relation to the sales and debtors cycle the level of substantive testing to be performed will be more rigorous
- Where a strong control environment has been identified the extent of substantive testing to be performed will be much less than the level of substantive testing to be performed in an entity where a weak control environment has been identified.

One key consideration when developing the audit plan will be the risk assessment made by the auditor on the client and the control environment. This is discussed in **Chapter 3** in detail. Points for the auditor to consider when making this assessment will include:

- Previous experience with the client, e.g. where a significant risk existed in the past in relation to recoverability of aged debtor balances the auditor will be alert to this in the current audit when performing testing in this area;
- Reliability of estimates made by the client in the past, e.g. where the basis of the bad debt provision determined by the client in the past was deemed unreliable resulting in

adjustments by the auditor being necessary to fairly state the provision, the auditor will be alert for this in the current audit when performing testing in this area;
- Robustness of accounting system, e.g. where cut-off errors where discovered in prior audit as a result of sales invoices being posted to the system in the incorrect period around the period end date, the auditor will remain alert for this when performing testing in this area in the current period;
- Complexity of business, e.g. where recognition of a sale occurs only after a number of key stages have been completed or actions taken, then the auditor will remain alert to the possibility that sales may have been recognised in the period which are not true sales i.e. sales have been accounted for in the period but all the necessary stages resulting in revenue recognition have not been completed before the period end;
- Scope for fraud-related activity – in relation to sales and debtors this could include:
  - creation of false customer accounts resulting in overstated sales figures and debtor balances
  - misappropriation of cash receipts where the business is cash based.

9.3 The Sales System

The components of a company's sales system should comprise a number of key steps. These steps together with the objectives and controls which should feature within each of these steps are as follows:

System Objectives

(a) Ordering and granting of credit
- Goods/services supplied to customers with good credit ratings (occurrence)
- Sales orders are recorded correctly (accuracy)
- Customer orders are fulfilled (occurrence)
- Goods and services returned are correctly recorded and reasons investigated (completeness)

(b) Despatch and invoicing
- Invoices generated by the company relate only to goods and services supplied by the business (occurrence)
- Despatches are accurately recorded (accuracy)
- Despatches are invoiced correctly (completeness and accuracy)
- Credit notes are only issued for valid reasons (completeness)
- Cut-off is applied to the recording of dispatch records (cut-off)

(c) Accounting
- Invoices/credit notes are correctly recorded in company's books (completeness and accuracy)
- Payments from customers are properly recorded (accuracy)

- Payments received relate to goods/services supplied by the business (completeness)
- Credit notes issued are properly recorded in books and records of business
- Entries made in sales ledger are posted to the correct customer account (accuracy)
- Bad debts (potential/actual) are identified on a timely basis (accuracy)
- Entries made to nominal ledger are posted to the correct account (classification)
- Cut-off is correctly applied (cut-off)

Each step within the sales system should feature a number of key controls in order to ensure the objectives discussed above are achieved. These controls also act to minimise the possibility of material misstatement due to fraud and error.

System Controls

(a) Ordering and granting of credit

Sales orders need to be checked for authenticity, acceptability of terms and conditions and availability of stock. Orders taken over the telephone should be assigned consecutive order numbers. The availability of goods in stock should be checked before accepting an order. Once a sales order is accepted, it should be recorded on a pre-numbered sales order form and signed by the person accepting the order.

It is recommended that customer credit approval should be separated from sales order acceptance as this minimises the risk that the sales department may accept orders from customers with poor credit ratings which could ultimately result in bad debts being borne by the company. Credit checks are made of every new customer and, based on the results of these checks, an appropriate credit limit should be set. For existing customers, a comparison should be made between a customer's credit limit and the current balance owed by the customer. An order should be refused if it would bring the customer over their credit limit and their account is already overdue. Controls over credit approval enable management to make a more accurate assessment of the bad debt provision required.

A summary of the main controls which should feature in this part of the sales process are summarised below:

• Organizational controls	written procedures authority for approving new customers credit checking procedures for new customers
• Segregation of duties	separation of staff responsible for taking orders and dispatching goods from those responsible for processing invoices and collecting money
• Physical controls	pre-numbered order forms safeguarding of blank order forms

- Authorization — changes in customer data appropriately authorized
  authorization for customer credit limits
- Arithmetical and accounting checks — customer discounts calculated correctly
  vat correctly calculated
  matching of orders, dispatch dockets

(b) Dispatch and invoicing

Control objectives relating to invoicing are as follows:
- All deliveries are invoiced to customers
- Only actual deliveries are invoiced
- Invoices issued should contain authorised prices and the invoice amount should be correctly calculated.

Control procedures to ensure these objectives are met include:
- Segregating invoicing function from other steps in the sales processing transaction
- Matching and checking details of the related dispatch docket and sales order to ensure accuracy before invoice is prepared and sent to customer
- Preparing sales invoices based on the price details in an authorised price list
- Performing independent checks on the accuracy of sales invoice details.

A summary of the main controls that should feature in this part of the sales process are summarised below:

- Organizational controls — written procedures
  authority levels for selling prices and discount arrangements
  authority for issuing credit notes
- Segregation of duties — separation of staff responsible for dispatching goods and services from those responsible for processing sales invoices
- Physical controls — monitoring condition/quality of despatches
  Pre-numbering of delivery notes, invoices, goods returned notes
  safeguarding of blank forms
  recording delivery of goods to customers (signed GDNs)
  recording returns of goods by customers (pre-numbered Goods Returned Notes)

- Authorisation and approval — authorization of discounts, goods on special terms or free of charge
  matching sales invoices with dispatch and delivery dockets
  matching credit notes with goods returned notes

(c) Accounting
- A Primary control which should exist here is to ensure sales invoices are recorded in the appropriate period.
- Where manual systems are in place, sales invoices are entered into a sales journal. Invoices are posted to the debtors ledger and the sales journals posted to the general ledger. The debtors ledger and general ledger balances should agree and regular checks should be performed to ensure that this is so. Invoices should be entered in numerical sequence and missing number check performed. Monthly customer statements should also be sent.
- Where On line computer systems exist, it is common that, when an order is entered into the online system, the computer checks customer credit limits etc., and instructions are issued to the dispatch department who in turn on delivery of the goods enter delivery details into the system. The system automatically produces an invoice and debtors ledger, stock records and general ledger are simultaneously updated. Controls in place here should relate to access controls and programme application controls.
- Access controls permit read only access to files except for those authorised individuals who are permitted to amend standing data.
- Programmed application controls allow only orders from those customers recorded on the master file to be accepted, documents should be kept in numerical order, and the duplication of document numbers prevented, unusual prices, quantities, dates should also be rejected.
- When payment from the customer is received the risk is that cash is misappropriated before it is recorded or that errors may occur in the subsequent processing of cash receipts.
- Where cash is received over the counter, the cash register is used to record the cash receipts. Controls in place here should include the issue of receipts to customers who have paid for goods/services, the presence of a supervisor to oversee the cash receipt process, the reconciliation of the cash in hand with the cash totals recorded by the till register.
- Where payment is received by mail, it is recommended that the mail should be opened by two responsible officials. Cheques received should be endorsed as this process prevents the cashing of the cheque by a person other than the person/company to whom the cheque is endorsed to. All cash receipts should be recorded in a cash book and all cash together with a cash receipt listing should be forwarded for banking, and details of the receipts along with remittances should be posted to the accounts receivable records.

- Where customers pay by credit transfer, these payments should be picked up during the bank reconciliation process and details recorded in the accounts receivable records.
- All cash receipts should be deposited in tact daily.
- Independent checks should be made to ensure the receipts posted to the ledgers agree with the actual receipts received, in addition, bank reconciliations should be performed by individuals not involved in the cash receipt/cash recording process.
- Sales transactions usually include a number of sales adjustments which include granting discounts, sales returns and bad debts. Where these adjustments are deemed to be material they can lead to errors and irregularities in the processing of sales transactions. There is a risk that these sales adjustments may be used as a means of concealing the misappropriation of cash receipts, for example, by writing off a customer debt as a bad debt but misappropriating the cash received from the customer.
- Controls to prevent such frauds include:
  - Appropriate authorization of all sales adjustments
  - The use of appropriate documents and records
  - Segregation of duties between the duties of those authorizing sales adjustments and those recording/processing cash receipts.

A summary of the main controls which should feature in this part of the sales process are summarised below:

• Organizational controls	written procedures authority to write off debts
• Segregation of duties	separation of staff responsible for posting invoices and maintaining customers' accounts from those responsible for recording receipts from customers
• Physical controls	sequential numbering of sales invoices Controls on processing of invoices (batch totals) Control over unused invoice sets Control over spoilt invoices Restriction of access to parts of accounting system not relating to sales
• Authorisation and approval	authorization to implement credit control procedures
• Arithmetical and accounting checks	checking of invoices for prices, calculations' prompt entry of invoices/credit notes in to accounting records, sending of statements to debtors

production of aged debtors analysis and credit control procedures

reconciliation of sales ledger control account with sales ledger balances

cut-off checks to ensure goods dispatched but not invoiced are dealt with in correct period

In order to assess the design, implementation and operating effectiveness of the controls in place in the various steps of the sales process, the following tests should be performed:

Audit testing

- Check new customer credit procedures are operating effectively
- Check new customer accounts/credit limits, properly authorized
- Check orders are only accepted from customers within credit limits
- Ensure sales invoices are supported by customer orders and signed delivery notes
- Check Invoices for tots, price, calculations and vat; that they are correctly coded with customer and nominal codes, entered in day books, ledger and stock records
- Test numerical sequence and enquire into missing numbers of sales orders, invoices, delivery notes and goods returned notes
- Check goods returned are supported by goods returned note, correspondence with customer and properly authorized
- Check non-routine sales for appropriate authorization, check evidence of arrangements for sale, check assets removed from plant register
- Check postings between day books, cash book and ledger
  - Customer receipts posted to correct accounts
  - Investigate payments on account/round sum amounts
  - Investigate sums received where no invoice issued
  - Check analysis in sales day books
  - Check additions
  - Check entries in stock records for despatches of goods
  - Cut-off procedures at period end
  - Check sales ledger control account reconciliations
  - Check aged debtor analysis and control procedures such as follow up on overdue debts
  - Obtain explanations for contra and journal entries in sales ledger
  - Examine records for large/unusual receipts.

9.4 Typical Components of an Efficient Sales and Debtors Cycle

When designing the process surrounding sales and debtors management, the auditor will be attempting to mitigate the following critical risks:

- sales are not complete i.e. all sales invoices raised are not recorded
- sales are not accurate i.e. sales invoices are not recorded at the correct amount
- customer accounts included on the debtors ledger do not exist
- payments received from customers are not lodged to the bank
- payments received from customers are not recorded in the correct customer account
- old debtor balances are not followed up resulting in bad debts for the business

The following are the typical components of an efficient sales and debtors cycle which help to mitigate the above risks:

Credit sales and debtors

1. Sales order is raised on receipt of a telephone/e-mail/written/over the counter request. Sales orders are raised in sequential order. If the customer is new to the business a suitable member of management must authorise the customer and create a new customer account
2. Sales order is passed to dispatch department
3. Order is prepared for dispatch and sales order details are agreed to goods prepared prior to delivery
4. Goods delivery note (GDN) is prepared in duplicate form, when delivery is dispatched customer signs the GDN and keeps one copy with the second being returned to the client
5. On receipt of a signed GDN from the customer a sales invoice is raised and sent to the customer. Sales invoices are raised in sequential order
6. The accounting system is updated for the sale i.e.
   Dr Accounts receivable xxxxxxx
   Cr Sales xxxxxx
7. On receipt of payment the manual cash received book is updated for the receipt and the accounting system is updated as follows:
   Dr Cash xxxxxx
   Cr Debtors xxxxxx
8. Cash received is lodged to the bank.

Cash sales

1. Customer visits business premise and selects goods for purchase
2. Sale is processed through cash register by sales assistant and invoice is automatically generated from the system for the customer. Accounting system is automatically updated for the sale i.e.
   Dr Cash xxxxxxx
   Cr Sales xxxxxxx

3. Payment is received from customer at point of sale either in cash or credit card
4. At the end of each shift a till reconciliation is performed by a supervisor as follows:
   a) X-Read printed off cash register which details total cash/credit card takings since start of shift
   b) Cash in till is counted and reconciled to totals per X-Read
   c) Till reconciliations are maintained for future reference
5. Cash counted at end of each shift is stored in a safe until lodgement to the bank takes place
6. Cash received is lodged to the bank

   In relation to credit sales, management should perform the following on a timely basis, e.g. monthly/quarterly:
   – review of aged debtor listing by management for large unusual balance, old balances and credit balances
   – reconciliation of aged debtor listing to trial balance
   – review of doubtful debt provision and assessment of the need for increase/decrease in provision in view of aged balances on the aged debtor listing
   – chasing of customers to secure payment for outstanding balances

   In relation to cash sales, management must ensure that:
   – till reconciliations are performed and reviewed by appropriate personnel
   – lodgements to bank of cash takings are not made by the same personnel who receive the cash across the counter to prevent misappropriation of cash.

Performance of the above will create a strong control environment surrounding the sales and debtors cycle within the business. For the auditor, this means that controls testing can be performed on the system in place and, where found to be robust, the level of substantive audit tests to be performed will be greatly reduced.

9.5 Controls Testing Over the Sales and Accounts Receivable Cycle and Related Assertions

The starting point when designing tests of controls is to gain a full understanding of how the cycle operates within a client's business. This will usually take the form of a meeting with management and the individuals involved in the cycle in order to discuss the process in place within the business for processing sales transactions and recording receipt of payment. Once this understanding is obtained a testing plan can be designed based on the key controls which are in operation. When designing such tests it is essential that the auditor remembers the assertions which must be addressed by the controls testing performed, and further keep in mind that the objective of tests of controls is to obtain sufficient appropriate audit evidence that the control operated effectively throughout the entire period under review. General information surrounding the performance of controls testing is discussed further in **Chapters 3 and 5.**

Examples of controls testing performed over the sales and debtors cycle are given in the table below together with the assertions addressed.

Test of Control	Assertion Addressed
A walkthrough test can be performed as follows:	Completeness, occurrence and accuracy of sales income
– inspect sales order raised and confirm that they have been raised by a person who has authority to do so	Completeness of accounts receivable balance
– inspect goods delivery notes (GDNs) relating to the sales orders tested and ensure the following:	
1. the items delivered agree to the items per the sales order	
2. the GDN has been authorised by a person who has the authority to dispatch an order e.g. stores manager	
3. GDNs are signed as evidence of receipt by the customer and the delivery person	
4. Inspect sales invoices raised in respect of GDNs and confirm that items per the invoice agree to the items delivered	
5. Confirm that sales invoices are posted to the sales ledger on the correct date and to the correct customer account	
6. Vouch payment of sales invoices to the cash received book and the bank statement	
7. Confirm that customer accounts on the debtors ledger have been updated for payment received	
Obtain a sample of sales orders and ensure that they have been raised in sequential order	Completeness of sales
Obtain a sample of sales invoices and ensure that they have been raised in sequential order	Completeness of sales
Inspection of aged accounts receivable listings for evidence of review by management	Accuracy of accounts receivable balance
Inspection of reconciliation of aged debtor listing to trial balance	Completeness and accuracy of accounts receivable balance
Inspection of evidence to validate and corroborate credit control procedures in place at the client site e.g. if customers are contacted via phone when debts become old, review of memos detailing response to these follow-up phonecalls or if customers are contacted via letter review of such letters	Valuation of accounts receivable balance

Test of Control	Assertion Addressed
Review of aged debt provision and evidence that it is updated by management on a regular basis to reflect old balances on the aged accounts receivable listing	Accuracy of accounts receivable balance
Inspection of client's policy for acceptance of new customers, including which personnel have the authority to accept a new customer and create a customer account, if credit worthiness checks are performed and how credit limits are assigned to customer accounts. Once procedures are determined validation and corroboration should follow as appropriate.	N/a

Depending on the nature of the tests of controls and the results obtained, low, moderate or high assurance will be obtained over the financial statement assertion areas.

When tests of controls are complete it is important for the auditor to consider the impact of the results on the audit plan.

Where the control environment is found to be robust, the auditor can conclude that reliance can be placed on the system surrounding the sales and accounts receivable cycle and the level of substantive testing to be performed can be reduced appropriately.

Where the control environment is found to have significant weaknesses, the auditor must consider what level of reliance, if any, can be placed on the system. Following on from this assessment, the level of substantive testing performed will be increased in order to gain sufficient appropriate audit evidence over the sales figure and accounts receivable balance included in the financial statements.

9.6 Substantive Testing

Substantive procedures are used to gather evidence in order to substantiate account balances e.g. debtors and classes of transactions e.g. sales. They are designed to address the risk of material misstatement at the financial statement assertion level. As discussed in **Chapter 5** substantive testing includes substantive analytical review and substantive tests of details.

When the auditor is designing substantive procedures the following should be considered:

- the materiality of the sales figure and the debtors balance to the financial statements; for example, where the accounts receivable balance is not material to the financial statements a limited amount of substantive testing will be necessary

- the impact of any significant risks surrounding the sales and debtors cycle and the tailoring of the audit approach to perform suitable substantive testing to gain sufficient appropriate audit evidence over the area of significant risk
- the results of controls testing performed and the assurance gained from these tests; the extent of substantive testing to be performed around sales and debtors will be dependent upon how robust the control environment surrounding the sales and accounts receivable process is.

9.7 Substantive Analytical Procedures

Assertions covered: accuracy, existence/occurrence, completeness, valuation, cut-off. Substantive analytical procedures can be used as the main test of the account balance or they can be used in conjunction with substantive tests of details that will be appropriately reduced in extent. Background behind the approach to the performance of substantive analytical procedures has been discussed in **Chapter 5.**

When performing substantive analytical procedures the following four steps should be considered by the auditor:

- an expectation for current year results, with the basis of expectation being explained and the reliability of the data used being assessed;
- a threshold level for further investigation where deviations between actual result and expectation occur (usually based on planning materiality level);
- calculation of the deviation occurring between actual results and expectation;
- performance of further substantive testing where deviation from expectation is greater than the threshold established.

The auditor can use the following when developing an independent expectation for current period sales:

- prior period results;
- current period sales budget as developed by management (provided that the budgetary process has been tested and is found to be robust);
- market expectations for the industry within which the company operates.

When developing an independent expectation for the current period results, the auditor must consider if any significant changes have taken place within the operations of the business during the period under review, compared to the prior period, which have impacted on the sales level for the current period. Considerations should be given to the following:

- is the duration of the period under review in line with the duration of the prior period?
- have any new divisions opened during the period under review?

- have any divisions been discontinued during the period under review?
- have new products been introduced?
- have products been discontinued?
- has the competitive environment changed?
- has the macroeconomic environment changed e.g. have consumer spending habits changed?
- have new sales personnel been employed during the period under review impacting on the trading results?
- have selling prices been increased during the period under review?
- comparison of current period gross margin to prior period margin.
- review and comparison of daily/weekly/monthly sales figures for current period compared to same period in prior year.

Depending on the answers to the questions above, the auditor must then consider how these will impact on the development of an expectation for current period sales, obtain relevant, reliable substantive evidence to support and/or quantify the known changes and build the effects of such changes on sales within the current period expectation.

The auditor can use the following when developing an independent expectation for the period end debtors balance: for example, in the motor industry it may be possible to reconcile stock movements precisely or indeed in the drink/bar trade business via weekly counts:

- prior period result
- current period budget as developed by management (provided that the budgetary process has been tested and is found to be robust).

When developing an independent expectation for current period results the auditor must consider if any significant changes have taken place within the operations of the business during the period under review, compared to the prior period, which have impacted on the period end debtors balance. Considerations should be given to the following:

– has the company expanded significantly resulting in increased sales and a corresponding increase in the period end debtors balance?
– has the company reduced operations significantly resulting in reduced sales and a corresponding decrease in period end debtors balance?
– have normal payment terms for customers been changed during the period e.g. from 30 days to 45 days i.e. change in debtor days ratio?
– have any one off sales contracts been taken on and completed during the period and remain due at the period end?
– has the macroeconomic environment changed e.g. have consumer spending habits changed?

Depending on the answers to the questions above, the auditor must then consider how these will impact on the development of an expectation for period end debtors balance and build in the effects of the known changes within the current period expectation.

When expectations are developed the auditor must compare the expectation to the actual result. Where the deviation is below the threshold established for further investigation no additional substantive testing is necessary. However, where the deviation is greater than the threshold, the auditor must perform further substantive testing to provide appropriate evidence around the unexpected deviation.

Worked Example – Substantive Analytical Procedures for Sales and Debtors

You are undertaking the sales and debtors sections of the audit for your client Holiday Heaven Ltd. You are at the phase of the audit where substantive analytical procedures are being performed. You have ascertained the following information from the work carried out by the audit team to date:

a) Sales levels for existing products have remained reasonably in line with prior period.
b) No products have been discontinued in the period.
c) Two new sales contracts have been won during the period, these are one off contracts, details as follows as agreed to signed contracts:
   (i) Contract 1 commenced in February 2007, contracting the client to produce and supply the customer with goods totalling €/£100k (sales value) per month
   (ii) Contract 2 commenced in October 2007, contracting the client to produce and supply the customer with goods totalling €/£45k (cost price) per month. Gross profit margin on this contract is expected to be 40%.
d) Selling price for all items increased by 5% in September 2007 – corroborated via inspection of letter sent out to customers outlining the above in August 2007.
e) Normal credit terms have increased from 30 days in prior period to 35 days in current period – corroborated via inspection of letter sent out to credit customers outlining the above in Jan 2007.
f) Dispute ongoing with a customer for payment of €/£300k which is 9 months outstanding at period end. This was a new customer accepted in the period under review. Audit team inspected invoices issued to customer and letters sent to customer demanding payment. Dispute confirmed as now being with client's legal representatives.

Other required information
Current period: 12 months to 31 December 2007
Current period sales: €/£6,690,000
Period end debtor balance: €/£930,000
Threshold for further investigation: 75% of planning materiality of €/£25,000 i.e. €/£18,750

Prior period: 15 months to 31 December 2006
Prior period sales: €/£6,575,000
Prior period end debtor balance: €/£540,410

Using the information above, sales substantive analytical review can be performed:

1. Develop expectation

Prior period sales	= €/£6,575,000 over 15 months
Prior period monthly sales	= €/£6,575,000/15
	= €/£438,333
Expected sales for current period using prior period monthly sales value	= (€/£438,333*8)+(€/£438,333*1.05*4) W1
	= €/£3,506,667+€/£1,840,999
	= €/£5,347,666

Adjustment for additional sales revenue won during the year:

Additional sales revenue from contract 1	= €/£1,100k	W2
Additional sales revenue from contract 2	= €/£225k	W3

Total expected sales for current period = €/£6,672,666

2. Outline deviation for further investigation
From information above, deviation threshold is €/£18,750

3. Compare actual result to expectation and calculate deviation

Actual sales	= €/£6,690,000
Total expected sales for current period	= €/£6,672,666
Deviation from expectation	= €/£17,334

4. Perform further investigation where deviation is above threshold for further investigation

As deviation is below threshold for further investigation no further work deemed necessary.

W1. Being 8 months sales at prior period monthly sales plus 4 months sales adjusting for 5% price increase in September 2007
W2. Being €/£100k per month over 11 months
W3. Being sales revenue of €/£75k over 3 months
Cost price = €/£45k
Gross margin = 40%
Cost price = 60%
Revenue = 100% being €/£45k/60*100

Using the information above debtors substantive analytical review can be performed:

1. Develop expectation

Expectation to be developed using the information ascertained in relation to debtor credit terms and ongoing dispute with customer – assuming that sales are spread evenly throughout the year.

Credit terms are 35 days as corroborated above
Actual sales are €/£6,690,000

Expectation can be developed using this information and the debtor days ratio: (assuming sales are spread evenly throughout the year)

$$\frac{Debtors * 365}{Sales} = Debtor\ days$$

$$\frac{Debtors * 365}{6,690,000} = 35$$

Debtors	= 35/365*6,690,000
	= 641,507
Add increase in period end debtors due to customer dispute	300,000
Expected debtors	=€/£941,507

> **2. Outline deviation for further investigation**
> From information above deviation threshold is €/£18,750
>
> **3. Compare actual result to expectation and calculate deviation**
>
> Expected debtors = €/£941,507
> Actual debtors = €/£930,000
> Deviation from expectation = €/£11,507
>
> **4. Perform further investigation where deviation is above threshold for further investigation**
> As the deviation is below threshold for further investigation, no further work deemed necessary.

Analytical review

Where moderate or high comfort has been obtained from the performance of controls testing and supplemented with substantive tests of details (discussed below), the auditor may decide that additional comfort is not required from substantive analytical procedures and may instead perform an analytical review of the movement between prior period and current period results, focusing primarily on the reasons for fluctuations between prior period results and current period results or where current period results are in line with prior period results, an assessment of whether non-movement is reasonable given other information obtained during the audit. When carrying out an analytical review it is not necessary to follow the four-step approach which is used when performing a substantive analytical review and it is not necessary to vouch explanations for fluctuations to supporting documentation.

This procedure will not provide any further comfort over financial statement assertions. However it will provide an overview of the reasons for the movements in balances and should corroborate auditor findings noted through performance of substantive tests of details.

9.8 Substantive Tests of Details

Where the results of controls testing and substantive analytical procedures do not reduce the risk of material misstatement to an acceptably low level, substantive tests of details should also be performed. The background to substantive tests of details is discussed further in **Chapter 5**. Outlined and discussed below are tests of details which can be used when performing work on sales and the debtors balance.

Testing recorded sales

Assertions covered: existence/occurrence, accuracy, completeness

When testing total sales recorded by the client in the period the auditor should consider/perform the following:

- verify that a sales invoice was issued for each sales amount recorded
- verify that the sale was accurately posted to the correct customer's account on the sales ledger
- test the mathematical accuracy of sales invoices
- test the selling price of items on an invoice by agreeing the amounts to the client's price list/sales catalogue and validate that any discount allowed has been authorised by the appropriate person
- verify that output VAT has been calculated properly on sales invoices.

Further, the auditor should consider performing testing around the actual delivery of sales orders to gain assurance around the existence of the sale. The auditor should select delivery documentation (e.g. goods delivery note) and perform the following:

- trace delivery documentation (e.g. delivery docket) to sales invoices and agree the quantity delivered to the quantity recorded on the invoice. Inspect customer acknowledgement signature as evidence of receipt of goods (i.e. basis for proof of delivery if there is a subsequent dispute)
- if delivery dockets are raised in a sequential order, verify the numerical sequence on a test basis
- obtain explanations for and corroborate where necessary significant adjustments made in sales accounts throughout the year.

Testing sales returns

Assertions covered: existence/occurrence, accuracy, completeness

When testing total sales returns recorded by the client in the period the auditor should consider/perform the following:

- test the mathematical accuracy of sales returns credit notes
- test pricing by checking credit note to sales invoice
- ensure that the credit note was approved by an individual authorised to issue credit notes
- ensure that the credit note has been correctly posted to the sales ledger and the customer's account
- verify that output VAT has been calculated properly on sales returns credit notes.

Testing sales discounts

Assertions covered: existence/occurrence, accuracy, completeness

Where the client issues discount to customers the auditor should perform testing to validate the following:

- sales discount has been approved by an individual authorised to do so and
- where discount has been issued due to damaged stock, the facts surrounding the discount should be validated through inspection of appropriate information held on file by the client
- obtain details of the company policy on the granting of discounts and ensure that it is being complied with.

Agreement of the Detailed Accounts Receivable Listing to the Trial Balance

Assertions covered: existence/occurrence, accuracy

The auditor should obtain the detailed accounts receivable listing and perform the following:

- The current periods opening balance should be agreed to the closing audited balances in the prior years audit working papers or signed financial statements
- Agree the balance per the listing to the balance per the trial balance. Reconciling items should be tested in order to obtain the desired level of assurance and agreed to supporting documentation
- Ensure each account is settled by the customer from time to time
- enquire into the reasons for any transfers between accounts or any amounts recorded in cash book as one amount but subsequently split into two or more amounts when recorded in the sales ledger as this could be evidence of fraud
- obtain comfort over the mathematical accuracy of the detailed listing
- review the listing for any unusual balances such as large balances, credit balances and old balances.

Analytical Procedures/Review

Auditors should carry out analytical review procedures as part of substantive testing and should include calculations such as

- Debtor days ratio (debtors/credit sales × 365)
- No of day sales in trade debtors v previous year
- Aged debtors v previous year in order to identify increased debtor ageing
- Where ever a change in relationships cannot be readily obtained or an unusual pattern is uncovered, auditors should seek explanations from management and corroborate the explanation received by performing additional tests of detail.

Debtors Circularisation (ISA 505 External Confirmations)

Assertions covered: existence/occurrence, rights and obligations

ISA 500 Audit Evidence states that audit evidence is influenced by its source, nature and is dependent on the individual circumstances under which it is obtained. It can be concluded therefore that audit evidence obtained independently from third parties can reduce the risk of material misstatement surrounding the particular account balance to an acceptably low level. With regard to accounts receivable balances, the performance of a debtors circularisation is a means of obtaining independent third-party confirmation of the accuracy of the year-end balance on the debtors ledger. Through performance of this substantive test the auditor seeks confirmation from customers as to whether they are in agreement with the balance per the client's debtors ledger at the year end.

Using debtors circularisations to test the year-end debtor balances have a number of advantages to the auditor including that they provide

- Direct external, third-party evidence which provides evidence over the existence and ownership of the debt and also the value of amount due
- They confirm the effectiveness of the system of internal control in operation within the company
- They assist in determining cut-off procedures by identifying invoices in transit over year end
- They provide evidence of items in dispute where the amount stated by the debtor differs from the amount recorded in the books of the company.

Using these circularisations also have their disadvantages which include the following

- Where customers are small businesses or private individuals, they are less likely to maintain accurate ledger balances to provide a reliable response
- Customers are less likely to admit to owing more than is shown on the confirmation letter
- Many trivial differences are likely to be reported as a result of cash/goods in transit
- The non-response rate may be high.

Two methods of confirming debtors balances exist, these are as follows:

1. **Negative circularisation**
   These circularisations request the customer to respond only if they are not in agreement with the balance stated.

   The problem with this is that it may be impossible to tell whether the customer agrees with the year-end balance stated or whether there is simply a failure on their part to reply. It can be concluded that negative confirmations provide less persuasive audit evidence than positive confirmations.

The proposed ED ISA 505 (revised and redrafted) External Confirmations, permits the use of negative confirmations (as the sole substantive procedure) when the auditor is satisfied that internal controls are operating effectively, concludes risk of material misstatement is low and the population subject to confirmation consists of a large number of small, account balances, very few exceptions are expected and the auditor has no reason to believe the recipients of the letters will disregard the confirmation request.

2. Positive circularisation

Here the customer is asked to reply whether they agree with balance or not. In some cases the customer is asked to supply the balance themselves.

The positive form is used when planned detection risk is low or individual customer balances are relatively large and generally produces statistically valid evidence, so long as non-responses are verified by other means. This is the favoured method but a combination of the two may be used in a single engagement.

The following should be considered when performing a debtors circularisation:

- the auditor must remain in control of the external confirmation process, meaning that the auditor must select the customers to be contacted, prepare and send the confirmation requests and ensure that responses are sent directly to the auditor and not via the client
- the debtors circularisation process should be carried out a suitable length of time prior to the commencement of the audit fieldwork in order to allow customers time to respond
- the auditor should target high value balances on the year-end debtors ledger in order to gain high assurance over the total balance. *Do not, however, omit nil balances, credit balances or accounts written off in the period*
- for responses returned which are not in agreement with the balance per the client's debtors ledger appropriate investigation into the differences arising should be conducted by the auditor with appropriate journal adjustments proposed if necessary in order to correct the balance per the client's ledger
- where responses are not returned the auditor should ordinarily consider contacting the customer via telephone in order to obtain a response; in the scenario where a response can still not be obtained, alternative procedures should then be performed to confirm the year-end balance per the debtors ledger (alternative procedures are discussed below)
- where management requests that the auditor does not perform a debtors circularisation, the auditor must consider if there are valid grounds for such a request

and obtain audit evidence to support the validity of management's request. If the auditor agrees to management's request and does not perform a debtors circularisation, the auditor should apply alternative audit procedures in order to obtain sufficient appropriate audit evidence regarding the year-end debtors balance (discussed below). If the auditor does not accept the validity of management's request and is prevented from carrying out the confirmations, there has been a limitation on the scope of the auditor's work and he/she should consider the possible impact on the auditor's report
- when considering the reasons provided by management the auditor should apply professional scepticism and consider if it raises any questions surrounding the integrity of management or possible instances of fraudulent behaviour within the business
- where responses are returned to the client directly, these cannot be accepted by the auditor on the grounds that the client may have manipulated the response.

When the auditor receives responses from the debtors circularised the following should then be considered:

- Where the customer confirms the balance due to the client, this confirms the accuracy of the balance for the auditor but it does not confirm the collectability and the valuation of the balance i.e. is recoverability of the balance likely? The auditor must consider this further when testing the allowance for doubtful debts (see below)
- Where the customer is not in agreement with the balance due per client's records work must be performed by the auditor in order to reconcile the difference. Differences arising can be due to the following:
  - timing differences e.g.
    - the customer has sent a cheque payment to the client but the client has not received the payment at the time of preparation of debtors circulars
    - the client has credited the customer account with discount for prompt payment but the customer has not yet received the credit note and updated their system
  - permanent differences e.g.
    - the client has posted an invoice incorrectly to the customer account either at the wrong amount or to the wrong customer account entirely
    - the customer has not posted a legitimate invoice to their system.

The auditor must carry out appropriate work to reconcile any differences arising.

The auditor must summarise findings from the debtors circularisation in a suitable manner. *The working paper should list each account selected for confirmation and the results obtained from each request, cross-referenced to the actual confirmation response. Differences should be investigated and discussed with management when deemed to be material.* A possible means of documenting audit work is shown in the table below.

Customer Name	Customer Code	Balance per Client Ledger	Balance Confirmed by Customer	Difference Arising	Further Audit Work Performed on difference Arising
Holly Hill Ltd	HH001	£/€23,241	£/€11,117	£/€12,124	Confirmed that client had posted 3 invoices totalling €/£12,124 to HH001 in error, invoices should have been posted to HH002. Inspected invoices and confirmed that they were in the name of Heads Up Ltd and not Holly Hill Ltd.

In the case where no responses are received, alternative procedures should be performed by the auditors. The two main alternative procedures are as follows: examining post-year-end receipts and vouching unpaid invoices and supporting documentation.

Post-year-end cash receipts testing

Assertions covered: existence/occurrence, completeness, valuation

A means of verifying the existence, completeness and valuation of year-end debtor balances is to confirm the amount of cash received post year in respect of such balances. In order to perform this test correctly the following should be considered:

- obtain a detailed breakdown of the sales invoices which make up the year-end balance per the debtors ledger for each customer;
- obtain details of cash received from selected customers post-year-end along with details of the sales invoices to which the receipts relate;
- vouch cash receipts to remittances or bank statements;
- where cash has not been received post-year-end from the customer the auditor should vouch the year-end debtor balance to *supporting documentation such as invoices, goods dispatch notes and customer orders in order to confirm the occurrence of the sale.*

Alternative Procedures where Cash is not Received

Open invoices should be traced to a dispatch note signed by the customer acknowledging receipt of the goods, or to the customer's original order.

It is important to determine the invoices outstanding at the year end in order to confirm post-year-end cash payments are in relation to invoices which have been included on the ledger at the year end.

If post-year-end cash receipts are discovered which relate to pre-year-end invoices which are not outstanding on the ledger, a cut-off error has occurred and the debtors ledger is understated. It will be necessary to propose an adjusting journal to correct for material pre-year-end sales invoices not included on the debtors ledger.

Sales/accounts receivable cut-off

Assertions Covered: Cut-off
Cut-off errors can arise when either of the following occurs:

- a pre-year-end dated sales invoice is not posted to the debtors ledger until post-year-end;
- a post-year-end dated sales invoice is posted to the debtors ledger before the year-end date.

When either of the above occurs the sale in question has been recorded in the incorrect period in the financial statements of the company.

In order to determine whether the client has undertaken appropriate cutoff procedures at the year end the auditor should perform appropriate tests. The following should be considered:

- the auditor should assess the high risk period i.e. the dates around the year end where the risk of a cut-off error occurring is deemed greatest, this could be the final week of trade pre-year end and the first week of trade post-year-end
- the auditor should target invoices posted to the sales ledger during the high risk periods
- the auditor should inspect the chosen sales invoices and the corresponding delivery documents in order to confirm that the sales have been recorded in the correct period.

Post-year-end returns

Assertions Covered: Cut-off
It is important for the auditor to consider post-year-end credit notes issued by the client. The auditor should consider the following:

- any significant post-year-end credit notes raised and if they have been accounted for in the correct period i.e. if a credit note has been raised post-year-end in relation to a pre-year-end sales invoice then the credit note has not been accounted for in the correct period and an adjusting journal will be necessary
- the level of credit notes raised post year end. Where there are unusual amounts of high value credit notes issued early in the new accounting period in relation to pre-year-end sales invoices, the auditor should consider the legitimacy of the sales invoices issued pre-year-end and consider the possibility of a cut-off error arising
- the reason for the returns and the credit notes being issued
- journal adjustments should be proposed to correct for post-year-end credit notes raised relating to pre-year-end invoices.

Reasonableness of the allowance for doubtful debts testing

Assertions Covered: Valuation
Most entities determine the provision for bad debts by:

- making a general provision which is usually determined by applying a percentage to balances overdue by more than a specified period
- making a specific provision which involves identifying customers who are known to be in financial difficulties or where payment is in dispute.

The Bad Debt provision is an estimate, ISA 540, Audit of Accounting Estimates therefore applies. The auditor is required to adopt one or more of the following approaches

- reviewing and testing the process used by management
- using an independent estimate
- reviewing subsequent events.

First approach, adopted for verifying general provision, is by obtaining management's procedures for determining the estimate and considering the reliability of them; ensuring the procedures have been followed and have been appropriately approved; considering the reasonableness of assumptions used in the calculation; checking calculations and considering reliability of prior year provisions.

Approaches usually adopted when considering specific provision include examining correspondence from customers, reviewing customer credit reports and financial statements and discussing collectability of debts with management.

The risk of doubtful debts occurring is a common risk for most businesses. The auditor must exercise caution and assess the aging of the balances outstanding on the year-end debtors ledger and consider if the balance has been provided for by the client and, if not, the auditor must consider if a provision is necessary. This assessment is crucial for the overall valuation of the debtor balance included within the financial statements.

The auditor should also consider the following:

- The adequacy of the system of internal controls relating to approval of credit terms and following up of overdue debts
- Period of credit allowed and taken
- Whether balances have been settled post-year-end
- Whether an account is made up of specific items or not i.e debtor paying amounts on account, this could indicate cash flow difficulties and a potential bad debt
- Whether an account is within maximum credit limit approved
- Reports on major debtors from collectors, agencies etc.
- Legal proceedings and legal status of debtor, e.g. in liquidation or bankruptcy.

The auditor should perform the following:

- review the aged debtor listing for debts aged 60–90 days and older. The auditor should also at this point review a sample of sales invoices included on the period end ledger to assess the reasonableness of the aging of the invoices by the system on the period-end ledger.
- confirm and verify if such balances have been received post-year-end.
- where balances have not been settled post-year-end, the auditor should enquire from management if there are any circumstances surrounding the non-payment of the balance; such as a dispute between the customer and the client, the customer being declared bankrupt or the customer experiencing cash flow difficulties
- where receipt of the balance outstanding on the aged listing at the year end is deemed unlikely after the above testing is performed, the auditor should consider if the client has provided for the balance
- where the client has not provided for the balance and the auditor deems that a provision is necessary, then an adjusting journal should be proposed.

The bad debt provision created by the client is known as an accounting estimate, as final payment amount which will be received from the customer is not known with certainty. It is the role of the auditor to assess the facts surrounding the aged balances and to determine if the provision appears reasonable based on what is known.

Where the client has included a general provision in the accounts i.e. a provision which is general in nature is not established in respect of a specific customer and balance, the auditor should understand the basis of the provision and inspect corroborating information and determine the reasonableness of the provision and if it is necessary.

9.9 Comfort Obtained from Controls Testing, Substantive Analytical Review and Substantive Tests of Details

When the auditor has performed controls testing, substantive analytical review and substantive tests of details it must be considered if sufficient appropriate audit evidence has been obtained over sales and debtors which give the appropriate level of comfort required over the assertions stated at the outset, these being:

- completeness
- valuation
- existence/occurrence
- cut-off
- valuation
- rights and obligations.

The auditor must also consider if the testing performed has appropriately addressed any key risks identified by the auditor surrounding the sales and debtors cycle and reduced the risk of material misstatement arising as a result of key risks to a suitably low level.

The auditor must consider the results of testing performed on the audit opinion to be issued:

- Where the auditor has obtained sufficient appropriate audit evidence over the sales and debtors balance, an unqualified opinion can be issued
- Where the auditor has been prevented, or could not carry out sufficient audit procedures surrounding sales and debtors, a limitation of scope may arise and a qualified audit opinion or a disclaimer of opinion may be necessary
- Where there is a disagreement between the auditor and management regarding the acceptability of the accounting policies selected relating to sales and/or debtors, the method of their application or the adequacy of financial statement disclosures, a qualified audit opinion or an adverse opinion may be necessary.

The auditor's report on financial statements is considered in detail in **Chapter 15**.

Disclosure requirements should also be assessed:

- Auditors must be aware of the disclosure requirements for trade receivables and sales under applicable financial reporting framework
- Review of sales ledger may indicate amounts owed from employees, officers, other group companies and related parties which should be specifically disclosed if found to be material
- Credit balances included in the debtors ledger may, if found to be material, require reclassification to current liabilities
- Evidence of such activities may be obtained through the review of minutes from board of directors' meetings and from inquiry of management
- Obtain management's representations on these matters in writing in a representation letter.

Summary

Key considerations for the auditor when performing audit procedures around sales and debtors:

- nature of the control environment surrounding sales and debtors
- tests of controls to be applied and the outcome of testing performed
- materiality of the sales figure and debtors balance to the overall financial statements
- identification of any significant risks around sales and debtors cycle
- designing suitable substantive testing in view of results of controls testing, materiality and existence of significant risks around sales and debtors
- performing substantive testing in the form of substantive analytical review and substantive tests of details and assessing the outcome of the results
- considering whether testing performed has provided assurance over relevant financial statement areas
- impact of outcomes of testing performed on the audit opinion

9.10 Loans

1. Loans other than to Directors
- Assess Internal Control evaluation – authority to lend
- Obtain schedule of loan agreements, interest calculations, repayments
- If material – confirm balance
- Examine terms of agreement – are terms being adhered to
- Loan secured – examine security, and assess value and recoverability
- If loan guaranteed – examine status of guarantor
- Review of bad debt provision

2. Loans to directors and connected persons

Audit procedures:
- Review all transactions involving directors which were outstanding at any time during year
- If approval is required by shareholders, ensure resolution approved
- Obtain certificate of confirmation of balance from the director
- Obtain evidence of approval in board minutes
- Ensure compliance with relevant company law
- Ensure full disclosure in the financial statements

QUESTIONS

Self-test Questions

1. What are the financial statement assertions in relation to debtors?
2. What are the principal stages in a sales system?
3. What are the advantages of using a debtors circularization?
4. Outline the role of analytical procedures when auditing debtors.

Review Questions

(See Solutions to Review Questions at the end of this textbook.)

Question 9.1

Describe two tests of controls which can be used to gain comfort over the completeness of the total sales figure in the financial statements.

Question 9.2

Where the controls process surrounding the sales and debtor cycle is found to be weak, explain the impact of this on the audit plan for the auditor.

Question 9.3

Where the controls process surrounding the sales and debtor cycle is found to be strong, explain the impact of this on the audit plan for the auditor.

Question 9.4

You are given the following information regarding total sales for Football Crazy Ltd:

	FY 2008 (1 Jan – 31 Dec 2008) €/£'000	FY 2007 (1 Jan – 31 Dec 2007) €/£'000	
DVDs	335	227	a) and b)
Sweatshirts	55	37	c)
Magazines	178	198	d)
	568	462	

(a) 5 new DVDs have been brought to the market during the financial year to 2008, details as follows:

DVD	Month of Introduction to Market	Selling Price	Budgeted Monthly Sales Volume (Units)
1	Feb 2008	€/£10	250
2	April 2008	€/£17	300
3	July 2008	€/£12	485
4	September 2008	€/£15	245
5	November 2008	€/£22	165

(b) 2 DVDs were discontinued in January 2008 due to poor sales in prior year, details as follows:

DVD	Selling Price	Prior Year Annual Sales Volume (Units)
1	€/£22	565
2	€/£19	500

(c) The sweatshirt range for adults has remained the same, however, a new range for children was introduced during the 2008 financial year, details as follows:
  − new sweatshirt range introduced for children for the final 2 months of the 12-month period under review
  − selling price range of sweatshirts on sale is €/£12–€/£15
  − based on market research expected monthly sales of sweatshirts is 650 per month.

(d) During financial year 2008 the company was forced to reduce magazine selling prices due to growing competition from competitors:

Magazine	Prior Year Selling Price	Prior Year Sales Volume	Prior Year Sales Revenue	New Reduced Price	Month of Price Cut
1	€/£2.50	20,000	€/£50,000	€/£2.30	Jan 08
2	€/£2.00	13,500	€/£27,000	€/£1.80	Jan 08
3	€/£4.75	10,000	€/£47,500	€/£4.45	March 08
4	€/£3.50	11,000	€/£38,500	€/£3.10	Jan 08
5	€/£1.25	28,000	€/£35,000	€/£1.10	June 08
			€/£198,000		

Requirement:

(i) Use the information above to develop an expectation for total sales revenue for the 2008 financial year, showing the overall expectation and an expectation for each individual revenue stream.

(ii) Outline for each particular sales component what additional information you would require in order to determine the reliability of the information used when developing the expectation above

(iii) Explain briefly the remaining three parts of the four-step approach which should be considered by the auditor when performing substantive analytical procedures.

Question 9.5

Quad Tec Engineering Ltd has a bad debt provision of €/£253,000 at the year end.

Requirement

Outline what your approach to the audit of this provision would be in order to gain comfort over the valuation of year-end accounts receivable balance.

List three other accounting estimates that can be included in financial statements and briefly describe the audit approach which should be adopted for these estimates.

Question 9.6

Ballycane Metals Ltd is a new audit client for your audit firm. The engagement leader and audit manager attended a preliminary meeting with the directors and the financial director of the company in the past few days. Audit fieldwork is due to commence in 1 week. The audit manager noted the following from the meeting:

1. In recent months the company has experienced severe competition and as a result has increased its payment terms for customers in order to attract new customers and maintain current customers
2. Debtors days ratio has moved from 35 days in prior year to 60 days in current year
3. The client is contemplating introducing a 3% discount for payment within credit terms
4. On review of the aged debtors listing half of the year-end debtors balance is aged greater than 90 days

Requirement:

(a) As audit senior of the team draft a memorandum to your audit team outlining how the team will approach the audit of debtor balances aged greater than 90 days old on the aged debtor listing at the year end. Memorandum should include general and specific guidance.
(b) If the client decides to implement a 3% discount for prompt payment explain how in future years the audit team could develop an independent expectation for total discount allowed during the performance of substantive analytical procedures.

Question 9.7

Explain how an audit team should approach the audit of credit balances on the debtors ledger.

Question 9.8

The following information has been gathered by an audit team carrying out fieldwork around the sales and debtors cycle of Mac Apple Ltd:

- Business is predominantly cash orientated with total weekly takings of approx €/£100k
- Customer accounts do exist and represent approx €/£30k of weekly takings
- Over the counter cash sales take place on a daily basis
- All sales are processed through front office sales and sales invoices are printed on process of every sale through the till
- The company has 3 separate locations, head office and two further sites (a and b) from which cash sales are made
- Tills at the 3 locations are not networked
- Daily cash takings are agreed to daily z reports printed from the till, however, the client stopped keeping the reconciliations at the start of the financial year as they take up too much space
- Cash takings are delivered to head office by an employee from locations a and b at the end of each trading week
- One lodgement is made per week for all 3 locations
- A manual cash lodgement book is not maintained by the client
- Receipts received from customers are posted to the customer account
- As a manual cash received book is not maintained the client is unable to provide an analysis of weekly lodgements split between cash sales, cheque sales and customer account receipts
- The client requested that the audit firm did not perform a debtors circularisation at the year end as relations with customers are sensitive

Requirement

(a) Explain the weaknesses in the above cycle and the impact on the auditor's ability to gain sufficient appropriate audit evidence over
   i) cash sales
   ii) year-end debtors balance.
(b) Outline 3 changes which the client could make to the above cycle in order to improve controls operating around the sales and debtors cycle.
(c) Explain the impact of the client request regarding the debtors circularisation on the audit plan. Could this request affect the audit opinion and if so how?

Question 9.9

As audit team manager you are considering carrying out a debtors circularisation on year-end trade debtors for one of your audit clients where the trade debtor balance is material to the financial statements.

Requirement

(a) Outline how you will perform the debtors circularisation.
(b) Give 3 circumstances where it is not necessary to perform a debtors circularisation.
(c) Where debtors circularised do not respond to your audit request, explain the alternative audit procedures which should be performed to gain comfort over these balances.

Question 9.10

Describe and discuss three potential risks surrounding the trade debtors balance and link these risks to the relevant financial statement assertions. Suggest testing which the auditor can perform to mitigate these risks.

Appendix 9.1 – Extracts from Audited Financial Statements

LARGE COMPANY LIMITED

STATEMENT OF ACCOUNTING POLICIES
(For the year ended 31 December 20X8)

Turnover

Turnover is stated net of trade discounts, VAT and similar taxes and derives from the provision of goods falling within the company's ordinary activities.

Comprehensive Income Statement

for the year ended 31 December 20X8

	Notes	20X8 €000	20X7 €000
Turnover – continuing operations	1	280,250	198,500
Cost of sales		(140,250)	(120,800)
Gross profit		140,000	77,700

Statement of Financial Position

as at 31 December 20X8

	Notes	20X8 €000	20X8 €000	20X7 €000	20X7 €000
Stocks	15		49,774		35,020
Debtors:					
amounts falling due after one year	16	8,700		10,250	
amounts falling due within one year	17	6,500		7,250	
			15,200		17,500

Notes

(forming part of the financial statements)

16. Debtors: amounts falling due after one year

	20X8	20X7
	€000	€000
Loan notes	6,000	8,000
Other debtors:		
Called up share capital not paid	685	875
Prepayments and accrued income:		
Pension prepayment	65	25
Other prepayments	1,950	1,350
	8,700	10,250

17. Debtors: amounts falling due within one year

	20X8	20X7
	€000	€000
Loan notes	1,500	1,500
Trade debtors	3,250	4,100
Other debtors	750	600
Prepayments and accrued income	1,000	1,050
	6,500	7,250

"Other debtors" include amounts advanced to finance the acquisition of shares in the company.

Trade debtors are stated net of a provision of €500,000 (20X7 - €750,000) for estimated bad debts based on historical experience.

Bad debts Provision	20X8	20X7
	€000	€000
Opening balance	750	700
Increase/(decrease) in provision	(50)	150
Bad debts written off	(200)	(100)
Closing balance	500	750

An aged analysis is utilised to determine the likelihood of payment default.

Aged analysis of trade debtors

	20X8 €000	20X7 €000
Current (within credit terms)	2,600	3,500
30-60 days	420	350
60-90 days	150	140
Greater than 90 days	80	110
	3,250	4,100

The directors consider the net trade debtor value to be representative of fair value.

CHAPTER 10

THE AUDIT OF BANK AND CASH

Learning Objectives

Be able to

- Select and apply appropriate audit procedures to typical income statement and balance sheet captions
- Select and apply audit procedures to typical accounting estimates
- Describe the procedures used by the auditor to gain assurance in relation to the audit assertions in respect of Bank and Cash
- Give an account of typical systems of internal control
- Identify the critical risks and related controls within those systems
- Select and apply appropriate tests to identified controls
- Select and apply appropriate substantive audit tests to typical financial captions, which address identified risks at the assertions level
- Describe the types of audit evidence available to support accounting estimates
- Select and apply audit procedures to typical/simple accounting estimates.

Checklist of Relevant Professional Statements:

ISA 315 – Obtaining an Understanding of the Entity and its Environment and Assessing the Risks of Material Misstatement
ISA 500 – Audit Evidence
ISA 505 – External Confirmations
ISA 501 – Audit Evidence – Additional Considerations for Specific Items
ISA 620 – Using the Work of an Expert

Introduction

This chapter will examine the audit procedures the auditor uses to obtain assurance in relation to the audit assertions in respect of Bank and Cash. In order to gain sufficient comfort over the Bank and Cash the auditor will need to assess the risk of material misstatement, examine the controls in place and the appropriate procedures that will respond to the identified risks.

Furthermore, the chapter will outline the various audit procedures that will enable the auditor to reach an opinion on whether the Bank and Cash balances as disclosed in the financial statements are fairly stated.

10.1 Assess the Risk of Material Misstatement

Step 1 – Identify what risks require mitigation, i.e. bank accounts misstated

According to ISA 315 the auditor should use professional judgement to assess the risk of material misstatement. As part of that judgement the auditor should consider prior experience with the client, industry knowledge and factors that are part of the economic climate (see **Chapter 3** the Risk Assessment Process). Risk factors relating to bank and cash include:

- Reliability of cash recording system
- Frequency of Bank Reconciliations (i.e. how often does the company receive bank statements and when are the reconciliations prepared)
- Physical controls over cash and its susceptibility to theft
- Risk due to fraud: false bank accounts, fraudulent or erroneous payments, rights over bank accounts (i.e. does the company you are auditing own the account or is it belonging to another company within the group) and does the company have rights to all of the cash in the bank account (directors of companies may have personal cash in company accounts)
- Cut-Off (i.e. have the payments and receipts been recorded in the correct period).

Consider whether other transactional risks exist that could result in a material misstatement if not mitigated e.g. credit card transactions.

Step 2 Document relevant internal controls

ISA 315 paragraph 41 states that "The auditor should obtain an understanding of internal control relevant to the audit" the auditor develops an understanding of internal control to identify types of potential misstatements, considers factors that affect the risks of material misstatement, and designs the nature, timing, and extent of further audit procedures.

The purpose of this step is to identify the existence of internal control that mitigates the risk factors listed in Step 1 above.

The most efficient way to get an overview of the controls in place is to perform a walkthrough of the process (See **Chapter 5,** Gathering Audit Evidence). There are various ways of documenting the controls in place such as:

- Flowcharts
- Narratives

The extent of documentation required will vary depending on the size, nature, and complexity of the entity and is a matter of professional judgment.

Some of the main controls over bank and cash are outlined below.

Controls over bank and cash

In summary controls over bank and cash should include the following:

- Payments are authorized
- Payments are made in respect of legitimate liabilities
- Receipts are collected and banked in tact
- Amounts are correctly recorded in books
- There is segregation of duties between person dealing with receipts and payments and persons who deal with sales/purchases transactions

The following procedures should be carried out:

1. Performance and Review of Bank Reconciliations on a regular basis.
2. Authorisation Signatures on account, i.e. only authorised staff can make payments ensured through the establishment of mandates with the bank. Where signatories on the account changed during the year, review the bank mandate form to ensure that this has been correctly updated.
3. Restrictions on the opening and closing of accounts, again only authorised staff or management can open bank accounts.
4. All bank accounts should be clearly identified.
5. Cheque books should be locked in a safe and only authorised personnel should have access to them.
6. Check authorisation signatures on cheques.
7. Review of Payment Run: ensure that a review of payments has been carried out and matched to appropriate invoices.
8. Check reconciliation and review of petty cash.
9. Review cash sales reconciliation and ensure that it has been reviewed by management.

When it has been established that the internal control has been properly designed and implemented (ensure that the controls are relevant to the audit) it is worth considering the following (See also **Chapter 5** Gathering Audit Evidence).

- What tests of the operating effectiveness of controls (if any) will reduce the need for other substantive testing? and
- What controls require testing because they cannot be tested substantively?

Tests of controls

- Inspect bank reconciliation between bank statements and general ledger balances, ensuring that they have been prepared and reviewed on a timely basis for all accounts.
- Check signatures on the account (i.e. obtain copies of bank mandate currently in force for each account and ensure that they are up to date and only include current staff).

- Test authorisation of closure of accounts.
- Check that all bank accounts exist.

Step 3: Design audit procedures in response to the audit risks identified

Use of Assertions in Obtaining Audit Evidence "The auditor should use assertions for classes of transactions, account balances and presentation and disclosure in sufficient detail to form a basis for the assessment of risks of material misstatement and the design and performance of further audit procedures" (ISA 500).

The specific audit objectives in relation to cash are as follows:

Transactions and Events During the Period

Assertion	Objective of Audit Evidence
Existence	To ensure that recorded bank and cash balances exist at the balance sheet date
Completeness	To ensure that all bank and cash balances are recorded in the correct period and included in the financial statements
Accuracy	To ensure bank and cash balances are accurately recorded in the financial statements
Valuation	To ensure Bank and Cash balances are properly valued, and a provision has been made for any balances that may not be recoverable
Cut-Off	All transactions have been accounted for in the correct accounting period
Rights and Obligations	To ensure the entity has the rights to all bank and cash balances shown at the balance sheet date
Presentation and Disclosure	To ensure cash balances are properly classified and disclosed in the balance sheet and that lines of credit, loan guarantees and other restrictions on bank and cash balances are appropriately disclosed

10.2 Audit Procedures that Address the Assertions Above

The auditor must design and perform audit procedures that address the relevant assertions detailed above. The list below links audit procedures to each assertion relevant to the audit of cash and bank.

Existence

- Obtain direct confirmation from the client's bankers for each account balance disclosed in the cash ledger (see below for bank confirmations and ISA 505).
- Attend the year-end cash count unannounced. The auditor should ensure the cash count is performed in the presence of the custodian, ensure the custodian signs the record of amount counted and agree the amount counted to the cash ledger, this should only be performed in companies where petty cash balance is likely to be material (e.g. retail companies).
- Ensure petty cash vouchers for payments are pre-numbered sequentially and review vouchers for omissions.
- Check that cash vouchers relate to authorised expenditure and have been included in the cash payments record.
- When cash funds include cheques cashed for employees or directors, the auditor should review these cheques and ensure they are currently dated and are not post-dated. The auditor should also check that they have subsequently cleared the bank account.

Completeness

- Carry out an analytical review of the balances and obtain explanations for any large or unusual variations.
- Review the bank confirmation letter, minutes of board meetings and enquire of management if any new accounts were opened during the period.
- Investigate whether separate bank accounts exist for the payment of payroll or petty cash, and ensure that all bank accounts are included at the balance sheet date.

Accuracy and cut-off

- Examine bank reconciliations in respect of all bank accounts held at the balance sheet date and obtain explanations for large or unusual reconciling items.
- Agree the total as per the reconciliation to the cash ledger, the bank confirmation letter and the bank statements.
- Tot the reconciliation.
- Trace any outstanding cheques at the balance sheet date to post-year-end bank statements. In the case of outstanding cheques taking a longer than expected time to clear after the year end, obtain explanations as to the delay and ensure that the cheques were actually issued by the client prior to the balance sheet date and not post the balance sheet date, depending on the number of outstanding cheques and lodgements, a sample of outstanding items may be tested.
- Trace outstanding lodgements to post-year-end bank statements.
- Agree a sample of lodgements to the lodgement book.
- For a sample of receipts and payments taken from the cash receipts/cheque payments book, ensure that items selected are either included on the bank statements prior to year-end or included on the list of outstanding lodgements/cheques.

- Examine the cash receipts book for evidence of a reversal of lodgements subsequent to the year-end.
- Review the bank statements, cash receipts book and cheque payments book for any large or unusual items.
- Ensure interest payable on loans is properly accrued and included in the financial statements.
- For a sample of items included within outstanding cheques and lodgements test to ensure that the items have been treated appropriately in year-end debtors and creditors, i.e. items included in outstanding lodgements have been removed from the debtors ledger, and items included within outstanding cheques have been removed from the creditors ledger.
- Obtain post-year-end bank statements and trace all prior year dated cheques to outstanding cheques listed on the bank reconciliation (could assist in finding prior year cheques not included as outstanding on the bank reconciliation and also that cheques listed as outstanding on the reconciliation have not yet cleared the bank) – if uncleared cheques are material it could indicate window dressing – where cheques are written on last day of the year but not mailed for several weeks until there are funds in the account to meet these payments, recipients do not usually delay in lodging cheques, should clear within a week. Make enquiries of management if delay in presentation of cheques is greater than two weeks). Trace deposits in transit on bank reconciliation to deposits on post-year-end bank statement (these should be one of the first items shown on the post-year-end bank statement, if not enquire into reason for time lag and corroborate explanation, significant delays in depositing receipts could indicate fraudulent practice of teeming and lading). Scan the statement for unusual items such as unrecorded bank debits/credits, bank errors and corrections.

Valuation

- Review relevant loan agreements or board minutes to determine whether there are any restrictions on the availability or use of bank balances or cash.

Ownership

- Obtain sufficient audit evidence in relation to bank balances from bank confirmation letters.
- Ensure all bank statements are in the name of the client.

Disclosure

- Review the response to the bank letter and ensure all items are properly accounted for and disclosed in the financial statements.
- Ensure all loans are properly disclosed in accordance with loan details.

- Ensure that loans payable within one year are classified as a current liability.
- Ensure overdrafts and loans are properly classified as creditors.

10.3 Bank Accounts

Bank confirmation request letters (example)

As part of the audit of Bank and Cash the auditor should obtain an audit confirmation. This will provide the auditor with independent reliable audit evidence (see **Chapter 5** Gathering Audit Evidence). The bank confirmation should disclose cash on deposit, loans and details of all accounts in the name of the audit client at the balance sheet date.

The confirmation can be subdivided into two categories: one which should detail standard information and the other which should detail supplementary information relating to trade finance and derivative and commodity trading, The bank confirmations should:

- Confirm all bank accounts the company has with the bank-this should also include nil balances and accounts opened/closed during the year)
- Credit limits/overdraft facilities
- Terms of loans/other borrowings
- Outstanding charges and interest accrued
- Outstanding bills of exchange, guarantees, acceptances etc.
- Foreign currency contracts
- Hire purchase/leasing agreements
- Items held in safe custody or as security for borrowings.

The request should be sent on the auditor's letterhead and clearly identify all of the information required. It is important the auditor maintains complete control over the process. The audit confirmation is a very important part of the audit of bank and cash as it provides the auditor with independent third-party audit evidence (see below for a sample of an audit request letter).

> **"When performing confirmation procedures, the auditor should maintain control over the process of selecting those to whom a request will be sent, the preparation and sending of confirmation requests, and the responses to those requests."** (ISA 500.30)

The confirmation of other arrangements with the banks should be conducted through the audit confirmation process. When returned, the audit confirmation should confirm guaranteed loans to third parties, bills discounted with recourse and any unused facilities. The bank confirm should be signed or stamped by the entity signatory and confirms should be obtained directly from the bank.

It is important to note that confirmations cannot be relied upon entirely. The confirmations include a disclaimer in favour of the bank and in essence the bank cannot be held liable if they provide incomplete/inaccurate information.

Example – Bank Confirmation Letter

STANDARD FORM OF REQUEST

This form has been approved by the Institute of Chartered Accountants in Ireland and the Irish Banks' Standing Committee and the Northern Ireland Bankers' Association.

The Manager
Worldwide Bank
123 Main Street
Ennis
Co Clare

Dear Sir,

Re: Joe Bloggs Ltd

I/We have read this document and I/we authorise you to provide the information requested herein in respect of the accounts of the above-named customer and also to disclose the number of joint accounts, if any, to which the above-named customer is party.

Please send this information to our auditor(s)

Mr Joe O'Connor
O'Connor and Co
123 Market Street
Kilkenny

Yours faithfully,

....
Authorised Signature(s)

Dear Sir,

We report that at the close of business on* .... 31/12/20XX .... the record of this branch showed:-

1. BANK ACCOUNTS

Description of a/cs (including deposit a/cs)	S/SX Note A	Date of last letter outlining terms/ conditions of borrowing	Balance Dr/Cr	Amounts accrued but not posted at above date (Note B) Estimated interest Dr/Cr	Est. Current Account Fees and other charges
			£/€	£/€	£/€

Note A Where a specific letter of set-off for principal exists affecting any of the above accounts, please indicate this by adding S to the account title. If the set-off refers to accounts other than those being reported on use SX.

(Other set-offs may arise either at law or on foot of a bank security document.)

Note B The provision of this information may entail work and costs. If the information is not essential this request should be deleted.

2. FULL TITLES AND DATES OF CLOSURE OF ALL ACCOUNTS CLOSED DURING PERIOD:-From 01/01/20XX to 31/12/20XX

3. CUSTOMER'S ASSETS

Nature of security held directly from customer (e.g. Deeds, Stocks, Shares etc.). Amount only of any guarantees held for the benefit of the customer.

4. CONTINGENT LIABILITIES

All known contingent liabilities

Date(s)   Amount £/€

(a) Total of bills discounted for your customer, with recourse

(b) Amounts and dates of each Guarantee, (excluding Acceptances) Bond or Indemnity given to you by the customer

		Date(s)	Amount £/€

(c) Amounts and dates of each Guarantee, (excluding Acceptances), Bond or Indemnity given by you on behalf of your customer

(d) Total of Bills drawn on and accepted by Bank on behalf of customers (excluding (f) hereunder)

(e) Total Forward Foreign Exchange Contracts

(f) Total of Outstanding Liabilities under Documentary Credits

(g) Others - Please give details:

The information available at branch contained herein is given in confidence for your use only, in your capacity as Auditor(s) and without responsibility on the part of the Bank or any of its officials.

Note: No information can or will be given which would disclose confidential information regarding other customers.

Signed:..Manager

....Date

Branch Brand

10.4 Cash

Where cash transactions are significant and inherent risk is high the auditor should:

- Consider if internal controls surrounding cash receipts and payments are sufficient
- Where the balance sheet cash balance is material:
  - Review operation of cash system
  - Count cash – at year end or surprise cash count at random point during audit
  - During the cash count ensure full control over all funds simultaneously to prevent funds from being swopped from one to another – count in the presence of independent client personnel - list details of notes and coins – ensure IOUS are recorded and collectible and that they are made within company's policy guidelines.

- Reconcile count to petty cash record, investigate differences
- Get cashier to initial reconciliation as evidence of agreement.

QUESTIONS

Self-test Questions

1 What audit benefits are derived from a standard bank letter confirmation?
2 Why is it important to check outstanding cheques at the year end?
3 What steps should the auditor take if their is evidence of "window dressing" at the year end?

Review Questions

(See Solutions to Review Questions at the end of this textbook.)

Question 10.1

Outline briefly the audit procedures you would perform in relation to gaining assurance over the balance included under bank loans in the financial statements.

Question 10.2

You are the manager in charge of the external audit of Green Ltd (Green) which operates a chain of retail outlets throughout Ireland. Green has an established internal audit function which undertakes monitoring procedures at head office and outlets. All outlets have electronic point of sale systems which record the sale of an item and update the inventory records. All takings are required to be banked daily.

In order to determine whether you can reduce the amount of detailed testing on bank and cash, set out the monitoring procedures you would expect internal audit to have conducted.

Question 10.3

Why is it important for the auditor to confirm all bank accounts held and operated by the entity during the year?

Question 10.4

What steps can the auditor take to ensure that all bank accounts have been confirmed at the balance sheet date?

Question 10.5

Explain the benefits to the company, in addition to the maintenance of its borrowing facility, of having a full audit.

Appendix 10.1 – Extracts from Audited Financial Statements

LARGE COMPANY LIMITED

Statement of Financial Position as at 31 December 20X8

	Notes	20X8 €000	20X8 €000	20X8 €000	20X8 €000
Current assets					
Stocks	15		49,774		35,020
Debtors:					
amounts falling due after one year	16	8,700		10,250	
amounts falling due within one year	17	6,500		7,250	
			15,200		17,500
Derivative financial instruments	25		390		170
Available-for-sale investments	18		4,200		5,000
Cash at bank and in hand			**104,200**		**105,530**

CHAPTER 11

THE AUDIT OF INVESTMENTS

Learning Objectives

Be able to

- Select and apply appropriate audit procedures to typical income statement and balance sheet captions.
- Select and apply audit procedures to typical accounting estimates
- Describe the procedures used by the auditor to gain assurance in relation to the audit assertions in respect of investments
- Give an account of typical systems of internal control
- Identify the critical risks and related controls within those systems
- Select and apply appropriate tests to identified controls
- Select and apply appropriate substantive audit tests to typical financial captions, which address identified risks at the assertions level
- Describe the types of audit evidence available to support accounting estimates
- Select and apply audit procedures to typical/simple accounting estimates.

Checklist of Relevant Professional Statements:

ISA 500 – Audit Evidence
ISA 505 – External Confirmations
ISA 501 – Audit Evidence – Additional Considerations for Specific Items; Valuation and Disclosure of Long-term Investments

Introduction

This chapter will examine the audit procedures the auditor uses to obtain assurance in relation to the audit assertions in respect of Investments. In order to gain sufficient comfort over the Investments the auditor will need to assess the risk of material misstatement, examine the controls in place and the appropriate procedures that will respond to the identified risks.

Furthermore, the chapter will outline the various audit procedures that will enable the auditor to reach an opinion on whether the Investments balances as disclosed in the financial statements are fairly stated.

Investment balances constitute ownership of securities issued by other entities and these may be in the form of certificates of deposit, shares, debentures or government bonds.

Such securities represent financial assets in the hands of the entity who own them. The accounting requirements for such investments are determined by IFRS7, Financial Instruments and IAS 39 Financial Instruments: Recognition and Measurement.

The accounting requirements for subsequent measurement of the four categories of financial assets as defined by IAS 39 are:

- Loans and receivables not held for trading – amortised cost using the effective interest method subject to impairment
- Held to maturity investments – amortised cost using the effective interest method subject to impairment
- Financial assets measured at fair value through profit or loss- fair value, with value changes recognized through profit or loss
- Available for sale assets and others not falling into any of the above categories – measured at fair value in the statement of financial position, with value changes recognized in other comprehensive income as an unrealized gain or loss, subject to impairment testing. If the fair value cannot be reliably measured, the asset is carried at cost.

A special category of investments is that held for the purpose of acquiring influences or control over another entity. Such entities must be classified as subsidiaries, associates and joint ventures. The main audit considerations related to consolidated financial statements are explained at the end of the chapter.

11.1 Assess the Risk of Material Misstatement

Step 1: Identify what risks require mitigation i.e. investments incorrectly valued

According to ISA 315 the auditor should use professional judgement to assess the risk of material misstatement. Risk factors relating to investments include:

- Reliability of investment recording system.
- Physical controls over investments held and the susceptibility to theft of investments physically held by the client or by an independent custodian. If the investment certificates are held by the client the auditor should ensure that they are adequately stored (i.e. in a securely locked safe).
- Physical controls over the purchase and sales of investments.
- Risk due to fraud: false investments and rights over investments (are the investments in the client's name or are they held in the name of a director or another entity).

Consider whether other transactional risks exist that could result in a material misstatement if not mitigated.

Step 2: Document relevant internal controls

ISA 315 paragraph 41 states that "The auditor should obtain an understanding of internal control relevant to the audit", uses the understanding of internal control to identify types of potential misstatements, to consider factors that affect the risks of material misstatement, and to design the nature, timing, and extent of further audit procedures.

Due to the fact that the purchase and sale of investments are often processed separately from all other purchases and sales, entities which hold substantial investments often adopt specific control procedures over investments.

Ideally the following should be present in the control environment:

- Authority and responsibility for investing activities should be given to an individual who is deemed to be a person of integrity and of sufficient knowledge and experience in dealing with investments.
- The information system in place should be one that is reliable and accurate at all times in the recording of the data required for accounting for the various categories of investments.
- Internal audit should closely monitor the effectiveness of controls over investing activities.
- Title to the investments usually in the form of a share or debenture cert should be safeguarded.

The purpose of the step is to identify the existence of internal control that mitigates the risk factors listed in Step 1. However, depending on the number of investments, it may be more appropriate for the auditor to test the balance substantively (if this is the case there is no need to continue with the tests of controls).

The most efficient way to get an overview of the controls in place is to perform a walk-through of the process as outlined previously.

The extent of documentation required will vary depending on the size, nature, and complexity of the entity and is a matter of professional judgment.

The following is a sample of the controls over investments:

Controls over investments

1. Perform a regular inspection of investments held by the company or ensure that the custodian still has the investment certificates if held by a third party.
2. Authorisation Signatures on the purchase and sale of investments. Board approval may be required for the purchase or sale of non-current investments.
3. Restrictions on the purchasing and sales of investments.
4 Dividend and interest cheques must be deposited promptly.

5. Transactions should be recorded on the basis of appropriate supporting documentation and the duties of recording and custody of the investments should be segregated.
6. Securities should be stored in safes or vaults with access restricted to authorized personnel.
7. Changes in value and circumstances relating to the appropriate classification of investments should be analysed regularly.
8. Management should undertake performance reviews to detect poor investment performances.
9. The classification of investment should be periodically reviewed.

Only when it has been established that the internal control relevant to the audit has been properly designed and implemented is it worth considering the following:

- What tests of the operating effectiveness of controls (if any) will reduce the need for other substantive testing?
- What controls require testing because they cannot be tested substantively?

Tests of controls

- Inspect controls over the custody of investments and obtain a confirmation of investments from all custodians of investments.
- Check the authorised signatures.
- Test authorisation of additions and disposals of investments.
- Check existence of all investments.

Step 3: Design audit procedures in response to the audit risks identified

Use of assertions in obtaining audit evidence

Audit Objectives

Transactions and Events During the Period

Assertion	Objective of Audit Evidence
Existence	To ensure that recorded investments exist at the balance sheet date
Completeness	To ensure all investments have been included in the financial statements
Accuracy	To ensure all investments are properly recorded and included in the financial statements

Cut-off	To ensure all additions and disposals of investments have been accounted for in the correct accounting period
Valuation	To ensure investments have been accurately valued and provision has been made for any investments whose carrying value exceeds realisable value
Rights and Obligations	To ensure the entity has the rights to all investments recorded at the balance sheet date
Presentation and Disclosure	To ensure investments are properly classified and disclosed in the balance sheet

Accuracy and completeness

- Obtain and review the reconciliation of the investment control account in the nominal ledger to the list of individual investments. Check the accuracy of the reconciliation and review the clearing of reconciling items subsequent to the year end. Agree opening investment balances to prior year audit working papers. Review the activity in the investment related accounts to identify entries that are unusual.
- Review the accounting policy adopted by the client for determining the carrying value of investments. Ensure that the policy adopted is in accordance with relevant legislation and accounting standards.
- Where investments have been acquired during the year, agree the cost of investments to supporting documents (contract notes or similar documentation).
- Agree disposal of investments to contract notes. Ensure disposal has been officially authorised and approved.
- Check the Profit or Loss on disposal of a sample of investments and ensure it has been correctly posted.
- For investments held in foreign currencies, ensure the correct translation into domestic currency. This can be done by independently obtaining appropriate foreign exchange rates ensuring that there is not a material difference in the rates used.
- Ensure additions and disposals of investments have been authorised and approved.
- For listed investments, check the market value to the stock exchange daily list, *Financial Times* or other reliable pricing source.
- For unlisted investments, if the valuation has been undertaken by the directors the auditor should discuss the basis of valuation with the client in order to ascertain whether the valuation has been made on the basis of reasonable criteria. The auditor may consider the need to acquire the advice of an expert.
- Perform analytical review to ensure completeness and obtain explanations for any material variances. Analytical procedures can be applied in comparing interest and dividends receipts to investment balances. Unexpected differences should be investigated as they could indicate misstatement.

- Check from the list of investments that all income due has been recorded and received. Vouch dividend/interest receipts to remittance advices which accompany payment. Recalculate the interest received by multiplying the par value of the debt by the interest rate to ensure complete or confirm the interest receipt with the issuer. View the investees financial statements in order to verify the dividends received.
- Check the posting of income to the correct account in the nominal ledger.

Existence and ownership

Where securities are held at the entity's premises these should be inspected and counted at the same time as the cash count (if applicable). Ensure the custodian is present at the time of the count, that a receipt is signed when the securities are returned and ensure that there is control over the securities until the count is complete.
- Where securities are held by the bank for safe keeping, ensure the bank seals the boxes on the date of the count and obtain confirmation from the bank that there was no access to the box (other than by the auditors) until count has been complete. Where count takes place on a date other than on the balance sheet date, a reconciliation should be prepared between the date of the count and the balance sheet date. All movements between these dates should be reviewed.
  - When inspecting securities, the following points should be observed:
    - Certificate number on the document
    - Name of owner
    - Description of security
    - Number of shares (debentures)
    - Face value of shares (debentures)
    - Name of issuer.

In addition all securities should be checked against records in the investment register and for securities purchased in prior years and, their details should be agreed to prior year audit working papers.

- Obtain direct third-party confirmation of investments held on behalf of the client and inspect documents of title.
- Securities held by outsiders for safekeeping must be confirmed as of the date on which the securities held by the entity are counted. The mailing of the confirmations must be under the control of the auditor and responses must be made directly to the auditors.
- Review board minutes and obtain representations of management to ascertain whether investments have been pledged as collateral or security for liabilities.
- Obtain direct third-party confirmation from borrowers in respect of loans made to them by the client.

Valuation

- Consider whether the value of any investments should be reduced to recognise a permanent diminution in value. The auditor should discuss any such diminution with management and obtain any independent information that will support the revaluation of investments.
- If an investment was written down in previous years and the reasons for the write down no longer apply, the auditor should check that the provision has been released.
- For financial assets valued on the basis of amortised cost, consider recalculation tests based on cashflows and interest rate used to discount the cash flows. Consider appropriateness of discount factor used. Also consider the need for adjustments because of the recoverability of the asset and other factors that give rise to impairment.
- Audited financial statements of the entity in which the investments are held can be used to assist in the valuation of unquoted shares, debentures and similar debt obligations.
- Check that the basis of the valuation is consistent with previous years. If there are any changes in the basis of the valuation the auditor should discuss this with management, ensure that the basis of valuation is reasonable and in line with the appropriate laws and regulations.
- Check market value calculations for listed investments to published prices, i.e. the *Financial Times*, Bloomberg, Reuters or independent stock broker prices. For infrequently traded securities, it may be necessary to seek advice from an independent broker as to the estimated market value at the balance sheet date.
- Confirm that directors' valuations of unlisted investments are reasonable. The auditor should obtain independent support of the valuation or written representations from the directors to support their valuation.
- For long-term investments "ISA 501 Audit Evidence – Additional Considerations for Specific Items, Part D: Valuation and Disclosure of Long-term Investments (para 39–41), requires sufficient appropriate audit evidence to be gathered regarding the valuation and disclosure of material long-term investments. Evidence must be gathered on the ability of the entity to hold onto the investments on a long-term basis written representations from management indicating their intention to hold onto the investments on a long-term basis must be obtained. Reviewing post-balance sheet events would also feature.
- In respect of loans, ensure repayments are being made on time and interest payments are being made.
- Discuss with management the recoverability of the loan and obtain independent confirmation of the value of and repayments on the loan.

Cut-off

- For a sample of additions and disposals during the period ensure they are accounted for in the correct accounting period.

Presentation and disclosure

- Ensure investments are properly classified as fixed or current assets
- Ensure separate disclosure of investments in associates or subsidiaries
- Ensure classification of financial asset investments into appropriate classes
- Ensure the financial position is accurately disclosed, for example, disclosures about fair values, reclassifications etc.
- Ensure factors relating to performance are disclosed such as recognition of dividends, interest etc.
- Ensure separate disclosure of income from group companies

QUESTIONS

Self-test Questions

1. Why is it important to assess the internal control procedures relating to investments?
2. List five ways in which fraud could be committed in respect of investments.
3. What valuation method should be used for trade investments?
4. Why is it important to inspect original supporting documentation for investments?

Review Questions and Solutions

(See Solutions to Review Questions at the end of this textbook.)

Question 11.1

Meridian Ltd is a large company with a number of financial investments in Ireland and internationally. You have been assigned to the investments section of the audit engagement and a member of the client's finance team has provided you with the following schedule:

Name of Investment	Investment €/£'000	Market Value €/£'000
Rainbow	1,243	1,721
Lilly	936	1,321
Golden	1,654	1,320
Yellow	1,111	300
Grenadier	1,879	2,012
Total Investments	**6,823**	

The client's member of staff has also provided you with the following information:

The investment in Rainbow was acquired during the year and the Yellow investment was sold before the year end for £/€300,000.

The investments' balance in the draft financial statements is €/£6,823,000. The company has a policy of recognising its investments at cost with any gains/losses only recognised on disposal.

Requirement

(a) Describe the general and specific audit work that you would plan in order to enable you to form an opinion on the investment account balance of Meridian.
(b) From the information above, list the potential audit issues in Meridian and state the additional audit work that you would perform.
(c) Assuming the information included in the schedule is correct and the client has no further information to provide, outline the adjustments to the investment balance that you would recommend to your audit partner.

Question 11.2

You have been assigned to the audit of WILCOX Ltd, a successful property development company. The audit area for which you will have direct responsibility is that of current assets. Your audit manager has informed you that the prior-year audit file did not contain a detailed audit plan for current assets but that he would like one prepared prior to the commencement of the current year's audit. You note from the prior-year audit file that the audit materiality figure was £/€100,000 and that the current assets at the previous year-end were made up as follows:

	£/€000
Trade investments (listed)	500
Trade investments (unlisted)	800
Prepayments	100
Bank balances	950
Cash balances	100
	2,450

Requirement

Set out the procedures that you would adopt in order to obtain the required assurance concerning the standard audit objectives for the current assets detailed above. You are to assume that the current asset balances for the current year are expected to be at a similar level to that of the prior year.

Appendix 11.1 – Extracts from Audited Financial Statements

LARGE COMPANY LIMITED

STATEMENT OF FINANCIAL POSITION
as at 31 December 20X8

	Notes	20X8 €000	20X8 €000	20X7 €000	20X7 €000
Current assets					
Stocks	15		49,774		35,020
Debtors:					
amounts falling due after one year	16	8,700		10,250	
amounts falling due within one year	17	6,500		7,250	
			15,200		17,500
Derivative financial instruments	25		390		170
Available-for-sale investments	**18**		**4,200**		**5,000**
Cash at bank and in hand			104,200		105,530

Notes *(forming part of the financial statements)*

18. Available-for-sale Investments

	20X8 €000	20X7 €000
Other unlisted equity investments	1,200	850
Listed equity investments	3,000	4,150
	4,200	**5,000**

The unlisted equity investments are recorded at cost. The directors consider that these shares have not diminished in value and that their market value at the balance sheet date is similar to their cost.

The listed equity investments (all of which are listed on the Irish Stock Exchange) are measured at fair value in line with the group's accounting policy.

Chapter 12

THE AUDIT OF PURCHASES AND CREDITORS

Learning Objectives

Be able to

- Select and apply appropriate audit procedures to typical income statement and balance sheet captions.
- Select and apply audit procedures to typical accounting estimates
- Describe typical systems of internal control
- Identify the critical risks and related controls within those systems
- Select and apply appropriate tests to identified controls
- Select and apply appropriate substantive audit tests to typical financial captions, which address identified risks at the assertions level
- Describe the types of audit evidence available to support accounting estimates
- Select and apply audit procedures to typical/simple accounting estimates.

Checklist of Relevant Professional Statements

ISA 500 – Audit evidence
ISA 501 – Audit Evidence – Additional Considerations for Specific Items
ISA 505 – External Confirmations
ISA 520 – Analytical Procedures
ISA 540 – Audit of Accounting Estimates

Introduction

Every business incurs costs in the process of generating goods and services which they subsequently sell to their customers. For example, a company involved in the manufacture of shoes will have to purchase leather in order to make its shoes and might employ the services of an advertising agency to promote its finished products. Where such transactions are not settled immediately via cash payments they give rise to trade payables. Such trade payables (or "creditors" as they are more commonly referred to) meet the definition of liabilities as set out in the Framework to International Financial Reporting Standards (Paragraph 49) which states that:

> A liability is a present obligation of the entity arising from past events, the settlement of which is expected to result in an outflow from the entity of resources embodying economic benefits.

It is the auditor's duty to ensure that both purchases and trade payables are reflected appropriately in the company's year-end financial statements. In simple terms, all goods and services which a company has received during the financial year should be recorded within their financial statements as purchases in the Income and Expenditure Account. Where amounts due to suppliers relating to purchases have not been settled at the year-end they should also be recorded as liabilities in the balance sheet, either within trade-payables where an invoice has been received or within accruals when the goods or services have been received but the invoice has not yet been received from the supplier.

The auditor devises tests in order to gain assurance that the key audit assertions over purchases and trade-payables/accruals are not misstated. You have been introduced to the concept of audit assertions earlier in **Chapter 1**. The key assertions on which the auditor focuses his work on purchases and trade payables/accruals are:

- Completeness

All purchases made during the period and related liabilities at the year-end have been included in the financial statements.

- Existence

All purchases and related liabilities which are included in the financial statements relate to transactions which have in actual fact occurred during the financial year.

- Accuracy

All purchases and related liabilities which are included in the financial statements have been recorded at the correct amount.

Failure to adequately focus work on the above assertions could lead to material errors in the financial statements going undetected. The most common circumstances giving rise to misstatements of purchases and trade payables/accruals are:

(a) Inappropriate/fraudulent payments recorded in the purchase ledger due to weaknesses in internal controls in the purchase system (see **Chapter 3** for a full discussion of internal controls)
(b) Misstatement of year-end creditors and accruals due to incorrect cut-off procedures being applied (i.e. transactions occurring pre-year-end not being recorded until the following period and conversely transactions occurring post-year-end being incorrectly recorded in the current period)
(c) Understatement of year-end creditors and accruals due to failure to record all outstanding liabilities because of fraud or error.

12.1 Audit of Internal Controls over Purchases and Creditors

A company will have in places various procedures and checks around its purchasing process in order to minimise the risks of misstatement highlighted above.

The purchases system can be divided into a number of key sections; below it has been classified into three distinct steps. These steps together with the objectives and controls which should feature within each of these steps are as follows:

Purchase cycle objectives

(a) Ordering
- All orders for goods and services are properly authorized and are for goods and services received and are used for the purposes of the company's business (occurrence)
- Purchase orders are only made to authorized suppliers (accuracy)

(b) Receipt of goods and invoicing
- Goods and services received are for the purpose of business use only (occurrence)
- Goods and services accepted only if ordered (completeness)
- Receipts of goods and services are accurately recorded (accuracy)
- Liabilities are recognized for all goods and services received (accuracy)
- Any credits due to the company for faulty goods have been claimed (completeness)
- It is not possible to record a liability for goods or services which haven't been received (completeness)

(c) Accounting
- All payments are properly authorized (occurrence)
- All payments are for goods and services which have been received (completeness)
- All expenditure has been correctly recorded in the books and records of the company (accuracy)
- All credit notes have been properly recorded in the books and records of the business (accuracy)
- All entries in the purchase ledger are to the correct supplier account (classification)
- All entries in the nominal ledger are to the correct account (classification)
- Cut-off has been correctly applied (cut-off)

System controls within the purchases system which are designed to achieve system objectives and to minimize the possibility of misstatment due to fraud and error are as follows:

(a) Ordering

• Organisational controls	written procedures
	policy on ordering from approved suppliers – ascertain best source of supply and obtain competitive bids

- Segregation of duties
  - authority levels for order limits
  - defined structure who can order what
  - separation of staff responsible for requisitioning and raising orders from those involved in processing and paying invoices in order to reduce the risk of fraudulent orders. For instance, the purchasing department are unlikely to issue a bogus order because they do not have access to goods delivered
- Physical controls
  - safeguarding of blank pre-numbered order forms
- Authorisation
  - all orders to be authorized by appropriate persons and signed. Original sent to supplier and copies distributed to accounting and receiving department
- Accounting checks
  - pre-numbered order forms
  - review of orders placed but not delivered or invoiced

(b) Delivery of goods and invoicing

- Organizational controls
  - written procedures
  - authority limits for approving invoices
  - procedures for obtaining credit notes from suppliers
- Segregation of duties
  - separation of staff responsible for checking goods received from those responsible from checking purchase and posting invoices
- Physical controls
  - monitoring quantity and condition of goods received – compare goods received with details on purchase order and inspect them for damage. Refuse to accept unordered goods
  - recording the receipt of goods on pre-numbered goods received notes. Copy for goods received note should be forwarded to accounts
  - recording returns of goods on pre-numbered goods returned notes

- Authorization and approval   matching of orders to invoices and GRNs – the receipt of a PO represents authorisation for the receiving department to accept goods delivered

  check on the sequence of goods received notes

  matching supplier credit notes with goods returned notes

  confirmation that orders and GRNs have been agreed to invoices

  Prior to recording the invoices which have been received, the invoices must be checked and put in numerical sequence, matched to the purchase order and goods receipt note, checked for tots, coded to the correct supplier account, signed by appropriate person as evidence of approval

(c) Accounting

- Organisational controls   written procedures – payment terms and invoices processed for payment on their due dates

  authority limits for making payments

  cheque signatories

- Segregation of duties   separation of staff responsible for checking and posting invoices from those responsible for payment

- Physical controls   numbering supplier invoices sequentially

  controls on processing invoices e.g. batch totals

  control over blank cheques and access to credit transfer facility

  restriction of access to parts of accounting system not relating to purchases

- Authorization and approval   authorization of invoices for payment – those signing cheques should have no involvement in initiating or processing purchase transactions. Cheque details agree to details on invoice being paid. Invoices should be stamped with date and cheque number. Control of the mailing of cheques

- Accounting checks   checking of invoices for prices, calculations, quantities

    invoices and credit notes entered into accounting system

    regular reconciliations of suppliers statements with purchase ledger balances

    cut off checks and accrual of goods received notes not matched to purchase invoices at year end

    checks on the cheque summary to amounts posted to creditors ledger

    regular independent preparation of bank reconciliations

In order to assess the design, implementation and operating effectiveness of the controls in place, the following work should be performed by the auditor:

Audit work to be performed

- Check evidence that invoices are supported by purchase orders and goods received notes
- Check evidence that invoices are checked for prices, calculations, are correctly coded with supplier and nominal codes and are entered in day books, ledgers and stock records
- Test numerical sequence and enquire into missing numbers of invoices, orders, goods received notes and goods returned notes
- Obtain explanations for items outstanding for a long time
- Check authorization of invoices approved for payment
- Check goods returned are supported by a goods returned note, there is evidence of correspondence with supplier, credit note is entered in the ledger and invoices are cancelled
- Check postings between day books, cash book and ledger
- Check payments to supplier are debited in full to correct account in ledger
- Check entries in stock records
- Check cut-off procedures at year end
- Check creditor reconciliations
- Check explanations for contra and journal entries in purchase ledger
- Examine records for large or unusual transactions

The typical purchase process within a business is illustrated in **Figure 12.1** below:

1. A purchase order is generated and sent to supplier
2. Goods or services are received from supplier
3. The Purchase Order is matched to the Goods Received Note and is recorded on the purchase ledger.

Dr Purchases
Cr Accruals

4. When the invoice is received from the supplier this is matched to the GRN and Purchase Order and the invoice amount is recorded within trade payables.

Dr Accruals
Cr Trade Payables

5. When the invoice is settled the trade payable is removed from the Balance Sheet

Dr Trade Payables
Cr Bank

Figure 12.1: Typical Purchase Cycle

There is a wide variety of control procedures that may be implemented by businesses to mitigate risks of misstatement within this process. These can vary significantly depending on specific circumstances unique to each business; however there are a number of key control procedures which are common to the majority of businesses. The auditor will generally test the design and implementation and the operating effectiveness of these controls in order to reduce the level of substantive testing he performs over purchases and trade payables/accruals.

In summary the key controls over the purchase cycles are:

- **Segregation of duties**
  In order to reduce the risk of fraudulent or erroneous purchases, it is common for an enforced segregation of duties to be built into the purchasing procedures whereby different members of staff are responsible for:
  - Raising purchase orders and accepting goods from suppliers;
  - Receiving goods from suppliers and recording purchase invoices on the purchase ledger; and
  - Raising purchase orders and processing payment.

- **Authorisation of purchase orders/purchase invoices**
  In order to mitigate the risk of unnecessary or fraudulent purchases it is common for only a small number of experienced staff to have the authority to raise purchase orders.

In addition, the value of purchases which a staff member can authorise often varies depending on their seniority and level of experience.

- **Three-way match of purchase orders, goods received notes and invoices**
  In order to mitigate the risk of purchases being recorded and payments being made in respect of goods and services which were not received, a physical matching of Purchase Order, Goods Received Note and supplier invoice is common.

- **Authorisation of supplier payments**
  In order to mitigate the risk of fraudulent or erroneous payments being made to suppliers it is common for only a small number of senior staff to be authorised to make supplier payments (i.e. through signing cheques).

- **Review of supplier statement reconciliations**
  Where the company received regular statements from its suppliers, it is common for these statements to be reconciled to the balance per the trade payables ledger and for any differences to be investigated.

As discussed in **Chapter 3**, the design and implementation of controls are tested through walkthrough tests and tests of control. In relation to purchases and trade payables the auditor may wish to take a purchase transaction from the period and trace its progress through each stage of the purchases cycle, noting various controls in operation along the way. For example, the auditor might search for evidence of:

- Purchase Order being raised by an authorised member of staff.
- Goods Received Note being matched to the Purchase Order and posted to the purchase ledger by a different member of staff than that member who raised the Purchase Order.
- Invoice being matched to both the Goods Received Note and Purchase Order and being posted to the Purchase Ledger.
- Invoice appearing on monthly supplier statement which is reconciled to the purchase ledger.
- Payment being made by an authorised member of staff and the trade payable balance being removed from the ledger.

In order to test the operating effectiveness of the key controls, the auditor will perform tests of operating effectiveness as described in **Chapter 3**. These will include testing of the operation of controls over a sample of transactions from the period and obtaining documentary evidence of the controls in operation.

Depending upon the results of tests of design and implementation and operating effectiveness of controls, the auditor will form an opinion of the control environment and effectiveness of controls around purchases and trade payables/accruals and will determine whether or not the level of substantive testing can be reduced.

12.2 Audit of Internal Controls over Payroll

For most businesses payroll costs are a significant cost component and the risk of misstatement or fraud is always a concern.

A company will have in place various procedures and checks around its payroll process in order to minimise the risks of misstatement. A company wants to ensure they only pay for work that has been done and that this is paid at a correct rate to the correct number of employees.

Features to consider when looking at wages and salaries include:

- All employees must have a contract of employment
- Rates of pay must be agreed
- All deductions statutory or voluntary are authorised by employee
- All tax calculations are the same for monthly paid and weekly paid employees
- All employees must be paid on time.

Audit objectives

- Payment of wages and salaries relate to work done for the company (occurrence)
- All payments of wages and salaries have been recorded (completeness)
- Deductions relating to wages and salaries have been calculated and recorded at correct amounts (accuracy)
- All payments and liabilities have been recorded in the appropriate period (cut-off)
- Payments of wages and salaries have been recorded in the appropriate nominal ledgers

Confidentiality

Payroll is a sensitive subject and it is crucial that auditors when they have access to such information should treat it with the utmost confidentiality and it should be documented in such a way in the audit work papers that information about individual employees should be kept to a minimum.

Controls

(a) Hiring Employees
- New employee details recorded on personnel authorization form which records job classification, starting wage/salary, etc. Details entered into HR masterfile and access to this should be restricted to authorised personnel. Copy of details should be sent to payroll department. Payroll masterfile changes report should be printed on a regular basis and checked by an independent person for accuracy.
- Segregating the responsibilities between HR and payroll reduces the risk of fictitious employees being added to the payroll. As HR have only access to change the masterfile and payroll have only access to process the payments.

(b) Authorising Payroll Changes
- All changes should be authorised in writing before being entered on the employee masterfile.

(c) Basis of Payroll Calculation
Once the payroll calculations have been posted, a number of reports may be generated, all of which should be reviewed by appropriate personnel:
- An exceptions and control report
- Copy of payroll register that is sent to payroll department for review
- Copy of the register and associated cheques/EFT listing which is sent to the chief accountant
- General ledger summary sent to the accounting department

The main controls can be summarised as follows:

- Organisational control — written procedures
  - Approved wage and salary rates
  - Starter and leaver procedures
- Segregation of duties — separation of staff involved in preparing wages and salaries from those involved in paying them
- Physical control — restriction of access to payroll office
  - restriction of access to parts of the accounting system responsible for payroll
- Authorization — for changes to rates
  - employee authorization for non-statutory deductions
  - authorisation for hours worked, bonuses, commission payments
- Accounting — correct basic rates set as basis for calculation of gross pay
  - correct overtime rates applied
  - tax codes applied to correct tax years
  - payroll upgrades received and applied following tax rate changes

12. THE AUDIT OF PURCHASES AND CREDITORS

(d) Payment of Wages and Salaries

Payroll cheques and or payroll EFT listing together with the payroll register (Gross to net report) is sent to the chief accountant for approval. Here the following should be performed:

- Agree the names and amounts listed on cheques and on EFT listing to the payroll register to ensure all is in agreement
- Payroll cheques should be signed by trusted employees who are not involved in the payroll process
- Access to cheque books etc; should be restricted to authorised personnel only
- Unclaimed payroll cheques should be stored in a safe for safekeeping until claimed.

The main controls can be summarised as follows:

• Organisational controls	written procedures
	separate payroll department from personnel department
	personnel file maintained for each employee
• Segregation of duties	separation of staff responsible for preparing payroll from those responsible for authorizing it
• Physical controls	filling and distribution of pay packets by those not involved in preparing payroll
	security of cash in transit and on premises
	controls for security of unclaimed cash wages
• Authorization	payroll authorised by responsible official before payment
	wages cheques and electronic payment transfers signed by authorised individuals not involved in payroll preparation process
• Accounting	preparation of a wages control account
	reconciliation of payroll between dates
	payment of PRSI/PAYE to revenue and preparation of PAYE/PRSI reconciliations.

12.3 Audit Work to be Performed

These tests are designed to ensure that internal controls are working and the scope of fraud is limited. However, this is not an exhaustive list of tests, but some key areas are required to ensure all employees exist, are paid at the correct rate, all deductions are correctly applied and calculated.

- Check authorised rates of pay are being used and applied
- Confirm authorization procedures are in operation over clock cards, time sheets etc., signed bonus lists and approved lists of commission payments to staff
- Check calculations of gross to net pay for a sample of employees
- Inspect authorised payment lists
- Observe delivery of cash payments to employees
- Test starter and leaver procedures applied to payroll (ensure leavers removed from payroll on correct date and joiners added on correct date)
- Check payroll summary to payroll and nominal ledger
- Check salary payments are in line with contracts of employment
- For payment of cash wages: check the packets to ensure each employee has one, attend wages payout and observe, ensure all employees sign for their packet, ensure no employee receives more than one pay packet, check unclaimed wages are entered in an unclaimed wages book and obtain reasons for unclaimed wages.

12.4 Substantive Audit Procedures over Purchases and Creditors

Initial procedures:

- The opening balance should be traced to prior year's audit working papers or signed financial statements.
- The activity in the general ledger should be reviewed for any unusual entries.
- A payables listing which shows amounts owed at the balance sheet date should be obtained from the client. This listing should be totted and the total balance agreed to general ledger.

The definition of substantive procedures has been covered in detail in **Chapter 5**. ISA 520 distinguishes between two types of substantive procedure, Tests of Detail and Substantive Analytical Procedures:

Tests of details

These are procedures that are used to substantiate a financial statement amount. They are used to obtain audit evidence regarding certain assertions. In the case of Purchases and Trade Payables/Accruals they are used to gain audit evidence over the Completeness, Existence and Accuracy assertions.

Substantive analytical procedures

These tests are designed to substantiate predictable relationships among both financial and non-financial data. They are mostly applicable to large volumes of transactions that tend to be predictable over time.

Within the context of the audit of purchases and trade payables/accruals, substantive analytical procedures are most suitable in order to gain audit evidence over the purchases figure in the financial statements. The purchases figure consists of a large volume of routine transactions that tend to be predictable over the course of a financial year. Tests of Details are more commonly used within the audit of trade payables and accruals.

Substantive testing of purchases

Substantive Analytical Procedures

As stated above, substantive analytical procedures are most effective in the audit of the purchases figure. In this process, it is necessary to review the understanding of the entity in order to establish whether changes to purchases/trade payables figure are to be expected.

Significant changes in amounts between the current year and the prior year should be identified. Ratios and trend analysis such as the gross profit ratio should be calculated.

The auditor will develop an expectation for the level of purchases in the year based upon key factors affecting the performance and operation of the business in that period. This could include:

- Prior year volumes of purchasing
- Movements in cost of key supplies
- Inflation
- Movements in levels of demand for finished goods.

The auditor will seek to quantify and substantiate the effects of each of these factors through obtaining documentary and other evidence where available. For example, prior-year purchase and sales volumes could be verified to prior-year audit working papers, movements in costs of key supplies could be verified by comparing current and prior-year supplier invoices and movements in demand levels for finished goods could be verified by comparing current and prior-year sales reports.

Once the auditor has developed his expectation for the current year purchases figure he will compare this to the actual figure reported in the financial statements. He will gain comfort over the Completeness, Existence and Accuracy of the purchases figure by confirming that his original expectation is within a pre-defined acceptable range of the actual figure reported in the financial statements. This acceptable range is a matter of judgement, however a commonly used range is reported purchases figure a within 5% of expected.

Analysis of expense accounts is also important. This is usually undertaken by comparing the ratio of each expense to sales in the current and prior period. An unusually low expense may indicate unrecorded liabilities. Wherever a change in relationships cannot be readily explained, the auditors must seek an explanation from management and corroborate it, usually by conducting additional tests.

Tests of Details over Purchases

Where the auditor does not feel that sufficient audit evidence over Purchases can be obtained from Substantive Analytical procedures alone, he may chose to perform additional Tests of Details to gain assurance over Existence and Accuracy of purchases.

This will involve agreeing a sample of reported purchases transactions to supporting documentation such as purchase orders, goods received notes, and supplier invoices, confirming that the amounts recorded are accurate and are recorded within the correct period. It is also importance to test the numerical sequence of purchase orders, and goods received notes and to trace them to purchase invoices and trade payables to confirm completeness. The auditor will often use a sampling tool (discussed in **Chapter 5**) as a method for generating an appropriate sample size.

Additional assurance over the Completeness of Purchases can be obtained from the performance of Unrecorded Liabilities testing which is discussed in more detail below.

Substantive testing of trade payables and accruals

Specific substantive testing over trade payables and accruals will tend to vary depending upon the nature of the client's operations. However, there are a number of key substantive tests that are common to the audit of the majority of audit clients. These will generally take the form of Tests of Details rather than Substantive Analytical procedures, and they are summarised below:

Confirming trade payables (all assertions)

Confirmation of trade payables performed less frequently because:

- Offers no assurance that unrecorded liabilities will be discovered
- External evidence such as invoices/supplier statements should be available to substantiate the balances
- It is recommended to confirm trade payables only when
  - The level of detection risk is low
  - And the suppliers being confirmed are those with which the company engaged in a substantial level of business and do not issue monthly statements and/or the statement is not available at the balance sheet date.

If confirmations are used to confirm trade payables, the auditors must be in control of the preparation and of the mailing of the requests. They must also ensure they receive the responses directly from the suppliers.

The positive form should be used in making the confirmation request and the amount due at the balance sheet date should not be stated on the request, the supplier should specify the amount due to them as recorded in their own records. The supplier should also provide details regarding purchase commitments and any collateral for the amount due.

Confirming the trade payables balance provides only a limited amount of evidence relating to the completeness assertion, due to the increased likelihood that the test may fail to identify suppliers with which the entity has unrecorded liabilities.

12.5 Search for Unrecorded Liabilities (Completeness)

The search for Unrecorded Liabilities is a fundamental test of detail over the Completeness of Trade Payables and Accruals common to almost every audit. The objective of the test is to gain assurance that all of a client's liabilities which were in existence at the year-end were recorded in the balance sheet. Intentional understatement of year-end liabilities is a key tool which could be used by a client engaging in "earnings management", i.e. by recording current year expenditure in the following period, current year costs are reduced with the result that profits are overstated. The auditor searches for Unrecorded Liabilities by examining various sources of evidence to identify pre-year-end transactions where goods or services have been received by the client before the year-end.

The auditor then checks to ensure that any such pre-year-end transactions are appropriately recorded within the year-end financial statements. The main sources of evidence are:

- Post-year-end payments identified from bank statements.
- Post-year-end invoices received.
- Goods Received Notes which have not been matched to invoices at the year-end.

For example, for a company with a 31 December year-end the auditor may identify from review of post year-end bank statements a significant payment for £100,000 made on 10 January. Upon investigation he ascertains that this payment relates to an invoice which was received on 3 January. On further examination the auditor finds that this invoice has been matched to a goods received note dated 31 December. As the goods were received pre-year-end the transaction should be recorded in current year purchases and accruals. If this is not the case, the year-end accruals and purchases figures will be understated.

Analytical procedures may also help identify unexpected differences between this year's and prior year's liability figure, which could indicate the presence of unrecorded liabilities.

An examination of contractual commitments may also indicate the existence of unrecorded liabilities such as progress payments on long-term contracts.

In addition the performance of a subsequent events and contingent liabilities review may also contribute to uncovering unrecorded liabilities.

- **Performance of purchases cut-off testing (Completeness, Existence and Accuracy)**
  Another key test performed in almost every audit of trade payables is the performance of purchases cut-off testing in respect of the purchase of goods. The objective of this test is to ensure that purchases close to the year-end are recorded in the appropriate accounting period.

  Unlike trade receivables it may take several weeks for transactions which have occurred before the balance sheet date to be invoiced by the supplier. The majority of entities do not have sufficient controls in place to ensure accurate distinction between the recording of transactions before and after the balance sheet date.

  The test is generally performed by examining Goods Received Notes received close to the year-end and confirming that they are appropriately recorded in the financial statements.

  Goods Received Notes issued in the days prior to the balance sheet date may be traced to purchase journal entries or purchase accruals, to ensure they have been recorded pre-year end.

  In addition, goods received notes issued after the balance sheet date will be traced to suppliers invoices to ensure they are recorded after the year end.

  The number of Goods Received Notes to be examined is again a matter of judgement, however, typically the auditor may examine the last 10 pre-year-end Goods Received Notes and the first 10 post-year-end Goods Received Notes. The auditor will typically obtain the last pre-year-end goods received notes at the time of attendance at the year-end inventory count and can then identify the first post-year-end goods received notes by following the numerical sequence.

- **Re-performance of Supplier Statement Reconciliations (Completeness, Existence and Accuracy)**
  Where the client receives monthly supplier statements from its suppliers, the auditor will seek to gain audit evidence over the Completeness, Existence and Accuracy of the trade payables balance by reconciling amounts appearing on year-end supplier statements to corresponding balances appearing on the creditor's ledger.

  The supplier statements are evidence which is generated external to the entity and therefore provides reliable audit evidence to the auditors as to the accuracy of year-end supplier balances. Photocopied or faxed copies of supplier statements should not be used in testing, instead the auditors in this case should request a copy of the statement from the supplier or confirm the balance directly with the supplier.

In selecting the accounts for testing, the focus should not centre on the year-end supplier balance but instead should centre on those suppliers with which the entity has had the greatest volume of business during the year, as the auditors' concern is that the recorded creditors balance is understated.

Differences between supplier statements and the recorded year-end trade payables balance should be investigated. The main reasons for differences can be attributed to goods and cash in transit and also amounts in dispute between both parties.

Accruals An accrual is an amount set aside for a specific liability i.e. where expenditure has been incurred in the period but for which no invoice has been received. Key audit procedures include:

- Determining how the client identifies all accruals required to be made – discover and test the procedures
- Checking the schedule of accruals for arithmetical accuracy.

- **Re-calculation of a sample of year-end accruals (Existence and Accuracy)**
  The auditor can gain audit evidence over the Existence and Accuracy of year-end accruals by recalculating a sample of accruals appearing on the year-end schedule. These calculations can be performed with the help of supporting documentation used by the client in their calculation. For example, for a company with a 31 December year-end there may be an accrual for electricity costs for December when the previous bill related to the quarter ending 30 November and the next expected bill covers the period 1 December to 28 February, the auditor may recalculate the year-end accrual by dividing the previous quarterly bill by three.

- **Comparison of year-end accruals to prior year (Completeness, Existence and Accuracy)**
  Generally accrual balances relate to similar items within a business year-on-year, e.g. rent, rates, electricity etc. It is possible to gain audit evidence over the Completeness, Existence and Accuracy of accruals by comparing items and amounts on the prior year accruals listing to those on the current year listing and identifying and examining any unusual omissions or additions.

- **Recalculation of payroll liabilities**
  Many entities must make a number of payroll accruals at the balance sheet date for amounts due to employees in respect of salaries, wages, bonuses, holiday pay and amounts due to the Revenue in respect of PAYE and PRSI due at the year end.

Assessing the implications of errors found during the course of substantive testing

As discussed in **Chapter 5**, errors identified during the course of substantive testing should be assessed against previously determined levels of materiality (discussed in **Chapter 1** and see also ISA 320). If an error is above the level of determined materiality, the auditor should request that the client make an appropriate adjustment to their financial statements. If the client is not willing to do this, the auditor should consider the implications for his audit report (discussed in **Chapter 15** and see also ISA 700).

Summary

In summary, the audit of purchases and creditors generally focuses on the three key assertions of:

- Completeness,
- Existence and
- Accuracy.

Audit evidence over these assertions is gained through a combination of tests of control and substantive procedures.

QUESTIONS

Self-test Questions

1. How does an auditor check that all liabilities in respect of the purchases of goods and services are included in the financial statements?
2. Why is the control over the ordering of goods and services so important?
3. What is the importance of cut-off tests?

Review Questions

Question 12.1

You are the audit senior on the audit of Kopite Cabinets, a manufacturer of trophy display cabinets, for the year ended 31 December 2008. You have instructed your junior to review the file of post-year-end invoices received. From your review your junior has identified the following:

(a) An invoice dated 1 January 2009 for timber with a value of €/£12,000. The goods received note for the timber is also dated 1 January 2009. The invoice is not recorded in creditors or accruals at the year-end.
(b) An invoice dated 7 January 2009 for glass with a value of £/€9,000. The goods received note for the glass is dated 31 December 2008. The invoice is not recorded in creditors or accruals at the year-end.
(c) An invoice dated 2 January 2009 for glue with a value of £/€5,000. The goods received note for the glue is dated 2 January 2009. The invoice is found to be included in year-end accruals.

(d) An invoice dated 1 January 2009 for nails with a value of £/€50. The goods received note is dated 31 December 2008. The invoice is not included in year-end creditors or accruals.

Requirement What action would you take as audit senior in respect of each of these items including, where appropriate, relevant audit differences.

Note: Audit materiality for the engagement has been set at £/€5,000.

Question 12.2

Lactic Ltd (LACTIC) is a client of your firm. You are the audit senior on the audit for the year end 31 May 2007.

Your assistant is responsible for the audit of the accounts payable and she has asked you to review, and provide guidance on, the following creditor reconciliation that she is about to audit.

Lactic Ltd – Accounts Payable Reconciliation

	£/€000	£/€000	£/€000
Balance per accounts payable listing			1,490
Balance per supplier's statement 28 May 2007			2,620
Difference			1,130
Reconciling items:			
– Payments made not on statement		(720)	
– Invoices on statement not on ledger			
24/05/07 No. 14255	540		
27/05/07 No 15105	650		
28/05/07 No. 15385	760		
		1,950	
			1,230
			100

The Financial Controller has noted that, in general, the audit fieldwork has always run smoothly, but there was a delay each year in the completion of the **statutory accounts.** The Financial Controller has indicated that a better understanding of the key financial statement completion steps would benefit the finance department of LACTIC in supporting the audit process.

Requirement Assuming that your assistant has not performed any audit work on the Lactic reconciliation, outline briefly the audit work and queries the assistant might consider.

Question 12.3

BISTRO Ltd (BISTRO) is a confectionery distributor that has been in business for the last 20 years and is managed by J Bistro. Your audit firm has been the auditor of this company since its incorporation. The audit partner is new to the engagement, following a required rotation. The company has performed well during the year ended 31 March 2005 with sales (€/£2,565,000) and profit before tax (€/£100,000) running at approximately 10% higher than prior-year performance.

The field work for the 2005 audit is complete and the partner has asked you to review the analytical review of operating expenses. The following is the schedule of analytical review work performed by the audit assistant on the operating expenses.

Description	2005 €/£000	2004 €/£'000	Comments
Insurance	20	10	The increase is due to rising insurance charges (J. Bistro)
Administration Salaries	113	98	The increase is attributable to the cost of hiring a temporary accounts clerk to cover maternity leave (J. Bistro)
Depreciation	12	10	Appears reasonable
Distribution costs	322	182	The company had a policy of splitting distribution costs between cost of sales and operating expenses 50:50 ratio, but in 2005 all distribution costs have been charged to operating expenses (J. Bistro)
Repairs and Maintenance	32	4	There were significant improvements made to the warehouse in 2005 (J. Bistro)
Computer Costs	9	8	Appears reasonable
Accountancy	12	11	Appears reasonable based on prior year fee
Rent and Rates	15	11	The local authority increased rates during the year (J. Bistro)
Total:	535	334	

Requirement

(a) Define substantive analytical procedures
(b) Draft a memorandum to the partner on this engagement, highlighting what further work should be performed on the analytical review of operating expenses
(c) J Bistro has just phoned you about an article he has read in an accountancy journal on CAATs. He has asked you to describe, briefly the ways in which CAATs could be used in the audit of BISTRO.

Question 12.4

BARROW Ltd (BARROW) manufactures electrical components for use in various electronic applications worldwide. The company has been a client of your firm for many years. It is a significant local employer with almost 400 permanent employees. It also recruits temporary staff at peak periods.

At the audit planning meeting you were informed that the company decided during the year to outsource its payroll function in order to cut costs. It has engaged OTTER Ltd, a well known payroll bureau, to carry out the payment functions.

The results of your audit testing have identified a number of control weaknesses in the payroll and also in other financial statement areas, including fixed assets, bank and cash and accounts payable.

Requirement

(a) State, as part of your audit planning, what further information you need to obtain arising from BARROW's decision to outsource its payroll function.
(b) State what additional audit procedures you would carry out as a result of the decision taken during the year to outsource the payroll function.
(c) Set out FIVE key considerations for the reporting of control weaknesses to the directors of the company.

Appendix 12.1 – Extracts from Audited Financial Statements

LARGE COMPANY LIMITED

COMPREHENSIVE INCOME STATEMENT
for the year ended 31 December 20X8

	Notes	20X8 €000	20X7 €000
Turnover – continuing operations	1	280,250	198,500
Cost of sales		(140,250)	(120,800)
Gross profit		140,000	77,700

Statement of Financial Position as at 31 December 20X8

	Notes	20X8 €000	20X8 €000	20X7 €000	20X7 €000
Creditors: amounts falling due within one year	19		(135,680)		(142,600)
Creditors: amounts falling due after more than one year	20	109,940		116,630	

Notes (continued) *(forming part of the financial statements)*

19. Creditors: amounts falling due within one year

	20X8 €000	20X7 €000
Bank and other loans (note 21)	4,250	9,650
Obligations under finance leases and hire purchase contracts (note 22)	2,500	4,000
Derivative financial instruments (note 25)	120	80
Trade creditors	109,320	114,650
Bills of exchange payable	150	230
Other creditors	16,150	10,500
Accruals and deferred income	500	750
	132,990	139,860

Tax creditors		
Corporation tax	2,310	2,280
PAYE	100	120
VAT	80	60
Capital Gains tax	120	80
Other tax	30	110
	2,640	2,650
Social welfare (PRSI)	50	90
	2,690	2,740
	135,680	**142,600**

Trade creditors include the following:

Due at the year end to suppliers who claim reservation of title	20,000	21,000

20. Creditors: amounts falling due after more than one year

	20X8 €000	20X7 €000
Bank and other loans (note 21)	20,350	27,560
Obligations under finance leases and hire purchase contracts (note 22)	85,000	85,000
Preference shares	3,000	3,000
Derivative financial instruments (note 25)	70	50
	108,420	115,610
Other creditors		
Government grants (note 23)	1,308	808
Pension commitments	212	174
Other		38
	1,520	1,020
	109,940	**116,630**

21. Bank loans

Current	20X8 €000	20X7 €000
Galway bank loan	1,000	1,000
Dublin bank loan	3,250	8,650
	4,250	9,650
Non-current		
Eurobond	3,750	350
Galway bank loan	14,000	15,000
Dublin bank loan	2,600	12,210
	20,350	27,560
Total Bank Loans	**24,600**	**37,210**

Analysis of loans

	20X8 €000	20X7 €000
Not wholly repayable within five years	13,050	17,720
Wholly repayable within five years	11,960	19,990
	25,010	37,710
Issue costs	(410)	(500)
Total	24,600	37,210
Included in current liabilities	4,250	9,650
Included in long-term liabilities	20,350	27,560

Loan maturity analysis

	20X8 €000	20X7 €000
Bank and other loans comprise amounts repayable:		
In one year or less, or on demand	4,250	9,650
Between one and five years	7,300	9,840
After more than five years	13,050	17,720
	24,600	37,210

The Eurobond is secured by a fixed charge on the land and buildings and a floating charge on the other assets of the company. It carries a fixed interest rate of 6.9%.

The Dublin bank loan is repayable in instalments over the next 6 years. It is subject to a variable interest rate based on EURIBOR. The weighted average interest rate during the year was 4.9% (20X7 – 4.9%).

The Galway bank loan is repayable in instalments over the next 8 years. It has a fixed interest rate for 75% of the loan at 5.5%, with the remainder at EURIBOR plus 2%. The weighted average interest for the period was 5.2% (20X7 – 5.1%).

22. Obligations under finance leases and hire purchase contracts

Analysis and maturity schedule

	20X8 €000	20X7 €000
Repayable within one year	2,500	4,000
Repayable between one and two years	2,500	2,500
Repayable between two and five years	12,000	13,300
Repayable after five years	83,000	82,200
	100,000	102,000
Finance charges and interest allocated to future periods	(12,500)	(13,000)
Total	87,500	89,000
Included in liabilities falling due within one year	2,500	4,000
Included in liabilities falling due after more than one year	**85,000**	**85,000**

Chapter 13

THE AUDIT OF SHARE CAPITAL AND RESERVES

Learning Objectives

Be able to

- Identify the audit objectives applicable to share capital and reserves
- Identify tests to audit share capital and reserves

Checklist of Relevant Professional Statements

ISA 500 – Audit evidence
ISA 501 – Audit Evidence – Additional Considerations for Specific Items
ISA 505 – External Confirmations
ISA 520 – Analytical Procedures
ISA 540 – Audit of Accounting Estimates

13.1 What is Share Capital?

Share Capital is the amount paid into the company by the shareholders (i.e. the owners) at the time(s) the shares were issued. Both called up share capital and called up share capital not paid must be disclosed on the balance sheet.

13.2 What are Reserves?

Reserves are the profits retained in the business and not distributed to the shareholders. Reserves are also known as retained earnings. The Companies Acts 1963–2009 require disclosure of the following categories of reserves:

- Profit and loss account
- Share premium account
- Revaluation reserve
- Other reserves e.g. capital redemption reserve.

13.3 Audit Objectives and the Audit of Share Capital and Reserves

In practice, this section of the audit requires the least amount of time. It should be noted that this is an important part of the audit. It is good practice to carry out a Companies Office search which will verify the existence of the company, its shareholders and directors.

Assertion	Objective of Audit Evidence
Existence	To ensure the company is in existence and is operating in line with its Memorandum and Articles of Association.
Completeness	To ensure any movement in share capital account has been recorded in the year under review. To ensure opening reserves are accurately stated and tie into the prior year closing reserves as per the last balance sheet filed.
Valuation and allocation	To ensure share capital is included in the financial statements at the correct value, often shares are allotted at a premium.
Presentation and Disclosure	To ensure reserves are correctly disclosed in the financial statements and that provisions in the Articles of Association are adhered to. To ensure share capital is appropriately disclosed in the financial statements. This includes disclosing: • Authorised share capital • Issued share capital • Directors' and secretary's interests in the share capital of the company or parent undertaking. To ensure share capital is presented correctly in the financial statements. In accordance with IAS 32 each class of share must be appropriately disclosed as equity or a financial liability. To ensure that dividends are not paid from capital.

13.4 Substantive Procedures for the Audit of Share Capital and Reserves

Reserves

The audit of reserves is completed as follows:

- Ensure the prior year closing reserves as stated in the signed financial statements tie into the current year opening reserves (i.e. reserves prior to inclusion of the current

year profit/loss). This is a simple audit procedure but is of the utmost importance as it ensures that the prior year audit adjustments have been posted.
- Prepare or obtain a schedule from the client detailing all reserve movements during the year. The auditor should vouch material movements to supporting documentation (e.g. board approving minutes) and ensure compliance with legal regulations. Such reserve movements need to be disclosed in the financial statements.

Company details

Share capital is primarily audited by obtaining third-party confirmation:

- Request a copy of the Company Search from the Companies Registration Office in the Republic of Ireland (CRO) or the Companies House in Northern Ireland. The company search details all the documents filed and available on public record for the company.
- Once the search has been obtained, review all documents filed during the period under review and where necessary request copies of the documents filed. The most common documents include the Annual Return form, change of registered office amendments or changes to the Memorandum and Articles of Association, changes in directors or company secretary and any changes to the share capital.
- It is important to ensure that any changes reflected in these documents are verified to board approving minutes and correctly updated and disclosed in the financial statements.
- The company search will give details of any changes to the share capital. Such changes include the issuing of shares, the redemption of shares, bonus shares, options taken up or issued, share splits and rights issues. It is important that these transactions are appropriately disclosed in the financial statements.
- The auditor should check the consideration received for any shares issued and agree amounts called up but not paid. In addition, the legality of any share repurchases should be investigated. The auditor also needs to determine whether a provision for premiums payable on redemption is required.
- The company search also details any charges or credits over the assets of the company.
- The authorised and issued share capital must be agreed to the company's Annual Return and also reflect any changes made since the annual return and the financial year end. The authorised share capital should also be agreed to the Memorandum and Articles of Association.
- The Memorandum and Articles of Association must also be reviewed to gain an understanding of the rights attaching to each class of share. As per IAS 32, consideration must be given to how equity instruments are treated, that is as liabilities or equity. Authorised and issued share capital should be analysed in the financial statements by each class of share. The auditor should examine significant shareholdings, in particular the register of members to issued share capital, and ensure correct disclosure of the directors' shareholdings.

The critical feature in differentiating a financial liability from an equity instrument is the existence of a contractual obligation of one party to the financial instrument to either deliver cash or another financial asset to the other party or to exchange another financial instrument with the holder under conditions that are potentially unfavourable.

Put simply:

If a contractual obligation exists => Instrument is a financial liability
If the instrument is redeemable at the option of the holder = DEBT
If no contractual obligation exists => Equity Instrument
If the instrument is redeemable at the option of the company = EQUITY

Example 1

Co A - Preference shares which carry right to cumulative fixed net dividend and repayment of share price on redemption

Should this be classed as a liability or equity?

Look at the substance of the arrangement:

Two obligations exist… Redeemable at the option of the holder…

=> Classed as a Financial Liability

Example 2

Co B has redeemable shares

Co B may redeem all or part of the shares at any time, holders are not entitled to payment of a dividend

Look at the substance of the arrangement

– Preference shares contain no obligations…Redeemable at the option of the company…

=> Should be classed as equity

Minutes of Shareholder meetings are also reviewed during the audit. It is a requirement under Company Law that companies hold shareholder meetings and maintain minutes.

Any changes to the Memorandum and Articles of Association or other company information should be noted in the minutes and confirmed by review of the documents filed with the Companies Office in the relevant jurisdiction.

Summary of Audit Tests

Audit Assertion	Audit Test
Existence/Occurrence	1) Confirm the total number of shares issued, dividends paid or payable, and other pertinent information directly with the independent registrar or transfer agent.
	2) Compare recorded amount of share capital and share premium to prior years and to expectations. Investigate deviations, if any.
	3) Scan the share capital accounts for large or unusual activity during the year.
	4) Scan the activity in the share premium account for large or unusual transactions.
	5) For dividends declared/paid on share capital (or a component) that is classified as a financial liability, ensure the dividend is recognised as an expense in the profit and loss account.
Completeness	1. Determine that the share capital and reserve accounts are complete:
	— Agree opening balances to the prior year's working papers.
	— Agree closing balances to the general ledger.
	— Review current year minutes, amendments to Memorandum and Articles of Association and other agreements.
	— Examine nature of charges or credits and determine the propriety of the entries.
	— Ensure that non-distributable reserves have only been applied for permitted purposes.
	2. Review the entity's detailed analysis of equity instruments:
	— obtain an analysis from the client and review the rights and obligations contained in the instrument by reference to the articles of association.

Audit Assertion	Audit Test
	– consider the obligations in respect of both share capital, options, warrants and dividend stream and ensure that the instrument has been properly classified as a financial liability, equity or a compound instrument. – in particular, ensure that any preference shares which exhibit the characteristics of liabilities are recognised as liabilities (or compound instruments) rather than equity as required by accounting standards.
Rights and Obligations	1) Examine documentation pertaining to rights, preferences or restrictions that may be imposed by various authorisations, agreements, or legal requirements: – Memorandum and Articles of Association or by-law provisions. – Trust deeds. – Voting rights. – Preference shares and other preferences. – Dividend arrears. – Rights to acquire share capital.
Presentation/Disclosure	1) Ensure that directors' and secretary's interests in shares of the company disclosed in the directors' report agree with the information extracted from the register of directors' interests during the performance of the capital, reserves and statutory records work. 2) Ensure that each class of share is appropriately presented as equity and/or a financial liability in accordance with the requirements of accounting standards. 3) Ensure proper disclosures are made of the accounting policies and methods adopted for equity instruments. 4) Consider whether disclosure of non-distributable reserves is required in order to give a true and fair view. 5) Enquire from management as to the name of the entity's controlling and, if different, its ultimate controlling party. Agree details to the register of shareholdings and other corroborating evidence.

QUESTIONS

Self-test Questions

1. Is it sufficient to check the company statutory records when auditing share capital and reserves?
2. What are the principal audit procedures used to audit reserves?
3. List the main external sources of information that an auditor could check as part of his audit of share capital.

Review Questions

(See Solutions to Review Questions at the end of this textbook.)

Question 13.1

You are the audit senior on XYZ Limited for year ended 31 March 2008. On receipt of the financial statements you notice ordinary share capital has increased from £/€100,000 in FY07 to £/€200,000 in FY08.

Requirement Outline the audit procedures you would undertake to audit the increase in share capital.

Question 13.2

You are the audit senior on PRINTER Limited (PRINTER) for the year ended 31 December 2007. Following review of the company search and the documents filed during the year you note that 50 shares were issued at €2 each during the year. The nominal price of the shares is €1. The issue of the shares has not been reflected in the draft financial statements provided to you by Printer Limited. Outline the audit procedures you would undertake to audit the above.

Appendix 13.1 – Extracts from Audited Financial Statements

LARGE COMPANY LIMITED
STATEMENT OF FINANCIAL POSITION
as at 31 December 20X8

	Notes	20X8 €000	20X8 €000	20X7 €000	20X7 €000
Capital and reserves					
Called up share capital	28		84,050		78,160
Share premium account	29		2,990		570
Other reserves	29		1,400		28,700
Profit and loss account	29		85,454		50,360
Shareholders' funds	30		173,894		157,790

Notes

(forming part of the financial statements)

28. Share Capital

	20X8 €000	20X7 €000
Authorised		
100,000,000 A ordinary shares of €1 each	100,000	100,000
5,000,000 10% redeemable preference shares of €1 each	5,000	5,000
Allotted, called up and fully paid		
84,050,000 (20X7 – 78,160,000) ordinary shares of €1 each	84,050	78,160
3,000,000 10% redeemable preference shares of €1 each	3,000	3,000

Preference shares
The preference shares, which were issued at par, are redeemable on 31 December 201Y at par. They carry a dividend of 10% per annum, payable half-yearly in arrears on 30 June and 31 December. The dividend rights are cumulative.

Share issue
On 30 June 20X8 5,890,000 ordinary shares were issued at €1.40 each.

Share option scheme
The company has a share option scheme under which options to purchase shares are granted to senior employees (see note 7).

29. Reserves and Dividends

	Share Premium	Other Reserves	Profit and Loss Account	Total
	€000	€000	€000	€000
At 1 January 20X8	570	28,700	50,360	79,630
Premium on share issue	2,356	–	–	2,356
Finance cost of share issue	(36)	–	–	(36)
Exchange difference on loan	–	(200)	–	(200)
Derivative financial instruments		100		100
Impairment of investment property		(10,000)	–	(10,000)
Revaluation of tangible assets	–	(17,200)	–	(17,200)
Actuarial gain on market value of defined benefit scheme's assets			200	200
Additional finance cost of preference shares to share premium account	100		–	100
Profit for the year	–	–	60,394	60,394
Dividends distributed in the year (note 11)	–	–	(25,500)	(25,500)
At 31 December 20X8	2,990	1,400	85,454	89,844

Analysis of profit and loss reserve:

	20X8	20X7
	€000	€000
Profit and loss reserve excluding pension asset	84,254	49,360
Pension reserve (note 8)	1,200	1,000
Profit and loss reserve	85,454	50,360

Other reserves:

	Currency reserve €000	Revaluation reserve[2] €000	Fair value reserve[3] €000	Total €000
At 1 January 20X8	250	28,300	150	28,700
Exchange difference on loan	(200)	–		(200)
Impairment of investment property		(10,000)		(10,000)
Revaluation of tangible assets		(17,200)		(17,200)
Derivative financial instruments		–	100	100
At 31 December 20X8	50	1,100	250	1,400

30. Reconciliation of movements in shareholders' funds

	20X8 €000	20X7 €000
Recognised gains and losses for the year	33,294	25,590
Dividends paid	(25,500)	(10,000)
New shares subscribed	5,890	–
Premium on new shares	2,356	–
Finance cost of issue	(36)	–
Additional finance cost of non-equity shares	100	90
Net increase in shareholders' funds	16,104	15,680
Opening shareholders' funds	157,790	142,110
Closing shareholders' funds	173,894	157,790

---

[2] There is usually a transfer from the revaluation reserve to the profit and loss reserves equal to the excess of the depreciation on the revalued amount, relative to the depreciation charge on the historical amount.

[3] Movements in the fair value of available-for-sale investments are included here (unless the movement brings the cumulative fair value of the investments to below cost, in which case the reduction below cost will be charged to the profit and loss account (see large consolidated proforma for an example).

Chapter 14

AUDIT WORK CONCLUSIONS

Learning Objectives

- Demonstrate a clear understanding of the appropriate framework for concluding an area of audit work.
- Demonstrate a clear understanding of Final Analytical Review Procedures and their importance in the conclusion of an audit.
- Distinguish between specific issues which can arise when concluding on an area of audit work.
- Prepare and formulate the appropriate double entry for a schedule of unadjusted differences.
- Distinguish between specific issues which can arise when concluding on an area of audit work and potential financial statement implications of these issues:
  - Disagreement over amount of an account caption or relating to the adequacy of a disclosure
  - Limitation of Scope where evidence ought reasonably to be available to the auditor but is unavailable
  - Significant uncertainty where the auditor is required to make a professional judgment based on evidence available
  - Appropriate double entry for the proposed adjustments of the above issues.

Checklist of Relevant Professional Statements:

ISA 220 – Quality Control for Audits of Historical Financial Information
ISA 260 – Communication of Audit Matters With Those Charged With Governance
ISA 320 – Audit Materiality
ISA 501 – Audit Evidence – Additional Consideration for Specific Items
ISA 520 – Analytical Procedures
ISA 560 – Subsequent Events
ISA 570 – Going Concern
ISA 580 – Management Representations
IAS 10 – Events after the Balance Sheet Date

Introduction

As the audit draws to a conclusion the auditor performs audit procedures to obtain further audit evidence in order to draw a conclusion and finalise the audit process. The auditor will perform the following when concluding on an entity's financial statements:

- Final Analytical Procedures
- Audit Differences
- Subsequent Events Review/Post Balance Sheet Events Review
- Provisions, contingent liabilities and contingent assets
- Going Concern
- Management representations (letter of representation)
- Management letter/letter of weakness

14.1 Final Analytical Procedures (ISA 520)

In concluding on the audit work performed the auditor should complete final analytical procedures to form an overall opinion on the financial statements.

"The auditor should apply analytical procedures at or near the end of the audit when forming an overall conclusion as to whether the financial statements as a whole are consistent with the auditor's understanding of the entity." (ISA 520.13)

This will allow the auditor not only to see if the financial statements "make sense" and if any unusual or unexpected relationships exist, but also whether the results are consistent with other information obtained by the auditor.

The following benefits will arise if the auditor performs analytical procedures at the end of the audit:

- During the course of the audit a previously unidentified risk of material misstatement may arise. Final Analytical Procedures will help reduce the detection risk.
- Unusual fluctuations or unexpected results that are inconsistent to other audit evidence will be highlighted.
- Final Analytical Procedures will ensure conclusions formed by the auditor during the audit financial statements can be supported.
- The auditor can conclude on the reasonableness of the financial statements with added comfort and support.

In concluding on the final analytical procedures, if the auditor identifies new risks, it may be necessary to reevaluate the audit procedures performed. Prior to conducting additional procedures the auditor should evaluate the misstatements identified and assess whether these misstatements have a material impact on the financial statements. In making this assessment, the auditor should consider the possibility of similar undiscovered misstatements that may require further investigation. **"When analytical procedures identify significant fluctuations or relationships that are inconsistent with other relevant information or that deviate from predicted amounts, the auditor should investigate and obtain adequate explanations and appropriate corroborative audit evidence"** (ISA 520.17).

Final analytical procedures are similar to the preliminary analytical procedures performed at the planning stages of the audit already covered in previous chapters. They allow the auditor to review the financial statements in their entirety to highlight any unusual balances or relationships (gross profit movements) which may not have been noted in the audit. Final analytical procedures may be performed by comparing current year figures to prior year financials or by using external knowledge sources as a benchmark. Based on the understanding of the client and the market, the auditor should identify an accurate and comparable benchmark. For example, if the audit client is a medium-sized hardware store, a large multinational hardware store should not be used for comparison purposes. It is important to keep this in mind when performing Final Analytical Procedures using an appropriate benchmark, the following are examples of Final Analytical Procedures:

- Customer acquisition – compare to the benchmark how many new customers have been acquired during the financial year; customer retention, compare to the benchmark how many customers have been retained during the financial year.
- Sales growth – compare sales growth to the benchmark during the financial year.
- Selling and marketing activities – compare selling and marketing activities to the benchmark.
- Determine the key performance measures that capture the business activities.

The Final Analytical Procedures conducted by the auditor supplement the other audit procedures conducted by the auditor during the course of the audit. They provide a comparison to the market and an overall assessment of the performance of the entity, however it is important to stress that they supplement other audit procedures and are not effective in any way on their own.

14.2 Audit Differences

"The objective of an audit of financial statements is to enable the auditor to express an opinion whether the financial statements are prepared, in all material respects, in accordance with an applicable financial reporting framework" (ISA 200.2).

During the course of the audit the auditor may note misstatements in the accounts of the entity which were not corrected by management and may need to be brought to the summary of unadjusted differences if, after discussions with management, are to remain uncorrected. It is important to consider materiality and tolerable error when examining audit differences. Once these have been set the auditor should evaluate the effect of the uncorrected misstatements, both individually and in aggregate, on the financial statements. Materiality is set at the planning stage of the audit. However, it should be reassessed throughout the audit. Generally, materiality is set on either a percentage of revenues or net assets. A lower level of materiality is often used in practice when bringing misstatements to the summary of unadjusted differences. The auditor should take into account any uncorrected misstatements from the prior period as this may increase the risk of the current period financial statements being materially misstated. The overall materiality level is then used to decide which adjustments need to be posted to the client's accounts.

Qualitative factors must also be taken into account when posting adjustments, for example classification errors which if not rectified could be in contravention of a financial reporting standard i.e. misclassification of goods for resale as fixed assets is in contravention of IAS 2. A discussion is held with management regarding the posting of adjustments to the accounts and if the client refuses to adjust the auditor must consider the effect on the auditor's report.

Set out below are examples of the reasons why adjustments may be required:

- A mistake in gathering or processing information from which financial statements are prepared.
- The exclusion of an amount or disclosure, for example if a new asset was purchased during the year which was not included in the fixed asset register.
- An incorrect accounting estimate arising from overlooking or clear misinterpretation of facts, for example if the accountant has omitted significant details that may impact on a provision in the accounts.
- Management's judgments concerning accounting estimates or the selection and application of accounting policies that the auditor considers unreasonable or inappropriate.

> *Example – an adjustment*
>
> During the course of the Audit the auditor noted that Company Y had incorrectly accounted for the capitalisation of fixed assets. As a result an adjustment had to be made.
>
> Dr. Profit and Loss – capital expense
> Cr. Balance Sheet – fixed assets
> Being the write off of incorrectly capitalised assets

An adjustment in itself may not be material; however a culmination of misstatements noted by the auditor could result in an overall material difference. The auditor should record a summary of errors in their working papers during the course of the audit. During the final phase of the audit the auditor must conclude on the cumulative effect of misstatements and the impact they have on the financial statements of the entity. An example of a summary of errors is set out below:

		Adjusted? (Yes/No)	Balance Sheet Dr £/€	Balance Sheet Cr £/€	Profit and Loss Account Dr £/€	Profit and Loss Account Cr £/€
Dr	Capital Expense				X	
Cr	Fixed Assets			X		

(being the write off of incorrectly capitalised assets).

In conclusion, the auditor will document the significance and severity of the misstatements. The documentation of a Summary of Errors allows the auditor to consider the cumulative effect of the errors and the impact they have on the financial statements. Remember the errors listed are material in terms of testing completed and not in the context of the overall financial statements. At the point of completion the auditor must conclude on the cumulative effect of the errors and consider whether collectively the errors will have a material impact on the financial statements (see **Chapter 15** Audit Reports).

Should management decide not to adjust for material errors, the auditor should seek a written representation from those charged with governance explaining their reasons for non-adjustment and that they believe the uncorrected misstatements are immaterial to the financial statements.

14.3 Subsequent Events Review (ISA 560)

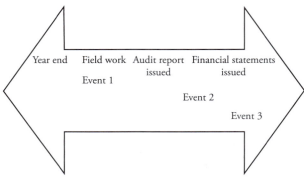

The auditor must ensure that there are no events post-year end that will materially impact the financial statements. "**The auditor should perform audit procedures designed to obtain sufficient appropriate audit evidence that all events up to the date of the auditor's report that may require adjustment of, or disclosure in, the financial statements have been identified**" (ISA 560.4).

ISA 560, Subsequent Events, defines subsequent events as both events occurring between the period end and the date of signing the auditor's report, and to facts discovered after the date of the auditor's report. The duty of the auditor is clear. Audit procedures should be designed to obtain sufficient appropriate audit evidence that all data up to the date of the audit report that may require adjustment or disclosure are identified.

IAS 10, Events After the Balance Sheet Date, also refers to events that occur between the balance sheet date and the date the financial statements are authorised for issue. These events can be described as adjusting or non-adjusting.

Ideally, the date the financial statements are signed by the board of directors and the date the auditors' report is issued should be the same date.

14.4 Types of Events

There are three types of subsequent events that the auditor must be aware off.

1. Events occurring up to the date of the audit report

As previously mentioned, IAS 10, Events After the Balance Sheet Date, categorises subsequent events that arise between the balance sheet date and the signing of the financial statements into both adjusting and non-adjusting.

Adjusting events provide evidence of conditions that existed at the balance sheet date and allow a more accurate valuation of balances and events at that date. These events must be reflected in the financial statements of the entity. Examples of such events are as follows:

- The settlement of a court case that confirms the entity has a present obligation at the balance sheet date
- The receipt of information after the balance sheet date which indicates an asset was impaired at the balance sheet date
- The determination after the balance sheet date of the cost of assets purchased or proceeds of assets sold before such balance sheet date
- Details of fraud or errors which show the financial statements are incorrect.

Non-adjusting events are not required to be reflected in the financial statements of the entity, as they do not provide additional evidence of events that existed at the balance sheet date. However, there are many non-adjusting events which do need to be disclosed by way of note to the financial statements due to their materiality. For example:

- The discontinuing of an operation after the balance sheet date
- Major restructuring plans
- A major business combination after the balance sheet date
- An issue of shares after the balance sheet date

(See IAS 10.21-22 for further examples.)

The auditor must design and perform procedures to obtain sufficient appropriate audit evidence that all events up to the date of the audit report that may require adjustment of, or disclosure in the financial statements have been identified (ISA 560.4). Such procedures should be performed in addition to the routine procedures applied to specific transactions occurring after period end to obtain audit evidence as to account balances at period end. There is no obligation on auditors to perform additional procedures to discover subsequent events from the date of signing of the audit report to the date of issue of the financial statements before the company. Should events be discovered within this time frame, they should discuss these with directors, evaluate the effect on the financial statements and take actions as deemed necessary.

The following are examples of audit procedures that can be performed:

- Review management procedures to ensure that subsequent events are identified
- Read original signed minutes of meetings held by management, shareholders and those charged with governance.
- Enquire of the client's legal counsel.
- Enquire of management of the following:
  - Any new commitments or borrowings entered into
  - Any major sale or acquisition planned
  - Any increase in capital or debt instruments
  - Any assets appropriated or destroyed by fire, flood etc.
  - Any developments in risk areas or where contingent liabilities were identified
  - Whether any events call into question the appropriateness of the accounting policies utilised.
- Review latest management accounts, budgets, cash flows etc., for unusual trends.
- Investigate risk areas and contingencies arising from the nature of the business.
- Calculate the current cash position and compare it to the overdraft limit and cash flow forecast and analyse movements since the year-end.
- Follow up on any matters cleared tentatively or on the basis of inconclusive information during the detailed fieldwork.
- Investigate unusual transactions occurring shortly before or after the balance sheet date.

- Review journal entries to ensure material adjusting events have been properly processed.
- Agree details of material non-adjusting events with the notes to the financial statements.

For any subsequent events that have been identified, the auditor should ensure that they have been appropriately disclosed and accounted for by management. If management are unwilling to amend the financial statements for the effect of a material and/or pervasive subsequent event, the auditor must consider the potential impact on their audit opinion. This will be discussed further in **Chapter 15** Audit Reports.

2. *Events occurring after the date of the audit report but before the financial statements are issued*

In compliance with International Standards on Auditing, the auditor does not have any responsibility to perform audit procedures or make any inquiry regarding the financial statements after the date of the auditors' report. It is the client's responsibility to inform the auditor of subsequent events that may affect the financial statements and which occurred between the date of the auditors' report and the date the financial statements were issued (ISA 560.8). If at this point the auditor becomes aware of a material subsequent event, they should examine the following:

- Consider whether the financial statements need to be amended as a result of the subsequent event.
- Discuss the subsequent event with management.
- Take the most appropriate action in the circumstances.
- Ensure the entity does not issue the financial statements and auditors' report to any third party until a decision has been made on the effect of the event.

If the directors decide to amend the financial statements, the auditor must perform further audit procedures to obtain evidence of the material subsequent event and its impact up to the date of the new audit report. New financial statements will then be issued and dated on the new date of issue.

If the directors decide not to amend the financial statements and the auditors are not in agreement with this decision, a qualified or adverse opinion will be issued. If the audit report has already been sent to the company, directors must be advised immediately not to forward the audit report and accompanying financial statements to third parties.

3. *Events that occurred after the financial statements are issued*

The auditor does not have a responsibility to perform audit procedures or make any inquiry regarding the financial statements after they have been signed (ISA 560.13). This includes the period after the financial statements have been issued, but before they have come before members. If a matter comes to the attention of the auditor which materially affects the "true and fair view" of the financial statements, the auditor must decide, through discussions with the directors, the implication for the audit report. If the financial statements have been issued but the AGM has not yet taken place, the auditors may request that the directors present at the meeting discuss this matter. The auditor, however, has a statutory right to attend the AGM and be heard on any part of the business of the meeting that is of concern to him. The auditor can make a statement about facts discovered after the date of the audit report. The auditor should consider what to do in relation to a subsequent event that comes to attention after the financial statements have been issued (ISA 560.13). The auditor ought to examine the following options:

- Whether the financial statements need to be amended as a result of the subsequent event.
- Discuss the subsequent event with management.
- Consider whether the action taken by management is appropriate in the circumstances.

Alternatively, they may decide to issue a revised set of financial statements. If this route is followed additional audit procedures may be necessary to cover the date to the new audit report and individuals already in receipt of the original financial statements will need to be informed of the revision. Depending on the circumstances, the audit report may need to be revised to cover the amendment or the auditor may just issue a new report on the revised financial statements.

Where a new report is issued on the revised financial statements an "emphasis of matter" paragraph will need to be included detailing the reasons for the revision. These details should also be included in a note to the accounts. The new report must also refer to the previous report issued on the original financial statements and be dated no earlier than the date of approval of the revised financial statements.

14.5 Provisions, Contingent Liabilities and Contingent Assets

Provisions

IAS 37, Provisions, Contingent Liabilities and Contingent Assets, states that a provision should only be recognized when an entity has a present obligation, legal or constructive, as a result of a past event and it is probable that a transfer of economic benefits will be required to settle the obligation and a reliable estimate can be made of the amount of the obligation.

The auditor must ensure that the disclosure of a provision is adequate to allow the user of the financial statements to understand:

- The nature of the obligation
- The expected timing of any resulting transfers of economic benefits
- The uncertainty surrounding the amount and timing of any transfers.

If the event does not qualify for the criteria of a provision (i.e. no present obligation, no probable transfers of economic benefits and it is not possible to evaluate the timing and amount of the obligation), it may however be classified as a contingent liability.

Contingent assets and liabilities

A contingency is described as a possible asset or liability that arises from past events and whose existence will be confirmed only by the occurrence or non-occurrence of one or more uncertain future events not wholly within the control of the entity.

Contingent liabilities are more of a concern for auditors than contingent assets as management may not be inclined to disclose them in the financial statements and because the events generally lie outside the accounting period. Examples of these include pending litigations, disputes etc. When performing his final audit procedures, the auditor should be searching for any undisclosed liabilities. The most common way to obtain such information is to:

- Review subsequent and post-balance sheet events up to the date of approval of the financial statements
- Enquire of management of any unresolved legal disputes and obtain an estimate of claims to be paid. This information should also be disclosed in the letter of representation
- Enquire of legal counsel and banks through review of solicitor's fee accounts and bank letters and other related correspondence
- Review original signed minutes of board and management meetings
- Review contracts and loan agreements entered into by the company
- Review current and previous years' tax returns
- Request written confirmation from the entity's lawyers, solicitors etc., of any known existing, pending or expected contingent liabilities.

(ISA 501, Audit Evidence Regarding Specific Financial Statement Account Balances and Disclosures, states that "direct communication with the entity's external legal counsel assists the auditor in obtaining sufficient appropriate evidence as to whether potentially material litigation and claims are known and management's estimates of the financial implications, including costs, are reasonable").

The entity does not recognise a contingent asset or liability, meaning they cannot be adjusted for in the financial statements. However, a contingent liability may be recognised as a provision when:

- It can be reliably measured
- It is probable the future event will occur
- The transfer of economic benefits is probable.

If none of these characteristics exists, the auditor must disclose the contingent liability in the notes to the financial statements providing the following information:

- An estimate of financial effect
- An indication of uncertainties relating to amount of timing of outflow of economic benefits
- The possibility of a reimbursement.

If the uncertainty identified is adequately disclosed, an unqualified audit report should be issued. If uncertainty identified is considered significant, the auditor should disclose such information in an "emphasis of matter" paragraph of his audit report without qualifying his audit opinion. However, where the auditor considers the disclosure made by management insufficient, he must qualify his opinion ("except for disagreement) or issue an adverse audit report. Again, this will be discussed further in **Chapter 15,** Audit Reports.

14.6 Going Concern

When planning and performing audit procedures and in evaluating the results thereof, the auditor should consider the appropriateness of management's use of the going concern assumption in the preparation of the financial statements (ISA 570.2).

The primary responsibility for assessing the appropriateness of the going concern assumption in which the financial statements are prepared rests with management and directors. The auditor has a secondary responsibility in respect of the going-concern assumption used in the preparation of the financial statements in that he must ensure the validity of management's assumptions. During the audit work conclusion stage, the auditor must reconsider and revise, if necessary, his initial assessment of the going concern basis for the preparation of the financial statements. It is recommended that there are early discussions between directors and auditors to discuss the assessment of going concern and any relevant disclosures. The going concern assumption is a fundamental principle in the preparation of the financial statements; as a result the auditor must ensure that the financial statements have been presented in this fashion. This principle is appropriate in respect of the planning and implementation of audit procedures; however it is during the completion of the audit that the auditor makes a decision on the going concern of the entity.

The going concern assumption focuses on the client being able to continue in business for the foreseeable future without an intention to liquidate the entity or that there are no conditions that might not allow it to continue (e.g. changing business environment or significant litigation that could impact on the future of the business).

The following factors are relevant to the judgement made (ISA 570, Para 7):

- The degree of uncertainty associated with the outcome of an event or condition increases significantly the further into the future a judgement is being made about the outcome of an event or condition.
- Any judgement about the future is based on information available at the time at which the judgement is made. Subsequent events can contradict a judgement which was reasonable at the time it was made.
- The size and complexity of the entity, the nature and condition of its business, and the degree to which it is affected by external factors all affect the judgement regarding the outcome of events or conditions.

Generally, the auditor will assess going concern for a period from one year from the date of approval of the financial statements. Where the period under consideration is less than one year, the auditor should consider disclosing the following in the financial statements:

- The time period being considered by the directors e.g. 7 months
- The reasons why they believe the period being considered is appropriate.

Company directors are required to make an assessment as to the company's ability to continue as a going concern and disclose any uncertainties that they are aware of when making this assessment when those uncertainties may cast doubt on the company's ability to continue as a going concern. It is the auditor's responsibility to consider the appropriateness of management's (or those charged with governance) going concern assumption in the preparation of the financial statements (ISA 570.9).

This is usually done by:

- Evaluating the means by which directors have satisfied themselves that the going concern basis of preparation is appropriate
- Judging the adequacy of the length of the period the directors have assessed and the systems by which directors have identified warnings of future risks and uncertainties
- Examining all appropriate audit evidence utilised in making the assumption e.g. review board minutes, cashflows, loan agreements, budgets, management accounts and other reports of recent activities etc.
- Assessing the sensitivity of the audit evidence to events and conditions both inside and outside the control of the entity
- Concluding on whether or not they are of the same opinion as the directors based on evidence available and reasonable assumptions about the outcome of future events

- Assessing the directors plans for resolving any matters on the going concern assumption
- Assessing whether the financial statements contain adequate disclosures
- Determining the implications for the audit report
- Preparing appropriate documentation documenting evidence and conclusions reached.

In considering the entity's ability to continue as a going concern the auditor should also examine the following:

- The knowledge of the client and its operating characteristics e.g. the company, its products, competitors and its environment.
- The industry and the economic conditions which surround it.
- Discussion with the client's principal officers on their assessment of the entity's ability to continue as a going concern.
- Gain an understanding of possible legal cases.
- Consider undisclosed arrangements or events which may hinder the entity's ability to continue as a going concern.

The following are examples of events that may have an impact on the going concern of an entity:

Financial

- The entity has not met necessary borrowing agreements.
- There is an indication of the withdrawal of financial support by debtors and other creditors for the entity.
- The entity has negative operating cash flows indicated by historical or prospective financial statements.
- The entity is unable to pay creditors on the appropriate due dates.
- The entity sells substantial fixed assets when it has no intention of replacing the assets.
- The entity has not complied with capital or other statutory requirements.
- Legislative changes that will adversely impact the entity.
- There is an inability to finance new products and product development.

Operational

- There has been a loss of key management or staff.
- There are labour difficulties and a shortage of key suppliers.
- There is a loss of a major market or a loss of a key supplier.
- There are fundamental changes in the marketplace or technology to which the company cannot respond.
- There is excessive dependence on a few products where the market is depressed.

Other

- Non-compliance with capital or other statutory requirements.
- Changes in legislation or government policy which may adversely affect the business.
- Pending legal claims against the company which cannot be met.

The auditor has to consider carefully of the factors that could influence the going concern of the entity, as this will have an impact on the audit report. These include:

- Adequacy of audit evidence
- Future periods considered by the directors
- Irresolvable uncertainty; and
- Disclosures in the financial statements.

If the auditor concludes that disclosures relating to going concern are not adequate, they are required to express a qualified or adverse opinion as appropriate. If the auditor concludes that there is material uncertainty that leads to doubt about going concern but that it has been adequately disclosed, the audit report must be modified for the inclusion of an emphasis of matter paragraph. The auditor should obtain written representation from directors and management confirming their view that the entity is a going concern for the foreseeable future. This should be supported by relevant assumptions and qualifications and should be noted in the letter of representation.

The auditor must also decide whether a financial statement disclosure is required on any uncertainties as to the continued existence of the entity. The auditor considers whether the financial statements:

- Adequately describe the principal events or conditions that give rise to the significant doubt on the entity's ability to continue in operation and management's plans to deal with these events or conditions; and
- State clearly that there is a material uncertainty related to events or conditions which could cast significant doubt on the entity's ability to continue as a going concern and, therefore, that it may be unable to realise its assets and discharge its liabilities in the normal course of business (ISA 570 Para 32).

The following table summarises the various types of audit report associated with uncertainty over the going concern basis of preparation of the financial statements.

Types of Disclosure	Type of Audit Report
Adequate evidence yet uncertainty over going concern assumptions and *is* fully disclosed in financial statements	Unqualified opinion to include an explanatory "emphasis of matter" paragraph in the "basis of opinion" section

Types of Disclosure	Type of Audit Report
Adequate evidence yet uncertainty over going concern assumptions but *not* fully disclosed in financial statements	Qualified opinion of an "except for" type due to disagreement over adequacy of disclosures
Directors have not fully considered the going concern assumptions for at least one year following the approval of the financial statements	Full disclosures of facts concerning the period under review – no reference in audit report If inadequate disclosures are made, then the period reviewed should be noted in the "basis of opinion" section of the report (report is not qualified)
Financial statements are found to be prepared on a going concern basis, however, this is not the case.	Adverse opinion should be issued as the financial statements do not give a true and fair view.

(See **Chapter 15**, Audit Reports for further details.)

14.7 Management Representations (ISA 580)

ISA 580 Para 3 states "the auditor should obtain audit evidence that management acknowledges its responsibility for the fair presentation of the financial statements in accordance with the applicable financial reporting framework and has approved the financial statements".

The auditor can obtain evidence:

- Through their own compliance and substantive tests e.g. physical verification of fixed assets
- Through third parties e.g. debtors circularisation
- Through entity specific documents e.g. relevant minutes of meetings of those charged with governance, a signed copy of the financial statements or verbal discussions with management and staff
- By obtaining a written representation from management on key aspects of the financial statements i.e. the Letter of Representation. By receiving such evidence in writing, it ensures that there is no conflict as to what was originally said and it leaves little room for misinterpretation or misunderstanding.

Representation should be specific and not relate to routine matters. Matters should be material in nature and no other independent corroborative evidence is available on the matter apart from the representation.

ISA 580, Management Representations, states the auditor should obtain representations from management with appropriate responsibilities for the financial statements before the audit report is issued. These representations are an important source of evidence to the auditor as not only do they confirm oral representations previously given by management and complement other audit procedures, e.g. going concern review, but they act as a form of audit evidence when other sufficient audit evidence cannot reasonably be expected to exist. It is important to note that representations by management cannot be a substitute for other evidence that the auditor could reasonable expect to be available.

The auditor should assess the reasonableness of the representations on material matters by:

- Obtaining corroborative evidence from inside or outside the entity
- Assessing the representations for inconsistency with other evidence obtained
- Considering whether those who made the representations can be expected to be well informed on the matter.

Representations can be either general or specific. General representations are a matter of course and include that:

- All transactions have been recorded and are reflected in the financial statements
- Directors have fulfilled their responsibility for preparing and presenting the financial statements as set out in the audit engagement letter and that the financial statements are prepared and presented in accordance with the applicable financial reporting framework
- Directors have provided the auditor with all relevant books, records and information as agreed in the audit engagement letter and as required by the Companies Act 2006
- It acknowledges its responsibility for the design and implementation of internal control to prevent and detect error; and
- It believes the effects of those uncorrected financial statements misstatements aggregated by the auditor during the audit are immaterial, both individually and in aggregate, to the financial statements taken as a whole. A summary of such items should be included in or attached to the written representations
- All subsequent events to the financial statements approval requiring adjustment or disclosed have been adjusted or disclosed
- All information relating to related party relationships and transactions is complete and has been accounted for and disclosed
- The selection and application of accounting policies are appropriate.

The auditor may in some instances require other specific representations to corroborate other audit evidence and ensure evidence obtained is complete. For example:

- Any subsequent events noted and their effect on the business
- The basis of estimates or provisions where evidence is minimal and the amounts are based on directors' judgements or averages

- The goodwill of the company is considered to be impaired and the value has been written down
- A legal claim has been settled and the directors do not anticipate any further action in this instance.

(See Appendix 2 to ISA 580 – Specific Management Representations the Auditor is required by other ISAs UK and Ireland to obtain.)

It is generally the auditor who drafts the representations on behalf of the entity, however, management should be encouraged to participate in its drafting. The auditor should not leave it until the end of the audit process to draft the letter of representation, instead noting any matters that may warrant inclusion in the letter in his working papers throughout his audit work. The letter must be on the company's own letterhead and signed and dated by an appropriate member of management and approved on a date as close as possible to that of the audit report and after the post-balance sheet events review has been concluded.

In some circumstances, management may refuse to cooperate in providing the necessary representations. In such cases the auditor should discuss the matter further with management, directors or the audit committee. The integrity of management must be evaluated and the effect of the non-representation on audit evidence. The auditor may conclude that he has not obtained all the information deemed necessary. This constitutes a limitation of scope and the auditor should express a qualified opinion or a disclaimer of opinion.

14.8 Management Letter/Letter of Weakness

Throughout the audit process, the auditor might observe areas of inefficiency and ineffectiveness in the entity's internal operations. These areas should be well documented in the related working papers to ensure they are not overlooked at the end of the audit. Ideally, the issues should be discussed first with the individual responsible for the accounting function when an issue is noted. Management could then be informed of all issues before a formal letter is submitted to the board.

The management letter is a constructive document, which not only highlights any weakness but also suggests practical changes to the existing system.

Its purpose is to:

- Allow the auditor communicate his/her findings on the accounting records, systems and controls of the entity to prevent them impacting on future audits
- Inform management of significant matters pertinent to the financial statements that may lead to material errors or misstatements

- Inform management of ways to make their systems more efficient and how resources and labour could be used more efficiently
- Provide solutions to management to rectify the problems found which may otherwise lead to a qualified audit report.

The basic elements of the management letter are as follows:

- A statement indicating that the accounting and internal control systems were audited to the extent that was deemed necessary to provide evidence for the purpose of the audit and not to provide assurances to management
- A list of the material weaknesses noted in the accounting and internal control procedures and any deficiencies in the books and records held
- Details of any accounting policies and practices deemed unsuitable for the entity
- Details of any non-compliance with accounting standards or legislation
- Explanations of the risks arising from each weakness and deficiency previously noted
- Suggestions by the auditor for improving the inefficiencies noted
- A statement informing the entity that they are not permitted to disclose contents of the document to third parties.

The management letter should be issued to management on a timely basis. In some cases two letters are sent – one in the interim and one in the final stage of the audit process. This not only demonstrates the auditor's continual interest in the welfare of the entity but it allows management to rectify any areas before the final signing of the financial statements. A written reply should be requested indicating any action intended to be taken. The auditor should bring the letter to the attention of the audit committee in the event of non-response or lack of action taken.

14.9 Audit Conclusion

The file is now ready for review by the reporting partner (who is the partner responsible for the audit engagement). The reporting partner examines the working papers and the information gathered over the course of the audit. The objective of the audit review is to evaluate the evidence obtained during the course of the audit and whether it constitutes "sufficient appropriate audit evidence", and the conclusions reached by the person preparing the working papers.

Whether "sufficient appropriate audit evidence has been obtained to support the conclusions reached and for the auditor's report to be issued" will depend on a number of factors:

- Significance of the potential misstatement in the assertion and the likelihood of its having a material effect, individually or aggregated with other potential misstatements, on the financial statements

- Effectiveness of management's responses and controls to address the risks
- Experience gained during previous audits with respect to similar potential misstatements
- Results of audit procedures performed, including whether such audit procedures identified specific instances of fraud or error
- Source and reliability of the available information
- Persuasiveness of the audit evidence
- Understanding of the entity and its environment, including its internal control.

In reviewing the audit work the partner thus ensures the following:

- Sufficient appropriate audit evidence has been obtained in each area of the audit process.
- The work performed by the auditor and the final financial statements are in compliance with statutory requirements (e.g. Companies Acts 1963–2009), accounting and auditing standards (e.g. IFRS/IASs, ISAs etc) and other relevant regulations (e.g. Combined Code on Corporate Governance).
- The nature, timing and extent of the audit procedures performed are in compliance with the applicable accounting reporting framework.
- The work completed by audit staff was accurate, thorough and in accordance with the audit programme.
- The judgements exercised by audit staff during the course of the audit were reasonable and appropriate and have been properly documented.
- All audit work has been completed in accordance with the conditions and terms specified in the engagement letter.
- The audit staff have properly resolved any significant accounting, auditing and reporting questions raised during the audit.
- The audit work is properly performed, documented in working papers and supports the audit opinion (see **Chapter 15** Audit Reports).
- Accounting policies adopted are in accordance with the applicable financial reporting framework, are appropriate to the entity and are consistently applied.
- The presentation of the final financial statements is appropriate in form, content and manner.
- Finally, the review should ensure the audit working papers have been documented in accordance with the International Statements on Auditing and that the firm's quality control policies and procedures have been met.

Paragraph 25 of ISA 230 duly notes "the auditor should complete the assembly of the final audit file on a timely basis after the date of the auditor's report". Paragraph 28 also states that "after the assembly of the final file has been completed, the auditor should not delete or discard audit documentation before the end of its retention period".

Checklists are common practice in ensuring that all aspects of the financial statements are covered, not only by the reporting partner, but also by the audit staff and audit manager.

Not only do they facilitate the review of the audit work performed but they act as evidence in showing a review has been carried out. The final analytical procedures and going concern analysis performed at the final phase of the audit will allow the auditor to make an informed conclusion on financial statements produced by the entity.

The final step the auditor should undertake before formulating his opinion is to communicate to the entity and to management any significant issues identified during the audit process which impacted on the audit process and procedures (ISA 260, Communication of Audit Matters with Those Charged with Governance). These can include:

- Difficulties in carrying out audit procedures, for example, incomplete books and records (limitation of scope)
- Views on accounting policies, estimates and financial statement disclosures
- Material unadjusted misstatements
- Summary of representations to be agreed by management
- Review of the going concern assumption and any related concerns
- Expected modifications to the audit report
- Any fraudulent activities identified or non-compliance with regulations.

Level of Matter Identified	Communicating Body
Significant	Written and verbal communication to audit committee or governing body
Less significant	Verbal discussion with management with authority to take appropriate action

It is now time for the auditor to consider the audit report (see **Chapter 15**, Audit Reports).

Audit issues

At this stage of the audit process the auditor now has to distinguish between specific issues that arose during the course of the audit. The auditor must examine details of evidence obtained and ensure that the following are appropriately addressed:

1. Disagreement over amount of an account caption or relating to the adequacy of a disclosure.
2. Limitation of Scope where evidence ought reasonably to be available to the auditor but is unavailable.
3. Significant uncertainty, where the auditor is required to make a professional judgment based on evidence available.

1. Disagreement During the course of an audit, circumstances can develop that give rise to disagreements between the auditors and the directors. The following are examples of issues that can give rise to a disagreement between the auditor and the directors:

- The application of inappropriate accounting policies. The auditor must ensure that the directors have used the appropriate IFRS accounting policies in the preparation of the financial statements.
- Disagreement as to facts or amounts to be included in the financial statements. This may occur if the auditor has found that the line items in the financial statements are not accurately disclosed or events have not been disclosed in the notes of the financial statements.
- Disagreement as to the manner or extent of disclosure.
- Failure to comply with relevant legislation.
- Failure to comply with accounting standards.
- Failure to comply with other regulatory requirements e.g. stock exchange or listing requirements.

The auditor must assess the nature of the disagreement and the appropriate course of action (see **Chapter 15**, for the impact on the audit report).

2. Limitation of Scope A limitation of scope will result where the auditor is unable to find sufficient evidence necessary to form an opinion. The auditor assesses the quality and type of evidence which would be expected to be available as support to a particular figure or disclosure in the Financial Statements. The possible effect on the financial statements will depend on the matter for which insufficient evidence is available (i.e. the potential materiality of the matter in question).

If the auditor is aware that the directors or those who appoint the directors will impose a limitation on the scope of the audit prior to accepting the engagement, which they consider likely to result in the need to issue a disclaimer of opinion, they should not accept the engagement unless required to do so by statute.

If the auditors become aware, after accepting an audit engagement, that the directors or those who appoint the directors, have imposed a limitation on the scope of their work which is likely to result in the need to issue a disclaimer of opinion, they should request the removal of the limitation. If the limitation is not removed the auditor should consider resigning from the audit engagement.

The following are factors that can lead to a limitation on the scope of the audit:

- Limitation imposed on the auditors, e.g. where the auditor is unable to obtain all accounting records or where the directors prevent a procedure considered necessary, by the auditor, from being performed.

- Limitations outside the control of the auditors and directors e.g. when the auditor has been appointed at such a time that attendance at the stock take is not possible or where the auditor is unable to gain access to an overseas business division due to political unrest.

3. Significant Uncertainty An inherent uncertainty will arise where the resolution of that uncertainty is dependent on uncertain future events outside the control of the entity, its management and directors. A significant uncertainty will arise where the magnitude of an inherent uncertainty is so great that it will impact negatively on the financial statements if it is not clearly disclosed.

The impact that an inherent uncertainty will have will be judged by reference to the risk of misstatement to the financial statements: where there is an estimate included in the financial statements that may change the range of possible outcomes and the consequences of those outcomes on the view shown by the financial statements.

The following are examples of uncertainties:

1. Bad debts provisions
2. Stock write off provisions
3. Depreciation charges, useful lives, residual values
4. Warranty costs.

QUESTIONS

Review Questions

(See Solutions to Review Questions at the end of this textbook.)

Question 14.1

What audit procedures should normally be followed to obtain details of subsequent events?

Question 14.2

What is the period with which the auditor is normally concerned with regard to post-balance sheet events?

Question 14.3

Is it possible for each individual item in financial statements to be fairly stated and for the financial statements as a whole to be misleading?

Question 14.4

Why at the end of an audit should an auditor review all working papers?

Question 14.5

How are final analytical review procedures useful to the auditor?

Question 14.6

You are the audit senior on MONITOR Ltd ("MONITOR") a security company. This is one of your firm's largest and most successful clients, with annual fee income (audit, tax and other services) in excess of €/£150,000 in each of the last three years.

The company, established in 1978, is owned 50:50 by Mike Greenwood and Dominic Clarke, who are the two directors of the company. You have been informed that Dominic Clarke is the brother-in-law of one of the tax partners in your firm, but that taxation services are provided by a different partner in the firm.

The 2002 audit field work was completed one month ago but the financial statements have not yet been approved by the directors due to the absence on leave of one of the directors. You understand that the financial statements are now due to be signed at the end of the week and you arranged a meeting with the Financial Controller. At the meeting the Financial Controller informed you of the following matters:

- One of the customers covered by the doubtful debts provision has gone into liquidation. However, MONITOR had ceased trading with this customer just after the year end and the debt due at the year end had been provided for in full.
- Subsequent to the audit field work, the company had changed all its banking arrangements to another bank which was offering lower overdraft rates. You were informed that, in the current difficult trading environment, the company was undertaking a review of all of its significant contracts.
- The company was considering a sale and leaseback of its premises to raise finance to repay certain commitments.
- It is hoped to pay the final balance of 20% of the previous year's audit fee within the next two months, with the current year's fee to be paid when the re-financing is put in place.

Requirement Draft a file note under the heading "SUBSEQUENT EVENTS PROCEDURES" which outlines the matters that have come to your attention since the completion of the audit fieldwork. The note should address each of the following:

- Further verification work required.
- Any other procedures which, based upon the above information, you consider may need to be carried out.

Question 14.7

Your audit of SANTA Ltd has uncovered the following:

(1) Prepayments of €/£50,000 have been included within the trade creditors balance in the trial balance, due to a misposting by the Accountant.
(2) Your payroll testing has identified bonus payments, in respect of the financial year, of €/£175,000 paid to staff subsequent to the year-end. However, the year-end bonus accrual was only €/£25,000.
(3) You have re-calculated the depreciation charge as €/£364,000, which compares with the balance of €/£320,000 included in the accounts.
(4) You were unable to agree the opening revenue reserves in the trial balance to the opening revenue reserves in the financial statements. This has been explained to you as being adjustments, which were processed through the prior year's financial statements, but which were posted into the accounting system in the current year.

The above matters have been brought to the attention of your client. However, no adjustments have been made to the accounts.

Requirement

(a) State what further audit work (if necessary) you would carry out in respect of each of the above matters.
(b) Draft the Schedule of Unadjusted Differences in respect of the above matters for review by the audit partner.
(c) Set out the factors that should be taken into account by the audit partner in his review of the Schedule of Unadjusted Differences.

Part IV

AUDIT REPORTING

Chapter 15

AUDIT REPORTS

Learning Objectives

Be able to

- Describe the principles underpinning audit reports, with reference to the relevant standards and legislation.
- Explain the differences between unqualified, modified and qualified audit reports.
- Identify typical scenarios in which audit reports might need to be modified/qualified.

Checklist of Relevant Professional Statements

APB Bulletin 2006/1 – Auditors reports on financial statements in the Republic of Ireland

ISA 570 – Going Concern
ISA 700 – The Auditor's Report on Financial Statements
ISA 701 – Modifications to the Independent Auditor's Report
ISA 710 – Comparatives
ISA 720 – Other information in Documents Containing Audited Financial Statements

15.1 Introduction

ISA 700 The Auditor's Report on the Financial Statements states:

> The Auditor's report should contain a clear written expression of opinion on the financial statements taken as a whole.

The auditor's primary task is to report to the shareholders on the truth and fairness of the financial statements prepared by the directors.

Auditors are also required by the Companies Acts to form an opinion as to whether

- Adequate accounting records have been kept by the company
- Proper returns have been received from branches not visited by the auditors
- The financial statements are in agreement with the underlying accounting records
- They have received all the information and explanations they required for the purposes of their audit
- The information given in the directors' report is consistent with the financial statements.

The auditor's report is the key deliverable from any audit engagement. It contains the auditor's opinion on the financial statements, an opinion which is based on the auditor's overall assessment and taking into account evidence gained during each phase of the audit process as described in the earlier chapters within this text. The auditor's report is, in simple terms, the "end product" of the audit engagement which users of the financial statements will look for to give them assurance over the contents of an entity's accounts.

The auditor can reflect a number of different types of opinion in his report, namely:

- Unqualified opinion – where the auditor is of the opinion that the financial statements show a true and fair view.
- Modified and Qualified opinion.

If the auditor's opinion is that the accounts do not give a true and fair view, or that something has prevented them from forming an opinion on all or part of the financial statements, the client will receive a modified audit report. There are a number of different types of modified audit reports:

- Limitation on scope – where the auditor is unable to form an opinion on the financial statements due to a limitation being imposed on his work
    - Except for – where the limitation relates to a specific account balance and the auditor can form an opinion on the financial statements except for that balance (Qualified)
    - Disclaimer – where the limitation is so material or pervasive that it prevents the auditor from forming any opinion on the financial statements (Modified)
- Disagreement – where the auditor disagrees with the financial statements prepared by the client
    - Except – where the disagreement relates to a specific account balance and the auditor can form an opinion on the financial statements except for that balance (Qualified)
    - Adverse – where the effects of the limitation on scope or disagreement are so material or pervasive that the auditor concludes that an except for opinion is not adequate to disclose the misleading or incomplete nature of the financial statements (Modified).

The audit opinion is contained in a separate paragraph within the body of the auditor's report. Guidance on what is required to be included in this report is found within two specific International Statements on Auditing (ISAs):

ISA 700   The Auditor's Report on Financial Statements
ISA 701   Modifications to the Independent Auditor's Report

Chapter 14 covered the process of evaluating audit evidence. This chapter will be structured to cover the following key areas:

- Basic aspects of the audit report
- Forming the audit opinion

- Matters that do not affect the auditor's opinion
- Examples of practical questions.

15.2 Basic Aspects of the Audit Report

The auditor's report to shareholders is a detailed document which should leave the reader in no doubt as to the way in which audit has been carried out and the reasoning behind the opinion reached.

Note The company's annual report often contains, in addition to the financial statements and auditor's report, some additional statements such as:

- Chairman's statement
- A five-year review
- A trading review of the year.

Auditors do not have to report on these and will exclude them from their report. Auditors do, however, have to ensure that, where figures etc., are quoted in these parts, that they are consistent with the financial statements.

ISA 700 (paragraph 17) sets out the following basic elements which must be included in the auditor's report:

1. **Title**
2. **Addressee**
3. **Introductory paragraph**
   - Identification of the financial statements audited
4. **Management's responsibility for the financial statements**
5. **Auditor's responsibility**
6. **Scope paragraph describing the nature of the audit**
   - A reference to the ISAs or relevant standards
   - A description of the work performed by the auditor
7. **Auditor's opinion**
   - a reference to the financial reporting framework used to prepare the financial statements
   - an expression of opinion on the financial statements
8. **Other reporting responsibilities**
9. **Other Matters**
10. **Auditor's signature**
11. **Date of the auditor's report**
12. **Auditor's address**

These components are explained and summarised in the following table which has been taken from IFAC's *Guide to Using International Standards on Auditing in the Audits of Small- and Medium-sized Entities (December 2007)*:

Component	Comments
Title	The title is "Independent Auditor's Report". Using the word "independent" distinguishes the independent auditor's report from reports issued by others.
Addressee	As required by the circumstances of the engagement or local regulations. It is usually addressed to the shareholders or those charged with governance of the entity being audited.
Introductory paragraph	• Identifies the entity whose financial statements have been audited. • States that the financial statements have been audited. • Identifies the title of each of the financial statements that comprise the complete set of financial statements. • Refers to the summary of significant accounting policies and other explanatory notes. • Specifies the date and period covered by the financial statements. Where supplementary information is presented, the auditor needs to ensure it is either clearly covered by the audit opinion or clearly differentiated as not being covered. Refer to paragraphs 25–27 of ISA 700 for additional guidance.
Management's Responsibility for the Financial Statements	State that management is responsible for the preparation and the fair presentation of the financial statements in accordance with the applicable financial reporting framework and that this responsibility includes: • Designing, implementing and maintaining internal control relevant to the preparation and fair presentation of financial statements that are free from material misstatement, whether due to fraud or error; • Selecting and applying appropriate accounting policies; and • Making accounting estimates that are reasonable in the circumstances.

Component	Comments
Auditor's Responsibility	a) State that the responsibility of the auditor is to express an opinion on the financial statements based on the audit. b) State that the audit was conducted in accordance with *International Standards on Auditing*. The auditor's report should also explain that those standards require that the auditor comply with ethical requirements and that the auditor plans and performs the audit to obtain reasonable assurance whether the financial statements are free from material misstatement. c) Describe an audit by stating that: • An audit involves performing procedures to obtain audit evidence about the amount and disclosures in the financial statements; • The procedures selected depend on the auditor's judgement, including the assessment of the risks of material misstatement of the financial statements, whether due to fraud or error. In making those risk assessments, the auditor considers internal control relevant to the entity's preparation and presentation of the financial statements in order to design audit procedures that are appropriate in the circumstances but not for the purpose of expressing an opinion on the effectiveness of the entity's internal control; and • An audit also includes evaluating the appropriateness of the accounting policies used, the reasonableness of accounting estimates made by management, as well as the overall presentation of the financial statements. d) State that the auditor believes that the audit evidence the auditor has obtained is sufficient and appropriate to provide a basis for the auditor's opinion.
Auditor's Opinion	The auditor's opinion of whether the financial statements give a true and fair view are presented fairly, in all material respects, in accordance with the applicable financial reporting framework or such similar wording as required by law or regulation. When *International Financial Reporting Standards* are not used as the financial reporting framework, the wording of the opinion should identify the jurisdiction or country of origin of the financial reporting framework (for example, …in accordance with accounting principles generally accepted in country X…).

Component	Comments
Other Matters	Standards, laws or generally accepted practice in a jurisdiction may require or permit the auditor to elaborate on matters that provide further explanation of the auditor's responsibilities in the audit of financial statements or of the auditor's report thereon. Such matters may be addressed in a separate paragraph following the auditor's opinion.
Other Reporting Responsibilities	In some cases auditors may be required to report on other matters such as performance of additional specified procedures or an opinion on specific matters, such as the adequacy of accounting books and records. Where the auditor is required/requested and permitted to report on other matters (supplementary to the auditor's opinion outlined above), they should be addressed in a separate section in the auditor's report that follows the opinion paragraph.
Auditor's Signature	The auditor's signature is either the firm name, the personal name of the auditor or both – whatever is appropriate for the particular jurisdiction. In certain jurisdictions, the auditor may also be required to declare: • The auditor's professional accountancy designation; or • The fact that the auditor/firm has been recognized by the appropriate licensing authority.
Date of Report	This date should be no earlier than the date on which the auditor has obtained sufficient appropriate audit evidence on which to base the opinion on the financial statements. This would include evidence that: • The entity's complete set of financial statements has been prepared; • The effect of events and transactions (of which the auditor became aware) that occurred up to the date have been considered (refer to ISA 560); and • Those charged with the recognised authority have asserted that they have taken responsibility for the financial statements.
Auditor's Address	Indicate the name of the location in the country or jurisdiction where the auditor practises.

An example of a complete auditor's report containing each of these basic components is included in the appendices to this chapter.

15.3 Forming the Audit Opinion

Chapter 14 explained how the final step of the audit process concentrates on evaluating evidence gained from audit procedures and reaching conclusions on each account balance and disclosure. Once the auditor has concluded on individual account balances and disclosures, he must consider all account balances and disclosures together in order to form an overall opinion on the financial statements. The concept of audit materiality, discussed in **Chapter 2**, is central to this assessment.

Materiality is an important consideration in arriving at an appropriate audit opinion. When the effect of the matter is below the materiality threshold, an unqualified opinion is appropriate.

When the effect of a disagreement or limitation on scope of the auditor's work is material, a qualified "except for" opinion is appropriate.

When the effect of a disagreement on the financial statements is pervasive (thereby affecting the view given by the financial statements as a whole) the auditor should issue an adverse opinion as the accounts are misleading.

A disclaimer of opinion should be expressed when the effect of a limitation of scope on the auditor's work is pervasive to the extent that the auditor is unable to form an opinion.

The opinion formed is then reflected in the audit opinion paragraph within the auditor's report. There are essentially two categories of audit report:

- Unmodified or Unqualified report (which is a clean report)
- Modified report (three types of which are as follows: a qualified (or an "except for") opinion, an adverse opinion and a disclaimer of opinion)

According to ISA (UK and Ireland) 700, Para 29, an auditor's report is modified in the following situations:

- Matters that do not affect the Auditor's opinion
  (a) emphasis of matter
- Matters that do affect the Auditor's opinion
  (a) qualified "except for" opinion
  (b) disclaimer of opinion or
  (c) adverse opinion

Guidance on each type can be found in ISA 700 and ISA 701.

15.4 Unqualified Audit Opinion

This is the most common form of audit opinion observed in practice. In reporting an unqualified audit opinion the auditor is confirming that he is of the opinion that the financial statements are free from any material misstatements which could be attributed, for example, to the use of inappropriate accounting policies, absence of required disclosures or incorrect use of the going concern concept.

True and fair view

ISA 700, paragraph 39 states:

> An unqualified audit opinion should be expressed when the auditor concludes that the financial statements give a true and fair view or are presented fairly in all material respects, in accordance with the applicable financial reporting framework.

Giving assurance of the truth and fairness of the financial statements was discussed in **Chapter 1** of this text as the key objective of the audit.

Relevant statutory and legislative reporting requirements

In addition to reporting on whether the financial statements give a true and fair view in accordance with applicable financial reporting framework, the auditor must also report on a number of areas of compliance with specific requirements under applicable Company Law. The opinion on these requirements may be separated from the opinion on the true and fair view, i.e. the auditor may report one opinion on the true and fair view and a different opinion on compliance with statutory requirements.

Relevant legislation is discussed in **Chapter 1**. The key statutory and legislative requirements impacting on the auditor's report are:

Republic of Ireland – Companies Acts 1963–2009

An auditor must report on the following:

- whether proper books of account have been kept by the company
- whether the information given in the Directors' Report is consistent with the financial statements
- whether he has obtained all the information and explanations necessary for the purposes of the audit
- whether the company's financial statements are in agreement with the books of account and
- whether any information specified by law regarding directors' remuneration and directors' transactions is not disclosed
- whether at the balance sheet date, there exists a financial situation requiring the convening of an extraordinary general meeting of the company.

The Act also requires that the auditor's report:

- Be qualified or unqualified and
- Include a reference to any matters to which the auditor wishes to draw attention by way of emphasis without qualifying the report {CA 2006 s.495(4)}.

Northern Ireland – Companies (Northern Ireland) Order 1986

Auditor must report on the following:

- whether information contained in the Directors' Report is consistent with the financial statements
- if the company has not kept proper accounting records
- if the auditor has not received all information and explanations required for the audit
- if information specified by law regarding directors' remuneration and other transactions is not disclosed.

These reporting requirements should be reflected in the audit report, and are often included in an "Other Matters" paragraph after the auditor's opinion paragraph (as referred to in the table above) or in the Opinion paragraph itself. Examples of this for both Republic of Ireland and Northern Ireland companies can be found in the appendices to this chapter.

Standard wording for an unqualified audit opinion

ISA 700 contains illustrative wording for an unqualified audit opinion. This standard wording is familiar to the majority of users of financial statements, making modifications to audit opinions quickly and easily identifiable. Below is an extract from ISA 700 (Paragraph 60) giving this standard wording, which should be included as a separate paragraph in the auditor's report:

> Opinion
>
> In our opinion, the financial statements give a true and fair view of (or "present fairly, in all material respects,") the financial position of ABC Company as of December 31, 20X1, and of its financial performance and its cash flows for the year then ended in accordance with International Financial Reporting Standards/UK or Irish Generally Accepted Accounting Principles.

What this means is that:

- the auditors agree that proper accounting records have been kept and proper returns have been made from any branches they haven't visited

- the financial statements agree with the underlying accounting records and returns
- all information and explanations they needed have been received from the staff and the directors and managers
- the auditors have had unrestricted access to the books and records
- details of all transactions involving the directors have been correctly disclosed
- there are no material errors or misstatements in the accounts.

The audit has been completed satisfactorily and the auditors have been able to gather all the evidence they need to support their unqualified opinion.

If, however, there is:

- a difference of opinion between the directors and auditors about something in the financial statements; or
- the auditors have experienced problems gathering the evidence they need the auditors may have to issue a qualified audit report.

Modified audit reports

Under ISA 700, "The Auditor's Report on Financial Statements", the auditor's report is considered to be modified in the following situations

- a qualified opinion
- a disclaimer of opinion
- an adverse opinion.

Effect of a qualified audit report

Generally, auditors believe that modifying their report is a last resort. In order to avoid having to issue a modified report, they will discuss the issues at great length with client's management. In most cases, directors are prepared to adjust the financial statements for any material errors or omissions which auditors have brought to their attention, as they would be keen to ensure the accuracy of the financial statements.

The Directors will also be ware that a modified report can have serious consequences for the company:

- it could affect shareholders' confidence in the company and its management
- it could discourage potential investors
- it could affect the willingness of lenders to continue offering a facility to the company
- it could affect the company's creditworthiness with its suppliers.

However, if the auditors feel a modified opinion is appropriate they must be able to justify the basis for the qualification and be able to explain this in the audit report.

The auditors must use their professional judgement to decide how serious the issues involved are, as this will influence which form of qualification to be included in the audit report.

The auditor must decide how seriously the issue/issues affect the truth and fairness of the financial statements.

If the issue is so significant that the accounts do not show a true and fair view, then the issue is said to be "pervasive".

However, if the issue is not detrimental to the accounts as a whole, but affects only part of them it is said to be "material but not pervasive". Here only part of the accounts is affected by the issue uncovered and the rest of the accounts will show a true and fair view.

15.5 Qualified Audit Opinion

If, as a result of the evaluation of the results of audit procedures, the auditor concludes that he is unable to issue an unqualified audit opinion, he may consider that a qualified audit opinion is appropriate.

A qualified opinion, which is often referred to as an "Except for" opinion, relates to instances where the auditor is unable to provide an unqualified opinion over the financial statements as a whole, but can give an unqualified opinion for some areas within the financial statements.

In this case, the issue is deemed to be material but not to the extent that the financial statements no longer give a true and fair view. The issue is not so material or pervasive as to require the auditors to disclaim an opinion or to give an adverse opinion but does require the auditors to draw attention of readers of the accounts to the issue which they have been unable to resolve.

Therefore, the auditor gives an unqualified opinion **except for** certain specific areas where his opinion is qualified. It represents a much lower level of assurance than that given by an unqualified opinion.

ISA 701 "Modifications to the Independent Auditor's Report" defines the circumstances which give rise to a qualified opinion.

Paragraph 12 of the standard states:

> A *qualified opinion* should be expressed when the auditor concludes that an unqualified opinion cannot be expressed but that the effect of any disagreement with management,

or limitation on scope is not so material and pervasive as to require an adverse opinion or a disclaimer of opinion. A qualified opinion should be expressed as being 'except for' the effects of the matter to which the qualification relates."

As intimated above, there are two types of qualified audit opinion, one relating to a Disagreement and one relating to a Limitation on Scope.

Limitation on scope

It is expected that auditors will obtain sufficient appropriate audit evidence in order to have the ability to express an opinion on the financial statemenets. When auditors cannot perform the necessary procedures or the procedures applied are unable to gather sufficient appropriate audit evidence, the auditor is said to have a scope limitation. Such limitations can be imposed by management or arise due to other circumstances.

Examples of scope limitations include: refusal by management to sign a management representation letter, refusal by management to permit confirmation of debtors, refusal to grant the auditor access to books and records.

ISA 700 requires that auditors do not accept appointment, or if already appointed, resign when faced with imposed limitation on scope. Where limitations are also imposed on the auditor's legal duties or ethical standards the audit should also be declined.

An example of a restriction attributable to circumstances is the timing of procedures i.e. appointing auditors too late to perform necessary procedures.

Scope limitations also exist when, in the opinion of the auditors, the client's accounting records are inadequate, but the auditors should try to carry out other procedures in order to overcome the scope limitation.

When a scope limitation exists the auditor should:

- describe the limitation and where possible quantify its effects on the financial statements
- express a qualified "except for" opinion where the matter is material but not pervasive
- issue a disclaimer of opinion if the matter is so material and so pervasive that the auditor is unable to form an opinion.

Disagreement

Auditors may disagree over the truth and fairness of the financial statements prepared by management over matters such as

- the relevance, reliability etc., of the accounting polices used
- the estimation techniques used in the formation of accounting estimates

- The adequacy of disclosures in the financial statements
- Compliance of the financial statements with relevant statutory and other requirements
- The appropriateness of the basis of accounting (for example where the financial statements have been prepared on a going concern basis but the auditors do not agree with management's assessment that the company is a going concern).

The auditor will take all necessary steps to overcome the source of the disagreement and will advise management to make the necessary adjustments. Where the source of disagreement remains, the auditors should amend the audit report accordingly.

Where such a disagreement exists the auditor should:

- express a qualified "except for" opinion where the matter is material but not pervasive
- issue an adverse opinion if the matter is so material and so pervasive that the auditor concludes that a qualification is not adequate to disclose the misleading or incomplete nature of the financial statements.

The concepts of Disagreement and Limitation on Scope have been discussed in detail in **Chapter 14** and are defined in ISA 701 (Paragraphs 16–21).

Circumstances giving rise to both types of qualified audit opinions are considered in the examples contained in the final section of this chapter.

Wording of qualified audit opinions

ISA 701 contains guidance on how qualified audit opinions should be expressed in the auditor's report.

A key requirement in this guidance is that the auditor must report the following in relation to the qualification:

- A description of the reasons/circumstances which give rise to the qualification
- A quantification of the possible effects on the financial statements, except where this is impracticable (i.e. a statement of how the financial statements could differ if the circumstances giving rise to the qualification had not arisen, e.g. if a different accounting policy had been applied, or an estimate of how a transaction for which information is incomplete may have impacted on reported figures).

(The above bullet points apply equally to Qualified and Modified audit opinions.)

Illustrations of how to report a qualified opinion arising out of a Disagreement and a Limitation on Scope are shown below. Essentially, what the auditors are saying is that the financial statements give a true and fair view, except for the matters in dispute. These are shown in the separate auditor's opinion paragraph within the auditor's report:

[Material not pervasive]

Disagreement on Accounting Policies—Inappropriate Accounting Method—Qualified Opinion

"We have audited ... (remaining words are the same as illustrated in the introductory paragraph – see paragraph 60 of ISA 700).

As discussed in Note X to the financial statements, no depreciation has been provided in the financial statements which practice, in our opinion, is not in accordance with International Financial Reporting Standards. The provision for the year ended December 31, 20X1, should be xxx based on the straight-line method of depreciation using annual rates of 5% for the building and 20% for the equipment. Accordingly, the fixed assets should be reduced by accumulated depreciation of xxx and the loss for the year and accumulated deficit should be increased by xxx and xxx, respectively.

In our opinion, *except for the effect on the financial statements of the matter referred to in the preceding paragraph*, the financial statements give a true and fair view of ... (remaining words are the same as illustrated in the unqualified opinion paragraph – see above)."

[Material not pervasive]

Limitation on Scope—Qualified Opinion

"We have audited ... (remaining words are the same as illustrated in the introductory paragraph – see paragraph 60 of ISA 700).

Except as discussed in the following paragraph, we conducted our audit in accordance with ... (remaining words are the same as illustrated in the auditor's responsibility paragraphs – see paragraph 60 of ISA 700).

We did not observe the counting of the physical inventories as of December 31, 20X1, since that date was prior to the time we were initially engaged as auditors for the Company. Owing to the nature of the Company's records, we were unable to satisfy ourselves as to inventory quantities by other audit procedures.

In our opinion, except for the effects of such adjustments, if any, as might have been determined to be necessary had we been able to satisfy ourselves as to physical inventory quantities, the financial statements give a true and fair view of ... [remaining words are the same as illustrated in the unqualified opinion paragraph – see above]."

15.6 Adverse Opinion and Disclaimer

This is the rarest form of audit opinion experienced in practice, as it effectively means that the auditor gives little or no assurance over the financial statements.

An **adverse opinion** arises out of a disagreement with management. It effectively states that the auditor fundamentally disagrees with the contents of the financial statements.

The issue is so material and pervasive, involving significant uncertainties or lack of disclosure, that it affects the truth and fairness of the financial statements as a whole.

ISA 701 (Paragraph 14) defines when an adverse opinion should be expressed:

> An *adverse opinion* should be expressed when the effect of a disagreement is so material and pervasive to the financial statements that the auditor concludes that a qualification of the report is not adequate to disclose the misleading or incomplete nature of the financial statements.

If auditors feel the items they are in dispute with the directors about are so serious that they mean that the financial statements are misleading they must issue an adverse opinion.

This opinion says that "the financial statements do not give a true and fair view".

A **disclaimer of opinion** arises out of a Limitation on Scope. It effectively means that the auditor is unable to reach any opinion on any part of the financial statements.

The auditors' work has been limited either by management or by lack of opportunity so they were not able to gather all the evidence they require.

Where management impose a limitation on scope of the audit, in the period following the acceptance of the engagement by the auditors and the auditors are of the opinion that this imposed limitation is likely to result in a qualified "except for" opinion or a disclaimer of opinion, the auditors should immediately request the restriction to be removed. Where the limitation is not removed, the auditors are required to perform alternative procedures to obtain sufficient appropriate audit evidence so as to enable an unmodified opinion to be expressed. Where the auditors are unable to perform such procedures the auditor must assess the potential impact this limitation will have on the audit report.

Is the matter material but not pervasive to the financial statements, so as to enable a qualified opinion to be expressed, or is the matter both material and pervasive, which in this case means the auditor must either:

- Resign from the audit, where the auditors must submit a written notice of their resignation to the company's registered office together with a statement of circumstances outlining their cessation of office and to notify the appropriate authority which in many cases is the Financial Reporting Council's Public Oversight Board or

- Express a disclaimer of opinion where resignation is not practicable before issuing the auditor's opinion. In this case the limitation on the scope of the audit should be expressed in the opinion paragraph of the report.

Where a limitation of scope is imposed before the auditor has accepted the audit engagement and the auditor believes that this scope limitation may result in the expression of a disclaimer of opinion on the financial statements, the auditor should not accept the engagement. Agreeing to conduct the audit subject to the limitation would seriously threaten the auditor's independence and would compromise the auditor's duties to **conduct the audit of the financial statements in accordance with applicable legislation, auditing and applicable ethical standards**.

In order to issue a disclaimer, the auditors must have been unable to gather sufficient appropriate audit evidence in order to support their opinion, either on the financial statements as a whole or a fundamental part of the financial statements, so that to issue any other opinion would be unsupportable.

Where the limitation has been imposed by the timing of circumstances such as appointment or by the inadequacy of the client's accounting records or where the auditor is unable to conduct an audit procedure they wish to, alternative audit procedures should be conducted by the auditors aimed at obtaining sufficient appropriate audit evident to support an unqualified opinion. Where this is not possible and a modified opinion is going to be expressed in the form of either a qualified "except for" or disclaimer of opinion, it should include a description of the limitation and indicate the possible adjustments which the financial statements would require to remove such a limitation.

ISA 701 (Paragraph 13) explains when a disclaimer of opinion should be expressed:

> A *disclaimer of opinion* should be expressed when the possible effect of a limitation on scope is so material and pervasive that the auditor has not been able to obtain sufficient appropriate audit evidence and accordingly is unable to express an opinion on the financial statements.

If the scope of the audit has been so limited that the auditors have been unable to carry out sufficient audit testing to the extent that they are unable to form a view on the financial statements, they must issue a disclaimer of opinion.

In essence, this says that "we cannot express an opinion because the scope of our work has been so restricted".

Circumstances giving rise to both adverse and disclaimer audit opinions will be looked at in the examples contained in the final section of this chapter.

ISA 701 again offers guidance on how each of these opinions should be reported. Illustrations of how to report an adverse or a disclaimer of opinion are shown below. These should be shown in the separate auditor's opinion paragraph within the auditor's report:

Pervasive — modified

Disagreement on Accounting Policies—Inadequate Disclosure—Adverse Opinion

"We have audited … (remaining words are the same as illustrated in the introductory paragraph – see paragraph 60 of ISA 700).

Management is responsible for … (remaining words are the same as illustrated in the management's responsibility paragraph – see paragraph 60 of ISA 700).

Our responsibility is to … (remaining words are the same as illustrated in the auditor's responsibility paragraphs – see paragraph 60 of ISA 700).

(Paragraph(s) discussing the disagreement.)

In our opinion, because of the effects of the matters discussed in the preceding paragraph(s), the financial statements do not give a true and fair view of (or do not present fairly, in all material respects,) the financial position of ABC Company as of December 20, 19X1, and of its financial performance and its cash flows for the year then ended in accordance with International Financial Reporting Standards."

Pervasive — modified

Limitation on Scope—Disclaimer of Opinion

"We were engaged to audit the accompanying financial statements of ABC Company, which comprise the balance sheet as of December 31, 20X1, and the income statement, statement of changes in equity and cash flow statement for the year then ended, and a summary of significant accounting policies and other explanatory notes.

Management is responsible for … (remaining words are the same as illustrated in the management's responsibility paragraph – see paragraph 60 of ISA 700).

[Omit the sentence stating the responsibility of the auditor.]

(The paragraph discussing the scope of the audit would either be omitted or amended according to the circumstances.)

(Add a paragraph discussing the scope limitation as follows:

We were not able to observe all physical inventories and confirm accounts receivable due to limitations placed on the scope of our work by the Company.)

Because of the significance of the matters discussed in the preceding paragraph, we do not express an opinion on the financial statements."

Auditors must make all reasonable efforts to find evidence they need before issuing a modified report. A modified report is very much a last resort.

Summarisation of options:

Audit Issue	Pervasive	Material but not Pervasive
Disagreement	Adverse opinion	Except for
Limitation of Scope	Disclaimer of opinion	Except for

Examples of Situations where Each Type of Report Could be Issued

Wording of Report	Examples where it Might Apply
"Except for" – issues are material but not pervasive	• Inadequate provision for doubtful debts • Non-disclosure in accounts of going concern problems • Disagreement over the value of some part of stocks
"Except for" – limitation of scope	• Limited evidence available for cash purchases • Records lost due to accidental flooding
Disclaimer of opinion – limitation of scope	• Appointed as auditors after year end and unable to attend stocktake where stock is a material balance in the financial statements • Directors deny access to information regarding significant claims against the company • No cashflow forecasts/cash budgets prepared so the going concern assumption cannot be considered
Adverse opinion	• Failure to comply with Companies Acts, accounting standards etc., without acceptable reason • Significant concern about the company's ability to continue as a going concern • Significant uncertainties regarding the existence, ownership, valuation or recording of assets and liabilities to a material extent

15.7 Matters That Do Not Affect the Auditor's Opinion – Emphasis of Matter

Another variation to the standard form of unqualified audit report which may arise relates to an "Emphasis of Matter" paragraph which does not modify the auditor's opinion. This is an additional paragraph included immediately after the opinion paragraph in the auditor's report.

This paragraph is used to highlight to users of financial statements that there is a serious concern over the company's ability to continue in operation for the next 12 months (i.e. its ability to continue as a going concern) or that there is a significant uncertainty impacting on the financial statements whose resolution is dependent on future events. It is important to note, however, that the inclusion of such a paragraph **does not** constitute a qualification of the audit opinion.

There are some circumstances which arise where the outcome of such circumstances are far from clear but the company has taken all steps it reasonably can to provide for any costs, if appropriate, and to draw attention of readers of the accounts to it, usually through the inclusion of a note to the accounts.

The auditors are therefore not qualifying their report but are drawing attention to the disclosure in the notes to the financial statements.

ISA 701 indicates clearly when such a modification of the auditor's report is required (Paragraphs 6 and 7). It states that for such a modification to be made there must be either:

- A material going concern problem
- A significant uncertainty (other than a going concern problem), the resolution of which is dependent upon future events and which may affect the financial statements. An uncertainty is more likely to be significant where the range of possible outcomes is sufficiently great as to have the potential for fundamentally affecting the entity.

Examples of situations which may give rise to an emphasis of matter paragraph in practice include:

- Ability to continue as a going concern dependent on the outcome of renegotiation and extension of loans with the company's bankers
- Completeness of provisions may be understated depending on the outcome of a particular court case involving the company. Although the auditor has been provided with all information relating to the case and agrees that the calculation of the provision represents a best estimate, due to the size of the potential liability in a worst case scenario it is appropriate to draw this to the attention of the users of the financial statements.

ISA 700 (paragraph 30) says that, when auditors use an emphasis of matter paragraph, they should:

- Use the heading "Emphasis of Matter" and place the paragraph immediately following the opinion paragraph
- Make clear reference in the paragraph to the matter being emphsised and to where in the financial statements the relevant disclosures describing the matter can be found
- Indicate that the auditor's report is not qualified in respect of the matter being emphasized.

ISA 701 (Paragraph 8) illustrates how an emphasis of matter paragraph should be reported:

> Without qualifying our opinion we draw attention to Note X to the financial statements. The Company is the defendant in a lawsuit alleging infringement of certain patent rights and claiming royalties and punitive damages. The Company has filed a counter action, and preliminary hearings and discovery proceedings on both actions are in progress. The ultimate outcome of the matter cannot at present be determined, and no provision for any liability that may result has been made in the financial statements.

15.8 Qualified Audit Reports and Dividends

Where a qualified audit opinion has been given on the last annual financial statements, the company's ability to make a distribution by reference to those financial statements could be in doubt unless they receive a statement from their auditors expressed under section 49c of the 1983 Companies Act concerning the company's ability to make a distribution (See details in Practice Note 9 Reports by Auditors under Company Legislation in the Republic of Ireland).

15.9 Further Disclosures within the Auditor's Report

Inconsistent other information

Audited financial statements are often bound together with other unaudited statements and reports which make up the entity's annual report. Some of the information such as the directors' report may be required by statute. Auditors have a statutory responsibility under the Companies Act 2006 to consider whether the directors' report is consistent with the financial statements.

ISA 720 The Auditor's Responsibility in Relation to Other Information in Documents Containing Audited Financial Statements, requires auditors to obtain details regarding the other information which the entity intends to include in its annual report, which may have a bearing on the information contained in the audited financial statements.

The auditor is required to read the other information contained in the annual report for material inconsistency with the audited financial statements and for material misstatements of fact before signing the audit report.

A material inconsistency may cause a reader to doubt the reliability of the information contained in the audited financial statements and the reliability of the audit opinion. A material misstatement of fact might undermine the credibility of the document containing the audited financial statements.

Where the auditor becomes aware of an inconsistency between the audited financial statements and the other information contained in the annual report, it is necessary to consider whether it is the financial statements themselves or the other information which requires revision and the matter should be discussed with management.

If it happens to be the financial statements that require revision and management refuse to make the necessary revisions, a qualified "except for" or adverse opinion should be expressed, depending on how material and pervasive the matter is.

If it is the other information that requires revision and management refuse, the auditor should consider including an emphasis of matter paragraph to describe the material inconsistency or use their right to address shareholders at the annual general meeting. Before doing this, the auditor should seek legal advice as to the possible consequences of taking such actions. As a last resort the auditors should resign and use the required statement issued on resignation to inform the shareholders

Under UK and Irish company law if the directors' report is inconsistent with the financial statements the auditor must make reference to these inconsistencies in their audit report. The audit report should be modified, without qualifying the audit opinion, by modifying the opinion on the directors' report.

(See ISA (UK and Ireland) 720 (Revised) Section B – The Auditor's Statutory Reporting Responsibility in relation to the Directors' Report.)

15.10 Listed Companies – Special Provisions

There are particular situations which apply to companies listed on the London Stock Exchange. Detailed guidance is provided in the APB Bulletin 2006/5, The Combined Code on Corporate Governance: Requirements of Auditors under the Listing Rules of the Central Bank and Financial Services Authority of Ireland and the Irish Stock Exchange.

- Auditors are required to comment on the disclosures made in the Directors' Remuneration Report. They will include a refererence to this in the second paragraph of their opinion.
- All companies whose shares are listed on the stock exchange are required to comply with the combined code on Corporate Governance or explain in the financial statements why they haven't complied. This is part of the listing rules.

If in the opinion of the auditor, the company has not complied and furthermore has not given any reason for non compliance in the financial statements, the auditors will comment on the non-compliance and non-disclosure in their report under the heading "Other Matter" which immediately follows the opinion paragraph.

If the auditors do not include a comment than the reader can assume all is well.

- As part of the Listing Rules, the directors are also required to review the internal control environment and include a statement on this review in the accounts. If the review reveals non-compliance, the auditors do not qualify their opinion but include a statement under "Other Matter" paragraph after the opinion section.

15.11 Other Reporting Considerations

15.11.1 Group reporting issues and consolidated financial statements

ISA 600 Special Considerations – Audits of Group Financial Statements, states that the Group or Principal Auditor is responsible for providing the audit opinion on the group financial statements and on the individual financial statements of components audited by the group auditor.

However, audit responsibility for the individual components of the group that may be audited by a different auditor (known as a component or other auditor) is that of the component auditor.

Where joint auditors are appointed to audit a component the responsibility and legal liability for the audit opinion is joint and several and is signed by both firms.

When forming the opinion on the consolidated financial statements the group auditor will need to consider the impact of any modifications to the audit report on the financial statements of the components. The group auditor will consider the materiality of the component, the form and reasons for the modification and its overall significance in the context of the financial statements.

For example, a qualified audit report on the financial statements of a component may be insignificant in terms of the consolidated financial statements and as a result would not be reported at group level.

It is necessary that the group auditor carry out procedures with respect to the work of the component auditor. If the group auditor concludes that reliance cannot be placed on the work of the component auditor and is unable to perform alternative procedures or the component auditor is uncooperative, there is a limitation on the scope of the audit (ISA 600 Para 16).

15.11.2 Comparatives

ISA 710, Comparatives distinguishes between

(a) Corresponding Figures – these are the amounts and other disclosures for the prior period that are presented on a comparative basis with those of the current period and as such form an integral part of the current period's financial statements; and
(b) Comparative Financial Statements - these are the amounts and other disclosures of the preceding period included for comparison with the financial statement of the current period, but do not form part of the current period financial statements.

15.11.3 Corresponding figures

The auditor has the responsibility to obtain sufficient appropriate audit evidence to ensure that the corresponding figures meet the requirements of the applicable financial reporting framework and that:

- Corresponding figures agree with the amounts and other disclosures presented in the prior period
- Accounting policies used for comparatives are consistent with those of the current period.

During the current year audit, if the auditor becomes aware of a possible misstatement in the corresponding figures further additional procedures should be performed. The circumstances considered in ISA 710 are:

1. Prior period opinion was modified Provided the matter has been resolved and has been properly addressed in the current year's financial statements an unqualified opinion is expressed for the current year.

It may be appropriate to include an emphasis of matter paragraph if the matter is material to the current period. However, the auditor's report for the current year will require a modification in respect of the corresponding figures if it is unresolved and 1) also results in a modification of the auditor's report in relation to the current year's financial information or 2) the unresolved matter, while not resulting in a modification of the auditor's report in the current period's financial information, is material in relation to the amounts and disclosures in the current period.

2. Subsequent Events A material misstatement may be discovered in the prior period financial statements on which the auditor has already expressed an unqualified opinion.

Where the financial statements have been revised and re-issued with a new auditor's report, the auditor should be satisfied that the corresponding figures agree with the new financial statements and if so issue an unqualified opinion.

If the prior periods financial statements were not revised, but the corresponding figures have been properly restated in the current period's financial statements, the auditors should issue an unqualified opinion and include an emphasis of matter paragraph.

The auditors should express a modified opinion with respect to the corresponding figures if the prior periods financial statements were not revised and the misstatement has not been properly restated in the current period's financial statements

15.11.4 Change of auditors

Where the previous year's financial statements were audited by a different auditor, there may be additional reporting requirements in some jurisdictions. The incoming auditor may be required to indicate:

- That the financial statements of the prior period were audited by another auditor and provide the name of the auditor
- The date of the previous auditor's report
- The form of opinion expressed by the former auditors
- The substantive reasons for any modification.

This information is not required under UK or Irish legislation and accordingly no reference to the existence of previous auditors or their reports is made.

15.11.5 Unaudited prior period financial statements

ISA 710 (Para 18) states that if prior period financial statements were not audited the incoming auditor should clearly state that the corresponding figures are unaudited. The auditor still has a responsibility to seek sufficient appropriate audit evidence to assess if the corresponding figures are misstated. If the auditor identifies a material misstatement, the auditor should request management to make the necessary revisions. If management refuse, the auditor should modify their audit report appropriately.

15.11.6 Comparative financial statements

ISA 710 (Para 20) requires the auditor to obtain sufficient appropriate audit evidence to ensure that the comparative financial statements meet the requirements of the applicable financial reporting framework.

When comparatives are presented as comparative financial statements ISA 700 requires the auditors to issue a report in which the comparatives are specifically identified because the auditor's opinion is on the financial statements of each period presented. For example, the auditor may express a modified opinion or include an emphasis of matter paragraph with the comparative financial statements for one period whilst expressing an unqualified opinion in those for another period.

15.11.7 Initial engagements

ISA 510, Initial Engagements – Opening Balances, requires the newly appointed auditor to obtain sufficient appropriate audit evidence that

- The opening balances do not contain misstatements that materially affect the current period's financial statements
- The prior period's closing balances have been correctly brought forward to the current period
- Appropriate accounting policies are consistently applied or changes to accounting policies have been properly accounted for and adequately presented and disclosed.

Where prior-period financial statements were audited by another auditor the current auditor may place reliance on the work of the predecessor auditor by reviewing their work papers and considering their professional competence and independence.

Other procedures may need to be performed where the prior period's financial statements were unaudited. The sufficient or lack thereof of appropriate audit evidence may lead to reporting conclusions as follows

- If the auditors were unable to obtain sufficient appropriate audit evidence, there is a limitation on the scope of the audit work. Accordingly, a qualified (except for) opinion or disclaimer of opinion should be issued as appropriate.
- If accounting policies are not consistently applied or the change has not been properly accounted for or adequately disclosed, a qualified (except for disagreement) or adverse opinion should be expressed as appropriate.
- Similarly if material misstatements in opening balances affect the current period's financial statements, a qualified (except for disagreement) or adverse opinion should be expressed as appropriate.

15.11.8 Electronic publication of financial statements

APB 2001/1 The Electronic Publication of Auditors' Reports refers to a number of matters which must be considered when a company makes their annual accounts available on their web site, such matters include:

- Where the financial statements are published in a form other than that of pdf, the auditor's report must identify the audited financial statements by name and date instead of using page numbers
- References to financial reporting and to auditing standards should specify the relevant nationality
- Documents loaded to the web must be identical to the hard copy version
- Hyperlinks should not inappropriately link the auditor's report to unaudited information.

15.11.9 Subsequent events and revised accounts

Where a material misstatement is discovered after the financials statements and auditor's report have been issued, revised financial statements may have to be re-issued, in this case the auditors should issue a new audit report on the revised financial statements.

15.11.10 Summary financial statements, interim reports and preliminary announcements

Auditors may have involvement in the issue of other reports such as summary financial statements which are issued in some countries by large quoted companies, some listed companies may also issue interim financial statements and may request the auditors to carry out a review of the interim financial information and provide a conclusion on it. The auditor has no statutory responsibility for the interim financial reports.

Where management wish to announce preliminary results the auditors are required to communicate their consent to the publication.

QUESTIONS

Self-test Questions

1. Who places reliance on the external auditor's report?
2. List the various forms of modified and unmodified audit reports.
3. What action must the auditor take where a material event takes place after the date of the audit report but before the financial statements are issued?

Review Questions

(See Solutions to Review Questions at the end of this textbook.)

Question 15.1

MERLIN Ltd ("MERLIN") is an established client of your audit firm. A broad range of professional services are provided to MERLIN. The audit fieldwork for the year ended 31 March 2007 was recently completed. Your firm's Cumulative Audit Knowledge and Experience (CAKE) is that there are relatively few audit issues. However, the following points have been noted from the audit:

(1) A repairs provision of €/£500k is included on the balance sheet for future repairs of the distribution warehouse. No contracts have been signed.
(2) From the Information Technology General Controls (ITGC) review, a number of weaknesses with regard to infrastructure security were noted.

(3) A consultancy payment of €/£10k to the brother of the Managing Director of MERLIN was made during the year; this item has not been disclosed in the financial statements.
(4) From a review of the fixed asset additions, the full salary costs of €/£100k relating to two employees have been capitalised. From discussions with management you have ascertained that 50% of the employees' time was spent on the related development project.
(5) A management bonus of €/£225k is provided for in the accounts. This is not due to be paid until July 2007 at which time the accounts will have been signed. The bonus is €/£75k higher than in the prior year without any significant improvement in the performance of the company during the year.

The draft financial statements, which do not contain any adjustments or disclosures relating to the matters above, show the following:

	€/£'000
Turnover	24,568
Profit before tax	1,609
Net current liabilities	(4,802)
Net assets	2,114

Requirement

(a) (i) For each of the points noted from your review, set out in bullet point format the potential audit report implications of each situation if treated individually.

Note *Your answer should explain briefly the reason for each of your opinions.*

(ii) In addition, outline and explain the overall audit opinion that you would provide, if no further adjustments or disclosures were made for the points noted.

NB *No sections of the audit report are to be drafted.*
(b) Outline briefly how an auditor would audit salary costs that have been capitalised as part of a development project.
(c) Prepare the accounting adjustments that you would recommend for the repairs provision and the capitalised employee costs for inclusion in the schedule of unadjusted differences.

Question 15.2

DENARK Ltd ("DENARK") is a client of your firm. You are audit senior on the assignment and the audit fieldwork for the year ended 31 December 2007 has just been completed. The following figures have been extracted from the draft financial statements.

	Year Ended 31 December	
	2007	**2006**
	€/£'000	**€/£'000**
Turnover	11,650	16,540
Profit before tax	331	590
(Loss)/profit after tax	(445)	540
Dividends proposed	(220)	(220)
(Loss)/profit for the year	(665)	320
Profit forward	810	490
Retained profit	145	810
Net assets	7,420	7,980

Audit Issues

1. On 6 December 2007 the creditor's ledger system unexpectedly crashed. As a result, all transactions posted to the creditor's ledger on 6 December were lost. The accounts payable team re-posted these transactions on 7 December 2007 once the system error had been corrected. The re-posting exercise was successful and proved to be reliable.
2. In January 2008, one of DENARK's customers went into liquidation owing the company €/£350,000 at that point. DENARK made sales of €/£100,000 to the customer in January 2008. The directors have indicated that the full debt will be provided for in the financial statements for the year ended 31 December 2008.
3. Bonus costs of €/£7,500 paid to two directors of the company have not been disclosed in the financial statements of DENARK. This information is commercially sensitive and the Finance Director has indicated that they are not willing to disclose the bonus costs.

Requirement

(a) Set out, in bullet point format, the potential implications for the audit report of DENARK for the year ended 31 December 2007 arising from the audit ISSUES 1-3 noted above. (*You may assume that DENARK is not willing to make changes to its draft financial statements.*)
(b) In respect of ISSUE 2 alone, draft any changes to the audit report that you deem necessary.
(*Note – Candidates are not required to draft a full audit report. However, paragraphs where a potential impact is noted should be drafted.*)

Question 15.3

WORLDGLOBAL Ltd ("WORLDGLOBAL") is a client of your firm. The company has experienced significant trading difficulties in recent years. The audit fieldwork for the year ended 31 December 2004 has been completed and the following matters have been noted.

1. WORLDGLOBAL was in breach of its bank covenant arrangements at the year end. Management have indicated that a meeting has been held with the company's bankers at which they received assurances from the bank that none of the financing facilities of the company would be withdrawn. WORLDGLOBAL has a 5-year term loan of €/£1.2 million and an overdraft facility of €/£500,000.
2. The company has a financial investment of €/£100,000 in a company called HORIZON Ltd ("HORIZON"). The investment does not qualify HORIZON to be treated as a subsidiary of WORLDGLOBAL. The client is unable to provide evidence to support the carrying value of the investment.

The results of WORLDGLOBAL for the year ended 31 December 2004 show a turnover of €/£16.2 million, a loss before tax of €/£1 million and net assets of €/£5.5 million. There were no other matters noted from the audit work performed.

Requirement

(a) Draft a memorandum to the audit partner setting out the audit evidence you would seek to obtain in respect of the matters noted and outlining their potential impact on the auditor's report.
(b) Assuming that the financial investment issue cannot be resolved, draft the qualification paragraph(s) required for the situation described.
(c) At the planning meeting for this engagement, the audit partner noted that the standard of audit reports being drafted by the audit seniors was poor. List a number of checks that should be performed on audit reports prior to signing.

Appendix 15.1 – Example of Unqualified Audit Report – Republic of Ireland Company

> **For use in the following circumstances:**
>
> - *Irish/UK GAAP used for company financial statements*

INDEPENDENT AUDITOR'S REPORT TO THE MEMBERS OF XYZ LTD

We have audited the financial statements of [name of entity] for the year ended [date] which comprise [state the primary statements such as the Profit and Loss Account, Balance Sheet, the Cash Flow Statement, the Statement of Total Gains and Losses] and the related notes. These financial statements have been prepared under the accounting policies set out therein.

This report is made solely to the company's members, as a body, in accordance with section 193 of the Companies Act 1990. Our audit work has been undertaken so that we might state to the company's members those matters we are required to state to them in an auditor's report and for no other purpose. To the fullest extent permitted by law, we do not accept or assume responsibility to anyone other than the company and the company's members as a body for our audit work, for this report, or for the opinions we have formed.

Respective Responsibilities of Directors and Auditors

The directors' responsibilities for preparing the Directors' Report and the financial statements in accordance with applicable law and the accounting standards issued by the Accounting Standards Board and promulgated by the Institute of Chartered Accountants in Ireland (Generally Accepted Accounting Practice in Ireland), are set out in the Statement of Directors' Responsibilities on page [number].

Our responsibility is to audit the financial statements in accordance with relevant legal and regulatory requirements and International Standards on Auditing (UK and Ireland).

We report to you our opinion as to whether the financial statements give a true and fair view and have been properly prepared in accordance with the Companies Acts 1963 to 2009. We also report to you whether, in our opinion: proper books of account have been kept by the company; whether at the balance sheet date, there exists a financial situation requiring the convening of an extraordinary general meeting of the company; and whether the information given in the Directors' Report is consistent with the financial statements.

In addition, we state whether we have obtained all the information and explanations necessary for the purposes of our audit, and whether the company's financial statements are in agreement with the books of account.

We also report to you if, in our opinion, any information specified by law regarding directors' remuneration and directors' transactions is not disclosed and, where practicable, include such information in our report.

We read the Directors' Report and consider implications for our report if we become aware of any apparent misstatements within it.

Basis of Audit Opinion

We conducted our audit in accordance with International Standards on Auditing (UK and Ireland) issued by the Auditing Practices Board. An audit includes examination, on a test basis, of evidence relevant to the amounts and disclosures in the financial statements. It also includes an assessment of the significant estimates and judgments made by the directors in the preparation of the financial statements, and of whether the accounting policies are appropriate to the company's circumstances, consistently applied and adequately disclosed.

We planned and performed our audit so as to obtain all the information and explanations which we considered necessary in order to provide us with sufficient evidence to give reasonable assurance that the financial statements are free from material misstatement, whether caused by fraud or other irregularity or error. In forming our opinion we also evaluated the overall adequacy of the presentation of information in the financial statements.

Opinion

In our opinion:

- the financial statements give a true and fair view, in accordance with Generally Accepted Accounting Practice in Ireland, of the state of the company's affairs as at [date] and of its [profit]/[loss] for the year then ended;
- the financial statements have been properly prepared in accordance with the Companies Acts 1963 to 2009.

We have obtained all the information and explanations which we consider necessary for the purposes of our audit. In our opinion proper books of account have been kept by the company. The financial statements are in agreement with the books of account.

In our opinion the information given in the directors' report is consistent with the financial statements.

The net assets of the company, as stated in the company balance sheet, are more than half of the amount of its called-up share capital and, in our opinion, on that basis there did not exist at … a financial situation which under Section 40 (1) of the Companies (Amendment) Act, 1983 would require the convening of an extraordinary general meeting of the company.

F Torres & Co
Chartered Accountants　　　　　　　　　　　　[Address]
Registered Auditor　　　　　　　　　　　　　　[Date]

Appendix 15.2 – Example of Unqualified Audit Report – Northern Ireland Company

> **For use in the following circumstances:**
>
> - *Irish/UK GAAP used for company financial statements*

We have audited the financial statements (the "financial statements") of [name of entity] for the year ended [date] which comprise the group profit and loss account, the group and parent company balance sheet, the group cash flow statement, the group statement of total recognised gains and losses, the group note of historical cost profits and losses and the related notes. These financial statements have been prepared under the accounting policies set out therein.

This report is made solely to the company's members, as a body, in accordance with Article 243 of the Companies (Northern Ireland) Order 1986. Our audit work has been undertaken so that we might state to the company's members those matters we are required to state to them in an auditor's report and for no other purpose. To the fullest extent permitted by law, we do not accept or assume responsibility to anyone other than the company and the company's members as a body for our audit work, for this report, or for the opinions we have formed.

Respective Responsibilities of Directors and Auditors

The directors' responsibilities for preparing the financial statements in accordance with applicable law and UK Accounting Standards (UK Generally Accepted Accounting Practice) are set out in the Statement of Directors' Responsibilities on page X.

Our responsibility is to audit the financial statements in accordance with relevant legal and regulatory requirements and International Standards on Auditing (UK and Ireland).

We report to you our opinion as to whether the financial statements give a true and fair view and are properly prepared in accordance with the Companies (Northern Ireland) Order 1986. We also report to you whether in our opinion the information given in the directors' report is consistent with the financial statements.

In addition we report to you if, in our opinion, the company has not kept proper accounting records, if we have not received all the information and explanations we require for our audit, or if information specified by law regarding directors' remuneration and other transactions is not disclosed.

We read the directors' report and consider the implications for our report if we become aware of any apparent misstatements within it.

Basis of Audit Opinion

We conducted our audit in accordance with International Standards on Auditing (UK and Ireland) issued by the Auditing Practices Board. An audit includes examination, on a test basis, of evidence relevant to the amounts and disclosures in the financial statements. It also includes an assessment of the significant estimates and judgments made by the directors in the preparation of the financial statements, and of whether the accounting policies are appropriate to the group's and company's circumstances, consistently applied and adequately disclosed.

We planned and performed our audit so as to obtain all the information and explanations which we considered necessary in order to provide us with sufficient evidence to give reasonable assurance that the financial statements are free from material misstatement, whether caused by fraud or other irregularity or error. In forming our opinion we also evaluated the overall adequacy of the presentation of information in the financial statements.

Opinion

In our opinion:

- the financial statements give a true and fair view, in accordance with UK Generally Accepted Accounting Practice, of the state of the group's and the parent company's affairs as at [date] and of the group's[profit]/[loss] for the year then ended;
- the financial statements have been properly prepared in accordance with the Companies (Northern Ireland) Order 1986; and
- the information given in the directors' report is consistent with the financial statements.

F Torres & Co
Chartered Accountants [Address]
Registered Auditor [Date]

Appendix 15.3 – Extracts from Audited Financial Statements – Independent Auditor's Report to the Shareholders of Large Company Limited

We have audited the financial statements of the Large Company Limited for the period ended 31 December 20X8 which comprise the Profit and Loss Account, Statement of Total Recognised Gains and Losses, Balance Sheet, Cash Flow Statement and the related notes. These financial statements have been prepared under the accounting policies set out therein.

Respective Responsibilities of Directors and Auditors

As described in the Statement of Directors' Responsibilities the company's directors are responsible for the preparation of the financial statements in accordance with applicable law and generally accepted accounting practice in Ireland including the accounting standards issued by the Accounting Standards Board and published by the Institute of Chartered Accountants in Ireland (Generally Accepted Accounting Practice).

Our responsibility is to audit the financial statements in accordance with relevant legal and regulatory requirements and International Standards on Auditing (UK and Ireland).

This report is made solely to the company's members, as a body, in accordance with section 193 of the Companies Act 1990. Our audit work has been undertaken so that we might state to the company's members those matters we are required to state to them in an auditor's report and for no other purpose. To the fullest extent permitted by law, we do not accept or assume responsibility to anyone other than the company and the company's members as a body for our audit work, for this report, or for the opinions we have formed.

We report to you our opinion as to whether the financial statements give a true and fair view in accordance with Generally Accepted Accounting Practice in Ireland and are properly prepared in accordance with the Companies Acts, 1963 to 2009. We also report to you whether in our opinion: proper books of account have been kept by the company, whether at the balance sheet date, there exists a financial situation requiring the convening of an Extraordinary General Meeting of the company and whether the information given in the directors' report is consistent with the financial statements. In addition, we state whether we have obtained all the information and explanations necessary for the purposes of our audit and whether the financial statements are in agreement with the books of account.

We report to the members if, in our opinion, any information specified by law regarding directors' remuneration and directors' transactions is not disclosed and, where practicable, include such information in our report.

We read the directors' report[5] and consider the implications for our report if we become aware of any apparent misstatements within it.

Basis of Audit Opinion

We conducted our audit in accordance with International Standards on Auditing (UK and Ireland), issued by the Auditing Practices Board. An audit includes examination, on a test basis, of evidence relevant to the amounts and disclosures in the financial statements. It also includes an assessment of the significant estimates and judgements made by the directors in the preparation of the financial statements, and of whether the accounting policies are appropriate to the company's circumstances, consistently applied and adequately disclosed.

We planned and performed our audit so as to obtain all the information and explanations which we considered necessary in order to provide us with sufficient evidence to give reasonable assurance that the financial statements are free from material misstatement, whether caused by fraud or other irregularity or error. In forming our opinion we also evaluated the overall adequacy of the presentation of information in the financial statements.

Opinion

In our opinion the financial statements:

- give a true and fair view, in accordance with Generally Accepted Accounting Practice in Ireland, of the state of the Company's affairs as at 31 December 20X8 and of its profit/(loss) and cash flows for the period then ended; and
- have been properly prepared in accordance with the requirements of the Companies Acts, 1963 to 2009.

We have obtained all the information and explanations that we consider necessary for the purposes of our audit. In our opinion, proper books of account have been kept by the Company. The financial statements are in agreement with the books of account.

In our opinion, the information given in the directors' report[6] is consistent with the financial statements.

---

[5] Include reference to any other information that is presented with the financial statements (including a detailed profit and loss if relevant).
[6] Include reference to any other information that is presented with the financial statements (including a detailed profit and loss if relevant).

The net assets of the company, as stated in the balance sheet, are more than half of the amount of its called-up share capital and, in our opinion, on that basis there did not exist at 31 December 20X8 a financial situation which, under section 40(1) of the Companies (Amendment) Act, 1983 would require the convening of an extraordinary general meeting of the Company[7].

Opinion & Co. [state date] *20X9*
Chartered Accountants
Registered Auditors
Balance Street
Dublin 2

---

[7] If the net assets were less than €250,000 the wording of this paragraph would change to 'The net assets of the Company as stated in the balance sheet on page 22, are less than half of the amount of its called-up share capital and in our opinion on that basis there did exist at 31 December 20X8 a financial situation which, under section 40(1) of the Companies (Amendment) Act 1983, may require the convening of an extraordinary general meeting of the Company'.

Appendix A

Past Exam Questions Reference List

(Auditing and Assurance)

Ethics
CA Proficiency 2 Sample Paper 1 Q1f
CA Proficiency 2 Sample Paper 2 Q2d
CA Proficiency 2 Summer 2009 Q1
Professional Three Summer 2007 Q1a
Professional Three Summer 2006 Q1e
FAE Autumn 2007 Q1a
FAE Autumn 2003 Q1a, Q1e

Laws and Regulations
CA Proficiency 2 Sample Paper 2 Q2a
Professional Three Autumn 2006 Q1a
Professional Three Summer 2005 Q1c

Tangible Fixed Assets
CA Proficiency 2 Summer 2009 Q2b, Q4
Professional Three Summer 2008 Q3
Professional Three Summer 2006 Q3
Professional Three Summer 2005 Q6
FAE Autumn 2005 Q3
FAE Autumn 2004 Q2

Intangible Fixed Assets/Research and Development
Professional Three Summer 2005 Q6
FAE Autumn 2006 Q5

Investments
Professional Three Summer 2007 Q1d
Professional Three Autumn 2006 Q3

Stock and Work in Progress
CA Proficiency 2 Sample Paper 1 Q1c, Q1d, Q1e
CA Proficiency 2 Summer 2009 Q1
Professional Three Summer 2008 Q4
Professional Three Autumn 2008 Q3
Professional Three Autumn 2007 Q3
Professional Three Autumn 2006 Q6
Professional Three Autumn 2005 Q4, Q5
FAE Autumn 2008 Q2
FAE Autumn 2005 Q1d
FAE Autumn 2005 Q4
FAE Autumn 2003 Q4

Sales and Trade Receivables
CA Proficiency 2 Sample Paper 1 Q1a, Q1b
CA Proficiency 2 Sample Paper 2 Q1a, Q1b, Q1e, Q3
CA Proficiency 2 Summer 2009 Q1
Professional Three Autumn 2008 Q4
Professional Three Summer 2007 Q1b, Q3
Professional Three Autumn 2007 Q1b, Q4
Professional Three Summer 2006 Q6
Professional Three Autumn 2006 Q1b
Professional Three Summer 2005 Q4
Professional Three Autumn 2005 Q1e
FAE Autumn 2007 Q2, Q4
FAE Autumn 2006 Q1a
FAE Autumn 2004 Q3
FAE Autumn 2003 Q3, Q5

Bank and Cash In Hand/Bank Loan
CA Proficiency 2 Summer 2009 Q1, Q2e, Q4
Professional Three Summer 2007 Q1e

Professional Three Summer 2006 Q3
Professional Three Summer 2005 Q1b, Q2
FAE Autumn 2008 Q5
FAE Autumn 2007 Q4

Purchases and Trade Payables
CA Proficiency 2 Sample Paper 1 Q3
CA Proficiency 2 Sample Paper 2 Q4
Professional Three Autumn 2008 Q6
Professional Three Autumn 2007 Q1a, Q5, Q6
Professional Three Summer 2006 Q4
Professional Three Autumn 2005 Q1c
FAE Autumn 2006 Q5
FAE Autumn 2004 Q5

Payroll
CA Proficiency 2 Summer 2009 Q3
Professional Three Summer 2008 Q6
Professional Three Summer 2007 Q2
Professional Three Autumn 2006 Q1c
Professional Three Summer 2005 Q3
Professional Three Autumn 2005 Q6
FAE Autumn 2005 Q5

Provisions
Professional Three Summer 2008 Q4
Professional Three Autumn 2007 Q2
Professional Three Summer 2006 Q1c, Q4
Professional Three Autumn 2005 Q5

Dividends
Professional Three Summer 2006 Q1b, Q3

Related Parties
Professional Three Summer 2008 Q1a
Professional Three Autumn 2008 Q4
Professional Three Summer 2007 Q6

Professional Three Autumn 2006 Q5
FAE Autumn 2006 Q3

Controls
CA Proficiency 2 Sample Paper 2 Q1c
CA Proficiency 2 Summer 2009 Q2a
Professional Three Summer 2008 Q6
Professional Three Summer 2007 Q5
Professional Three Summer 2006 Q1d, Q5
Professional Three Autumn 2005 Q4, Q6
FAE Autumn 2007 Q4

Audit Planning
FAE Autumn 2006 Q3
FAE Autumn 2004 Q4

Engagement Letter
Professional Three Autumn 2008 Q1b
Professional Three Summer 2005 Q1a
FAE Autumn 2005 Q1a

Audit Sampling
CA Proficiency 2 Sample Paper 2 Q1d
Professional Three Autumn 2007 Q1c
Professional Three Summer 2006 Q1a
Professional Three Autumn 2005 Q1a

Materiality
Professional Three Summer 2007 Q6
Professional Three Summer 2006 Q5, Q6
FAE Autumn 2007 Q1d
FAE Autumn 2004 Q1a

Audit Risk
CA Proficiency 2 Sample Paper 2 Q2b, Q2c
Professional Three Summer 2008 Q5

Professional Three Autumn 2008 Q5, Q6
Professional Three Summer 2007 Q5, Q6
Professional Three Autumn 2006 Q4
Professional Three Summer 2005 Q1d
Professional Three Autumn 2005 Q5
FAE Autumn 2008 Q3

Audit Completion
Professional Three Autumn 2008 Q2
Professional Three Summer 2007 Q4
Professional Three Autumn 2007 Q5
Professional Three Autumn 2006 Q1e

Audit Reports
CA Proficiency 2 Summer 2009 Q4
CA Proficiency 2 Sample Paper 1 Q2
CA Proficiency 2 Sample Paper 2 Q3
Professional Three Summer 2008 Q2
Professional Three Autumn 2008 Q2
Professional Three Summer 2007 Q2
Professional Three Autumn 2007 Q2
Professional Three Summer 2006 Q2
Professional Three Autumn 2006 Q2
Professional Three Summer 2005 Q2
Professional Three Autumn 2005 Q2
FAE Autumn 2008 Q2
FAE Autumn 2007 Q3
FAE Autumn 2006 Q2
FAE Autumn 2005 Q2
FAE Autumn 2004 Q1c, Q2
FAE Autumn 2003 Q2

Subsequent Events and Going Concern
Professional Three Summer 2008 Q1e
FAE Autumn 2008 Q4
FAE Autumn 2004 Q1b

Management Representations/Letter of Representation
Professional Three Summer 2008 Q1b
Professional Three Autumn 2006 Q5
Professional Three Autumn 2005 Q1b
FAE Autumn 2003 Q1b

Fraud
Professional Three Autumn 2007 Q1d
Professional Three Summer 2005 Q4
Professional Three Autumn 2005 Q3
FAE Autumn 2008 Q5

Internal Audit
CA Proficiency 2 Sample Paper 2 Q5
Professional Three Summer 2008 Q1c
FAE Autumn 2008 Q1b

Miscellaneous
CA Proficiency 2 Summer 2009 Q2c, Q2d
CA Proficiency 2 Sample Paper 1 Q4
Professional Three Autumn 2008 Q1a, Q1c, Qd
Professional Three Autumn 2008 Q1e
Professional Three Summer 2007 Q1c
Professional Three Autumn 2007 Q1e
Professional Three Summer 2005 Q1e, Q5
Professional Three Autumn 2005 Q1d
FAE Autumn 2008 Q1a, Q1c, Q1d
FAE Autumn 2007 Q1b, Q1c
FAE Autumn 2006 Q1b, Q1c, Q1d, Q4
FAE Autumn 2005 Q1b, Q1c
FAE Autumn 2004 Q1d
FAE Autumn 2003 Q1c, Q1d

Appendix B

LARGE COMPANY LIMITED

Directors' Report and Financial Statements
Year Ended 31 December 20X8

Registered Number (Specify)

October 2008

NOTE: REQUIREMENT FOR LARGE COMPANY STATUS

To qualify the company must satisfy at least two of the following criteria for two years in a row.

Turnover greater than:	€15,236,856
Gross assets greater than:	€7,618,428
Employees greater than:	250

(Note: These Financial Statements are for Illustrative Purposes only, and are NOT intended as the Study Source for Financial Reporting.)

LARGE COMPANY LIMITED

Directors' Report and Financial Statements

CONTENTS

Directors, Advisors and other Information	353
Directors' Report	354
Statement of Directors' Responsibilities	359
Independent Auditor's Report to the Shareholders of Large Company Limited	360
Statement of Accounting Policies	363
Comprehensive Income Statement	369
Statement of Financial Position	371
Cash Flow Statement	373
Notes (forming part of the financial statements)	375

LARGE COMPANY LIMITED

Directors, Advisors and other Information[8]

Directors (Executive)	Thomas Hogan (Chairperson)
	Mark Hogan (Managing director)
	Kevin Byrne
	Linda Connolly
	Deirdre Hogan
	David Stuart (British)
Directors (Non-Executive)	Francis Day
	John Night
	Fred Afternoon (American)
Secretary	Timothy Byrne
Auditors	Opinion & Co
	Chartered Accountants
	Balance Street
	Dublin 2
Bankers	General Bank Limited
	Money Street
	Dublin 9
Solicitors	Legal and Co
	Barrister Street
	Dublin 2
Registered office	123 Principal Street
	Dublin 5

---

[8] There are no requirements to provide this information; however, it is good practice to do so.

LARGE COMPANY LIMITED

DIRECTORS' REPORT

The directors present their report and audited financial statements for the year ended 31 December 20X8.

Principal Activities and Review of the Business

The company's principal activity continued to be the manufacture of furniture.

Turnover has increased by 41% to €280,250,000. The directors believe that this trend will continue for the foreseeable future as a new line of furniture has effectively broken into the luxury market. Demand for this range has also increased in foreign countries with €42,625,000 of the increase being attributable to exports.

All other ranges are selling successfully and are expected to do so for the coming year.

Future Developments

The directors are hopeful that the new line of furniture will expand into the United States. At present all sales are either in Ireland or in the United Kingdom. Market research has indicated that turnover could as much as double in the next three years if the major retail outlets in the United States accept the range. Negotiations are ongoing and should be completed by July.

Results and Dividends

	€000
The profit for the financial year amounted to	60,394
It is recommended that this be dealt with as follows:	
Ordinary dividends	
– dividends paid [*State date*] 20X8 of 30.34c per share	(25,500)
	34,894
Profit and loss account at beginning of year	50,360
Reserve movements	200
Profit and loss account at end of year	85,454

Research and Development

The company is involved in the development of two new ranges of furniture for future commercial production. These ranges are the "Authentic Mexican Pine range" and the

"Mahogany Cast Iron range". An additional employee has been employed to investigate these designs and to develop accompanying accessories.

Branch operations

The company has overseas branch operations as follows

Name of branch	**Country of operation**
Wood kit	Northern Ireland
Wood fit	England

Directors

The present membership of the Board is set out on page 3. Details of directors' shareholdings, related interests and transactions are provided in note 6 to the financial statements.

Mr Kevin Byrne and Ms Linda Connolly retire from the board by rotation in accordance with the Articles of Association and, being eligible, offer themselves for re-election. Ms Deirdre Hogan was appointed to the board during the year and, in accordance with the Articles of Association, retires and offers herself for election. Mr John Hogan retired from the board during the year and the directors express their sincere appreciation for his contribution to the company over the many years he served as a director.

Political Donations[9]

The company made the following disclosable political donations in the current year:

- Party A   –   €60,000
- Party B   –   €60,000
- Party C   –   €5,500

Principal Risks and Uncertainties

Financial risk management objectives and policies

The company uses financial instruments throughout its business. It uses derivatives to manage interest rate and currency exposures and to achieve a desired profile of borrowings. All transactions in derivatives are designed to hedge against risks without engaging in speculative transactions. The core risks associated with the company's financial instruments (i.e. its interest-bearing loans and debt, cash and cash equivalents, short-dated liquid investments

---

[9] Disclosure required if the cumulative donations in the year to which the report relates exceeds €5,078.95 (section 26 of the Electoral Acts, 1896 to 1977).

and finance leases, on the operational level trade receivables and payables) are currency risk, interest rate risk, credit risk and liquidity risk. The board reviews and agrees policies for the prudent management of these risks as follows:

Currency risk

The company's activities in the UK are conducted primarily in sterling, this results in low levels of currency transaction risk, variances affecting operational activities in this regard are reflected in operating costs or in cost of sales in the profit and loss account in the years in which they arise. The principal foreign exchange risk is translation-related arising from fluctuations in the euro value of the company's net investment in sterling. The company manages its borrowings, where practical and cost effective, to partially hedge the foreign currency assets. Hedging is done using currency borrowings in sterling (same currency as the assets), or by using currency swaps.

Finance and interest rate risk

The company's objective in relation to interest rate management is to minimise the impact of interest rate volatility on interest costs in order to protect recorded profitability. A long-term strategy for the management of the exposure considers the amount of floating rate debt that is anticipated over the period and the sensitivity of the interest charge on this debt to changes in interest rates, and the resultant impact on reported profitability. The company has a mix of fixed and floating rate debt and uses interest rate swaps to exchange at predetermined intervals the difference between fixed and floating interest rates by reference to a predetermined notional principal. The majority of these swaps are regarded as hedging financial instruments.

Liquidity and cash flow risk

The company's objective is to maintain a balance between the continuity of funding and flexibility through the use of borrowings with a range of maturities. The company's policy is to ensure that sufficient resources are available either from cash balances, cash flows and near cash liquid investments to ensure all obligations can be met when they fall due. To achieve this the company ensures that its liquid investments are in highly rated counter-parties; when relevant it limits the maturity of cash balances and borrows the majority of its debt needs under term financing.

Credit risk

The fair value of the company's financial assets are provided in the following table:

	20X8	20X7
	€000	€000
Cash and cash equivalents	104,200	105,530
Trade and other receivables	15,200	17,500

Derivative financial instruments	2,290	1,630
Other financial assets	44,450	21,350
	166,140	146,010

Other financial assets includes holding in listed and unlisted share capital.

The company's credit risk is predominantly attributable to its trade debtors. Provisions for bad debts are made based on historical evidence and any new events which might indicate a reduction in the recoverability of cash flows. The company's debtors are made up of a large number of customers and hence the risk of default is reduced. In addition, the company uses credit insurance when allowing credit to more risky customers, requests letters of credit, parent company guarantees or cash collateral.

The company may be exposed to credit-related loss in the event of non-performance by counterparties in respect of cash and cash equivalents and derivative financial instruments. However, the company considers the risk to be negligible as it only transacts with financial institutions that are rated as investment grade or above. Information on the derivative financial instruments is provided in note 25. This note has been prepared in compliance with FRS 29 *Financial Instruments, Disclosures*.

Payment of Creditors

The directors acknowledge their responsibility for ensuring compliance with the provisions of the EC (Late Payment) Regulation 2002. Procedures have been implemented to identify the dates upon which all invoices fall due for payment and to ensure that payments are made by such dates. Such procedures provide reasonable assurance against material non-compliance with the regulations.

Books of Account

The measures taken by the directors to ensure compliance with the requirements of Section 202, Companies Act, 1990, regarding proper books of account are the implementation of necessary policies and procedures for recording transactions, the employment of competent accounting personnel with appropriate expertise[10] and the provision of adequate resources[11] to the financial function. The books of account of the company are maintained at [*address/es*].

---

[10] Directors will consider whether the accounting personnel:
  1. Are suitably qualified – for example, hold a professional qualification as an accountant or accounting technician.
  2. Have the knowledge and experience needed to understand the business and how its particular circumstances impact the books of account.

[11] Directors consider whether the relevant personnel are able, without undue difficulty, to ascertain at all times the financial position and results of the company.

Post-Balance Sheet Events

Details of important events affecting the company which have taken place since the end of the financial year are given in note 33 to the financial statements.

Auditors

In accordance with Section 160 (2) of the Companies Act, 1963, the auditors, Opinion & Co., Chartered Accountants, will continue in office.

On behalf of the board

| Thomas Hogan | Mark Hogan | [*state date*] 20X9 |
| *Director* | *Director* | |

LARGE COMPANY LIMITED

STATEMENT OF DIRECTORS' RESPONSIBILITIES[12,13]

The directors are responsible for preparing the Annual Report and the financial statements in accordance with applicable Irish law and generally accepted accounting practice in Ireland including the accounting standards issued by the Accounting Standards Board and published by the Institute of Chartered Accountants in Ireland.

Irish Company law requires the directors to prepare financial statements for each financial year which give a true and fair view of the state of affairs of the company and of the profit or loss of the company for that period. In preparing those financial statements, the directors are required to:

- select suitable accounting policies and then apply them consistently;
- make judgements and estimates that are reasonable and prudent;
- prepare the financial statements on the going concern basis unless it is inappropriate to presume that the company will continue in business.

The directors confirm that they have complied with the above requirements in preparing the financial statements.

The directors are responsible for keeping proper books of account which disclose with reasonable accuracy at any time the financial position of the company and to enable them to ensure that the financial statements are prepared in accordance with accounting standards generally accepted in Ireland and with Irish statute comprising the Companies Acts, 1963 to 2009. They are also responsible for safeguarding the assets of the company and, hence, for taking reasonable steps for the prevention and detection of fraud and other irregularities.

The directors are responsible for the maintenance and integrity of the corporate and financial information included on the company's website. Legislation in Ireland governing the preparation and dissemination of financial statements may differ from legislation in other jurisdictions.[14]

---

[12] It can be included in the directors' report or separate as shown above. If it is not disclosed in the annual report then the directors' responsibilities must be detailed in the auditor's report.

[13] The new "Compliance Policy Statement" and the "Annual Compliance Statement" as required by the Companies (Auditing and Accounting) Act 2003 have not been commenced at this stage for large entities.

[14] It is assumed that large company limited makes its financial statements available on its website.

INDEPENDENT AUDITOR'S REPORT TO THE SHAREHOLDERS OF LARGE COMPANY LIMITED

We have audited the financial statements of Large Company Limited for the period ended 31 December 20X8 which comprise the Comprehensive Income Statement and Balance Sheet, Cash Flow Statement and the related notes. These financial statements have been prepared under the accounting policies set out therein.

Respective Responsibilities of Directors and Auditors

As described in the Statement of Directors' Responsibilities the company's directors are responsible for the preparation of the financial statements in accordance with applicable law and generally accepted accounting practice in Ireland including the accounting standards issued by the Accounting Standards Board and published by the Institute of Chartered Accountants in Ireland (Generally Accepted Accounting Practice).

Our responsibility is to audit the financial statements in accordance with relevant legal and regulatory requirements and International Standards on Auditing (UK and Ireland).

This report is made solely to the company's members, as a body, in accordance with section 193 of the Companies Act 1990. Our audit work has been undertaken so that we might state to the company's members those matters we are required to state to them in an auditor's report and for no other purpose. To the fullest extent permitted by law, we do not accept or assume responsibility to anyone other than the company and the company's members as a body, for our audit work, for this report, or for the opinions we have formed.

We report to you our opinion as to whether the financial statements give a true and fair view in accordance with Generally Accepted Accounting Practice in Ireland and are properly prepared in accordance with the Companies Acts, 1963 to 2009. We also report to you whether in our opinion: proper books of account have been kept by the company, whether at the balance sheet date, there exists a financial situation requiring the convening of an Extraordinary General Meeting of the company and whether the information given in the directors' report is consistent with the financial statements. In addition, we state whether we have obtained all the information and explanations necessary for the purposes of our audit and whether the financial statements are in agreement with the books of account.

We report to the members if, in our opinion, any information specified by law regarding directors' remuneration and directors' transactions is not disclosed and, where practicable, include such information in our report.

We read the directors' report[15] and consider the implications for our report if we become aware of any apparent misstatements within it.

Basis of Audit Opinion

We conducted our audit in accordance with International Standards on Auditing (UK and Ireland), issued by the Auditing Practices Board. An audit includes examination, on a test basis, of evidence relevant to the amounts and disclosures in the financial statements. It also includes an assessment of the significant estimates and judgements made by the directors in the preparation of the financial statements, and of whether the accounting policies are appropriate to the company's circumstances, consistently applied and adequately disclosed.

We planned and performed our audit so as to obtain all the information and explanations which we considered necessary in order to provide us with sufficient evidence to give reasonable assurance that the financial statements are free from material misstatement, whether caused by fraud or other irregularity or error. In forming our opinion we also evaluated the overall adequacy of the presentation of information in the financial statements.

Opinion

In our opinion the financial statements:

- give a true and fair view in accordance with Generally Accepted Accounting Practice in Ireland, of the state of the Company's affairs as at 31 December 20X8 and of its profit/(loss) and cash flows for the period then ended; and
- have been properly prepared in accordance with the requirements of the Companies Acts, 1963 to 2009.

We have obtained all the information and explanations that we consider necessary for the purposes of our audit. In our opinion, proper books of account have been kept by the Company. The financial statements are in agreement with the books of account.

In our opinion, the information given in the directors' report[16] is consistent with the financial statements.

The net assets of the company, as stated in the balance sheet, are more than half of the amount of its called-up share capital and, in our opinion, on that basis there did not exist at 31 December 20X8 a financial situation which, under section 40(1) of the Companies

---

[15] Include reference to any other information that is presented with the financial statements (including a detailed profit and loss if relevant).
[16] Include reference to any other information that is presented with the financial statements (including a detailed profit and loss if relevant).

(Amendment) Act, 1983, would require the convening of an extraordinary general meeting of the Company[17].

Opinion & Co. [state date] 20X9
Chartered Accountants

Registered Auditors
Balance Street
Dublin 2

---

[17] If the net assets were less than €250,000 the wording of this paragraph would change to 'The net assets of the Company as stated in the balance sheet on page 22, are less than half of the amount of its called-up share capital and in our opinion on that basis there did exist at 31 December 20X8 a financial situation which, under section 40(1) of the Companies (Amendment) Act 1983, may require the convening of an extraordinary general meeting of the Company'.

LARGE COMPANY LIMITED

STATEMENT OF ACCOUNTING POLICIES
(for the year ended 31 December 20X8)

The following accounting policies have been applied consistently in dealing with items which are considered material in relation to the company's financial statements[18].

Basis of Preparation

The financial statements have been prepared on the going concern basis and in accordance with accounting standards generally accepted in Ireland and Irish statute comprising the Companies Acts, 1963 to 2009. Accounting Standards generally accepted in Ireland in preparing financial statements giving a true and fair view are those published by the Institute of Chartered Accountants in Ireland and issued by the Accounting Standards Board.

Revenue

Revenue is stated net of trade discounts, VAT and similar taxes and derives from the provision of goods falling within the company's ordinary activities.

Goodwill

Goodwill represents the excess of the cost of an acquisition over the fair value of the identifiable net assets acquired at the date of acquisition. After initial recognition, goodwill is stated at cost less any accumulated impairment losses, with the carrying value being reviewed for impairment at least annually, and more frequently if events or changes indicate that the carrying value may be impaired.

Other Intangible Assets

Intangible assets acquired separately from a business are capitalised at cost. They are amortised using the straight-line basis over their estimated useful lives. For example, the cost of a patent for a new design of furniture is amortised over the term of the patent, which is 3 years on a straight-line basis.

---

[18] There are no changes to any accounting policy in the year (or the prior year). If a change had occurred a brief explanation of why the new accounting policy is thought more appropriate, the effect of the prior-period adjustment on the results of the preceding period, and an indication of the effect of the change on the results for the current period is required. If it is not practicable to provide the information on the results of both years, a statement of that fact, together with the reasons, should be disclosed.

In all cases intangible assets are reviewed for impairment at the end of the first full financial year following acquisition and in other periods if events or changes in circumstances indicate that the carrying value may not be recoverable.

Investment Properties

Investment properties are recognised using the fair value model, revalued annually and are not depreciated or amortised. This treatment is a departure from the requirement of Company Law to provide depreciation on all fixed assets, which have a limited useful life. However, these investment properties are not held for consumption but for investment. The directors believe that the policy of not providing depreciation is necessary in order for the financial statements to give a true and fair view, since the current value of investment properties, and changes to that current value, are of prime importance rather than the calculation of annual depreciation.

Changes in fair value are recognised in the comprehensive income statement.

Property, Plant and Equipment

All tangible fixed assets are initially recorded at historic cost. Freehold land and buildings (all non-specialised properties) are revalued on the basis of fair values.

Revaluation gains are recognised in other comprehensive income.

Revaluation losses caused by a clear consumption of economic benefits are recognised in other comprehensive income to the extent that there is a revaluation surplus relating to the asset. Beyond this the loss is recognised as an expense in the comprehensive income statement.

Finance costs directly attributable to the construction of freehold buildings are capitalised as part of the cost of these assets. The capitalisation rate used is the weighted average rate of general borrowing outstanding during the period.

Depreciation

Depreciation is provided on all tangible fixed assets, other than freehold land and investment properties, at rates calculated to write off the cost or valuation, less estimated residual value, of each asset systematically over its expected useful life, as follows:

Freehold buildings	– straight-line over 50 years
Leasehold land and buildings	– straight-line over the term of the lease
Plant and machinery	– reducing balance over 5 to 15 years
Motor vehicles	– reducing balance over 5 years

The carrying values of tangible fixed assets are reviewed annually for impairment in periods if events or changes in circumstances indicate the carrying value may not be recoverable.

Available for Sale Securities

The company usually holds certain equity securities (listed and unlisted) which are classified as available-for-sale and are measured at fair value, less incremental direct costs, on initial recognition. At the reporting period end the investments are revalued to fair value and any increase in value is credited to equity. Impairments are debited to equity (fair value reserve) to the extent that they were previously credited to equity, with further reductions in value beyond this amount being charged to the comprehensive income statement. When the investment is derecognised (for example on sale) the cumulative revalued amount to that point is released from the fair value reserve to the comprehensive income statement.

Government Grants

Grants are recognised when there is reasonable assurance that the grant will be received and all attaching conditions have been complied with. Grants towards capital expenditure are credited to deferred income and are released to the comprehensive income statement over the expected useful life of the related assets, by equal annual instalments. Grants towards revenue expenditure are released to the comprehensive income statement as the related expenditure is incurred.

Stocks and Work in Progress

Stocks are stated at the lower of cost and net realisable value. In the case of finished goods and work in progress, cost is defined as the aggregate cost of raw material, direct labour and the attributable proportion of direct production overheads based on a normal level of activity. Net realisable value is based on normal selling price, less further costs expected to be incurred to completion and disposal.

Research and Development

Research expenditure is written off to the comprehensive income statement in the year in which it is incurred. Development expenditure is written off in the same way unless the directors are satisfied as to the technical, commercial and financial viability of individual projects. In this situation, the expenditure is deferred and amortised over the period during which the company is expected to benefit.

Leasing and Hire Purchase Commitments

Assets held under finance leases and hire purchase contracts are capitalised in the balance sheet and are depreciated over their useful lives with the corresponding lease or hire purchase obligation being capitalised as a liability. The interest element of the finance lease rentals is charged to the comprehensive income statement over the period of the lease and represents a constant proportion of the balance of capital repayments outstanding.

Operating lease rentals are charged to the comprehensive income statement on a straight-line basis over the lease term.

Provisions for Liabilities

Provisions for the expected legal costs are charged against profits when an action against the company commences. The effect of the time value of money is not material, therefore the provisions are not discounted.

Income Taxes

Current tax assets and liabilities are measured at the amount expected to be recovered or paid to the taxation authorities, based on tax rates and laws that are enacted or substantively enacted by the balance sheet date.

Deferred income tax is recognized using the balance sheet liability method, providing for temporary differences between the tax bases and the accounting bases of assets and liabilities. Deferred tax is calculated on an undiscounted basis at the tax rates that are expected to apply in the period when the liability is settled or the asset is realised, based on tax rates and laws enacted or substantively enacted at the balance sheet date.

Foreign Currencies

Functional and presentation currency

Items included in the financial statements are presented in euros, the currency of the primary economic environment in which the entity operates (the "functional currency").

The principal exchange rates used for the translation of results, cash flows and balance sheets into euro were as follows:

	20X8	20X7
	€1=Stg£	€1=Stg£
Average	0.682	0.673
Year end	0.698	0.690

Transactions and balances

Transactions in foreign currencies are recorded at the rate ruling at the date of the transaction. Monetary assets and liabilities denominated in foreign currencies are retranslated at the rate of exchange ruling at the balance sheet date or the contracted rate. All differences are taken to the comprehensive income statement. Translation differences are disclosed separately in a "foreign currency reserve", within equity reserves.

Dividends

Dividends to the company's equity shareholders (holders of ordinary shares) are recognised as a liability of the company when approved by the company's shareholders. Preference share dividends are cumulative and cannot be waived, therefore they are treated in the same manner as debt interest and are accrued for, if not paid when due.

Derivative Financial Instruments

The company users foreign exchange contracts, interest rate swap contracts and commodity price contracts to hedge the risks of changes in foreign currency exchange rates, interest rates and commodity prices. These derivatives are stated at fair value.

The fair value of forward exchange contracts and commodity contracts is calculated by reference to current forward exchange rates for contracts with similar maturity profiles and equates to the market price at the balance sheet date (i.e. the present value of the quoted forward price). The fair value of interest rate swaps is the present value of future cash flows, estimated using forward rates from third-party market price quotations.

Changes in the fair value of derivative financial instruments which are designated at effective hedges of future cash flows are recognised directly in equity and the ineffective portion is recognised immediately in the income statement. Amounts deferred in equity are recognised in the comprehensive income statement in the same period in which the hedged item affects net income or expense.

Changes in the fair value of derivative financial instruments that do not qualify for hedge accounting are recognised in the comprehensive income statement as they arise.

Hedge accounting is discontinued when the hedging instrument expires or is sold, terminated or exercised, or no longer qualifies for hedge accounting. At that time, any cumulative gain or loss on the hedging instrument recognised in equity is kept in equity until the hedged transaction occurs. If a hedged transaction is no longer expected to occur, the net cumulative gain or loss recognised in equity is transferred to the comprehensive income statement.

Pension Costs

The company operates both defined benefit and defined contribution schemes. The asset recognised in the balance sheet represents the fair value of the scheme assets offset by the present value of the scheme liabilities.

Defined contribution scheme

Pension contributions in respect of defined contribution schemes for employees are charged to the comprehensive income statement as they become payable in accordance with the rules of the scheme. The assets are held separately from those of the company in an independently administered fund. Differences between the amounts charged in the comprehensive income statement and payments made to pension funds are treated as assets or liabilities.

Defined benefit scheme

For defined benefit retirement benefit plans, the cost of providing benefits is determined using the Projected Unit Credit Method, with actuarial valuations being carried out at each balance sheet date. Actuarial gains and losses that exceed 10 per cent of the greater of the present value of the company's defined benefit obligation and the fair value of plan assets as at the end of the prior year are amortised over the expected average remaining working lives of the participating employees. Past service cost is recognised immediately to the extent that the benefits are already vested, and otherwise is amortised on a straight-line basis over the average period until the benefits become vested.

The retirement benefit obligation recognised in the balance sheet represents the present value of the defined benefit obligation as adjusted for unrecognized actuarial gains and losses and unrecognised past service cost, and as reduced by the fair value of the plan assets. Any asset resulting from this calculation is limited to unrecognised actuarial losses and past service cost, plus the value of available refunds in future contributions to the plan.

Stock Compensation Scheme

Certain employees have been granted stock options with an exercise price less than the quoted market price on the date of grant. This is recorded as deferred compensation within shareholders' equity and recognised in the profit and loss account over the vesting period (three years) of the stock options. To hedge the related exposure the company buys, or transfers from existing portfolios, the number of shares necessary to satisfy all potential outstanding obligations under the plan.

Capital Instruments

Shares are included in shareholders' funds. Other instruments are classified as liabilities if not included in shareholders funds and if they contain an obligation to transfer economic benefits. The finance cost recognised in the comprehensive income statement in respect of capital instruments other than equity shares is allocated to periods over the term of the instrument at a constant rate on the carrying amount.

Issue Costs of Capital Instruments

The cost of issue of preference shares and debentures are charged to the comprehensive income statement on a straight-line basis over the life of the instrument. A corresponding amount is transferred from reserves to the share premium account.

LARGE COMPANY LIMITED

COMPREHENSIVE INCOME STATEMENT

for the year ended 31 December 20X8

	Notes	20X8 €'000	20X7 €'000
Revenue	1	280,250	198,500
Cost of sales		(140,250)	(120,800)
Gross profit		140,000	77,700
Other operating income		750	700
Investment revenue	3	350	330
Distribution costs		(23,000)	(20,000)
Administration costs		(35,000)	(34,000)
Profit/(loss) on sale of tangible fixed assets	2	420	(120)
Loss on disposal of available-for-sale investments	2	(120)	–
Impairment of investment property		(10,000)	–
Finance costs	4	(550)	(550)
Profit before tax		72,850	24,060
Income tax expense	10	(12,456)	(8,500)
Profit for the year	29	60,394	15,560
Other comprehensive income			
Unrealised surplus on revaluation of investment property		–	10,000
Impairment of revalued investment property		(10,000)	–
Unrealised deficit on revaluation of freehold property		(17,200)	–
Actuarial gain on market value of the defined benefit pension scheme's assets and liabilities (note 8)		200	80
Currency translation effects on foreign borrowings		(200)	150
Fair value movement on effective cash flow financial instruments		100	(200)

Income tax on other comprehensive income	–	–
Other comprehensive income net of tax	(27,100)	10,030
Total comprehensive income for the year	33,294	25,590

Thomas Hogan   Mark Hogan   [*state date*] 20x9
Director   *Director*

LARGE COMPANY LIMITED

STATEMENT OF FINANCIAL POSITION

as at 31 December 20X8

	Notes	20X8 €'000	20X7 €'000
ASSETS			
Non-current assets			
Property, plant and equipment	13	130,050	140,500
Other intangible assets	12	1,150	1,140
Derivative financial instruments	25	1,900	11,460
Financial assets	14	12,200	110,200
Pension asset		1,200	1,000
		246,500	254,300
Current assets			
Inventories	15	49,774	35,020
Trade and other receivables	16–17	15,200	17,500
Derivative financial instruments	25	390	170
Available for sale investments	18	4,200	5,000
Cash and other cash equivalents		104,200	105,530
		173,764	163,220
Total assets		420,264	417,520
EQUITY AND LIABILITIES			
Equity attributable to owners			
Capital and Reserves			
Share capital	28	84,050	78,160
Share premium account	29	2,990	570
Retained earnings	29	85,454	50,360
Other components of equity	29	1,400	28,700
Total equity		173,894	157,790

Non-current liabilities

Long-term borrowing	20	20,350	27,560
Other liabilities	20	89,590	89,070
Long-term provisions	24	750	500
Total non-current liabilities		**110,690**	**117,130**

Current liabilities

Trade and other payables	19	109,320	114,650
Short-term borrowing	19	4,250	9,650
Other	19	19,420	15,560
Current tax payable	19	2,690	2,740
Total current liabilities		135,680	142,600
Total liabilities		246,370	259,730
Total equity and liabilities		**420,264**	**417,520**

Approved by the directors on (*specify date*) 20X9

On behalf of the board
Thomas Hogan   Mark Hogan
Director   *Director*

LARGE COMPANY LIMITED

CASH FLOW STATEMENT

for the year ended 31 December 20X8

	Notes	20X8 €'000	20X7 €'000
Net cash inflow from operating activities	31	148,931	83,360
Income tax paid		(13,086)	(7,420)
Net cash generated by operating activities		135,845	75,940
Cash flows from investing activities			
Interest received		120	130
Dividends received		230	200
Purchase of property, plant and equipment		(117,250)	(102,300)
Purchase of available-for-sale investments (net)		(22,120)	–
Purchase of other non-current assets		(510)	(200)
Receipts from the sale of non-current assets		29,715	31,200
Receipt of government grant		2,000	1,000
Decrease/(increase) in short-term loan notes		2,000	(1,000)
Decrease in current asset investments		800	1,000
Net cash used by investing activities		(105,015)	(69,970)
Cash inflow before financing		30,830	5,970
Cash flow from financing activities			
Interest paid		(450)	(460)
Equity dividends paid		(25,500)	(10,000)
Issue of ordinary share capital		8,436	–
Share issue costs		(36)	–
Repayment of long-term loans		(7,210)	(5,000)
Repayment of capital element of finance leases and hire purchase contracts		(151,500)	(78,000)

New finance lease obligations	150,000	42,800
Net cash movement in derivative financial instruments	(500)	200
Net cash used by financing activities	(26,760)	(50,460)
Net increase/(decrease) in cash and cash equivalents	4,070	(44,490)
Cash and cash equivalents at beginning of period	95,880	140,370
Cash and cash equivalents at end of period	99,950	95,880

LARGE COMPANY LIMITED

NOTES (*FORMING PART OF THE FINANCIAL STATEMENTS*)

1. Revenue and Segmental Analysis[19]

The company operates in one industry and within two geographical markets, Ireland and the United Kingdom.
Area of activity

	Ireland		United Kingdom		Total	
	20X8	20X7	20X8	20X7	20X8	20X7
	€000	€000	€000	€000	€000	€000
Revenue by origin						
Continuing	168,150	129,025	112,100	69,475	280,250	198,500
Revenue by destination						
Continuing	180,000	140,000	100,250	58,500	280,250	198,500
Profit						
Continuing	68,714	24,674	22,476	13,286	91,190	37,960
Common costs						8,840	13,950
Operating profit						82,350	24,010
Exceptional items						(9,700)	(120)
Investment and other income						200	170
Profit on ordinary activities before taxation						72,850	24,060

---

[19] If operating in more than one class of business disclose this information for each class. In addition, if part of a group, disclose total sales, intersegment sales and sales to third parties, with comparatives.

Net assets
Continuing   190,728   186,180   63,042   46,170   253,770   232,350

Unallocated net
  liabilities   (81,076) (75,560)
Total net assets   172,694   156,790

Unallocated net liabilities comprise some dividends, taxation and net debt.

2. Exceptional Items

	20X8	20X8	20X7
	€000	€000	€000
Recognised in arriving at operating profit			
Bad debts		(1,000)	—
Recognised below operating profit			
Profit/(loss) on sale of tangible fixed assets	420		(120)
Impairment of investment property	(10,000)		
(Loss) on disposal of fixed asset investments	(120)		—
		(9,700)	
		(10,700)	(120)

Details of the impairment of the investment property is disclosed in note 14 to the financial statements.

The company also disposed of a rare cutting machine. This transaction resulted in the above exceptional gain of €420,000.

Shares costing €1,700,000 were also disposed off, resulting in an exceptional loss of €120,000.

3. Investment Revenue

	20X8 €000	20X7 €000
Available-for-sale fixed asset investment income	210	209
Available-for-sale current asset investment income	75	71
Other investment income	10	9
Net return from defined benefit pension scheme (note 8)	20	11
Bank interest receivable	30	23
Other interest receivable and similar income	5	7
	350	330
Of which derived from listed investments	215	205

4. Finance Costs

	20X8 €000	20X7 €000
On bank loans, overdrafts and other loans wholly repayable within 5 years	95	98
On other loans	15	19
Mark to market of designated fair value hedges and related debt*	5	8
Finance lease interest in respect of finance leases and hire purchase contracts	18	20
Finance costs in respect of completed freehold building	12	15
On overdue tax	5	-
Dividends on preference shares	300	300
Additional finance costs of financial liabilities	100	90
	550	550

* The company uses interest rate swaps to convert fixed rate debt to floating rate debt. Fixed rate debt which has been converted to floating rate debt using interest rate swaps is stated in the balance sheet at adjusted fair value to reflect movements in the underlying interest rates. The movement in this adjustment, together with the offsetting movement in the fair value of the swaps, is taken to the profit and loss account each year.

5. Statutory and Other Information

	20X8 €000	20X7 €000
Operating profit is stated after charging/ (crediting):		
Depreciation and amounts written off assets[20]:		
Depreciation of tangible fixed assets owned	48,580	42,200
Depreciation of tangible fixed assets held under finance leases	32,625	31,300
	81,205	73,500
Amortisation of development costs (see below: also included in research and development)	250	225
Amortisation of patents	200	200
	450	425
Exceptional item - Impairment in value of investment property	10,000	–
Total depreciation, amortisation and impairment in value of fixed assets	91,705	73,975
Exchange differences	25	23
Provision for legal costs charged	50	15
Provision for legal costs released	(15)	–
Operating lease rentals	800	800
Government grants amortised	(1,500)	(850)

	20X8 €000	20X7 €000
Auditor's remuneration:		
Ireland audit services	45	42
United Kingdom audit services	11	10
	56	52
Research and development:		
Amortisation of deferred development expenditure	250	225
Expenditure written off	1,800	1,530
Total research and development	2,050	1,755

---

[20] If appropriate – where there is a change in useful life, or change in estimate of residual value or a revaluation during the period which has had a material impact on depreciation or amortisation of a fixed asset, the effects should be explained and identified.

6. Directors' Remuneration and Transactions

6a. Directors remuneration

Staff costs include the following in respect of directors of the company:

	20X8 €000	20X7 €000
Fees	250	235
Amounts paid to third parties for the service of directors	25	20
Company pension contributions to money purchase schemes	45	36
Pensions to former directors	15	5
Amounts receivable under long-term incentive schemes	15	25
Compensation for loss of office (note 6h)	10	-
	360	321
	No.	*No.*
The number of directors for whom benefits accrued under the money purchase scheme during the year were:	6	6
The number of directors for whom retirement benefits are accruing under defined benefit schemes amounted to:	1	1

6b. Loans to directors

Included in "Other debtors" (note 17) is a loan to a director, Deirdre Hogan, to purchase a house. The loan is permitted by the Companies Act 1990, to enable Deirdre Hogan to carry out her duties as director. It is an unsecured interest-free loan repayable in monthly instalments.

	20X8 €	20X7 €
At 1 January 20X8	58,000	66,000
Monies advanced by company during the year	25,000	30,000
Amount repaid during the year	(23,000)	(38,000)
At 31 December 20X8	60,000	58,000

The maximum amount outstanding during the year was €62,000 (20X7 - €68,000).

An amount of €20,000 is included in debtors in respect of goods supplied at favourable rates by the company to Mr Byrne. The total arm's-length value of the transaction was €22,000. The whole amount has been paid since the balance sheet date. The maximum amount outstanding from Mr Byrne to the company at any time during the year was €5,000.

6c. Directors and secretary and their interests[21]

The directors at 31 December 20X8 and their interests in the share capital of the company were as follows:

	At 31 December 20X8		At 1 January or on Subsequent Appointment	
	Ordinary Shares	Preference Shares	Ordinary Shares	Preference Shares
Thomas Hogan	26,601,000	100,000	26,600,000	100,000
Mark Hogan	130,500	-	130,000	-
Kevin Byrne	131,000	-	130,000	-
Linda Connolly	750	-	-	-
Deirdre Hogan	200,250	100,000	200,000	100,000
David Stewart	101,000	-	100,000	-
Timothy Byrne	550,500	-	550,000	-

On 20 February 20X9 Timothy Byrne acquired another 2,000,000 shares in the company, increasing his total holding to 2,550,500 shares. In all other respects the interests of the directors were unchanged as shown above, except for exercising options to purchase shares.

6d. Interests in the share option scheme

The group operates a directors' share option scheme and in addition to the interests disclosed above certain directors have options to acquire shares in Large Company Ltd. Full details are as follows:

---

[21] If the directors do not have any interests in the company a nil statement is required.
An alternative to the above is to disclose particulars of directors' interests in the director's report. Directors' interests include those of their spouses, children and step-children (if under the age of 18).

	Number of Options Over Ordinary Shares of €1 Each in Large Company Limited				Exercise price	Market Price at Date of Exercise	Date from Which Exercisable	Expiry Date
Directors	01/01/08	Granted	Exercised	31/12/08				
T. Hogan	5,000	-	1,000	4,000	€1.10	€1.35	Jan 20X7	Jan 20Y1
M. Hogan	5,000	-	500	4,500	€1.20	€1.40	Jan 20X7	Jan 20Y1
K. Byrne	5,000	-	1,000	4,000	€1.20	€1.37	Jan 20X8	Jan 20Y2
L. Connolly	1,000	-	750	250	€1.10	€1.42	Jan 20X6	Jan 20X9
D. Hogan	5,000	-	250	4,750	€1.05	€1.56	Jan 20X7	Jan 20Y1
D. Stewart		2,000	1,000-	1,000	€1.25	€1.58	Jan 20X9	Jan 20Y1
T. Byrne		1,000	500	500	€1.25	€1.49	Jan 20Y1	Jan 20Y2
	21,000	3,000	10,000	14,000				

No options lapsed during the year. The market price of the shares at 31 December 20X8 was €1.60 and the range during the year was €1.30 to €1.72. See the accounting policy and note 8 for further details of the option scheme.

6e. Controlling party

Thomas Hogan, the chairman of the company, is considered by the directors to be the company's ultimate controlling party as he holds 60% of the ordinary share capital of the company. Included in this are 5,000,000 shares which are held in trust for his children.

6f. Material interests of directors in contracts with the company

The following information relates to transactions between the company and companies in which Thomas Hogan is considered to have an interest:

(a) The Pine Timber Company supplied materials to the value of €3,500,000 (20X7 – €3,000,000) for the pine bedroom range of furniture. The maximum amount outstanding at any time during the year was €300,000. Nothing was outstanding at the year end.
(b) The company has a loan from Wood Timber Company of €200,000 (20X7 – €250,000). This loan is included in bank and other loans (note 21). €50,000 is repayable within one year, the balance being repayable after more than one year.

(All transactions were made at arm's length).

Trading transactions

These are summarised below:

	€000
Aggregate sales to the directors of the company	1,005
Aggregate purchased from the directors of the company (including the €3,500,000 mentioned above)	4,000
Aggregate net amounts due from the directors of the company	60
Aggregate value of all the arrangements with directors at the end of the year expressed as a percentage of the company's relevant assets at the time.	1.1%

All the transactions were made on normal trading terms.

6g. Dividends

Details of the director's shareholdings in the company are set out in the Report of the Directors.

The rates of dividends on all shares are set out in note 11 of the financial statements.

6h. Other

John Hogan retired as director on 30 April 20X8 and was paid compensation for loss of office of €10,000. There were no amounts due to or from John Hogan at the balance sheet date.

During the year security was provided on a bank loan of €4,000 for J. Matthews, a senior officer of the company. The maximum amount owing on the loan in the year was €4,000. The balance on the loan at the year-end was €3,800.

7. Staff Costs

	20X8 €000	20X7 €000
Wages and salaries	9,256	8,856
Social security costs	1,110	954
Pension costs (see note 8)	1,523	1,230
	11,889	11,040

The average number of persons employed by the company (including executive directors) during the year analysed by category, was as follows:

	20X8 No.	20X7 No.
Management	39	37
Administration	56	54
Production	208	198
Research and development	7	3
Sales	23	18
	333	310

Directors and senior management staff are entitled to participate each year in a share option plan without payment if the company achieves, on average, a 5% increase in profitability each year, for the next three years. The benefits consist of the right to buy Large Company Limited shares at a predetermined price. This plan started on 1 August 20X5 and has a rolling seven-year duration, with the rights being vested after three years.

In order to hedge the related exposure the company buys – or transfers from existing treasury portfolios – the number of shares necessary to satisfy all potential outstanding obligations under the plan when the benefit is awarded and holds them until the maturity of the plan or the exercise of the rights.

Movements in the options and the relevant prices are as follows:

Number of Options Over Ordinary Shares of €1 Each in Large Company Limited				Exercise price	Weighted Average Price at Date of Exercise	Date from Which Exercisable	Expiry Date
01/01/X8	Granted	Exercised	31/12/X8[22]				
25,000	–	15,000	10,000	€1.10	€1.35	Jan 20X8	Jan 20Y0
15,000	–	10,000	5,000	€1.20	€1.40	Jan 20X8	Jan 20Y0
15,000	–	7,500	7,500	€1.20	€1.37	Jan 20X8	Jan 20Y0
10,000	–	5,000	5,000	€1.10	€1.42	Jan 20X8	Jan 20X9
15,000	–	2,000	13,000	€1.05	€1.56	Jan 20X8	Jan 20Y0
	200,000	–	200,000	€1.25		Jan 20X9	Jan 20Y2

---

[22] No options were forfeited or expired during the period, otherwise they would have been separately disclosed.

	150,000	-	150,000	€1.25	Jan 20X9	Jan 20Y2
80,000	350,000	39,500	390,500			

The weighted value of the share options granted in the period was 50c. This was measured using a binomial model which incorporated the following assumptions:

	20X8
Weighted average share price	€1.58
Exercise price	€1.25
Expected volatility	17%
Option life (average from date granted)	4 years
Expected dividend	10c per year
Risk-free interest rate	5%

Expected volatility is based on an annualised standard deviation of the continuously compounded rates of return on the share price over time. It is assumed that market conditions will not change materially and the probability of the company achieving the target profitability is estimated at 60%.

Amount included in the wages and salaries expense relating to the bonus accrued for the option compensation scheme is as follows:

	20X8 €000	20X7 €000
Granted 20X8[23]	35	–
Total charge for the period	35	–

8. Pension information

Analysis of the total amount charged to operating profit:

	20X8 €000	20X7 €000
Current service cost	1,338	1,075
Past service cost	150	125
Cost of other post-retirement benefits (note 9)	35	30
Total operating charge (note 7)	1,523	1,230

---

[23] 350,000 options x 50c x 60% = €105,000/3 years until vestment = €35,000 provided each year.

The company operates both defined benefit and defined contribution schemes in Ireland. The majority of the schemes are defined contribution with defined benefit schemes still in existence for those employees who joined before 1985 who did not want to transfer benefits to the contribution scheme.

The total pension cost for the company was €1,338,000 (20X7—€1,075,000) of which €1,200,000 (20X7—€975,000) relates to the defined contribution schemes and €138,000 (20X7—€100,000) to the defined benefit schemes.

Defined contribution scheme

The company operates the defined contribution scheme, Pension Scheme Fund, for its employees. The assets of the scheme are held separately from those of the company in an independently administered fund.

Defined benefit scheme

The pension cost of the defined benefit scheme is assessed on an annual basis in accordance with the advice of qualified actuaries using the projected unit method. The funding policy for this scheme is to make the maximum annual contributions that are deductible for income tax purposes.

A full actuarial valuation was carried out at 31 December 20X7 and updated to 31 December 20X8 by an independent qualified actuary. The major assumptions used by the actuary are as follows:

	At 31/12/X8	At 31/12/X7
Rate of increase in pensionable salaries	4.0%	5.5%
Rate in increase in pensions in payment	5.0%	3.0%
Discount rate	6.0%	7.0%
Inflation assumption	4.1%	3.0%
Life expectancy:	Years	Years
Current pensioners (at age 60) – males	23.1	23.1
Current pensioners (at age 60) – females	25.9	25.9
Future pensioners (at age 60) – males	23.9	23.9
Future pensioners (at age 60) – females	26.6	26.6

The life expectancy assumptions are based on standard actuarial mortality tables and include an allowance for future improvements in life expectancy.

The valuation at 31 December 20X8 shows a net pension asset of €1.2 million (20X7 – €1 million). A 0.1% increase/decrease in the assumed discount rate would decrease/increase the net pension asset by €500,000. A 0.1% increase/decrease in the assumed inflation rate would increase/decrease the net pension liability by €450,000.

The assets and liabilities of the scheme and the expected rate of return are:

	Long-Term Rate of Return Expected at 31/12/X8	Value at 31/12/X8 €000	Long-Term Rate of Return Expected at 31/12/X7	Value at 31/12/X7 €000
Equities	7.2%	1,900	7.0%	1,650
Bonds	5.0%	400	4.9%	350
Property	6.0%	450	7.2%	320
Total market value of assets		2,750		2,320
Present value of scheme liabilities		(1,450)		(1,230)
Surplus in the scheme		1,300		1,090
Related deferred tax liability		(100)		(90)
Net pension asset		1,200		1,000

The expected rate of return on equities is based on the expected average return over the long-term. The expected rate of return on bonds is measured directly from actual market yields for ROI gilts and corporate bonds. The expected return on property is based on predicted rent revenues and increases in the capital value of the properties.

Changes in the market value of assets

	20X8 €000	20X7 €000
Market value of assets at beginning of the year	2,320	2,001
Movement in year:		
Expected return	73	68
Contributions from employer	128	200
Contributions from scheme members	120	80
Benefits paid	(228)	(170)
Actuarial (loss)/gain	337	141
Market value of assets at end of the year	2,750	2,320

The company's contributions to the defined benefit scheme during the year included a special contribution of €80,000 (20X7—€150,000). The company expects to make total contributions to the defined benefit scheme of €60,000 in the next year.

Changes in the market value of liabilities

	20X8 €000	20X7 €000
Value of liabilities at beginning of the year	1,230	1,102
Movement in year:		
Interest cost	53	57
Current service cost	138	100
Contributions from scheme members	120	80
Benefits paid	(228)	(170)
Actuarial loss	137	61
Present value of liabilities at end of the year	1,450	1,230

Analysis of the amount charged to operating profit:

	20X8 €000	20X7 €000
Current service cost	138	100
Past service cost	150	125
Total operating charge	288	225

Analysis of amount credited to other finance income:

	20X8 €000	20X7 €000
Expected return on pension scheme assets	73	68
Interest on pension scheme liabilities	(53)	(57)
	20	11

Analysis of amount recognised in other comprehensive income.

	20X8 €000	20X7 €000
Actual return less expected return on pension scheme assets	337	141
Experience gains and losses arising on the schemes liabilities	(64)	(5)

Changes in assumptions underlying the present value of the scheme liabilities	(73)	(56)
Actuarial gain recognised in other comprehensive income	200	80

The full actuarial valuation at 31 December 20X7 showed an increase in the scheme surplus from €990,000 to €1,090,000. Improvements in benefits costing €58,000 were made in 20X8 and contributions increased to €120,000 (5% of pensionable pay). It has been agreed with the trustees that contributions for the next three years will remain at that level.

History of experience gains and losses

	20X8 €000	20X7 €000	20X6 €000	20X5 €000	20X4 €000
Actuarial gain/(loss) on assets	337	141	(18)	27	(44)
Actuarial gain/(loss) on liabilities	(137)	(61)	3	13	11
Total amount recognised in the statement of total recognised gains and losses	200	80	(15)	40	(33)

	20X8 €000	20X7 €000	20X6 €000	20X5 €000	20X4 €000
Market value of assets	2,750	2,320	2,001	1,980	1,900
Market value of liabilities	(1,450)	(1,230)	(1,102)	(1,180)	(1,350)
Net pension liability	1,300	1,090	899	800	550

Balance sheet amounts

In addition to the amounts included as a provision for pension and similar obligations under provisions for liabilities and charges, the following amounts are included in the balance sheet:

	20X8 €000	20X7 €000
Prepayments and accrued income		
Pension costs prepaid	65	25
Accruals and deferred income		
Other creditors – unpaid contributions	202	166
Accrued "Medical & Golf Fund" contributions	10	8
	212	174

9. Post Retirement Benefits Other than Pension Schemes

The company operates a plan which provides employees with over 30 years' service benefits, other than pensions. The liabilities in respect of these benefits are assessed by qualified independent actuaries, applying the projected unit method. The charge for the year is €35,000 (20X7—€30,000).

	Medical & Golf Fund
Main assumptions	
Discount rate for obligations (% per annum)	8.5%
Inflation rate (% per annum)	5%

10. Income Tax Expense

(a) Analysis of charge in period

	20X8		20X7	
	€000	€000	€000	€000
Current tax:				
ROI corporation tax on profits of the period	12,275		7,628	
Adjustment in respect of previous period[24]	–		–	
	12,275		7,628	
Double taxation relief	(22)		(19)	
Total ROI current tax		12,253		7,609
Foreign tax on income for the period	23		21	
Adjustment in respect of previous period[25]	–		–	
Total foreign current tax		23		21
Total current tax (note 10 (b))		12,276		7,630
Deferred tax:				
Origination and reversal of timing differences		150		830
Effect of increased tax rate on opening liability		27		36
Derivative financial instruments		3		4
Total deferred tax (note 24)		180		870
Tax on profit on ordinary activities		12,456		8,500

---

[24] None in this example
[25] None in this example

The tax effect on the profit and loss account relating to the exceptional items recognised below operating profit is a charge of €90,000 (20X7 – Credit of €36,000).

(b) Factors affecting the tax charge for the period:

The tax assessed for the period is lower than the standard rate of corporation tax in the ROI (31%). The differences are explained below:

	20X8 €000	20X7 €000
Profit on ordinary activities before taxation	72,850	24,060
Profit on ordinary activities multiplied by standard rate of corporation tax in the ROI of 31% (20X7 30%)[26]	22,584	7,218
Effects of:		
Expenses not deducted for tax purposes	864	2,352
Capital allowances for period in excess of depreciation	(9,076)	(1,472)
Utilisation of tax losses	(2,100)	(470)
Rollover relief on profit on disposal of property[27]	–	–
Higher tax rates on overseas earnings	4	2
Adjustment to tax charge in respect of previous periods[28]	–	–
Current tax charge for period (note 10 (a))	1 2,276	7,630

(c) Factors that may affect future tax charges

Based on current capital investment plans, the company expects to continue to be able to claim capital allowances in excess of depreciation in future years but at a slightly lower level than in the current year. The company has now used all brought-forward tax losses, which have significantly reduced tax payments in recent years.

Suggested disclosure where there has been a gain on revaluation.

The company's overseas tax rates are higher than those in Ireland because the profits earned in the United Kingdom are taxed at a rate of 45%. The company expects a

---

[26] Fictional rate change to show disclosures impacted on by a change in rate.
[27] None in this example
[28] None in this example

reduction in future tax rates following a recent announcement that the rate of tax in the United Kingdom is to reduce to 40%[29].

11. Dividends

	20X8 €000	20X7 €000
Equity dividends on ordinary shares[30]		
Dividend paid of 30.34c (20X7 – 12.79c) per share	25,500	10,000
	25,500	10,000

A dividend is proposed of €15,500 (18.44c per share); (20X7: €25,500 (30.34c per share))

12. Other Intangible Assets

	Patents €000	Goodwill €000	Development Costs €000	Total €000
Cost:				
At 1 January 20X8	600	1,000	415	2,015
Additions	–	–	510	510
At 31 December 20X8	600	1,000	925	2,525
Amortisation:				
At 1 January 20X8	200	600	75	875
Provided during the year	200	50	250	500
At 31 December 20X8	400	650	325	1,375
Net book value				
At 31 December 20X8	200	350	600	1,150
At 1 January 20X8	400	400	340	1,140

---

[29] Fictional rates are used.
[30] When relevant, disclose dividend income arising on own shares purchased.

13. Property Plant and Equipment

	Freehold Land and Buildings €000	Plant and Machinery €000	Motor Vehicles €000	Total €000
Cost:				
At 1 January 20X8	400,000	113,625	28,800	542,425
Additions	–	82,250	35,000	117,250
Deficit on revaluation	(355,000)	–	–	(355,000)
Disposals	–	(49,000)	(14,655)	(63,655)
At 31 December 20X8	45,000	146,875	49,145	241,020
Depreciation				
At 1 January 20X8	319,800	61,725	20,400	401,925
Charge for year	18,000	48,705	14,500	81,205
Elimination on revaluation	(337,800)	–	–	(337,800)
Disposals	–	(29,000)	(5,360)	(34,360)
At 31 December 20X8	–	81,430	29,540	110,970
Net book value				
At 31 December 20X8	45,000	65,445	19,605	130,050
At 1 January 20X8	80,200	51,900	8,400	140,500

Freehold land and buildings

Freehold land (€15,000,000) which is not depreciated is included in land and buildings. On 31 December the land was valued at its original cost by the external surveyors (details in next paragraph).

The freehold buildings were valued at €30,000,000 being their value in use, in accordance with the Appraisal and Valuation Manual of the Royal Institution of Chartered Surveyors, on 31 December 20X8 by external professional surveyors, Big Value Valuers and Co., Chartered Surveyors. The property had been revalued to €385,000,000 but by 31 December 20X8 was depreciated to €47,200,000. The sudden decline in value of the freehold buildings was caused by the upsurge of political trouble and the exit of commercial businesses in the local area. The total reduction in the net book value is €17,200,000. The year-end valuation (€30,000,000) is not materially different to the open market value.

Modified historical cost

Particulars relating to revalued land and buildings are given below:

	20X8 €000	20X7 €000
Opening book amount	65,200	95,200
Depreciation	(18,000)	(30,000)
Adjusted book amount	47,200	65,200
Revaluation gain/(loss[48])		
Recognised in the statement of total recognised gains and losses	(17,200)	–
Closing book amount	30,000	65,200

Finance costs

Where applicable finance costs were capitalised at 10% (20X7 – 12%). The cost of Freehold buildings includes €5,000,000 of finance costs, which were capitalised in 20X7. No finance costs were capitalised in 20X8.

Historical cost information for the property included at valuation:

On the historical cost basis, land and buildings would have been included as follows:

	€000
Cost:	
At 1 January 20X8 and 31 December 20X8	100,000
Cumulative depreciation based on cost	
At 1 January 20X8	74,320
Charge for the year	6,500
At 31 December 20X8	80,820
Net book values	
At 1 January 20X8	25,680
At 31 December 20X8	19,180

Other tangible fixed assets are included at cost.

Assets held under finance leases or hire purchase agreements

	Plant and Machinery €000	Motor Vehicles €000	Total €000
Net book values			
At 1 January 20X8	81,500	6,500	88,000
At 31 December 20X8	92,750	17,250	110,000
Depreciation charge for the year			
To 31 December 20X8	31,000	1,625	32,625
To 31 December 20X7	27,000	4,300	31,300

14. Financial Assets

	Investment Properties €000	Available-for-Sale Investments €000	Total €000
Fair value:			
At 1 January 20X8	100,000	10,500	110,500
Additions	–	23,700	23,700
Diminution in value	(20,000)	–	(20,000)
Disposals	–	(1,700)	(1,700)
At 31 December 20X8	80,000	32,500	112,500
Provision for diminution in value			
At 1 January 20X8	–	300	300
Charge for year	–	–	–
Disposals	–	–	–
At 31 December 20X8		300	300
Net book value			
At 31 December 20X8	80,000	31,400	112,200
At 1 January 20X8	100,000	9,400	110,200

Fixed Asset Investments

The balance sheet value of €112,200,000 reflects the market value of the company's investment properties and available for sale investments as at the year end (20X7: €110,200,000). In accordance with the company's accounting policy, these assets are held at fair value. The available-for-sale investments represent an equity stake in an unlisted entity. The stake is classified as available for sale as the company has no power to exercise any influence over the underlying entity.

Investment properties

The investment properties were valued at €80,000,000, being their fair value for existing use, in accordance with the Appraisal and Valuation Manual of the Royal Institution of Chartered Surveyors, on 31 December 20X8 by Big Value Valuers and Co., Chartered Surveyors. This has resulted in an impairment in value to €10,000,000 below the original cost price.

The historical cost and aggregate depreciation based on historical cost calculated at a rate of 5% per annum are as follows:

	€000
Cost	
At 1 January 20X8 and 31 December 20X8	90,000
Cumulative depreciation based on cost	
At 1 January 20X8	18,000
Charge for the year	4,500
At 31 December 20X8	22,500
Net book values	
At 1 January 20X8	72,000
At 31 December 20X8	67,500

True and Fair View Override

Had the investment properties been depreciated in accordance with companies legislation, the reported profit for the year would have been €4,500,000 less and assets and reserves in the balance sheet €12,500,000 lower.

15. Inventories

	20X8 €000	20X7 €000
Raw materials and consumables	9,320	7,770
Work in progress	12,530	10,750
Finished goods and goods in transit	27,924	16,500
	49,774	35,020

There are no material differences between the replacement cost of inventories and the balance sheet amounts.

16. Trade and Other Receivables

Due after One Year

	20X8 €000	20X7 €000
Loan notes	6,000	8,000
Other debtors:		
Called up share capital not paid	685	875
Prepayments and accrued income:		
Pension prepayment	65	25
Other prepayments	1,950	1,350
	8,700	10,250

17. Trade and Other Receivables

Due Within One Year

	20X8 €000	20X7 €000
Loan notes	1,500	1,500
Trade debtors	3,250	4,100
Other debtors	750	600
Prepayments and accrued income	1,000	1,050
	6,500	7,250

"Other debtors" include amounts advanced to finance the acquisition of shares in the company.

Trade receivables are stated net of a provision of €500,000 (20X7—€750,000) for estimated bad debts based on historical experience.

	20X8 €000	20X7 €000
Opening balance	750	700
Increase/(decrease) in provision	(50)	150
Bad debts written off	(200)	(100)
Closing balance	500	750

An aged analysis is utilised to determine the likelihood of payment default.
Aged analysis of trade receivables:

	20X8 €000	20X7 €000
Current (within credit terms)	2,600	3,500
30-60 days	420	350
60-90 days	150	140
Greater than 90 days	80	110
	3,250	4,100

The directors consider the net trade receivable value to be representative of fair value.

18. Available-for-Sale Investments

	20X8 €000	20X7 €000
Other unlisted equity investments	1,200	850
Listed equity investments	3,000	4,150
	4,200	5,000

The unlisted equity investments are recorded at cost. The directors consider that these shares have not diminished in value and that their market value at the balance sheet date is similar to their cost.

The listed equity investments (all of which are listed on the Irish Stock Exchange) are measured at fair value in line with the company's accounting policy.

19. Trade and other Payables: Amounts Falling Due within One Year

	20X8 €000	20X7 €000
Bank and other loans (note 21)	4,250	9,650
Obligations under finance leases and hire purchase contracts (note 22)	2,500	4,000
Derivative financial instruments (note 25)	120	80
Trade payables	109,320	114,650
Bills of exchange payable	150	230
Other creditors	16,150	10,500
Accruals and deferred income	500	750
	132,990	139,860
Tax creditors		
Corporation tax	2,310	2,280
PAYE	100	120
VAT	80	60
Capital Gains tax	120	80
Other tax	30	110
	2,640	2,650
Social welfare (PRSI)	50	90
	2,690	2,740
	135,680	142,600

Trade creditors includes the following:

Due at the year end to suppliers who claim reservation of title	20,000	21,000

20. Creditors: Amounts Falling Due after More than One Year

	20X8 €000	20X7 €000
Bank and other loans (note 21)	20,350	27,560
Obligations under finance leases and hire purchase contracts (note 22)	85,000	85,000

Preference shares	3,000	3,000
Derivative financial instruments (note 25)	70	50
	108,420	115,610
Other creditors		
Government grants (note 23)	1,308	808
Pension commitments	212	174
Other	–	38
	1,520	1,020
	109,940	116,630

21. Bank Loans

	20X8 €000	20X7 €000
Current		
Galway bank loan	1,000	1,000
Dublin bank loan	3,250	8,650
	4,250	9,650
Non-current		
Eurobond	3,750	350
Galway bank loan	14,000	15,000
Dublin bank loan	2,600	12,210
	20,350	27,560
Total Bank Loans	24,600	37,210

Analysis of loans

	20X8 €000	20X7 €000
Not wholly repayable within five years	13,050	17,720
Wholly repayable within five years	11,960	19,990
	25,010	37,710
Issue costs	(410)	(500)
Total	24,600	37,210

Included in current liabilities	4,250	9,650
Included in long-term liabilities	20,350	27,560

Loan Maturity Analysis

	20X8	20X7
	€000	€000
Bank and other loans comprise amounts repayable:		
In one year or less, or on demand	4,250	9,650
Between one and five years	7,300	9,840
After more than five years	13,050	17,720
	24,600	37,210

The Eurobond is secured by a fixed charge on the land and buildings and a floating charge on the other assets of the company. It carries a fixed interest rate of 6.9%.

The Dublin bank loan is repayable in instalments over the next six years. It is subject to a variable interest rate based on EURIBOR. The weighted average interest rate during the year was 4.9% (20X7 – 4.9%).

The Galway bank loan is repayable in instalments over the next 8 years. It has a fixed interest rate for 75% of the loan at 5.5%, with the remainder at EURIBOR plus 2%. The weighted average interest for the period was 5.2% (20X7 – 5.1%).

22. Obligations Under Finance Leases and Hire Purchase Contracts

Analysis and Maturity Schedule

	20X8	20X7
	€000	€000
Repayable within one year	2,500	4,000
Repayable between one and two years	2,500	2,500
Repayable between two and five years	12,000	13,300
Repayable after five years	83,000	82,200
	100,000	102,000
Finance charges and interest allocated to future periods	(12,500)	(13,000)
Total	87,500	89,000
Included in liabilities falling due within one year	2,500	4,000
Included in liabilities falling due after more than one year	85,000	85,000

23. Government Grants Deferred

	Government Grants €000
At 1 January 20X8	808
Grants received during the year	2,000
Amortisation in the year	(1,500)
At 31 December 20X8	1,308

Under agreements between the company and [*state name of agency*] which are dated on various dates between 20X6 and 20Y2, the company has a contingent liability to repay in whole, or in part, grants received amounting to €500,000 (20X7: €300,000) if certain circumstances set out in those agreements occur within [*ten*] years of the date of the agreement.

The agreements to which the company was a party were signed between 20X6 and 20Y2 and the amounts received under those agreements amounted to €800,000 (20X7: €350,000).

24. Provision for Liabilities

	Deferred Tax €000	Legal Costs €000	Post Retirement Benefits €000	Total €000
At 1 January 20X8	250	15	235	500
Charged to profit and loss account	180	50	35	265
Utilised during the year	–	(15)	–	(15)
At 31 December 20X8	430	50	270	750

For details on the movements to the legal costs provision see note 36.

Deferred taxation[31]

	20X8 €000	20X7 €000
Accelerated capital allowances	430	270
Tax losses carried forward	–	(20)
Undiscounted provision for deferred tax	430	250

25. Derivative Financial Instruments

The company's principal risks and uncertainties and the financial risk management objectives and policies used to manage these, including the use of derivative financial instruments to hedge forecasted transactions and the exposure of the company to credit risk, liquidity risk, interest rate risk and cash flow risk are included in the directors' report. Derivative financial instruments recognised as assets and liabilities in the balance sheet are analysed as follows:

20X8	Foreign Exchange Contracts €000	Commodity Swaps €000	Interest Rate Swaps €000	Total €000
Non-current assets	–	1,800	100	1,900
Current assets	100	200	90	390
Current liabilities	(10)	(80)	(30)	(120)
Non-current liabilities	(10)	(30)	(30)	(70)
At 31 December 20X8	80	1,890	130	2,100
20X7				
Non-current assets	–	1,380	80	1,460
Current assets	30	120	20	170
Current liabilities	(10)	(40)	(30)	(80)
Non-current liabilities	(5)	(15)	(30)	(50)
At 31 December 20X7	15	1,445	40	1,500

---

[31] Had the deferred tax balance been an asset then this note would have been classified under debtors, or as a separate subheading of debtors where material.

Foreign exchange contracts – cash flow hedges

The company has entered into foreign exchange contracts in respect of a proportion of the forecast euro costs of its sterling supplies for the year ended 31 December 20X9. The timing and amount of these foreign exchange contracts match the forecast requirements and the contracts are considered to be effective hedges. At 31 December 20X8 the fair value of the foreign exchange contracts was €80,000 (20X7 – asset of €15,000). At 31 December 20X8 an unrealised gain of €60,000 (20X7 – gain of €12,000), net of deferred tax of €18,000 (20X7—€2,500), relating to foreign exchange contracts is included in equity. During the year, realised gains of €12,000 (20X7—€20,000) were removed from equity and are included within the cost of sales in the profit and loss account in respect of completed hedges.

During the year no gains or losses (20X7—€10,000 gains) were realised in respect of foreign exchange contracts for which hedge accounting was discontinued due to the hedge designation being revoked. No gains or losses (20X7—€10,000 losses) were realised in respect of foreign exchange contracts that did not qualify for hedge accounting.

The fair value of foreign exchange contracts has been calculated by applying the forward price derived from third-party market price quotations.

Commodity swaps – cash flow hedges

The company has entered into commodity swap contracts in respect of a proportion of its forecast wood purchases up to 31 December 20Y1. The timing of an amount of the swap contracts match the forecast requirements and the contracts are considered to be effective hedges. At 31 December 20X8 the fair value of the commodity swaps was €1,890,000 (20X7 – asset of €1,112,000). At 31 December 20X8 an unrealised gain of €1,640,000 (20X7 – gain of €1,020,000), net of deferred tax of €258,000 (20X7—€198,000), relating to commodity swaps is included in equity. During the year, realised gains of €420,000 (20X7—€320,000) were removed from equity and are included within the cost of sales in the profit and loss account in respect of completed hedges.

During the year no gains or losses (20X7 – losses of €100,000) were realised in respect of foreign exchange contracts for which hedge accounting was discontinued due to the hedge designation being revoked. No gains or losses (20X7 – gain of €100,000) were realised in respect of commodity swap contracts that did not qualify for hedge accounting.

The fair value of commodity swap contracts has been calculated by applying the forward price derived from third-party market price quotations.

Interest rate swaps – cash flow hedges

The company has entered into interest rate swap contracts whereby it pays a fixed rate of interest and receives a variable rate of interest on the outstanding principal of certain sterling-denominated borrowings. The terms of the swap contracts match the forecasted interest payment profile and the contracts are considered effective hedges.

At 31 December 20X8 the fair value of interest rate swaps was an asset of €130,000 (20X7 – asset of €40,000). At 31 December 20X8 an unrealised gain of €90,000 (20X7 – gain of €30,000), net of deferred tax of €20,000 (20X7—€6,000), relating to interest rate swaps is included in equity. During the year, realised losses of €5,000 (20X7—€nil) were removed from equity and are included within finance costs in the profit and loss account in respect of completed hedges.

The fair value of commodity swap contracts has been valued by calculating the present value of future cash flows, estimated using forward rates from third-party market price quotations.

26. Sensitivity Analysis – Financial Instruments

Interest rate risk

At 31 December 20X8, if interest rates had been 1% lower with all other variables held constant, post-tax profit for the year would have been €12,000 higher (in 20X7 post-tax profits would have been €13,000 higher), arising mainly as a result of lower interest expense on variable borrowings, and other components of equity would have been €11,000 (20X7 €11,800) higher, arising mainly as a result of an increase in the fair value of fixed rate financial assets classed as available for sale.

If interest rates had been 1% higher with all other variables held constant, post-tax profits would have been €9,500 lower (in 20X7 post-tax profits would have been €11,000 lower), arising mainly as a result of higher interest expense on variable borrowings, and other components of equity would have been €12,950 (20X7 €11,500) lower, arising mainly as a result of an increase in the fair value of fixed rate financial assets. Profit is more sensitive to interest rate decreases than increases because of borrowings with capped interest rates. The sensitivity is lower in 20X7 than in 20X8 because of the increase in outstanding borrowings (see note 21).

Foreign currency exchange rate risk

At 31 December 20X8, if the euro had weakened 10% against sterling with all other variables held constant, post-tax profits for the year would have been €56,000 lower (in 20X7 the post-tax profit would have been €21,000 lower), and other components of equity would have been €18,000 (20X7 €17,000) higher.

Conversely, if the euro had strengthened 10% against sterling with all other variables held constant, post-tax profits for the year would have been €56,000 higher (in 20X7 the post-tax profit would have been €25,000 higher), and other components of equity would have been €18,000 (20X7 €17,000) lower. The lower foreign currency exchange rate sensitivity in losses/profits in 20X8 compared with 20X7 is attributable to an increase in foreign denominated debt. Equity is more sensitive in 20X8 than in 20X7 because of the increased use of hedges of foreign currency purchases, offset by the increase in foreign currency debt.

Commodity price rate risk

At 31 December 20X8, if the price of wood had increased in value by 10% with all other variables held constant, post-tax profits for the year would have been €186,000 lower (in 20X7 the post-tax profit would have been €121,000 lower).

Conversely, if the price of wood had decreased in value by 10% with all other variables held constant, post-tax profits for the year would have been €186,000 higher (In 20X7 the post-tax profit would have been €121,000 higher). The higher commodity price rate sensitivity in losses/profits in 20X8 compared with 20X7 is attributable to an increase in purchases to meet increased sales demand.

27. Management of Capital

The company's objectives when managing capital are:

(a) to safeguard the entity's ability to continue as a going concern, so that it can continue to provide returns for shareholders and benefits for other stakeholders, and
(b) to provide an adequate return to shareholders by pricing products and services commensurately with the level of risk.

The company sets the amount of capital in proportion to risk. The company manages the capital structure and makes adjustments to it in light of changes in economic conditions and the risk characteristics of the underlying assets. In order to maintain or adjust the capital structure, the company may adjust the amount of dividends paid to shareholders, return capital to shareholders, issue new shares, or sell assets to reduce debt.

Consistently with others in the industry, the company monitors capital on the basis of the debt-to-capital ratio. This ratio is calculated as net debt to capital[32]. Net debt is calculated as total debt (i.e. loans and finance lease liabilities) less cash and cash equivalents. Capital comprises all components of equity (i.e. share capital, share premium, minority interest, retained earnings, other equity reserves and revaluation reserve).

---

[32] Some companies regard some financial liabilities (i.e. some forms of subordinated debt) as part of capital. Other entities regard capital as excluding some components of equity (for example components arising from cash flow hedges). In these instances the capital figure is amended to include the financial liabilities and to remove the impact of the cumulative reserves built up in respect of cash flow hedges. The amended figure is called "adjusted capital".

During 20X8, the company's strategy, which was unchanged from 20X7, was to maintain the debt-to-capital ratio at a level which did not exceed 1:1, in order to secure access to finance at a reasonable cost by maintaining an AAA credit rating. The debt-to-capital ratios at 31 December 20X8 were as follows:

	20X8 €000	20X7 €000
Total debt	(107,850)	(116,560)
Less: cash and cash equivalents	111,650	110,380
Net debt	3,800	(6,180)
Total equity	173,894	157,790
Debt-to-capital ratio	–0.02:1	0.04:1

The reduced debt-to-equity ratio during 20X8 resulted primarily from a reduction in fixed rate interest bearing debt. As a result of this reduction in net debt, improved profitability and lower levels of managed receivables, the dividend payment was increased to €25.5 million for 20X8, from €10 million for 20X7.

28. Share Capital

	20X8 €000	20X7 €000
Authorised		
100,000,000 A ordinary shares of €1 each	100,000	100,000
5,000,000 10% redeemable preference shares of €1 each	5,000	5,000
Allotted, called up and fully paid		
84,050,000 (20X7 – 78,160,000) ordinary shares of €1 each	84,050	78,160
3,000,000 10% redeemable preference shares of €1 each	3,000	3,000

Preference shares

The preference shares, which were issued at par, are redeemable on 31 December 201Y at par. They carry a dividend of 10% per annum, payable half-yearly in arrears on 30 June and 31 December. The dividend rights are cumulative.

Share issue

On 30 June 20X8, 5,890,000 ordinary shares were issued at €1.40 each.

Share option scheme

The company has a share option scheme under which options to purchase shares are granted to senior employees (see note 7).

29. Reserves and Dividends

	Share Premium €000	Other Reserves €000	Profit and Loss Account €000	Total €000
At 1 January 20X8	570	28,700	50,360	79,630
Premium on share issue	2,356	–	–	2,356
Finance cost of share issue	(36)	–	–	(36)
Exchange difference on loan	–	(200)	–	(200)
Derivative financial instruments		100		100
Impairment of investment property		(10,000)	–	(10,000)
Revaluation of tangible assets	–	(17,200)	–	(17,200)
Actuarial gain on market value of defined benefit scheme's assets		200	–	200
Additional finance cost of preference shares to share premium account	100		–	100
Profit for the year	–	–	60,394	60,394
Dividends distributed in the year (note 11)	–	–	(25,500)	(25,500)
At 31 December 20X8	2,990	1,600	85,254	89,844

Analysis of profit and loss reserve:

	20X8 €000	20X7 €000
Profit and loss reserve excluding pension asset	84,054	49,360
Pension reserve (note 8)	1,200	1,000
Profit and loss reserve	85,254	50,360

Other reserves:

	Currency Reserve €000	Revaluation Reserve €000	Fair Value Reserve €000	Total €000
At 1 January 20X8	250	28,300	150	28,700
Exchange difference on loan	(200)	–		(200)
Actuarial gains	–	–	200	200
Impairment of investment property		(10,000)		(10,000)
Revaluation of tangible assets		(17,200)		(17,200)
Derivative financial instruments		–	100	100
At 31 December 20X8	50	1,100	450	1,600

30. Reconciliation of Movements in Shareholders' Funds

	20X8 €000	20X7 €000
Recognised gains and losses for the year	33,294	25,590
Dividends paid	(25,500)	(10,000)
New shares subscribed	5,890	–
Premium on new shares	2,356	–
Finance cost of issue	(36)	–
Additional finance cost of non-equity shares	100	90
Net increase in shareholders' funds	16,104	15,680
Opening shareholders' funds	157,790	142,110
Closing shareholders' funds	173,894	157,790

31. Reconciliation of Operating Profit to Net Cash Inflow from Operating Activities

	20X8 €000	20X7 €000
Operating profit	73,050	24,280
Depreciation of tangible assets	81,205	73,500

Amortisation of intangible assets	500	475
Impairment of investment property	10,000	–
(Profit)/loss on disposal of tangible assets	(420)	120
Loss on disposal of available-for-sale asset investments	120	–
Deferred government grants released	(1,500)	(850)
Provision for legal costs	35	15
Increase in stocks	(14,894)	(12,310)
Decrease in debtors	710	1,800
Decrease in creditors	(90)	(3,800)
Increase in provision for deferred tax	180	100
Increase in provision for post-retirement benefits	35	30
Net cash inflow from operating activities	148,931	83,360

32. Analysis of Net Funds

	1 January 20X8 €000	Cash Flow €000	Mark to Market €000	Translation Adjustment €000	31 December 20X8 €000
Net cash					
Cash at bank and in hand	105,530	(1,330)	-	-	104,200
Bank overdraft	(9,650)	5,400	-	-	(4,250)
Increase in cash	95,880	4,070	-	-	99,950
Liquid resources					
Available-for-sale investments	5,000	(800)	-	-	4,200
Loan notes	1,500	-	-	-	1,500
	6,500	(800)	-	-	5,700
Long-term resources					
Loan notes	8,000	(2,000)	-	-	6,000
Debt					
Finance leases	(89,000)	1,500	-	-	(87,500)

Debts falling due after one year	(27,560)	7,210	–	–	(20,350)
	(116,560)	8,710	–	–	(107,850)
Net (debt)/funds before derivative financial instruments	(6,180)	9,980	–	–	3,800
Derivative financial instruments	1,500	500	50	50	2,100
Net (debt)/funds after derivative financial instruments	(4,680)	10,480	50	50	5,900

The equivalent disclosure for the prior year is as follows:

	1 January 20X8 €000	Cash Flow €000	Mark to Market €000	Translation Adjustment €000	31 December 20X7 €000
Net cash					
Cash at bank and in hand	145,530	(40,000)	–	–	105,530
Bank overdraft	(5,160)	(4,490)	–	–	(9,650)
Increase in cash	140,370	(44,490)	–	–	95,880
Liquid resources					
Available-for-sale investments	4,000	1,000	–	–	5,000
Loan notes	2,500	(1,000)	–	–	1,500
	6,500	–	–	–	6,500
Long-term resources					
Loan notes	8,000	–	–	–	8,000
Debt					
Finance leases	(124,200)	35,200	–	–	(89,000)
Debts falling due after one year	(32,560)	5,000	–	–	(27,560)
	(156,760)	40,200	–	–	(116,560)

Net (debt)/funds before derivative financial instruments	(1,890)	(4,290)	–	–	(6,180)
Derivative financial instruments	1,900	(200)	(100)	(100)	1,500
Net (debt)/funds after derivative financial instruments	10	(4,490)	(100)	(100)	(4,680)

33. Post-Balance Sheet Events

The company sold a franchise licence in Cork on 28 February 20X9 and realised a gain on disposal of €10,000,000.

34. Capital commitments

At the balance sheet date the company had entered into contracts for future capital expenditure amounting to:

	20X8 €000	20X7 €000
Contracted	3,000	–
Authorised but not contracted	750	500
	3,750	500
Government grants reclaimable in respect of the above future capital expenditure are estimated at:	1,500	–

35. Other Financial Commitments

Finance leases and hire purchase contracts

In addition to the capital commitments set out above, the company has entered into contracts whose inception occurs after the year-end amounting to:

	20X8 €000	20X7 €000
Finance leases and hire purchase contracts	750	1,000

Operating lease commitments

Annual commitments exist under non-cancellable operating leases as follows:

	20X8 Land and Buildings €000	20X8 Other €000	20X7 Land and Buildings €000	20X7 Other €000
Expiring:				
Within one year	300	500	300	500
Between two and five years	800	2,000	800	2,000
More than five years	400	200	100	700
	1,500	2,700	1,200	3,200

The rentals payable in respect of leases of land and buildings are subject to rent review at three yearly intervals as specified in the lease agreement.

36. Contingent Liability and Subsequent Provision

A customer who purchased furniture in 20X7 has commenced an action against the company. He claims that the furniture is defective. The company's solicitors have advised that the action is unlikely to succeed therefore no provision for any liability has been made.

A provision of €65,000 for legal costs in connection with the defence has been provided for under other provisions (**Note 24**). €15,000 of this provision has been utilised in the year leaving a closing balance on the provision account of €50,000.

It has been estimated that the maximum liability should the action be successful is €150,000 to the plaintiff with an additional €50,000 in court costs. No provision has been made for these costs based on the solicitor's advice and the directors' judgement on the matter.

37. Approval of Financial Statements

The board of directors approved these financial statements for issue on [*state date*].

SUGGESTED SOLUTIONS TO REVIEW QUESTIONS

CHAPTER 1

Solution 1.1

There are a number of threats to integrity, objectivity and independence arising in the case of Trafford Limited.

- *Familiarity Threat*

Your firm has been auditor of Trafford Limited for 10 years, indeed the company has not had any other auditors. In addition, your audit partner appears to have a close relationship with the client's Managing Directors and has been audit partner on the engagement for 10 years. All these factors indicate a familiarity threat which could potentially impact on your firm's ability to adequately challenge the client's management where required, thus impacting on the firm's ability to arrive at the correct audit opinion.

- *Intimidation Threat*

The Managing Director of the client, Arnold Ferguson, appears to be a rather domineering figure and has shown tendencies towards intimidating members of the audit team in the past. This increases the risk that your firm may be pressurised into accepting his judgements even where these may not be appropriate. This may result in your firm issuing an inappropriate audit opinion.

- *Self-Interest Threat*

The fees generated by the audit of Trafford Limited are now extremely significant in the context of your firm's total income from audit activity, over 20% of total audit income. As a result, the loss of this audit client could have a serious impact upon your firm's income in the future. This may lead to your firm being reluctant to challenge management on difficult issues for fear of displeasing client management resulting in the client changing auditors.

- *Self-Review Threat*

Arnold Ferguson has recently raised the idea that your firm may wish to perform internal audit services for Trafford Limited. Should your firm accept this internal audit engagement, it may result in reliance being placed on work performed by your firm in its capacity as internal auditor being relied upon by your firm in its capacity as external auditor. This is a clear self-review threat, as the adequacy of internal audit work needs to be assessed by the external auditor prior to placing reliance on it.

- *Action to be taken:*

Prior to accepting the external audit engagement for the next financial year, your firm should assess whether adequate safeguards have been put in place to guard against each of the threats identified above, and reduce the threat to an acceptable level. This is in accordance with the APB's Ethical Standard number 1.

Solution 1.2

Memo

To: Mr Rick Parry, Istanbul Limited

From: XYZ Chartered Accountants

Subject: Corporate Governance practices in listed companies

- The standard for best practice in corporate governance is contained within the "Combined Code on Corporate Governance" which was issued in June 2006.
- If Istanbul Limited are to become listed, they would be required under Stock Exchange listing rules to report within their financial statements annually on their compliance with the requirements of this code.
- Some of the key structures/practices that the Directors in Istanbul should consider implementing in advance of listing include:
  - Undertaking a thorough review of the effectiveness of the systems of internal control. This review should be updated on an annual basis going forward.
  - Holding formal board meetings on a regular basis.
  - Appointing a number of non-executive directors to the company's board, ensuring that there is a reasonable balance on the board between non-executives and executives.
  - Establishing an audit committee to liaise with external and internal auditors and to manage the appointment of auditors. This committee should be chaired by an independent non-executive director.
  - Separating the roles of chairman and chief executive of the board.
  - Establishing a formal, rigorous and transparent procedure for appointing new directors to the board.

- Ensuring all board members are supplied with information on a timely basis prior to board meetings
- Establishing a procedure whereby the Board undertakes an annual review of its own performance.
• By establishing the above procedures and practices, corporate governance procedures will be enhanced and the transition to listed status will be eased.

CHAPTER 2

Solution 2.1

CAT Ltd

(A)

The prospective engagement partner should consider the following matters when deciding whether to accept a new client:

(i) The integrity of the prospective client's management and the integrity of its principal owners.
(ii) The legality of the entity's activities, and entity's reputation.
(iii) The entity's business environment and who will use the financial statements.
(iv) The entity's financial position and prospects.
(v) The likelihood that the scope of the audit will be restricted or subject to an unacceptable time constraint.
(vi) Discuss any key accounting policy issues.

Before accepting a new engagement, the auditor should determine that a sufficient number of **competent staff** will be available to provide the services that the client has requested.

Before commencing any services on an engagement for a new client, the auditor should determine whether the firm is **independent** with respect to that client. It should also be confirmed that the firm has no potential conflict of interests.

Where a registered auditor is a corporate practice it should obtain written confirmation from a potential audit client or associated undertaking that it **holds no interests** in the firm, before accepting the audit appointment.

(B)

Addressee

For clients incorporated under the Companies Act/Order, the auditor should address the engagement letter to the directors of the company.

Agreeing the terms of the engagement

The auditor should always discuss the scope of the engagement with the client's management, and should then confirm the matters agreed in the engagement letter. In the case of a new engagement, the auditor should normally discuss and agree the contents of the engagement letter with the client's management before accepting the audit appointment.

The auditor should obtain the client's confirmation of the terms of the engagement by sending an additional copy of the engagement letter and asking the client to sign this and return it.

In the case of a company, the auditor should request that the letter be tabled at a board meeting or, where the board delegates this responsibility, at a meeting of a suitable committee of the board, and for the approval of the letter to be minuted.

A copy of the engagement letter should be filed with the audit working papers.

Contents of the letter

Firms may wish to send their corporate clients an engagement letter covering additional services e.g. corporate tax advice and assistance in preparing tax computations.

Corporate Finance Clients

If the only incidental investment business the firm is likely to undertake for the client consists of corporate finance type activities, and the client has agreed that it is appropriate for the firm to treat the client as a "corporate finance" client, the engagement letter should include a specific paragraph highlighting this.

If the client does not agree to be treated as a corporate finance client, or the investment business anticipated would not be a corporate finance activity the engagement letter should include an appropriate paragraph.

Other matters which may be dealt with in the engagement letter include:

- fees and billing arrangements;
- procedures where the client has a complaint about the service;
- where appropriate, arrangements concerning the involvement of
  - other auditors and experts in some aspect of the audit;
  - internal auditors and other staff of the entity;
  - any restriction of the auditors' liabilities to the client;
  - where appropriate, the country by whose laws the engagement is governed;
  - a reference to any further agreements between the auditors and the client;
  - a proposed timetable for the engagement.

Solution 2.2

Engagement Letters – Leoville Ltd

The Board of Directors,

Leoville Limited

Re: PROPOSED PRESENTATION TO YOUR BANKERS

Dear Sirs,

I refer to our recent meeting. It is our understanding that Leoville proposes to raise funding of €4 million to fund its investment in Las Cases Ltd.

We further understand that your shareholding in Las Cases Ltd will be 50% of the share capital; the balance of the share capital will be held by Poyferre Ltd.

The purpose of this letter is to set out the basis on which we are to assist Leoville Ltd in its formal presentation to your bankers of:-

- A business plan for the new venture Las Cases Ltd, and
- The preparation of management accounts of Leoville Ltd, for the six months ended 30 June 2006.

Each of the above issues is dealt with separately below.

Leoville's management accounts for the six months ended 30 June 2006

As directors of the company, you are responsible for ensuring that the company maintains proper accounting records and for the preparation of the management accounts based on such accounting records.

Our responsibility is to *review* the accounts as prepared by you and to discuss any issues arising therein with the management of the company. We will not carry out an audit on the management accounts and, accordingly, we will *not* express an audit opinion.

We will review the balance sheet and related statements of profit and loss and cash flow and will report on this review to the directors of the company. Our report on the management accounts is at present expected to read as follows:

> Our review consisted principally of obtaining an understanding of the process for the preparation of the financial statements, applying analytical procedures to the underlying financial data, assessing whether accounting policies have been consistently applied, and making enquiries of management responsible for financial and accounting matters. Our review excluded audit procedures such as tests of control and verification of assets and liabilities and was therefore substantially less in scope than an audit performed in accordance with Auditing Standards. Accordingly, we do not express an audit opinion on the financial information.

On the basis of our review

- we are not aware of any material modification which should be made to the financial information as presented; and
- in our opinion the financial information has been prepared consistent with the accounting policies set out on pages — to —.

Clearly, the limited nature of our review work will thus be conveyed to your bank who will examine the management accounts of which our report will form a part.

Business plan for Las Cases Ltd

The drafting of a business plan and preparation of trading projections for this company for the period from 1 January 2007 to 31 December 2008 is a matter for which the directors of Las Cases Ltd are solely responsible. We further understand, from our recent discussions, that you will retain specialist textile industry consultants to advise on particular aspects of this new venture. Our responsibility will be to report to the directors of Leoville Ltd on our management of the plan's preparation. As the nature of the plan and the trading projections relate to a future accounting period, we clearly cannot offer any audit opinion on these matters.

The responsibilities of the directors of Las Cases Ltd are to make the underlying commercial assumptions which will form the basis of the plan. In this respect you will use the input of senior management of Leoville and Poyferre to assist you in the preparation of this plan and the related projections. You are also solely responsible for engaging the input of consultants and for deciding on the scope and nature of their engagement. Furthermore, your responsibility is to select appropriate accounting policies in line with generally accepted accounting principles and which reflect the activities of the proposed business.

Our report on the trading projections for the new venture is at present expected to read as follows:-

> We have reviewed the accounting policies and the calculations for the trading projections of Las Cases Ltd for which the directors are solely responsible. In our opinion, the forecasts so far as the accounting policies and the calculations are concerned have been properly compiled on the basis of the assumptions made by the directors of the company. Also the projections are presented, in our opinion, on a basis consistent with the accounting policies normally adopted by the company.

Other issues

Unless otherwise agreed, it will not be our responsibility to undertake or assist in the formal presentation to your bankers in relation to the application for finance.

Additionally, in order to ensure that the work we have agreed to can be done in sufficient time to enable the presentation to be made four weeks from now, we must have your agreement to the timetable set out in the Appendix to this letter. You should be aware that without adhering to the numerous deadlines for information identified in this Appendix, it will not be possible to complete the assignment within the given timescale.

Our fees are based on the time required by the individuals assigned to the engagement plus direct out-of-pocket expenses. Individual hourly rates vary according to the degree of responsibility involved and the experience and skill required.

We would be grateful if you would confirm in writing your agreement to these terms by signing and returning the enclosed copy of this letter to indicate that it is in accordance with your understanding of the arrangements in relation to the preparation of the business plan for the new venture and Leoville's management accounts for the six months ended 30 June 1996. Alternatively, you should inform us if your understanding of the proposed arrangement is not in accordance with the terms of the engagement as set out in this letter.

Yours faithfully,

_____

We agree to the terms of this letter.

_____

Signed for and on behalf of Leoville Ltd

NOTE TO STUDENTS

The Appendix referred to does not form part of the solution.

Solution 2.3

Conway Chartered Accountants

Memorandum

To: Audit Trainees

From: Audit Senior

Re: Planning, Controlling and Recording of an Audit

In order to ensure an effective and efficient audit it is essential that the audit is properly planned, recorded and controlled. Auditors are required by professional standards and guidelines to adequately plan, control and record their work.

(a) PLANNING

The nature of the planning required will vary from audit to audit and will be dependent on the complexity of the client's business, the auditor's knowledge of the client and his business and the reporting requirements to which the audit is subject.

Adequate Planning:

(i) establishes the intended means of achieving the audit objectives;
(ii) assists in the direction and control of the work;
(iii) helps to ensure that attention is devoted to the critical areas of the audit; and
(iv) helps to ensure that the work is completed expeditiously.

Business Review

One of the first stages of the audit planning process is to carry out a review of the clients business. This will comprise gaining an understanding of the business, carrying out preliminary analytical review, reviewing significant accounting policies and making a preliminary assessment on materiality.

Evaluating Inherent Risk

Audit risk can be divided into two main categories:

The risk of material misstatement. This is the risk that items in the financial statements either individually or in aggregate will be materially misstated and that the client's controls will not be effective in detecting those misstatements.

Detection risk. This is the risk that misstatements will not be detected by the audit work.

It should be possible for the auditor to assess the risk of misstatement, this will be done through his assessment of inherent risk and control effectiveness. The auditor can in some way control detection risk by varying the nature, extent and timing of his audit tests.

Inherent risk is the susceptibility of an account balance or type of transaction to material misstatement through fraud or error, before taking into account the effectiveness of the client's internal controls.

The auditor should carry out a search for inherent risks, evaluate the significance of those risks and relate such risks to account balances, classes of transactions and his audit objectives. The auditor's assessment of these risks will form the basis of his audit testing and will impact on his audit emphasis.

Review of internal controls for audit strategy purposes

A business must have some form of internal control systems in order to function. The nature and complexity of these systems will vary from business to business and will depend on the complexity of the business. An internal control structure can be divided into three main categories:

- The control environment
- The accounting system
- The internal controls.

The control environment is the overall attitudes, abilities, awareness and actions of the individuals in the organisation, particularly those of management, concerning the importance of control and the emphasis attached to it.

Accounting systems normally comprise the financially significant computer applications and the computer environment within which these are developed, implemented, maintained and operated. These systems will form the basis for the preparation of periodic financial statements and other information required by management to control the business.

Internal accounting controls are the specific procedures established by management to ensure that transactions are completely and accurately processed, transactions are recorded as authorised by management, assets are safeguarded and that the accounting systems are reliable and the account balances are correct.

The auditor's initial assessment of the control environment is crucial. If he forms the opinion that the control environment is unfavourable he is unlikely to carry out further procedures to assess the controls with a view to placing reliance on them in performing his audit.

Regardless of whether he is going to place reliance on internal controls he will need to understand the accounting systems. This will enable him to design his audit tests to ensure an efficient and effective audit.

If the auditor decides to rely on the internal control system he will need to make a detailed assessment of that system in order to design his compliance tests.

The review of the internal control systems will influence the audit strategy and is therefore a crucial element of the audit planning stage.

Determining the strategy

The audit strategy sets out the principal features of the planned audit approach. The auditor develops his strategy by considering his knowledge of the client together with more up to date information obtained through the business review and the preliminary assessment of internal control.

Substantive testing plan

Having determined his audit strategy the auditor can then set about developing his substantive testing plan. This forms the link between the audit strategy and the detailed tests to be performed during the audit.

In respect of each audit area the substantive testing plan should set out the following information:

- the audit objectives that are relevant to the particular account balance or class of transactions;
- an evaluation of the inherent risks;
- a general assessment as to the extent to which control effectiveness reduces those risks and any specific control risks identified;
- decisions as to the nature, extent and timing of the substantive tests.

Administrative matters

For a new client it is necessary to ensure that all necessary steps regarding the firm's appointment have been carried out. This includes clearance from previous auditors and agreeing the terms of the engagement with the client.

The staff needed to carry out the audit must be assigned, ensuring that they have the experience required to carry out the assignment and that there is no conflict of interest.

Consideration needs to be given as to whether it will be necessary to engage the services of other experts and the timing and nature of their report.

The audit partner and manager will then set timetables, time and fee budgets.

Before the audit work is commenced it is essential that all staff are properly briefed.

(b) CONTROLLING

The reporting partner needs to ensure that the audit work is being performed to an acceptable standard and that problems are quickly identified and brought to the attention of the partner or manager. The most important elements of control are the direction and supervision of audit staff and the review of the work they have done.

Roles of partners and managers

An audit team usually comprises people of different levels of experience and seniority. It is usual for all work to be reviewed by a person more senior than the person who performed the work. In some cases, for larger, high-risk clients it is usual to have a second partner review.

Procedures

The nature of the procedures needed to control an audit and the extent to which they need to be formalised will depend on the organisation of the audit firm and the degree of delegation of the audit work. The procedures established should be designed to ensure:

- work is allocated to audit staff who have the appropriate training, experience and proficiency;
- audit staff of all levels clearly understand their responsibilities and the objectives of the procedures they are carrying out;
- the working papers provide an adequate record of the work done and the conclusion reached;
- the work performed is reviewed by a more senior member of staff, this should ensure that the work was adequately performed and to confirm that the results obtained support the audit conclusions reached.

Quality assurance inspection

Each Registered Auditor is required by the "audit regulations and guidance" to establish and maintain quality control procedures appropriate to its circumstances. The firm's programme of quality assurance inspection has, as its main objective, to ensure that the audits are conducted in accordance with the relevant policies and procedures.

(c) DOCUMENTING

The quantity, type and content of audit working papers will vary with the circumstances, but they must meet the following overall objectives:

- assist in the efficient conduct of work;
- enable the work carried out to be independently reviewed;
- demonstrate that the auditor has properly performed all the audit work necessary to enable an opinion to be formed on the financial statements.

For this reason the following procedures are important:

- remove all lists of outstanding work once the work required has been completed;
- record all relevant information received and its source when questions of principles or judgement arise;
- the working papers should be consistent with the financial statements and audit report given;
- each working paper should be dated, record the preparer's initials, give the client's name;
- record the period covered by audit;
- detail the subject matter;

- show evidence of review;
- no unnecessary information should be kept on file;
- appropriate conclusions on the result of work performed should always be recorded;
- all working papers should be kept confidential.

CHAPTER 3

Solution 3.1

(a)

- Choose a sample of stock items and test the post-period end sale of the items of stock.
- Inspect the sales invoice raised when these items were sold.
- Consider whether the year end valuation is appropriate based on the following concept: Stock should be valued at cost or net realisable value (NRV) whichever is lower.
- Where the NRV is lower than the carrying value of stock items, year end stock has been overstated and a stock provision against these stock items will be necessary.
- Calculate a reasonable stock provision which will restate stock at a value which is not overstated.
- Adjust stock for the provision.

(b)

For five months in the year in the absence of supplier statements reconciliations and daily till reconciliations, the controls around the following areas and financial statement assertions have been absent:

- accounts payable: completeness, accuracy and existence/occurrence
- purchases: completeness, accuracy, existence/occurrence
- sales: completeness, accuracy, existence/occurrence.

Accounts payable: In the absence of controls comfort period end, accounts payable balance must be tested substantively through the performance of period end supplier statement reconciliations. A greater amount of creditor balances may need to be reconciled in order to test the balance down to the materiality level, whereas if the control was operating effectively during the year the level of substantive testing would be reduced.

Sales: As this is predominantly a cash business, in the absence of daily till reconciliations, gaining comfort over the completeness, accuracy and existence/occurrence of total sales figure per the financial statements may not be possible. The auditor may not be able to express an opinion on the financial statements given the inability to validate the assertions noted above in relation to cash sales. As a result a qualified audit opinion may be issued.

(c)

This will be a contract with a related party and as a result has inherent risk attached to it. As the company is experiencing a downturn in sales, the related party relationship with Gorgeous Shoes Ltd could be manipulated in order to improve the sales figures for Oh So

Chic Ltd through sales invoices being raised at overstated amounts. When performing an audit with such a related party relationship the auditor will have to inspect and review all sales invoices raised in respect of Oh So Chic Ltd and ensure that sales have been made on an arm's length basis i.e. that they have neither been inflated – which would be likely in this scenario – or reduced to an unrealistic selling price due to the related party relationship.

The auditor must also ensure that the following are disclosed in the financial statements in relation to related parties:

- the names of all related parties
- the basis of how the related party relationship has arisen
- the nature and amount of transactions with related parties which took place during the period – period end balances with related parties.

Solution 3.2

The key risk to the audit is the ability of the company to continue to trade as a going concern. The auditor should discuss with the company's directors their assessment of the going concern of the company and what this is based on. The auditor must consider the cash position of the company and the interest payments which the company must make on loan balances.

When performing the audit the auditor must remain alert for fraudulent accounting which could be used by the company directors in order to present results going forward which do not represent a going concern risk, for example, fictitious sales and debtor balances.

Solution 3.3

- Select a sample of weekly time sheets and confirm that they have been reviewed by line managers.
- From weekly time sheets select a sample of employees and confirm that the correct number of hours has been input onto the payroll system for processing.
- Select a sample of employees and agree hourly wage rate per personnel records to hourly wage rate per payroll system.
- Select a sample of employees and obtain payslips for each employee; recompute PAYE and NIC charges and compare to deductions from the employees' payslips. Assess for reasonableness.
- Select a sample of BACS payment listings and agree total per BACS listing to total per payroll report.
- Validate that the BACS payments listings selected above have been authorised by payroll manager.
- Observe payroll manager and accounts manager processing weekly wages and validate that authorisation codes are required.

Solution 3.4

The existence of dominant directors introduces the risk of override of internal controls resulting in misstated financial statements which do not reflect accurately the trading activity of the company for any given period. The following are some risks which may arise as a result of dominant directors running a company:

- creation of fictitious customer accounts and sales transactions;
- creation of fictitious supplier accounts and purchases;
- overstatement of stock value in order to increase assets of the company;
- risk of hidden bank accounts;
- inaccurate valuation of tangible fixed assets and investments;
- directors may limit the auditor's access to books and records therefore hindering performance of audit work; and
- directors may attempt to manipulate auditor's or provide false representations.

Possible Risks	Auditor Response
Creation of fictitious customer accounts and sales transactions	Performance of debtors circularisation. Unexpected visit to customer premises where significant doubt exists.
Creation of fictitious supplier accounts and purchases	Investigate existence of supplier by phonecall or research on the Internet. Unexpected visit to supplier premises where significant doubt exists.
Overstatement of stock value in order to increase assets of the company	Perform period end stock count. Visit premise unexpectedly and inspect site to ensure similar levels are maintained during the year. Perform NRV testing.
Risk of hidden bank accounts	Contact bank and confirm accounts held and period end balances.
Inaccurate valuation of tangible fixed assets such as land and buildings	Use professional valuers who are independent of the client.
Directors may limit the auditor's access to books and records therefore hindering performance of audit work	Qualified audit opinion may be issued.
Directors may attempt to manipulate auditors or provide false representations	Qualified audit opinion may be issued.

CHAPTER 5

Solution 5.1

(a)

Test of Detail	Financial Statement Area	Financial Statement Assertions Covered by Test
Recompute depreciation charge	Fixed Assets and P+L depreciation charge	Accuracy
Search for unrecorded liabilities	Accruals and accounts payable	Completeness Cut-off
Perform debtors circularisation	Accounts receivable	Existence/Occurrence Rights and Obligations

(b)

- Review client procedures for identifying and making obsolete stock provisions
- Examine any quality control reports available and discuss with management
- Check system in place to monitor the aging of stock
- Compare stock quantities held at year end with past and projected sales performance and with customer orders on hand
- Physically inspect the condition of the stock at the stocktake and subsequently follow up on any points noted during the stocktake
- Check outcome of previous provisions to consider how accurate management estimates have been in the past

Solution 5.2

(i)

- Examine documentation e.g. minutes of meetings of shareholders or board of directors that support the dividend amount issued to shareholders
- Ensure that dividends paid during the year were recorded at the appropriate amount e.g. inspection of the payment of dividends to shareholder by tracing cheque payments to bank statements
- Ensure that dividends payable at the year end were recorded at the appropriate amount e.g. inspection of post-year end payment of dividends to shareholder by tracing cheque payments to bank statements
- Ensure dividends payable at year-end were posted to the correct accounts by inspecting the actual postings made by the client

- Determine when dividends were declared and authorised by the board in order to ensure dividends paid and payable have been recorded in the proper period via inspection of board minutes. Under IAS 10 dividends declared to shareholders after the balance sheet date should not be provided for as a liability in the financial statements but should be disclosed in the notes to the financial statements.
- Ensure the transactions were authorized and approved via inspection of board minutes
- Ensure that any dividend paid was not paid illegally i.e. review reserves and confirm that there were sufficient reserves available to issue the dividends during the year

(ii)

- Gain or update understanding of how management organises and controls the process for determining fixed asset valuations and disclosures for fixed assets
- Obtain information as to who performed the revaluation e.g. directors or chartered surveyors
- Consider how the revaluation has been accounted for and if this is in line with UK GAAP, if the disclosures are appropriate and if the method of valuation is applied consistently or if changes are appropriate
- For external valuations obtain and inspect the valuation report issued by the surveyor, gain an understanding of how the valuation has been performed and assess the reasonableness of the valuation
- For internal valuations performed by directors gain an understanding of how the valuation has been performed and assess the reasonableness of the valuation
- Verify asset recording is appropriate, including depreciation calculation and valuation reserves

(iii)

- Verify whether any of this stock has been sold post-year end and paid for
- Confirm whether any of this stock will be recovered from the customer, review correspondence with the liquidator
- Confirm whether the client is attempting to secure contracts with new customers for the sale of this stock
- Consider if the stock has been recorded in the financial statements at an appropriate amount – if it is probable that the stock will not be sold it should be considered if it should be treated as obsolete stock

(iv)

- Contact the client's solicitor and confirm details of the pending litigation such as the nature of the claim, the status of the claim, the probability of an economic outflow arising and the probable amount of any such outflow

- Consider if a provision is necessary in the financial statements for any possible losses arising from the case
- If no provision is necessary consider if disclosure of a contingent liability is necessary in the financial statements

Solution 5.3

- Conduct a numerical sequence check on sales invoices to ensure that all sales are recorded
- Review and vouch the debtors control account reconciliation to underlying books and records
- Perform detailed cut-off testing
- Carry out analytical procedures

Solution 5.4

(i) Supplier statement reconciliations are a good procedure as they verify each financial statement assertion:
   (a) existence: the liability exists at the year end
   (b) rights and obligations: the liability pertains to the entity at the year end
   (c) occurrence: the purchase took place which pertains to the entity during the relevant period
   (d) completeness: there are no unrecorded liabilities
   (e) valuation: the liability is recorded at an appropriate carrying value
   (f) measurement: the creditor is recorded at the proper amount and the purchase is allocated to the prior period

(ii) Request the following of the audit assistant:

A – verify the actual reason for not recording the invoice and establish if there is a cut-off error

D – ensure the assistant follows up as to the reason for not posting the credit note. If it is an error it should be recorded on the summary of unadjusted differences

R – bring to schedule of unadjusted differences and no further work necessary

W – get the assistant to establish why there is a delay in the posting of the October payment. This could have implications for the reliance the auditor places on the system of internal control. Ensure the assistant enquires as to the present status of the discount claim. If there is no evidence that the discount is to be given then bring it to the summary of unadjusted differences as an error.

CHAPTER 6

Solution 6.1

ABC & Co

Chartered Accountants

Belfast

The Board of Directors

Druid Limited

Belfast

22 June 1999

Gentlemen

Thank you for this opportunity to explain how I would apply Computer Assisted Audit Techniques ("CAATs") to your company's debtors ledger if I were appointed auditor.

CAATs involve writing programmes or using application programme packages or test data to perform or assist the auditor in the performance of their audit procedures. They can also utilise audit/reporting functionality on many of the accounting packages etc., on the market today.

Writing programmes from scratch is expensive. Instead, I propose to use a specialist audit software package which allows the auditor analyse and parse data at a mouse click. These packages are known in computer jargon as "application programme packages" and are available "off the shelf". There are several available to the auditor. An example would be the IDEA packages developed by the Canadian Institute of Chartered Accountants.

This is a Windows-based package and is relatively easy to use. To use IDEA, the auditor obtains a copy of the data – in your case, the files containing the data for the debtors ledger for the year. Once the auditor has the data loaded, the auditors then use the package to perform a variety of tasks.

Druid has 260,000 debtors accounts, 125,000 of which are classed as active or semi-active. In view of the large number of accounts, it appears sensible that the auditor would use some form of computer aid audit testing.

The majority of packages in the area (including IDEA) allow the auditor to carry out the following auditing procedures on debtors:

- Selection of accounts for debtors circularization – stratifying the ledger by account type and by value of balance
- Preparing confirmation letters and associated control lists and summaries

- Reperforming calculations such as ledger totals and aged analysis of debtors
- Checking classification of accounts between active, semi-active and dormant
- Identifying all balances over 60 days old
- Identifying balances in excess of credit limits
- Identifying accounts with credit balances
- Reviewing for unusual items
- Accounts with names, addresses, contact numbers corresponding to similar details on employee payroll
- Accounts having unusual transactions
- Items for which set approval procedures have not been applied
- Abnormal credits in debtors accounts
- Billings at unusually high or low prices
- Accounts with no credit limits or limits that have not been amended in over one year or limits that are unusually high
- Identifying suspense items
- Identifying long outstanding unallocated cash.

I will also develop and use a pack of test data and run that through the debtors system to confirm that the system operates as intended.

I set out some detail relating to the above tests in the appendix to this letter. [**Note to candidates – the level of detail given in the appendix was not required in order to gain full marks for this part of the question and should be viewed as a learning tool**].

All the working papers generated on the audit, including those relating to the debtors ledger, will be generated and stored using a Lotus Notes package.

I trust you find this letter helpful. Please do not hesitate to contact me if you require any further information or explanation.

Yours sincerely,

ABC & Co.

Appendix

General Requirement

In order to run the IDEA package, I will require to liaise with your IT manager with a view to getting an electronic copy of your debtors ledger for the year under review. Care will be needed to ensure that the data is in an appropriate electronic format and also that the ledger totals reconcile back to the debtors information that will be reflected in the financial statements. Once reconciled, this data will be loaded by a computer expert member of the audit team into the IDEA package. The package will then be used to analyse the data as a basis for general audit tests.

Tests

Selection of Accounts for Debtors Circularization

Druid has an interesting profile of debtors. Good audit coverage can be obtained by examining the large balance accounts. However, the small accounts do accumulate into material amounts and, accordingly, we will wish to get comfort that the smaller balances are also correctly stated.

Preparing Confirmation Letters and Associated Control List and Summaries

We have already set up the text of the confirmation lettering on the package and it will automatically produce all the debtors continuation letters ready for your signature. If you wish we can also set the package so that a statement is also produced to support the balance we request the debtor to confirm.

The package will also produce a control list so that our staff can record responses received and promptly follow up outstanding responses. The package will also allow us to send reminder letters to debtors not responding to the original confirmation.

Reperforming Calculations Such as Ledger Totals and Aged Analysis of Debtors

The package can be used to recalculate the totals of the ledger and the aged analysis of debtors. This is very important in relation to ensuring the mathematical accuracy of the actual operation of the debtors ledger software. It will also save considerable time as such tests could take many days manually.

The programme used can check the total of all individual debtors accounts and check that the calculated total agrees with the actual total per the debtors ledger.

IDEA can also be used to total each balance on the ledger and check that calculation against the reported balance for all debtors on the system. IDEA can also be used to check that the number of accounts with a balance is the same as printed out by the debtors ledger system.

Checking Classification of Accounts Between Active, Semi-Active and Dormant

The classification of accounts can be easily checked by the package by checking the incidence of transactions on the accounts and reporting accounts that do not meet the criteria of the classification to which they have been assigned.

Identifying All Balances Over 60 Days Old

As balances over 60 days old are likely to be balances to be considered in relation to the bad debt reserve, it is useful to be able to identify them separately. The IDEA package will produce a separate print out of all such balances for further consideration.

Identifying Balances in Excess of Credit Limits

Balances in excess of credit limits may indicate that limits have become out of date and require revision. Alternatively, they may mean that the balance is likely to prove irrecoverable. The IDEA package will allow us to identify these balances and report them to you. Material balances identified will require further investigation in the course of the audit.

Identifying Accounts with Credit Balances

A credit balance often indicates an error – e.g. cash posted but no invoice raised, or credit note booked twice. IDEA can be used to produce a list of such balances for further investigation.

Reviewing for unusual items

Accounts with names, addresses, contact numbers corresponding to similar details on employee payroll

The IDEA package facilitates the comparison of different data sets. Accordingly, it will be possible for us to compare data from the debtors ledger to data on other systems such as payroll information including contact telephone numbers, addresses, and other information (e.g. bank account numbers). This test will help identify accounts which require further investigation.

Accounts Having Unusual Transactions

Accounts may have unusual items which might go undetected, the IDEA package allows the auditor define certain conditions and the package will trawl through the data and report any occurrences of the conditions identified.

The package can be used to examine for transactions such as unusually large journal entries or debits other than sales in the debtors ledger.

Items for which Set Approval Procedures Have Not Been Applied

The IDEA package can be set to look for appropriate approvals for certain transactions. This includes multiple sign-offs where procedures require more than one person to sign off on high value items.

Abnormal Credits in Debtors Accounts

Usually high or poorly explained credits in a debtors ledger normally require follow up. IDEA can be programmed to identity such amounts for further investigation. Credits can include amounts on credit notes, or other write offs, either discounts or bad debts. It is important to ensure that all such credits have been appropriately approved – see previous test.

Billings at Unusually High or Low Prices

The package can be set to examine for abnormal pricing procedures and report same for further investigation.

Other issues which can be tested for include:

- Accounts with no credit limits or limits that have not been amended in over one year or limits that are unusually high
- Identifying suspense items
- Identifying long outstanding allocated cash
- Test data

Solution 6.2

(a) **Definitions and examples**

Input, processing and output controls are all application controls as opposed to general computer controls,

Input Controls are controls to ensure data entered into the computer system is genuine, complete, accurate and valid. They include authorisation controls e.g. signature approval of invoice batches before data can be input and validation checks on data as it is entered e.g. edits check that dates are in fact in date format. The importance of input controls is illustrated by the truism "garbage in, garbage out" which is often quoted where there is a lack of such controls.

Processing Controls are controls to ensure the validity, completeness and accuracy of the computer processing and to detect and report items not fully or properly processed. A check of run-to-run totals is a typical example.

Output Controls are designed to ensure the output is valid, accurate, genuine and complete and distributed to the appropriate authorised personnel. Exception reports and controls over valuable pre-printed stationery such as cheques are examples of such controls.

(b) Security controls over the transmission of data by modern or other electronic media can include the following;

- caller dial-back facility
- challenge response facility

- use of ex-directory telephone numbers
- the switching to a leased or dedicated line, possibly an ISDN line for faster and more confidential transmission
- the use of well-designed encryption software to encode/decode data being sent/received
- installation of recognised anti-virus software with regular updating
- restrict access to limited parts of the computer network
- use password controls in conjunction with automatic logging of calls with regular exception reporting and review

Solution 6.3

(a)

(i) **Physical access controls** are implemented to secure computers, programmes and computer records based on restricting actual access to authorised personnel. Examples are securing computer locations by means of physical locks or swipe card systems.

(ii) **Logical or programmed access controls** are those controls such as passwords that are required by a computer system before it grants access to its data or allows its programmes to be altered.

(b)

(i) Computer lock; Sign on passwords; Menus; Use of encryption software; use of security software to restrict access – *no access; read only; edit access; full access*

(ii) as (i) with network software which allows the administrator to grant varying degrees of access based on log-in IDs; limit actions to certain terminals e.g. only PCs based in sales department can access sales invoice details

(iii) as (i) and (ii) above with the possibility of implementing an ex-directory telephone number for computer access; restrict knowledge of number to those with access; challenge response; call back; leased line; restrict access via telephone to only certain parts of system

(c)

– System software monitoring access and set to alert administrator in event of attempted unauthorised access. Review of system log for incidences of attempted access
– Review of exception reports detailing failed log on attempts
– Review of exception report of persons denied access to system or component of system

Solution 6.4

(a) Sales and trade debtors: software to re-tot ledger; analysis and stratify sales appropriately; identifying large round sum amounts; complete debtors circularisation; select sales; credit notes or debtors in excess of a given value; select negative sales/debtors; select sales/debtors in excess of credit limits; select sales/debtors matching records on employee masterfile; analysis of transactions with VAT not at standard rates; reperform debtor ageing; select credit notes not appropriately authorised or not matched to sales invoices; report post-reporting date cash receipts; report unallocated cash; identifying mis-sequencing of invoice numbers.

(b) Stocks: Report negative balances; report stocks in excess of one months sales; stratify and analyse stock balance; report unusual/unapproved stock movements; report slow moving/obsolete/aged stock; reperform stock ageing; retot stock ledger; identifying mis-sequencing of invoice numbers; selecting credit balances; identifying large round sum amounts; select items below re-order level; comparing stock cost to purchase ledger records; examining cut-off.

(c) Purchases and trade creditors: software to re-tot ledger; analyse and stratify purchases appropriately; select purchases; credit notes or creditors in excess of a given value; identifying large round sum amounts; select negative purchases/creditors; select purchases/creditors in excess of credit limits; select purchases/creditors matching records on employee masterfile; analysis of transactions with VAT not at standard rates; select credit notes not appropriately authorised or not matched to purchase invoices; identifying mis-sequencing of invoice numbers.

(d) Wages and salaries: retot ledger; report gross wages in excess of a given figure; report duplicates; report tax and other third-party deductions above a given % of salary; report differences between personnel's masterfile and payroll records; identifying mis-sequencing of records; identifying large round sum amounts.

(e) Fixed assets: retot ledger; report fully depreciated assets still in use; analyse and stratify balance; recalculate depreciation; identifying mis-sequencing of records; identifying large round sum amounts; identifying items for physical verification; identifying aged and obsolete assets; identify credit balances.

Solution 6.5

(a) General computer controls are controls over the environment in which the computer operates. They ensure that applications run smoothly and free from trouble. General controls consist of development controls, organisational controls and security controls.

(b) The development controls that I would expect to see operating in Beta include an appropriate organisational structure e.g. project team, to ensure the data processing development is subject to the highest standards in development and completion and to ensure that the project follows an appropriate life cycle:

- preliminary survey
- feasibility study
- system design and programme specification
- programming and drafting of operating instructions

- system review and testing by system analysts
- pilot study: system review and testing by user department; and by auditors
- implementation and
- post-implementation review.

A typical project team might be chaired by a senior representative of the Board of Directors and include systems analysts, programmers and operators, end user representatives and the internal auditors. Input might also be sought from New Dolphin in their role as the original software suppliers. The development process should be fully documented including:

- preliminary survey
- feasibility study
- system flowcharts
- program specification
- program logic
- test records
- summary of problems encountered and solutions thereto
- controls to minimise effect of system breakdown
- appropriate level
- good pilot cost control
- budgeting and monitoring
- controls to ensure all users are appropriately trained and introduced to the new system
- controls to ensure all data converts appropriately to the new system
- controls to ensure any unauthorised amendments to the system are detected and that unauthorised changes are prevent in so far as possible – including errors
- review of system once implemented to ensure that system development has achieved its objective and to learn from experience.

(c) The organisational controls that one would expect to see operating in Beta include:

- segregation of duties: segregation of user departments and the data processing department
- user department retention of control over data
- formal transfer of data between user department and the data processing department
- maintenance of data control logs in both user department and the data processing department
- clear lines of authority within the data processing department
- segregation of duties of the systems analyst, programmer and operator. This means programmer should not be able to test programme amendments with live programmes and/or data
- a reporting system that allows exceptions in data processing to be reported to those who can take appropriate action

- authorisation of any pre-programmed or computer generated actions e.g. orders for goods generated automatically when stock re-order level reached review of computer generated actions by appropriate officials.

Solution 6.6

(a) Computerised systems are very prevalent in the hotel business. The system used by the hotel is a sophisticated one with integrated functions from bedroom bookings to food and drink dispensing, stock control and gross profit reporting, virtually on an instantaneous basis. The risk and benefits from the use of such a system are as follows:

(i) Room Revenue Risks

- The system is a state of the art integrated point of sales system – the general manager or head receptionist may not have the necessary expertise in this type of computer system and may not fully understand it. This could lead to room revenue not being recorded properly etc.
- Inputting the wrong rate will lead to miscalculation of all invoices.
- System controls can be overridden and rates on the system changed by the General Manager or Head Receptionist.
- If the system controls are overridden and information is not accurate, then wrong decisions may be made.
- Systems such as these are usually designed to limit the volume of printed data, and there is the potential for loss of audit trail.

Room Revenue Benefits

- Quicker and more accurate calculation of invoices and there is less chance of human error associated with manual calculation.
- The software is state of the art and will facilitate quicker checkout times and improve guest services in general.
- There is a clearer trail of transactions and computation of various expenses by guests, which will lead to a more accurate bill calculation.
- The system will generate analysis of the performance of the various departments in the hotel.
- The system will lead to real time responses to room availability and occupancy.
- The system will allow the hotel to maximise its rate structure and occupancy levels (Demand Forecasting/Yield Management).
- The system will record customer details, which can be used for marketing purposes.
- It will allow the hotel to reallocate labour resources through reduction of manual back of house processes.
- The system will allow analysis of profitability by customer.
- The system will improve the skill sets of its reception employees.

(ii) Bar and Restaurant Revenue Risks

- The wrong standing prices may be applied leading to customer undercharging and loss of revenue.
- If the system is not properly set up, system controls can be overridden and rates on the system changed.
- Systems such as these are usually designed to limit the volume of printed data, and there is the potential for loss of audit trail.

Bar and Restaurant Revenue Benefits

- Once the system is set up it cannot be tampered with by staff.
- Using a pas system reduces the risk of mispricing compared with a system of manual input of prices into till machines.
- The system facilitates automatic review and control of margins.
- The control of margins acts as a deterrent to staff to commit fraud.
- The system facilitates immediate review of the most profitable product lines.
- There is a clearer trail of all transactions.
- Such a system is integrated with the stock system and facilitates reconciliation by product to stock movements.

(b) There are two main groups of Computer Assisted Audit Techniques (CAATs) – Audit software, which are computer programs used to examine the contents of the entity's computer files and test data which are used to test the operation of the entity's computer programs.

The following are among the CAATs that could be used on the audit of the Silver Birch Hotel.

Technique	Benefit
Access controls on reservations and room system	To test that only authorised staff have access to the system
Run off standing data and test it to approved rate card.	To test correct rate applied to room revenue
Reconciliation of reservations to revenue	To ensure completeness of revenue
CAAT to test the depreciation calculated by the fixed asset register	To test accuracy of the depreciation calculation
Processing of all turnover on to the ledger	To ensure completeness of income
Stratification of debtors	To be used in the audit of debtors e.g. selection for debtors circularisation etc.

| Selection of sample sizes | Quicker and more accurate selection of items for testing throughout the audit |
| Reconciliation of other revenue system e.g. telephone, laundry charges, etc. | To ensure correct recording of income |

Solution 6.7

(a)

ABC and Co
Chartered Accountants
and Registered Auditors
9 Main Street
Cork

Mr John Murphy
Managing Director
Elegant Limited
4 IT Disaster Road
Cork
15 October 2002

Dear John

I refer to our conversation on the review of your IT maintenance and security system and respond as follows:

(i) The procedures that should be put in place for the maintenance of the computer systems would include –

- A list should be drawn up of all the computer systems within the company.
- Ensure the proper management of the maintenance of the computer system by keeping a log record of system changes, employing staff with proper skills and experience etc.
- There should be specific authorisation checks to track any changes to the system e.g. signatures, initials etc.
- There should be a process for updating system facilities and arrangements.
- There should be a procedure for reporting system malfunctions.
- There should be a procedure for testing both the system unit and user.
- There should be a procedure for authorising the transfer of the system to the live environment.
- There should be a procedure for updating technical and user documentation.
- There should be proper training of all users to minimise the possibility of loss or damage to hardware.

(ii) The steps that I will take in order to carry out a review of the security of an IT environment are as follows:

- Obtain the company's written IT security plan.
- Review the company plan for completeness.
- Review the company's disaster recovery and backup procedures.
- Assess the adequacy of the company's software security system e.g.
  - safeboot passwords
  - encryption
  - network login
  - logical access controls
  - firewalls.
- Review the physical security procedures in place such as
  - raised floors for servers
  - locked rooms to deny unauthorised users access etc.
- Assess the procedure for reporting information security breaches.
- Evaluate management's attitude and response to previous weaknesses.
- Carry out tests on security weaknesses I detected.
- Review the training procedures for users in relation to security issues.

Should you wish to discuss any of the above please do not hesitate to contact me.

Yours sincerely

Etc.

(b)

Memo

To: Audit partner

From: Audit senior

Re: Installation of new accounting system at Elegant Limited

The following are the proposed headings I intend to use for my review of the installation of the new accounting system at Elegant Limited.

- Users – review of access controls such as passwords, network logins etc.
- Coding structure – review of coding structure used.
- Security – review of disaster recovery plans, back up procedures, physical security etc.
- Capacity – review of capacity requirements and capability of the system to meet users' needs.
- Transfer of balances – review procedures for transferring balances to the new system.

- Audit trail – review of paper trail to ensure a proper trail is kept of all inputs to the new system.
- Data transfer – review procedures for transferring data to the new system.
- Training – review planned training for users of the system.
- Support from supplier – review supplier support contracts for adequacy.
- Other installations – review other installations to establish how they interact with the accounting system.

Can you revert to me with any comments etc.

Solution 6.8

(a)

> J Ryan& Co.
> Chartered Accountants &
> Registered Auditors
> Penrose Street
> Dublin

Mr P. Hourigan
Finance Director
UGARS Ltd
Ballymount Industrial Estate
Dublin

Dear Sir,

In response to your recent request please find set out below a description of the various security settings that we as auditors would want to consider when reviewing remote and local security controls within the new computer system that your company has recently acquired and implemented.

- Minimum password length – best practice would indicate that this should be a minimum of 6 characters.
- Maximum "force change" periods – best practice would suggest that the maximum age of a password before forced expiry should be in the region of 30–45 days.
- Password history – the password history will retain a list of the user's previous used passwords to ensure that the practice of reuse or rotation of passwords is not adopted.
- Lockout settings – should be reviewed, ideally these should be set to lock out an access attempt after 3 unsuccessful login attempts, with the lockout duration being "forever" until administrator intervention.
- The setting for the last recorded login should be analysed to check for redundancy of accounts where the last login date is "aged".

- The settings that restrict the access times of staff to systems should be reviewed to ensure that they are set to restrict access where operationally possible.
- Ensuring the desktop has a time out enabled that will automatically invoke a password protected screensaver where the keyboard has not been used for "n" minutes.
- The access rights of individual users which restrict their actions in an application system and provide an expected level of segregation of duties.
- The access permissions granted on folders and files within Public Groups on a shared/network drive.

If you have any queries concerning the matters outlined above please do not hesitate to contact me.

Kind Regards,

J. Ryan

(b)

- The auditor should be aware that materiality does not solely have a quantitative element, there is also a qualitative element.
- The auditor has to consider overall materiality at overall financial statement level and in relation to classes of transactions, account balances and disclosures.
- The auditor should be aware that "ballpark" may not be sufficient for some disclosures under statutory law. An expected degree of accuracy may be required for certain disclosures.

(c)

The implementation of the new computer system may allow the auditor to apply Computer Assisted Audit Techniques (CAATs) to increase the efficiency and effectiveness of the audit and also to reduce the amount of substantive audit testing required.

CHAPTER 7

Solution 7.1

Select a sample of additions from the fixed asset registers and ensure they have adequate supporting documentation.

Solution 7.2

It is more economical to audit fixed assets using substantive testing because of the relatively few associated transactions compared with other balances.

Solution 7.3

To:	Audit Assistant
From:	Audit Senior
Date:	1 May 2005
Re:	Builder Limited
	Audit of Tangible Fixed Assets
	Year ended 31 March 2005

The following is the audit programme to be followed when auditing Builder tangible fixed assets:

- Prepare or obtain a fixed asset register showing the date of purchase of assets and the make up of the opening balance.
- Agree the client's fixed asset schedule to the closing nominal ledger. Check the tots on the schedule.
- Agree opening balances to prior-year signed financial statements.
- Physically verify assets. Ensure assets brought forward have been inspected.
- Vouch additions to supporting documentation.
- Vouch disposals to supporting documentation.
- Examine title documents (if not held as security). Ensure title is in the name of the company.
- Examine vehicle registration documents. Note details of model and user.
- Review hire purchase and lease agreements and ensure the assets and related obligations have been properly accounted for in accordance with IAS17.

Solution 7.4

The following audit tests should be completed on each of the reconciling items:

(1) Plant held on operating lease – as per IAS 17 "Lease payments under an operating lease shall be recognised as an expense on a straight line basis over the lease term". The

operating lease agreement should be reviewed and the transaction should be traced through the P&L.

As per IAS 17 assets held under operating leases should not be capitalised, therefore Handitel are correct in omitting this from its final tangible fixed asset listing.

(2) Repairs posted to fixed asset register – These items should be vouched to purchase invoices to verify that they are in fact repairs and not of a capital nature. An analytical review should also be completed on the repairs and maintenance expenses and fluctuations should be discussed with the client.

(3) Assets purchased on 5 January 2008 – Vouch receipt of goods to Goods Despatch note and invoice and vouch payment for goods to the bank. Enquire of management when the asset was brought into use.

From enquiries and tracing to backup documentation determine if it is correct to capitalise 20% or 100% of the cost of the asset.

(4) Assets excluded from register – Vouch receipt of goods to Goods Despatch notes and invoices. Vouch payment to the bank. If receipted before year end then it is correct to capitalise them at year end.

Review the depreciation on these assets and ensure it is accurate and complete.

(5) Adjustment for capitalisation of interest – As per IAS 23 interest can be capitalised if it is directly attributable to the construction of fixed assets. Capitalisation should cease when the asset is ready to be brought into use. The interest capitalised should be recomputed.

Ensure there is consistency in treatment across all fixed asset classes.

Ensure the new accounting policy is reflected in the notes to the financial statements.

(6) Assets constructed internally – Inspect the supporting documentation for labour costs, materials and overheads, ensure they are directly attributable and cease when the asset is ready to be brought into use.

Verify that only expenditure relating to design, construction or installation of the asset is capitalised and that no profit or abnormal costs are included. Review the depreciation policy and review if depreciation has been charged since October.

CHAPTER 8

Solution 8.1

(a) CASTLELYONS INVENTORY SCHEDULE TESTING

- Check tots, costs and calculations of the schedule
- Verify that the cost of each Product No. is correct to supporting purchase invoices
- Ensure that stock is valued at lower of cost or net realisable value in accordance with IAS 2, Inventories
- The Net Realisable Value of the stock should be tested by agreeing sales to recent sales invoices
- Review stocktake reports for evidence of obsolescence
- Agree stock figures to nominal ledger
- For products where the components can be sold separately, the component value should be tested
- Discuss with management the saleability of all products and substantively test the responses e.g. look at orders placed and post-year end sales
- Review the level of sales of the products in the last few months to determine if any provision maybe required

(b) Stocktake Error

- Contact person who attended the stocktake and enquire if they remember anything unusual
- Inquire from management how the error was detected
- Recount the stock of the products relating to the errors as soon as possible
- Reconcile the movement of the stock from the year end to the subsequent
- Recount the movements should be agreed to the sales and purchases ledgers
- Review stocktake error and consider whether it has any material impact for the audit report

(c)

Current Assets: Inventory €/£808,264

Explicit assertions:

– inventory exists (existence)
– the correct amount of inventory is €/£808,264 (valuation)

Implicit assertions:

– all inventory that should be reported has been included (completeness)

- all reported inventory is owned by the entity (ownership) – there are no restrictions on the use of the inventory (presentation and disclosure)

Solution 8.2

(a) Ensure that adequate stocktaking instructions were given to all counters
   - Check that there is no movement of stock during the count
   - Review for slow-moving stock
   - Check that all stock has been counted
   - Perform test counts from the stock sheets to the floor to test existence of stock and counts from the floor to the sheet to test the completeness of the count sheets
   - Obtain cut-off information i.e. Last GRNs and despatch dockets

(b) Test cut-off at the stocktake

Purchases cut-off: Select the last goods received notes for goods delivered pre stocktake and check that they have been recorded in the book stock before the stocktake. Also select a sample of goods received notes for stock received after the stocktake and ensure they were not recorded in the stock system until after the stocktake.

Sales Cut-off: Select the last despatch dockets for goods despatched pre stocktake and ensure the sale has been recorded before the stocktake. Select the first despatch dockets for goods despatched after stocktake and ensure the sale has been recorded after the stocktake.

Test cut-off at year end

Purchases cut-off: Select the last goods received notes for goods delivered pre year end and check that they have been recorded in the book stock before the year end. Also check to ensure that the purchase invoice relating to the goods received note has been recorded in the purchases ledger or accruals at year end. Also select a sample of goods received notes for stock received after the year end and ensure they were not recorded in the stock system until after year end. Also check to ensure that the purchase invoice relating to the goods received note has not been recorded in the purchases ledger or accruals at year end.

Sales Cut-off: Select the last despatch dockets for goods despatched pre year end and ensure the sale has been recorded before the year end. Select the first despatch dockets for goods despatched after year end and ensure the sale has been recorded after the year end. Also trace the despatch documentation through to the relating sales invoice and ensure the sales invoice was posted to debtors and sales in the correct period.

   (i) Check the level of adjustment posted to book stock at the end of each stocktake. If there are only minor adjustments posted this will give the auditor comfort that the stock system at any one time is fairly accurate.

(ii) Obtain a summary report from the stock manager which details how often all stock was counted and ensure that all stock was counted at least 3 times a year.
(iii) Check the level of adjustments posted near year end.
(iv) Review the inventory listing for negative items and ensure that they are treated correctly.
(v) Test completeness of raw material receipts between the stocktake and the year end. This may be tested through checking the sequence of GRNs and tracing a sample of the GRNs to the raw material sub ledger.
(vi) Test the completeness of the transfer in to WIP from raw materials and the transfer out of WIP to finished goods. This may be completed by testing a sample of journals for transfers of EIP to FG and WIP to raw material.
(vii) Check completeness of despatches of FG. This should be tested by checking the sequence of despatch notes and tracing a sample of items in Sales/COS reports to the FG sub ledger.

CHAPTER 9

Solution 9.2

Where the controls process surrounding the sales and debtors cycle is weak this means that a greater level of substantive testing will be necessary in order to gain comfort over the assertions surrounding total sales and the period end debtors balance.

- the auditor may consider vouching sales down to the materiality level to invoices raised/contracts/rental agreements depending on the nature of the business in order to gain comfort over accuracy of total sales
- the auditor may perform a debtors circularisation in order to gain comfort over the existence/occurrence of the balances
- the auditor may perform post-year end cash receipts testing on balances which are not confirmed via the debtors circularisation in order to confirm the existence/occurrence of the balances
- the auditor may perform cut-off testing to verify that sales invoices around the period end have been included in the correct period in order to gain comfort over the cut-off of the debtors balance and total sales included in the accounts
- the auditor may perform a substantive analytical review on trade debtors
- the auditor may consider credit notes issued post-period end by the client and determine if any adjusting journals are necessary

Where the control environment is weak the auditor will perform a further substantive testing to compensate for the lack of controls comfort obtained, for example, when performing debtors circularisation and post-period end cash receipts testing down to materiality will be necessary in contrast to a strong control environment where testing down to materiality will not be necessary and a lower level of substantive testing will be supplemented by controls comfort.

Solution 9.3

Where the controls process surrounding the sales and debtors cycle is strong this means that a lower level of substantive testing will be necessary in order to gain comfort over the assertions surrounding total sales and the period end debtors balance.

- substantive testing of sales in the form of vouching total sales to invoices raised/contracts/rental agreements depending on the nature of the business in order to gain comfort over accuracy of total sales will not be necessary. Performance of substantive analytical procedures over sales will be sufficient along with strong controls comfort to gain assurance over total sales
- the auditor may perform a debtors circularisation in order to gain comfort over the existence/occurrence of the balances

- the auditor may perform post year end cash receipts testing on balances which are not confirmed via the debtors circularisation in order to confirm the existence/occurrence of the balances
- the auditor may perform cut-off testing to verify that sales invoices around the period end have been included in the correct period in order to gain comfort over the cut-off of the debtor balance and total sales included in the accounts
- the auditor may perform an analytical review on trade debtors instead of a substantive analytical review given the strong control environment
- the auditor may consider credit notes issued post period end by the client and determine if any adjusting journals are necessary

Where the control environment is strong the auditor will perform a lesser extent of substantive testing due to the significant comfort obtained from controls work, for example, when performing debtors circularisation and post period end cash receipts testing down to materiality will not be necessary in contrast to a weak control environment where testing down to materiality would be necessary and a greater level of substantive testing will be necessary to compensate for lack of controls comfort.

Solution 9.4

1. (i)

	€/£	
Total sales to 31/12/07	462,000	
Increase in revenue due to new DVDs brought to market	130,280	See a) below
Decline in revenue due to DVDs discontinued	(21,930)	See b) below
Increase in revenue due to introduction of children's sweatshirt range	17,550	See c) below
Decline in revenue due to reduction in magazine prices	(15,800)	See d) below
Total expectation for sales to 31/12/08	**572,100**	

Expected Sales FY 2008	
DVDs	335,350
Sweatshirts	54,550
Magazines	182,200
Total	572,100

(ii)
New DVDs

- determine basis of budgeted figures, understand budget and assess how robust the budget is
- consider who prepares the budget
- consider who authorises the budget
- determine if actual results are traced to budget on a timely basis and if remedial action is taken
- understand why budgeted figures have not been achieved and validate the reasons for this
- confirm month of introduction of new DVDs to market for example by inspection of sales catalogue or sales records
- validate selling prices of DVDs, for example, by inspection of sales catalogue or sales invoices

Discontinued DVDs

- confirm that selling prices for DVDs 1 and 2 were €/£22 and €/£19 respectively for all of prior year
- confirm month of discontinuation of DVDs to market, for example, by inspection of sales catalogue or sales records

Sweatshirts

- confirm month of introduction of children's sweatshirts to market, for example, by inspection of sales catalogue or sales records
- validate selling prices of children's sweatshirts for example by inspection of sales catalogue or sales invoices
- inspect market research and assess reliability of data and confirm expected monthly sales figure
- consider if average selling price is a reliable basis for use when determining expectation

Magazines

- assess reliability of using prior year sales volume when determining expectation
- view sales records to confirm selling price cut for amount of price cut and date of price cut e.g. inspect invoice before and after date and confirm that price cut has taken place

(iii)
- develop threshold for further investigation based on planning materiality of €/£10,000, for example 75% of €/£10,000 i.e. €/£7,500
- compute difference between expectation and actual result

Expected sales	€/£572,100
Actual sales	€/£568,000
Difference	€/£4,100

– Where difference is greater than threshold, for further investigation perform additional testing: not deemed necessary as difference is below threshold for further investigation

(a) New DVDs

DVD	Number of Months on the Market	Expected Revenue (No. of months on market × selling price × budgeted monthly sales)
1	11	11 × €/£10 × 250 = €/£27,500
2	9	9 × €/£17 × 300 = €/£45,900
3	6	6 × €/£12 × 485 = €/£34,920
4	4	4 × €/£15 × 245 = €/£14,700
5	2	2 × €/£22 × 165 = €/£7,260
Expected increase in revenue		€/£130,280

(b) Discontinued DVDs

DVD 1
Lost revenue = €/£22 × 565
= €/£12,430

DVD 2
Lost revenue = €/£19 € 500
= €/£9,500

Expected decline in revenue = €/£21,930

(c) Children's Sweatshirts

Number of months on the market = 2

Average selling price = €/£13.50

Expected monthly sales = 650

Expected increase in revenue = 2 × €/£13.50 × 650

= €/£17,550

(d) Magazines

Price Cut	No. of Months During Which Price Cut was in Operation	Prior Year Annual Sales Volume	Lost Revenue
€/£0.2	12	20,000	€/£0.2 × 20,000 = €/£4,000
€/£0.2	12	13,500	€/£0.2 × 13,500 = €/£2,700
€/£0.3	10	10,000	€/£0.3 × 10/12 × 10,000 = €/£2,250
€/£0.4	12	11,000	€/£0.4 × 11,000 = €/£4,400
€/£0.15	7	28,000	€/£0.15 × 7/12 × 28,000 = €/£2,450
Decline in revenue			**€/£15,800**

Solution 9.5

(a)

- Obtain an analysis of the bad debt provision which shows which customer balances have been provided for by the client
- Obtain an analysis of the invoice numbers, invoice dates and invoice amounts which have been provided for
- Discuss with management/directors how provision amounts have been determined and assess reasonableness and basis of provision amounts
- Consideration should be given to the following when considering the amount provided for by the client and if it is necessary or adequate:

(a) Has the customer gone bankrupt? If so the total customer balance on the ledger should be provided for in full.
(b) Is there a dispute over a balance which has been provided for?
(c) Is the customer experiencing financial difficulties?
(d) How long has the balance which has been provided for been outstanding?
(e) How recent was the last payment received from the customer? The greater the length of time the greater the risk that future payments will not be received
(f) Is the customer account on hold or is the client still trading with the customer?
(g) Is the client actively chasing the debt?

— It will be important for the auditor to confirm any of the circumstances above in order to validate the need for the provision amount:

(a) Bankruptcy should be known publicly and can be validated with reasonable ease
(b) Where balances are disputed inspect correspondence with the customer (letters/e-mails/faxes) discussing the dispute
(c) A review of the customer's payment patterns may indicate cashflow problems; for example, if the customer is making round sum payments on a timely basis such as €/£1,000 each month, this could suggest that the customer is experiencing difficulties and may cast doubt over the recoverability of the balance and confirm the need for a provision
(d) Inspect invoices which have been provided for and confirm the age of the invoices
(e) By inspection of customer accounts and cash receipts book, verify the date of the final payment made by the client
(f) Inspect accounting system to confirm if the customer account is on hold or if it remains active
(g) Inspect correspondence with the customer (letters/e-mails/faxes) requesting payment for aged balances

In view of information obtained from testing the auditor must consider if the provision is adequate i.e. has an over/under provision been made. The auditor should consider if correcting audit adjustments are necessary.

(b)

Estimate	Audit Approach
Accruals	— discuss with management the method of determining balance and understand the basis of the accrued amount; — evaluate whether the assumptions used are consistent with each other, the prior year, supporting data, relevant historical data, and industry data

	– consider whether accounting estimates are in compliance with generally accepted accounting policies
	– recompute accrued amounts
	– apply analytical procedures
	– assess reasonableness of period end balance
	– confirm that significant estimates are disclosed appropriately in the financial statements
	– verify post year end payment of accrued amounts
Depreciation	– consider reasonableness of depreciable life
	– consider appropriateness of depreciation policy
	– recompute depreciation for significant fixed asset classes and assess reasonableness
	– where significant differences arise investigate reasons for differences
Stock provision	– discuss with management the method of determining balance and understand the basis of the stock provision
	– evaluate whether the assumptions used are consistent with each other, the prior year, supporting data, relevant historical data, and industry data
	– apply analytical procedures
	– assess reasonableness of period end balance
	– confirm that significant estimates are disclosed appropriately in the financial statements
	– investigate post period end sale of stock items and confirm that selling price is greater than carrying value in the accounts i.e. confirm that stock balance is not overstated

Solution 9.6

(a)

To:	All members of engagement team

From:	Audit Senior

Re:	Audit approach to testing of debtor balances aged greater than 90 days

Date:	June 2008

On review of aged debtor listing for Ballycane Metals Ltd it is clear that half of the year end balance is aged 90 days plus. The total balance is material to the financial statements therefore it is important that we perform suitable audit procedures around the aged balances in order to gain sufficient comfort over the valuation of the debtor balance and the recoverability of the aged debts. In order to obtain sufficient appropriate audit evidence I suggest that the following is obtained/considered:

1. Obtain an analysis of all debts aged 90 days plus by customer name which provides a breakdown of all invoices making up the aged balance
2. Obtain an analysis of the bad debt provision (if a provision has been made) and consider how much has been provided for in relation to debts aged 90 days plus
3. Confirm aging of invoices on the debtors ledger is accurate by reperforming the aging of a sample of customer invoices
4. Discuss with the credit controller/financial controller/directors the circumstances surrounding each aged debt as each balance will likely have unique circumstances. The following should be given consideration:
   (a) Has the customer been declared bankrupt suggesting that the balance is not recoverable?
   (b) Is the customer experiencing cashflow problems? This could be noted on review of payment pattern by the customer; for example if the customer is making round sum payments on a timely basis such as €/£1,000 each month, this could suggest that the customer is experiencing difficulties and may cast doubt over the recoverability of the balance
   (c) How recent was the last payment received from the customer? The greater the length of time the greater the risk that future payments will not be received
   (d) Confirm if the customer account remains active. Has the account been put on stop or is the client still supplying the customer? Where the account has been put on stop this suggests that a dispute is ongoing between the customer and the client
   (e) Is there a dispute ongoing between the customer and the client over particular invoices, for example, due to faulty stock being supplied or the customer being invoiced for goods which they did not receive? Have credit notes been issued post period end to correct account balance? Are audit adjustments necessary to reflect this in the year end accounts?
   (f) Has payment been received from the customer post period end? If so payment should be vouched to cash receipts book
   (g) Is the client actively chasing the aged debt? Confirm via inspection of letters which the client has sent to the customer seeking payment or memos detailing phone calls which the client has made for same reason
   (h) Based on experience are any of the customers notoriously slow payers?
   (i) Are all customer balances legitimate? Is there any issue of existence? If so include customers with aged debtor balances within the debtors to be circularised.

It is essential that at all times you keep in mind the valuation of the debtors balance included in the period end accounts and the recoverability of the balances:

- Have all balances which are unlikely to be recovered in view of investigations performed by the audit team been adequately provided for? Should the provision be increased? Are audit adjustments needed?
- Has the debtor balance been overstated?
- If significant debts are written off what are the implications on the trading results of the company?

(b)

In determining an expectation for prompt payment discount the auditor should consider the following:

- Is the discount available to all customers or only to key customers?
- If available only to key customers obtain details of activity on the customers' accounts during the period under review i.e. total value of goods invoiced to the customer, determine expectation by calculating 3% of total sales value (assuming that all key customers always took advantage of prompt payment discount – this can be confirmed by reviewing a sample of invoice dates and when they were paid by the customer throughout the period under review to determine whether they generally made payment promptly).
- Where discount is available to all customers ascertain from sales manager which customers generally during the period under review have taken advantage of the discount available. Unlikely that all customers will avail of the facility. For all named customers validate if they have paid promptly during the period by performing the same review of invoices and payments as noted above. Review customer activity to ascertain total sales value to customers using prompt payment facility and calculate expected discount in same way as above.

Solution 9.7

The auditor should scan the period end debtors listing and review for any credit balances. Where credit balances are noted the auditor should:

(a) determine why the balances have arisen i.e. are they deposits received from customers, payments on account, overpayments or amounts posted in error to the debtors ledger?
(b) when the reason for the credit balances appearing on the ledger are ascertained the auditor should consider if any correcting audit adjustments are necessary
(c) where credit balances are deposits received from customer the auditor should vouch the receipt of the deposits to the cash receipts book/bank statement and inspect any supporting documentation such as a signed agreement with the customer for the deposit. Where deposits are refundable the balances should be disclosed within other creditors instead of being netted off against the total debtor balance

(d) where credit balances are payments on account the auditor should vouch the receipt of the deposits to the cash receipts book/bank statement. Where payments on account are refundable the balances should be disclosed within other creditors instead of being netted off against the total debtor balance
(e) where credit balances are overpayments by the customer the auditor must determine whether the client has informed the customer of the overpayment. Where the customer has not been informed the possibility of money laundering should be considered. Where the customer has been informed the auditor must verify this via inspection of correspondence with the customer notifying them of the overpayment. Overpayments should be disclosed within other creditors instead of being netted off against the total debtor balance
(f) where credit balances have arisen due to amounts being posted in error to the debtors ledger the auditor must obtain the details of how the error arose and understand the impact of the error on the financial statements i.e. should a correcting audit adjustment be made to correct the disclosure per the accounts?

Solution 9.8

(a)

- No controls exercised by head office over cash sales at sites (a) and (b) as tills are not networked
- Till reconciliations are retained therefore no evidence of reconciliations being performed, lack of control could result in misappropriation of cash
- Transfer of cash from sites (a) and (b) is not secure
- Lodgements are not made to bank on a timely basis, increasing the risk of loss due to theft
- Manual cash lodgement book is not maintained by the client and analysis of weekly lodgements to the bank is not possible meaning that a cash audit trail does not exist

(b)

- Maintain a manual cash received book
- Retain till reconciliations
- Network tills between head office and sites (a) and (b) and implement head office review of till reconciliations for sites (a) and (b) on a weekly basis

(c)

- Alternative testing must be performed to gain comfort over period end trade debtors balance e.g. post year cash receipts testing
- Request raises suspicion over existence of customer balances when the client does not want the auditor to contact customer

- Alternative procedures may not provide adequate comfort
- Qualified audit opinion may be necessary where sales/trade debtors balance cannot be confirmed

Solution 9.9

(a) A debtors circularisation should not be performed where any of the following are identified:
- Debtors balance is immaterial to the financial statements
- The use of confirmations is deemed to be ineffective e.g. based on past audit experience the auditor is unlikely to get an adequate response rate to the confirmations or that responses are known or expected to be unreliable and, in such cases, the auditor may conclude that the use of confirmations would be ineffective.
- Based on the auditor's assessment of risk and comfort from controls testing, the risk in relation to the debtors balance has been reduced to an acceptably low level to allow alternative forms of substantive testing.

b) Where debtors do not respond to the debtors circularisation the auditor should perform alternative procedures which include the following:
- agree period end debtor balance to invoice/sales invoice/goods delivered note
- vouch post-period end payment of the debtor balance by agreeing payment to the client's cash receipts book and bank statement and verify that post-period end payment is in respect of invoices included on the debtors ledger at the period end
- consider whether it is necessary to confirm the existence of the customer, for example, by visiting the business premises or telephoning the customer

Solution 9.10

Risk	Financial Satement Assertion	Testing Performed to Mitigate Risks
1. Recoverability of the trade debtors balance i.e. will the customer recover the trade debtor balance in full	Valuation	(a) testing of post-period end receipts from customers in respect of period end balances (b) review of aged debtor balances e.g. all balances aged greater than 90 days and discussion with relevant personnel of the reason why the balances have not been settled at the period end (c) consideration of the bad debt provision and its adequacy in view of findings from (b) above

2. Are all customer balances legitimate i.e. do the balances represent real sales made to real customers	Existence/ Occurence	(a) Performance of a debtors circularisation to confirm existence of customer and agree period end balance per client records
3. Have all sales invoices raised during the period under review been posted to the debtors ledger	Completeness	(a) Select a sample of invoices raised during the period and confirm that they have been posted to the debtors ledger
		(b) Perform period end cut-off procedures and confirm that invoices raised around the period end – where the greatest risk exists – have been posted to the ledger in the correct period i.e. vouch that only pre-period end invoices have been posted to the ledger and that post-period end invoices have only been posted to the ledger post period end
		(c) Review credit notes issued to customers post-period end by the client in respect of pre-period end invoices and consider if adjusting journals are necessary to correct the sales figure and debtors balance included in the financial statements

CHAPTER 10

Solution 10.1

The auditor could first obtain the year-end bank statement for the loan account. He should then review the year-end bank reconciliation performed by the client to agree the figure disclosed in the financial statements if there is a difference between the figure in the accounts and the figure on the bank statements (e.g. due to a repayment in transit etc.). A bank confirmation letter should also be obtained directly from the bank, and the auditor should check that interest accrued on the loan has been properly accounted for.

Solution 10.2

You would expect internal audit to have conducted the following in order to determine whether you can reduce the amount of detailed testing on bank and cash.

Branch visits involving:

– checking compliance with standard procedures
– cash counts to confirm amounts agree with point of sale record
– all branches to be covered on a rotational basis.

A review of bank reconciliations to ensure:

– reconciliations performed
– amounts banked agree with point of sale record
– delays in banking investigated.

Internal audit should also investigate the use and review of exception reports for identifying and investigating the differences between the book amount and the actual amount.

Ideally, the retail outlet should undertake weekly stock counts and reconcile stock movements to sales. The internal auditors should attend these counts and review the reconciliations.

Solution 10.3

The request should be sent on the auditors' letterhead and clearly identify all information required and the auditor must maintain complete control over the process. The audit confirmation is a very important part of the audit of bank and cash as it provides the auditor with reliable independent third-party audit evidence.

Also the bank confirmation should disclose cash on deposit, loans and details of all accounts in the name of the audit client at the balance sheet date.

Solution 10.4

In order to ensure that all bank accounts are confirmed at the year end the auditor should obtain details of accounts held by and on behalf of the entity by:

- Enquiring of management details of bank accounts held by the entity
- Reviewing details of any new accounts opened
- Enquiring from the bank for details of any changes to banking arrangements.

Solution 10.5

An audit provides management with assurance that it is complying with statutory duties and that information filed with the registrar of companies meets legal requirements. It also provides other stakeholders such as the tax authorities with assurance on the credibility of the figures.

Audited financial statements are more reliable and will result in more informed decisions by management. The company will also benefit from the by-products of an audit such as the identification of weaknesses and recommendations for reducing risk and improving performance.

An audit imposes discipline which is useful for control purposes in a growing company.

Audited financial statements will assist a future sale of an entity by providing a basis for the determination of the purchase consideration.

CHAPTER 11

Solution 11.1

(a)

Investment Audit Work

- Vouch each of the investments to supporting documentation
- Verify that each of the investments are in the name of Meridian
- Obtain a copy of the investment reports to confirm the net market values of each of the investments
- Investigate where cost of investment is greater than market value i.e. GOLDEN and YELLOW
- Where the cost of the investment is greater than its market value enquire from management if the investment has been impaired and assess the need for an impairment review
- For any new investments, agree purchase to supporting documentation in the year of purchase and consideration paid should be agreed to bank statements
- The YELLOW investment should not have been included in the client schedule, as it had been sold before year-end
- The sale of the YELLOW investment should be vouched and the loss reviewed to ensure that it is appropriately calculated and correctly accounted for and disclosed

(b)

Audit Issues

– The market value of the investment in GOLDEN equals €/£1,320,000 which is €/£334,000 lower than the cost of the investment, therefore an impairment of €/£334,000 exists.
– The impairment in investment may need to be adjusted for as the investment in YELLOW is still appearing on the client year end schedule despite the fact that it has been sold before the year end.
– We need to investigate the circumstances surrounding this.

(c)

Proposed Adjustments

Please find outlined below the adjustments to the investment balance that I would recommend:

	€/£'000	€/£'000
Dr. Profit and Loss – loss on sale	€/£811	
Cr. Balance Sheet – Investment		€/£811
Being the sale of the investment not recorded		
Dr. Profit and Loss – impairment provision	€/£334	
Cr. Balance Sheet – Investment		€/£334
Being the recording of the investment at the lower of cost or market value		

Solution 11.2

The procedures that should be adopted in order to obtain the required assurance concerning the standard audit objectives for the current asset balances detailed are as follows:

TRADE INVESTMENTS (LISTED AND UNLISTED)

Completeness

The auditor will normally obtain sufficient assurance on the completeness objective for investments from work in conjunction with other objectives, particularly that relating to existence and to rights and obligations.

Recomputation in total is an efficient method of auditing income from fixed interest investments such as loans, debentures, fixed rate preference shares, and government securities. The auditor should recompute the total income by using the principal amount and a known interest rate.

A substantive analytical review may, for example, be based on a comparison of the average recorded yield and the investment portfolio (or outstanding loans) with prior years and with budget. Alternatively, the audit may develop an estimate by applying an average yield to the average market value of investments.

Accuracy

The auditor will obtain part of the required assurance concerning the accuracy objective from work on the other objectives. For example, the work carried out to verify the existence and ownership of investments should provide secondary assurance that those investments have been accurately recorded. However, it is still necessary to check the following:

– The control account reconciliation
– The carrying values of investments

- The classification of investments in subsidiaries and associates
- That the amounts in the financial statements agree with the accounting records

Where there is an investment control account in the general ledger, the auditor should check the reconciliation of the control account with the total of the individual investment balances by:

- Tracing the totals to the general ledger
- Testing individual balances with the investment ledger (or equivalent records)
- Checking the additions of the reconciliation

As part of the business review, the auditor should review the client's accounting policies for determining the carrying value of investments. This should include checking that such policies conform with relevant legislation and accounting standards, that they are appropriate to the circumstances, and have been consistently applied.

The auditor should examine supporting documents for additions (e. g. broker's contract notes), ascertain that the transaction was properly authorised and approved and trace the acquisition to the investment ledger or equivalent detailed record.

The auditors should examine supporting documents such as broker's contract notes ensuring that disposals have been authorised and approved. The disposals should be checked to the investment ledger or equivalent detailed records. The correct calculation and recording of any gain or loss on disposals should also be checked. If only part of the investment has been sold, the auditor should check that the unsold balance is recorded correctly.

It is not normally necessary to investigate the selling price if it is possible to rely on the independence of the broker who has originated the contract note. However, if there is any doubt about the independence of the broker, or if the investment is not listed, it is important to consider whether the sale price appears reasonable. If necessary, the auditor should make reference to a stock exchange official list (if the investment is listed), or to audited financial statements or PE ratios of similar companies (if the investment is not listed).

If there are any investments carried at a valuation the auditor should check the market value to the stock exchange daily list or the *Financial Times* (for listed investments). For unlisted investments, the valuation by the directors is often based on the underlying net assets or a PE ratio of similar companies using reports or valuations made by experts. The auditor should discuss the basis of the valuation with the client, review the available financial statements, and inspect any reports of the experts on whom the directors have relied.

Existence: Rights and Obligations

The principal substantive test for the existence and ownership of investments is the inspection of documents of title, or confirmation from third parties (normally independent, reliable authorised custodians) that they are holding such documents on behalf of the client. The auditor should also obtain direct confirmation of loans.

To ascertain whether investments have been pledged as collateral or as security for liabilities (either the client or a third party), the auditor should enquire of client management, and review board minutes, loan agreements and other appropriate documentation.

Cut-off

The auditor will normally obtain sufficient assurance relating to the cut-off objective from work carried out on the completeness, accuracy, existence and rights and obligations objectives. For example, work on additions and disposals will also provide evidence that purchases and sales of investments and income from investments have been recorded in the appropriate period.

Valuation

Clients may classify investments as either fixed or current assets and the treatment of any diminution in value will vary accordingly. In the case of fixed asset investments, provision is required for any permanent diminution in value whereas for current asset investments carried at cost, provision is also required for any temporary diminution in value (i.e. so that the current asset is carried at the lower of cost and net realisable value).

There are two complementary procedures that the auditor may use with regard to assessing any diminutions in value. These are:

- Checking individual investments and making specific enquiries into their current status and prospects; and
- Reviewing the investment portfolio in the light of background knowledge of the client acquired during the business review, and discussing the portfolio with members of management who possess an adequate level of knowledge and seniority.

For listed investments carried at cost, a significant decrease in the market value may suggest a permanent diminution in value. However, market value might not be an appropriate indicator if the market in the shares is small or infrequent, or if the dealings have been suspended. In these cases the auditor may need to follow the procedures relating to unlisted investments.

Unlisted investments should be examined by reference to all the available information, such as recent financial statements, reports by independent accountants or investment advisers, and operating forecasts and budgets produced by the investee. The auditor should consider the marketability of the investment and, in the case of overseas investments, any restriction on the remittances of funds.

Management is frequently reluctant to recognise that an apparent reduction in the value of an investment is permanent, particularly if the client is committed to some form of continued support to the investee. Whilst it is important to recognise that decisions concerning the permanent impairment of value involve judgement, the auditor should not accept unrealistic optimism on the part of management.

Presentation and Disclosure

To help achieve the objective the auditor should, at the end of the audit, review the financial statements and consider the matters set out in a GAAP checklist.

PREPAYMENTS

The auditor should be aware that the prepayments balance in total only equals the audit materiality balance and, as such, only limited work should be carried out.

The auditor should carry out a substantive analytical review of prepayments based on prior period amounts adjusted for any relevant changes in the business. The auditor should be aware of the client's major items of income and expenditure from which prepayments, accrued income and other debtors might arise.

Examination and checking of supporting documents should only be carried out where prepayments appear to be out of line with the expected amount and where the difference is material (say one-third of the audit materiality level).

BANK AND CASH BALANCES

Completeness

The auditor should derive the required assurance that all bank balances have been identified and accounted for principally from the understanding of the business which has been acquired through the business review.

In particular, the auditor should consider whether the number of bank accounts appears adequate for the level of business.

Additionally, the following procedures may be appropriate:

- Reviewing the list of balances at the previous balance sheet date and enquiring into any changes
- Scrutinising bank confirmations, cash books, bank statements and board minutes for evidence of accounts opened during the period.

Accuracy

Detailed checking of the bank reconciliations should normally provide sufficient assurance that bank and cash transactions have been accurately processed. The auditor should normally check the bank reconciliation at the same date confirmation of balances are obtained from the bank.

The auditor should carry out the following work:

- Checking the balances on the reconciliations to the general ledger, the bank confirmations and the bank statements.
- Testing the additions of the reconciliations, and of the lists of unpresented cheques and outstanding lodgements.
- Tracing entries in the cash records before the substantive testing date to the bank statements or reconciliations.
- Checking unpresented cheques and outstanding lodgements recorded in the bank reconciliation to the cash records and the bank statement.
- Investigating and verifying any other reconciled items.

The auditor should select from the receipts and payments recorded in the cash records for the period before the substantive testing date, and should ensure that the items selected are either:

- Recorded on bank statements prior to the substantive testing date; or
- Included in the bank reconciliation as unpresented cheques or outstanding lodgements.

The auditor should check that any material payments to creditors, identified in work on creditors' reconciliations and not recorded on the creditors' statement at the reconciliation date are traced to the unpresented cheque listing.

The auditor should review the detailed list of represented cheques for all large amounts (especially any large round sum amounts) that have not been cleared by the bank since the substantive testing date, and should trace these cheques to original documentation and discuss with the client why they have not been cleared.

With regard to unpresented cheques not cleared by the time the work is carried out, the auditor should:

- Obtain explanations for any large or unusual items;
- Investigate any cheques which have been outstanding for more than six months and consider whether they should be added back to the bank balance.

Existence

The auditor would normally acquire sufficient evidence that recorded bank and cash balances exist by obtaining direct confirmation from the client's bankers. Confirmation should cover all banks with which the client held an account during any part of the period under audit, including payroll and dividend accounts, even though the account might have been closed before the balance sheet date. This should be done to identify possible unrecorded bank borrowings and contingent liabilities.

Many clients' cash balances are immaterial and, depending on the assessment of the risk of misstatement, the auditor may decide not to carry out any substantive testing on them.

In the current circumstances, however, the cash balances are very material and the auditor will need to specifically address them.

The auditor should attend the year end cash count – unannounced. To avoid any possibility that a shortfall could be blamed on the audit staff, it is essential to count cash in the custodian's presence, insist that he or she stays until the count is completed, and ask the custodian to sign the record of the amount counted to confirm acceptance of the findings. The auditor should check the amount counted to the general ledger and to the petty cash records.

Cash funds often include cheques that have been cashed for directors or employees. However, shortages of cash are often concealed by the inclusion of fictitious, forged, or worthless cheques and IOUs in the funds. The auditor should therefore:

- Examine cheques carefully and ensure that they bear a recent date and are not post-dated
- Check that they are subsequently banked and cleared
- Check that there is authority for the issue of IOUs and test that they are repaid subsequently.

Cut-off

The auditor should normally obtain much of the required assurance concerning the cut-off of bank and cash balances from the work on bank reconciliations.

The auditor should identify any significant transfers of funds between two or more of the company's bank accounts in the period prior to the balance sheet date. In respect of such transfers, the auditor should check that receipts and payments are recorded in the accounting records in the same accounting period and that any such items not reflected by the bank in the same accounting period appear in the appropriate bank reconciliation.

The auditor should review the accounting records for evidence of the inclusion of lodgements which were physically received after the balance sheet date.

The auditor should review the lapse of time between the date of issue of unrepresented cheques as recorded in the accounting records and the date of their subsequent presentation at the bank and consider whether any of these cheques might not have been released by the client until after the balance sheet date.

Valuation

If balances are held with reputable banks the auditor should not need to question recoverability.

If there are substantial balances in other countries or currencies, the auditor should determine whether there are any restrictions on the transferability of funds which could affect the value of the asset or which, for any other reason, should be disclosed in the financial statements.

Rights and Obligations

As a rule this objective should be accomplished through the normal bank confirmation procedures.

Presentation and Disclosure

The auditor will normally achieve this objective at the end of the audit by reviewing the financial statements and considering the matters set out in the GAAP checklist. Also, it is important to be alert for any matters that require disclosure or reclassification.

CHAPTER 12

Solution 12.1

The audit test being performed by the audit junior is a typical audit procedure used to search for unrecorded liabilities to gain assurance over the completeness of creditors within the financial statements.

Issue (a)

This relates to goods delivered post year-end. There is therefore no liability in existence at the year-end. The current treatment of this transaction by the company is therefore appropriate, and no audit adjustment is required.

Issue (b)

Although the invoice for these goods has not been received until post year-end, the goods themselves have been delivered pre year-end, and should therefore be accounted for within the December 2008 financial statements. As the value of the goods involved (€/£9,000) is greater than materiality (€/£5,000), an audit adjustment is required to account for this transaction:

Dr	Purchases	£/€9,000
Cr	Accruals	£/€9,000
Dr	Stock (BS)	£/€9,000
Cr	**Stock (IE)**	**£/€9,000**

Issue (c)

This invoice relates to goods received post year-end, and therefore should not be accounted for in the December 2008 accounts. However, the goods are currently included within year-end accruals. This is incorrect, and assuming the goods have also been included within year-end stock, represents an overstatement of accruals and stock in the balance sheet. As the amount involved is material, an audit adjustment is required:

Dr	Accruals	€/£5,000
Cr	Purchases	€/£5,000
Dr	Stock (IE)	€/£5,000
Cr	Stock (BS)	€/£5,000

Issue (d)
Although this invoice relates to goods received pre-year-end which have not been accounted for in the correct period, the amount involved is immaterial and indeed is clearly trifling. As a result no audit adjustment is required.

Solution 12.2

Creditor Reconciliation

- Agree balance per accounts payable to the actual creditors' listing at 31 May 2007
- Agree balance per supplier's statement to actual statements received from supplier
- Check mathematical accuracy of the accounts payable reconciliation
- The payment made of €/£720,000 should be agreed to supporting documentation
- Invoices on statement not on ledger, need to verify that these amounts were not received by LACTIC before the year end or if received have been appropriately accrued
- The auditor should enquire about the date of the statement – 28 May, as it does not coincide with the year end
- Enquire as to why invoice No. 14255 has not been posted to the ledger
- Investigate the reasons for the remaining unreconciled difference of €/£100,000

Solution 12.3

(a)

Analytical procedures means the analysis of relationships between items of data (financial or non-financial) deriving from the same period, or comparable information from different periods or entities, in order to identify consistencies, predicted patterns, significant fluctuations or unexpected relationships, and to investigate the results thereof.

Analytical procedures can be used to obtain audit evidence directly, at the substantive testing stage, in order to detect material misstatements in the financial statements.

(b)

Memorandum

To: Audit Partner
From: Audit Senior
Re: BISTRO Ltd
        Analytical review of operating expenses year ended
        31 March 05
Date: 08/06/05

Expense	Work Required
Insurance	Vouch to insurance to corroborate the explanation given for the increase in insurance costs.

Administration Salaries	Vouch temp salary to payroll records and payments made to person on maternity leave.
Depreciation	Cross-reference and agree to work on fixed assets.
Distribution Costs	– Policy adopted in current year not consistent with prior year. This seems a change in accounting policy and would require a prior year adjustment. This requires further investigation.
	– Sales have increased by 10%. I would expect a direct correlation with distribution costs, but overall distribution costs have decreased. This requires further investigation.
Repairs and Maintenance	– Vouch to supporting invoices.
	– Investigate whether any amounts expensed should have been capitalised and cross-reference to the tangible fixed asset section of file.
Rent and Rates	Vouch to supporting documentation from local authority and cheque payments.

(c) Computer Assisted Audit Techniques could be used in the audit of each significant account balance. Generally they could be used to:-

- Perform additions and calculations
- Select a sample of items for testing e.g. select a sample of trade debtors for confirmation or stock items to test the accuracy of the pricing of items
- Re-perform calculation of extraction of items from stock, debtor and creditor lists
- Perform analytical procedures and comparisons
- Compare data elements in different files for agreement.

Solution 12.4

BARROW Ltd

(a)

At the planning stage the auditor needs to identify audit risks, i.e. the risk that an auditor may give an inappropriate audit opinion on the financial statements. As part of this process the auditor is required to obtain a knowledge of the business to enable them to identify and understand transactions and events that affect the financial statements. The outsourcing of the payroll function is such an event and the following is the information that will need to be obtained.

First, the auditor will need to obtain and document an understanding of the contract between the company and the payroll bureau, and how the company monitors the work carried out by the payroll bureau.

The auditor will need access to the documents to carry out audit work and should enquire who holds the payroll records and, if it is the payroll bureau, arrange with them to gain access to the records.

The degree of authority delegated to the payroll bureau will have to be assessed in the context of evaluating the internal controls of the company. Such issues as who approves payroll payments, who authorises payroll changes, what controls are in place for authorising overtime etc., will form part of this assessment.

The auditor will have to assess the quality of the work of the payroll bureau and this should be planned at the start of the audit. The auditor will assess, at the planning stage, the reputation and expertise the service organisation has in this area.

The auditor will have to report, as part of their audit opinion on Barrow Ltd, whether the company has kept proper accounting records. The quality of the payroll bureau's work will need to be assessed in this context and this should be considered at the planning stage.

(b)

Additional audit procedures may not be necessary as a result of the decision to outsource the payroll function. As part of systems testing the auditor will have assessed control risks relating to the payroll bureau. Provided that the auditor is satisfied that the bureau has the expertise and a good reputation within the industry, it may be possible to reduce the auditor's detailed testing and rely on evidence produced by the bureau. In order to do this the auditor may need to review information from the payroll bureau concerning the design and operation of its control system.

When considering whether to rely on work undertaken by the payroll bureau the auditor considers the professional qualifications, experience and resources of the bureau's personnel.

The auditor will need to obtain representations to confirm balances and transactions from the payroll bureau and inspect records and documents held by them. In some cases the auditor may decide that they need to visit the premises of the bureau to obtain audit evidence.

(c)

The following are the key considerations for the reporting of control weaknesses to the directors of the company:

- SAS 610 *Communication of Audit Matters* obliges the auditor to report "any material weaknesses in the accounting and internal control systems identified during the audit".
- There is a need for the auditor to document the weaknesses based on audit findings.

- There is a need for the auditor to report the potential impact of the weaknesses.
- The auditor will need to consider if further audit work is required as a result of control weaknesses.
- The auditor needs to consider the effects of the weaknesses on the financial statements in arriving at their audit opinion.

CHAPTER 13

Solution 13.1

The following are the audit procedures which would be undertaken in the audit of the increase in share capital:

- Obtain a copy of a company search print out for XYZ Limited
- Review the documents filed during the period under review
- Request/Obtain a copy of the share issue certificates.
- Agree the increase in share capital to the share issue certificates.
- If shares issued were to a director or secretary ensure this is appropriately disclosed in the financial statements.
- Ensure the issue was within the remit of the Memorandum and Articles of Association.
- Vouch the transaction and trace the cash receipt to the Bank Statement.

Solution 13.2

The new shares have been issued at a premium. The following should be completed:

- Ensure the issue of share capital at a premium is in line with the Memorandum and Articles of Association.
- Determine the correct disclosure for the financial statements.
- Propose an audit adjustment to reflect the issue of the new shares.
- Ensure the issue of shares at a premium is correctly disclosed in the financial statements.
- Vouch the transaction.
- Enquire as to why the transaction was not included in the draft accounts.

CHAPTER 14

Solution 14.1

The auditor should conduct the following in order to ensure that they have obtained sufficient evidence about the entity's subsequent events:

- Review management procedures to ensure that subsequent events are identified.
- Read minutes of meetings held by management, shareholders and those charged with governance.
- Enquire of the client's legal counsel.
- Enquire of management.
- Review latest management accounts for unusual trends.

Solution 14.2

The most important period for auditor after the balance sheet date is the time between the year end and up to and including the signing of the audit report.

Solution 14.3

The review of audit papers ensures the following:

- The work completed by audit staff was accurate, thorough and in accordance with the audit programme.
- Judgements exercised by audit staff during the course of the audit were reasonable and appropriate and have been properly documented which will support the audit opinion.
- All audit work has been completed in accordance with the conditions and terms specified in the engagement letter.
- The audit staff have resolved any significant accounting, auditing and reporting questions raised during the audit.
- The review will ensure the audit working papers have been documented in accordance with the International Statements on Auditing and that the firm's quality control policies and procedures have been met.

Solution 14.4

The benefits of final analytical procedures are as follows:

- Final analytical procedures will help reduce the detection risk and may identify a previously unidentified risk of material misstatement that may arise.
- Final analytical procedures will ensure conclusions formed by the auditor during the audit of the financial statements can be supported.
- The auditor can conclude on the reasonableness of the financial statements with added comfort and support.

Solution 14.5

The following are the benefits that arise from performing final analytical procedures:

- Final analytical procedures will help reduce the detection risk and may help identify a previously unidentified risk of material misstatement
- Final analytical procedures provide support for the audit conclusions
- The auditor can conclude on the reasonableness of the financial statements with added comfort and support.

Solution 14.6

Memo to Monitor Limited File

From: A. Senior

Re: Subsequent events procedures

Date: 01/07/XX

Following my meeting with the financial controller on 11 June 20XX the following post-balance sheet events require attention:

Customer gone into liquidation
Further verification work required

- Confirm that the debt was fully provided for and no further provision is required.
- Inspect any liquidator's report to determine if the company will recover any of its debt.
- Consider if any further doubtful debt provisions are necessary in light of this customer going into liquidation.

Other procedures that may need to be carried out:

- Evaluate the effect the loss of this customer will have on future trading and on the going concern assumption.

Change of banking arrangements, review of contracts and proposed sale and leaseback

Further verification work required:

- Inspect latest post-year-end management accounts.
- In light of this new information, extend going concern audit procedures.
- Enquire of management what is their exact intention regarding contracts and what stage they are at regarding the proposed sale and leaseback of premises.

Other procedures that may need to be carried out:

- Consider if there are any further going concern disclosures required in the accounts.
- Consider if there is any impact on the audit opinion based on the revised going concern review.
- Consider if there are any post-balance sheet disclosures required in the financial statements in accordance with IAS 10.
- Consider the accounting impact the proposed sale and leaseback will have on next year's financial statements.

Solution 14.7

(a) Further work

(1) No further work required – bring error straight to schedule of Unadjusted Differences
(2) Verify that bonus should have been accrued in full at the year end and if this is the case enquire as to why it was not.
(3) Confirm that your calculation is correct, e.g. you may have included fully written down assets in your calculation in error.
(4) Verify adjustments to prior-year working papers, ensuring that closing reserves are correct and can be agreed to the closing trial balance.

(b)

CLIENT: SANTA LIMITED

PERIOD END:

Schedule of Unadjusted Differences

Reference Accounting Entries Profit and Loss A/C Balance Sheet

		Balance Sheet		Profit and Loss Account	
		Dr £/€	Cr £/€	Dr £/€	Cr £/€
Dr	Prepayments			50,000	
Cr	Trade Creditors				50,000
	Being correction of misposting				
Dr	Staff bonus costs			150,000	

Cr	Accruals		150,000
	Being correction of understatement of Bonus Costs		
Dr	Depreciation (P/L)	44,000	
Cr	Fixed Assets (B/S)		44,000
	Being correction of depreciation charge		

(c)

The audit partner will need to take the following into account when reviewing the schedule of unadjusted differences (SUDs):

- Materiality of each error – if material the financial statements should be adjusted.
- The reason for the error in payroll – if there is evidence of fraud then this should be reported to the directors and the auditor may have an obligation to report to a third-party regulator.
- The need for further investigation of any matters.
- Whether any of the errors found impact on other aspects of the audit e.g. the reliance the auditor places on internal controls, the auditor's analysis of the integrity of management etc.
- The year on year impact, i.e. may have to review prior-year SUDs.
- The result of any discussion with the client and explanations received.

CHAPTER 15

Solution 15.1

(a)

Implications for Audit Report

Individual Items

Repairs Provision

- MERLIN Ltd is not committed to repairs at year end, as such the provision is not justified in accordance with IAS 37.
- This will result in a qualified opinion disagreement in accounting treatment if the provision is not reversed prior to the approval of the financial statements.

Information Technology General Controls Review

- No audit report implications arise as a result of the weaknesses identified with regard to infrastructure security.
- Whilst an issue exists, this issue does not have any significant impact on the financial statements.

Consultancy Payment

- No impact on the audit report.
- Amount is immaterial and doesn't impair the true and fair view of the financial statements.
- Possible Related Party transaction in accordance with IAS 24 as may be material to the brother. Further audit investigation required. Possible qualified audit report if the auditor considers that appropriate disclosure was not made.

Fixed Assets

- This item has not been correctly treated in accordance with IAS 16.
- However, the amount is immaterial and does not impair the true and fair view of the financial statements.
- As a result, no impact on the audit report.

Management Bonus

- No impact on the audit report.
- Assuming no further information can be obtained to verify the increases on the prior year, the amount is immaterial and doesn't impair the true and fair view of the financial statements.

Overall Opinion

- Any decision regarding the overall opinion is a matter of professional judgement.
- The most likely outcome is a qualified opinion arising as a result of disagreement in accounting treatment regarding the repairs provision, capitalisation of employee costs and management bonus.

(b)

Salary costs included in fixed assets

- Verify that the individuals are employees of the company
- Agree the salary costs to supporting documentation
- Verify that the estimate of percentage involvement of the employee in the capital project is reasonable, by looking at supporting documentation evidencing involvement in the project e.g. attendance at meetings, compilation of reports, timesheets
- Obtain a copy of calculation and check the arithmetic accuracy

(c)

Merlin Limited

Uncorrected Misstatements – Year ended 30 March 2007

Uncorrected Misstatement	Balance Sheet Dr	Balance Sheet Cr	Profit and Loss Dr	Profit and Loss Cr
1				
Repairs Provision				
Provisions	500,000			
Operating expenses				500,000
–				
Repair and Maintenance				
Being provisions not relating to				
Financial year				
2				
Capital Project				
Fixed assets		50,000		

Operating expenses		50,000		
Wages and Salaries		—		
Being expense items incorrectly capitalised				
Total	**500,000**	**50,000**	**50,000**	**500,000**

Solution 15.2

(a) Implications for Audit Report

Issue 1

- This could potentially result in a limitation of scope of the auditor's work if the crash resulted in a loss of evidence that could not be corroborated by alternative audit means.
- However, the creditor information was only lost for one day and this information has been reposted.
- On the basis that there is no issue with the reposted information and it is supportable by source documentation, there is no limitation on scope.
- Therefore on this basis there is no impact on the audit report arising from the crash in the creditor's system.

Issue 2

- IAS 10 states that the bankruptcy of a customer that occurs after the balance sheet date usually confirms that a loss existed at the balance sheet date on a trade receivable and that the entity needs to adjust the carrying amount of the trade receivable.
- Consequently the amount of £/€250,000 should be provided for at the year end.
- In addition the £/€100,000 of additional business would be disclosed as a non-adjusting post-balance sheet event – IAS 10, as the sale took place in the post-balance sheet period.
- The effect of the incorrect treatment has resulted in profit before tax being overstated by £/€250,000 and net assets overstated by the same amount. The level of misstatement is material from an audit reporting point of view as it represents 75% of PBT.
- If unadjusted this would cause the financial statements to be misleading – therefore an adverse opinion will be issued on the basis of a disagreement with management.

Issue 3

- The amounts are quantitatively immaterial.
- They are required to be disclosed by the Companies Acts and consequently will result in a disagreement over the adequacy of disclosure.
- This will likely result in a qualified audit opinion (Except for) and the information omitted from the financial statements will be disclosed in the audit report.

(b)

Adverse Opinion

As more fully explained in Note X to the financial statements, no provision has been made in the financial statements for a significant debtor that went bankrupt in January 2008....

In our opinion, this is not in accordance with International Accounting Standards. In line with IAS 10 "Events after the balance sheet date"....

The bankruptcy of a debtor in the post-balance sheet period confirms that a loss existed at the balance sheet date and consequently provision should have been made for the amount of the irrecoverable debt....

Accordingly, trade debtors and profit for the year should be reduced by €250,000....

In view of the effect of the matter referred to in the preceding paragraph, the financial statements do not give a true and fair view of (or "do not present fairly, in all material respects") the financial position of DENARK Limited as of 31 December 2007, and of its financial performance for the year then ended.

In all other respects, in our opinion, the financial statements have been properly prepared in accordance with the Companies Acts....

Solution 15.3

(a)

Memo to:	Audit partner
From:	A. Senior
Re:	WORLDGLOBAL Limited
	Year ended 31/12/04
Date:	08/06/05

The following is the audit evidence I require and the implication that I see for the audit opinion in respect of the matters raised regarding the above company:

Breach of Covenants

Management has indicated that they have received assurances from their bank that none of the financing facilities would be withdrawn. With the client's permission, I propose communicating with the bank directly and requesting them to confirm this to us in writing. Should we receive such confirmation, this would form part of the basis for our conclusion as to whether the entity is a going concern. The net assets of the company are €/£ 5.5 million. Whether the entity can continue as a going concern in the foreseeable future will depend on the working capital of the entity which I will investigate further. Provided that this investigation proves positive, then the matter will have no implications for our audit report.

If no confirmation is received from the bank and they state that they have not given assurances that none of the financing facilities would be withdrawn, then a going concern issue exists and requires further consideration.

If we conclude, post our analysis of all the pertinent facts, that it is appropriate to prepare the financial statements on a going concern basis and the relevant disclosures in the financial statements are adequate' then an explanatory paragraph should be given in the audit report referring to the relevant disclosures.

If we consider the disclosures to be inadequate but that the entity is a going concern, we should qualify the audit report on the basis of an except for disagreement type qualification as well as giving an explanatory paragraph outlining the going concern uncertainty.

If the financial statements are prepared on a going concern basis and we disagree with that basis and the effect of using that basis is so material or pervasive that the financial statements are seriously misleading, an adverse audit qualification should be given.

Carrying Value of Investment

The company cannot provide us with the evidence we require to support the carrying value of the investment in Horizon Limited. We need to establish if there is any alternative evidence we can use to support the carrying value. I will try to obtain the last financial statements issued by Horizon and review the net asset position of the company. If there is no alternative evidence available then there is a potential limitation of scope issue. The maximum impairment is €/£100k which would reduce the net assets of the company and increase the loss by that amount. Given the loss-making nature of the entity, it could be argued that the amount is material and if we conclude this to be the case then this would lead to an "Except for" limitation in scope qualification.

(b)

The following are the changes required to the standard unqualified audit report:

As normal as far as basis of opinion –

We planned our audit so as to obtain all the information and explanations …. Whether caused by fraud or other irregularities or error. However, the evidence available to us was limited because we were unable to obtain sufficient appropriate audit evidence regarding the carrying value of the financial investment in the balance sheet amounting to €/£100,000. Any adjustment to this figure would have a consequential effect on the loss for the year. There were no other satisfactory audit procedures that we could adopt to confirm that the carrying value of the financial investment was correct.

In forming…

Qualified Opinion Arising from Limitation in Audit Scope

Except for any adjustments that might have been necessary had we been able to obtain sufficient evidence concerning the carrying value of the financial investment, in our opinion the financial statements give a true and fair view….

As indicated above we were unable to satisfy ourselves that the carrying value of the financial assets was correct. In all other respects:

(1) We have obtained all the information and explanations we consider necessary for the purpose of our audit: and
(2) In our opinion proper books of account have been kept by the company.

… Rest as for unqualified opinion

(c)

The following are the checks that should be performed on audit reports prior to signing –

- ensure legal references are correct,
- ensure the page references refer to the actual pages of the financial statements being audited,
- the correct result is reflected in the opinion paragraph i.e. a profit or a loss,
- ensure consistency with relevant GAAP,
- check name of company being audited and year end is correct,
- ensure final audit opinion is correct i.e. unqualified or qualified,
- ensure consistency with audit firm's standard audit report wording,
- two members of staff should "call over" the audit report to ensure the wording is correct.

INDEX

acceptance 15–17
Accounting for Leases (IAS 17) 148
accounting frauds *see* fraud
accounting policies 54
accounts, revised 334
accounts receivable *see* sales and debtors
accuracy
    bank and cash 229–30
    inventory 175–6
    investments 241–2
    purchases and creditors 248
    tangible fixed assets 254–5
additions 145–8
adjustments 285–6
adverse audit opinion 323, 325, 326
aggressive earnings management 80
agreement of balances 207
Allied Crude Vegetable Oil Refining Corporation of New Jersey 165
analytical procedures
    final 283–4
    inventory 170–71
    overview 20, 36, 99, 116–18
    purchases and creditors 259–60
    risk assessment 51
    sales and debtors 200–205, 207
    tangible fixed assets 145
Analytical Procedures (ISA 520) 36, 99, 170–71, 283–4
APB *see* Auditing Practices Board
application controls 124, 126–8
Arthur Andersen 10–11
assertions *see* audit assertions
assessed risks 26, 27–30, 62–8
assets
    contingent 291–2
    misappropriation of 79
    see also tangible fixed assets

assurance engagements 5–7
attribute sampling 112
audit assertions
    bank and cash 228
    inventory 168–9, 172–81
    overview 27–9, 94–6
    purchases and creditors 248
    sales and debtors 188–90
    tangible fixed assets 154–6
audit differences 284–6
Audit Documentation (ISA 230) 33, 35, 300
audit evidence
    analytical procedures 116–19
    and audit assertions 94–6
    audit sampling 108–13
    definition of term 92
    evaluation of 34–5, 68–9, 100
    methods of obtaining 96
    reliability 92–3
    substantive testing 103–4
    sufficiency and appropriateness 34–5, 68–9, 92, 214–16, 299–300
    tests of controls 100–103
    tests of details 104–8
    work of experts 113–16
Audit Evidence (ISA 500) 27–8, 91–2, 93, 94, 168, 187, 208, 228, 231
Audit Evidence – Additional Considerations for Specific Items (ISA 501) 165, 291
audit issues 301–3
audit juniors 24–5
audit materiality *see* materiality
Audit Materiality (ISA 320) 22–4, 35, 38, 183
Audit of Accounting Estimates (ISA 540) 171, 213
audit opinion 38, 309–10, 315
    adverse 323, 325, 326
    disclaimer of opinion 323–6

490 INDEX

qualified 319–22
unqualified 315–19
audit plans 18, 25–30, 32, 144
audit procedures
    for bank and cash 225–36
    designing 27–30
    extent of 64
    for fraud detection 82–4
    for inventory 168–83
    for investments 237–46
    nature of 62–3
    performing 32–4
    for purchases and creditors 247–64
    for sales and debtors 187–216
    for share capital and reserves 272–81
    for tangible fixed assets 145–50
    timing of 30–31, 63–4
    types of 64–8
    see also testing
audit process
    acceptance 15–17
    completion 34–8, 299–303
    documentation 32
    extent of testing 31–32
    communications 17–18, 20, 37
    performing the audit 32–4
    planning 18–30
    timing of procedures 30–31
audit reports
    audit opinion 315–28
    basic aspects 311–14
    electronic publication 333
    further disclosures 328–9
    modified 315, 318–19
    other reporting considerations 330–34
    overview 309–11
    qualified 328
    provisions for listed companies 329–30
audit reviews 299–301
audit risk 18, 46–9, 69–70
audit sampling 108–13
Audit Sampling and Other Means of Testing (ISA 530) 102, 107, 108, 111–12
audit seniors 24, 25
audit strategies 18, 19–25, 32

audit teams 24–5, 81–2
Auditing Practices Board (APB) 10, 80
The Auditor's Procedures in Response to Assessed Risks (ISA 330) 25, 34, 61, 62, 65, 66–7, 100–101, 104
The Auditor's Report on Financial Statements (ISA 700) 35, 183, 309–10, 311, 315–18, 320, 328, 332
The Auditor's Responsibility in Relation to Other Information in Documents Containing Audited Financial Statements (ISA 720) 328–9
The Auditor's Responsibility to Consider Fraud in an Audit of Financial Statements (ISA 240) 76, 78, 79, 81, 83, 85, 87–8
auditors
    change of 16, 332
    liability for negligence 5
    responsibilities 8, 80–81, 86–7
audits 3–7
    see also audit procedures; audit process

bad debts provisions 213–14
balances, agreement of 207
bank
    audit procedures 228–34
    risk of material misstatement 226–8
bank confirmation letters 231–4
block sampling 112
Borrowing Costs (IAS 23) 146
business risk 46, 54–5

CAATs *see* computer-assisted audit techniques
case law 75, 165
cash
    audit procedures 228–31, 234–5
    risk of material misstatement 226–8
cash receipts testing 211–12
circularisation, debtors 208–11
client integrity 15–16
Combined Code on Corporate Governance 12
Communication of Audit Matters With Those Charged With Governance (ISA 260) 37, 301

communications 17–18, 20, 37, 61–2, 81
comparative financial statements 331, 332
Comparatives (ISA 710) 331, 332
competency 16
completeness
    bank and cash 229
    inventory 175
    investments 241–2
    purchases and creditors 248
    share capital and reserves 276–7
    tangible fixed assets 254
computer-assisted audit techniques 85, 128–31, 181–2
computers and auditing
    approach 123–4
    computer-assisted audit techniques 128–31
    controls 124–8
    e-commerce 131–2
confirmation 98
conflicts of interest 16
consolidated financial statements 330
contingent assets 291–2
contingent liabilities 291–2
continuance 15–17
continuous stocktaking 174–5
control risk 48, 144, 167
controls
    application 124, 126–8
    assessment of 21–2
    bank and cash 226–7
    computerised environment 124–8
    correction 124–5
    detection 124–5
    general 124–6
    input 127
    internal control 21–2, 56
    inventory 166–8
    investments 239–40
    limitations 56
    output 128
    payroll 255–7
    preventative 124–5
    processing 128
    purchases and creditors 249–54

    sales system 191–5
    weaknesses in 61–2
    see also tests of controls
conventional costing system 177–8
corporate governance 11–12
correction controls 124–5
corresponding figures 331–2
costing systems
    conventional 177–8
    standard 177, 179
creditors *see* purchases and creditors
cut-off testing
    bank and cash 229–30
    inventory 180
    investments 243
    purchases and creditors 262
    sales and debtors 212–13

debtors *see* sales and debtors
debtors circularisation 208–11
depreciation 149–50
details, tests of *see* tests of details
detection controls 124–5
detection risk 46, 48–9, 144
directors
    loans to 216
    responsibilities 8, 80–81
disagreement 302, 320–21
disclaimer of opinion 323–6
disclosures
    adequacy of 68
    bank and cash 230–31
    inventory 181
    investments 244
    sales and debtors 215
    share capital and reserves 277
    tangible fixed assets 152–4, 156
discounts 207
disposals 148–9
dividends 328
documentation
    audit plans and strategies 32
    filing and retention 38
    fraud detection and prevention 87–8
    performance of audit 33–4, 69

492   INDEX

results of testing 69
tangible fixed assets 151–2

e-commerce 131
earnings management 80
emphasis of matter 327–8
employee records 89
engagement letters 17–18, 39–40
engagement teams *see* audit teams
Enron 5, 10–11
Enterprise Resource Planning systems 122
entity, understanding of 49–56
ERP *see* Enterprise Resource Planning systems
error
    expected 111
    and fraud 76–81
    tolerable 111
ESs *see* Ethical Standards
ethical framework 10–11
Ethical Standards (ESs) 10–11
Events After the Balance Sheet Date (IAS 10) 287, 288
evidence *see* audit evidence
existence
    bank and cash 229
    inventory 172–5
    investments 242
    purchases and creditors 248
    share capital and reserves 276
    tangible fixed assets 154
expected error 111
expenses 61
experts, work of 113–16
External Confirmations (ISA 505) 208–11

fictitious suppliers 89
final analytical procedures 283–4
Financial Instruments (IFRS 7) 238
Financial Instruments: Recognition and Measurement (IAS 39) 238
financial performance 55
financial reporting, fraudulent 78–9
financial reporting framework 53
financial statements
    comparative 331, 332

consolidated 330
electronic publication 333
summary 334
users of 4–5
finished goods 165, 177–9
fixed asset registers 152
fraud
    accounting frauds 5
    aggressive earnings management 80
    and CAATs 85
    case law 75
    characteristics 78–80
    and current environment 88–90
    detection policies and procedures 82–4
    discussion among engagement team 81–2
    documentation 87–8
    duty and right to report 86–7
    and error 76–81
    management representations 85
    risk factors 78
    steps to prevent 90
fraud risk 61, 78
fraud triangle 76–7
fraudulent financial reporting 78–9

general controls 124–6
going concern 37, 49, 292–6
Going Concern (ISA 570) 37, 292–3, 295
group reporting 330

identity theft 89–90
IFAC *see* International Federation of Accountants
IFRSs *see* International Financial Reporting Standards
impairment 150
Impairment of Assets (IAS 36) 150
independence 16
industry conditions 53
inherent risk 48, 144
initial engagements 333
Initial Engagements – Opening Balances (ISA 510) 333
input controls 127
inquiry 50–51, 96–7

INDEX   493

inspection 20, 51, 97
Integrity, Objectivity and Independence (ES 1) 11
interim reports 334
internal control *see* controls
International Federation of Accountants (IFAC) 10
International Financial Reporting Standards (IFRSs) 313
International Framework for Assurance Engagements (IAASB) 5
International Standards on Auditing (ISAs) 6, 10, 313
Inventories (IAS 2) 171, 176, 181
inventory
    audit procedures 168–83
    controls over 166–8
    counting 172–5
    definition of term 165
    risk of material misstatement 166
    theft of 89
    valuation 176–9
inventory provisions 179–80
Investment Property (IAS 40) 149
investments 237–46
Irish Woollen Co Ltd vs Tyson and Others 75
ISAs *see* International Standards on Auditing
IT *see* computers and auditing
IT operations 125
IT security 125–6
IT system change controls 126

judgmental sampling 109

Kingston Cotton Mill Co Ltd 75, 165

letters of weakness 298–9
liabilities 247
    contingent 291–2
limitation on scope 302–3, 320
listed companies 7, 329–30
loans 216

maintenance 148
management letters 298–9
management override 61, 79

management representations 85, 296–8
Management Representations (ISA 580) 296–8
managers 24, 25
material misstatements, risk of 46, 47–8, 49–50, 57–61, 166, 226–8, 238–40
materiality 22–4, 35, 49, 69–70, 111
McKesson and Robbins Inc 165
misappropriation of assets 79
misstatements, evaluation 35
    see also material misstatements
Modifications to the Independent Auditor's Report (ISA 701) 38, 310, 315, 319–20, 321, 323, 324, 327–8
modified audit reports 318–19
monetary unit sampling *see* value weighted selection
multi-stage sampling 112

negative circularisation 208–9
negligence 5
net realisable value 176, 177

objectives 54–5
Objectives and General Principles Governing and Audit of Financial Statements (ISA 200) 4, 10, 17, 47–8, 49, 84, 284
obligations *see* rights and obligations
observation 20, 51, 98
Obtaining an Understanding of the Entity and its Environment and Assessing the Risks of Material Misstatement (ISA 315) 21, 45, 46, 49–50, 52, 56, 59–60, 104, 166, 182, 226, 238–9
opening balances 145, 169–70, 333
output controls 128
ownership
    inventory 180–81
    investments 242
    tangible fixed assets 151–2, 156

Parmalat 5
partners 24–25, 299–300
payroll 255–8
Planning an Audit of Financial Statements (ISA 300) 16, 18, 24, 32

positive circularisation 209
post-year-end cash receipts testing 211–12
post-year-end returns testing 212–13
preliminary announcements 334
presentation
   adequacy of 68
   inventory 181
   investments 244
   share capital and reserves 277
   tangible fixed assets 156
preventative controls 124–5
processing controls 128
Property, Plant and Equipment (IAS 16) 141, 145–8, 151, 152–4
provisions 290–91
Provisions, Contingent Liabilities and Contingent Assets (IAS 37) 290
purchases and creditors
   audit procedures 249–54, 258–64
   controls 249–54
   overview 247–8
   payroll 255–8

qualified audit opinion 319–22, 328
Quality Control for Audits of Historical Financial Information (ISA 220) 15, 34

random sampling 111
raw materials 165, 177
recalculation 98–9
recession and fraud 88–90
recorded sales testing 206
regulatory bodies, audit of returns to 7
regulatory framework 10
repairs 148
re-performance 99
reserves 272–81
retained earnings *see* reserves
retention of title 172
returns testing 206, 212–13
revaluation of fixed assets 151
revenue recognition 61
revised accounts 334
rights and obligations
   share capital and reserves 277
   tangible fixed assets 156

risk
   assessed risks 26, 27–30, 62–8
   audit risk 18, 46–9, 69–70
   business risk 46, 54–5
   control risk 48, 144
   detection risk 46, 48–9, 144
   fraud risk 61, 78
   inherent risk 48, 144
   of material misstatement 46, 47–8, 49–50, 57–61, 166, 226–8, 238–40
   significant risks 59–61
risk assessment process
   audit risk 46–9, 69–70
   business risk 46
   communication of weaknesses 61–2
   documentation 69
   presentation and disclosure 68
   procedures 21–2, 50–52
   response to assessed risks 62–8
   risk of material misstatement 49–61
   sufficiency of audit evidence 68–9
roles, audit team members 24–5

sales and debtors
   analytical procedures 200–205, 207
   assertions 188–90
   components of efficient cycle 195–7
   loans 216
   overview 187–8
   sales system 190–95
   substantive testing 199–200
   sufficiency of audit evidence 214–16
   tests of controls 197–9
   tests of details 205–14
sales discounts testing 207
sales returns testing 206, 212–13
sampling 108–13
share capital 272–81
significant risks 59–61
significant uncertainty 303
simple random sampling 111
Special Considerations – Audits of Group Financial Statements (ISA 600) 330
standard costing system 177, 179
statutory framework 7–9

statistical sampling 110
stock *see* inventory
stocktaking 172–5
strategies 54–5
   see also audit strategies
stratified sampling 112
Subsequent Events (ISA 560) 286–90
subsequent events reviews 36–7, 286–90, 334
substantive testing
   computerised environment 130–31
   overview 29–30, 67–8, 103–4
   purchases and creditors 258–64
   sales and debtors 199–200
   see also analytical procedures; tests of details
summary financial statements 334
summary of errors 285–6
suppliers, fictitious 89
systematic selection 112
systems-based audit approach 40

tangible fixed assets
   associated risks 142
   audit objectives 142–4
   audit procedures 145–50
   definition 141
   disclosure requirements 152–4
   documentary evidence 151–2
   fixed asset register 152
   impairment review 150
   revaluation 151
Terms of Audit Engagements (ISA 210) 17–18, 39–40, 80
testing
   extent of 31–2, 64
   nature of 29–30, 62–3
   see also audit procedures; substantive testing; tests of controls; tests of details

tests of controls
   appropriateness of 26
   bank and cash 227–8
   computerised environment 129–30
   extent of 67
   inventory 168
   investments 240
   nature of 65–6
   overview 29–30, 100–103
   purchases and creditors 252–4, 258
   sales and debtors 197–9
   timing of 66–7
tests of details
   inventory 171–2
   overview 104–8
   purchases and creditors 258, 260–64
   sales and debtors 205–14
   tangible fixed assets 145, 150
timing, audit procedures 30–31
tolerable error 111

understanding of the entity 49–56
unqualified audit opinion 315–19
Using the Work of an Expert (ISA 620) 113–14, 151, 171

valuation
   bank and cash 230
   inventory 176–9
   investments 243
   tangible fixed assets 155
value weighted selection 112

work in progress 165, 177–9
work of experts 113–16, 151
World-Com 5

Xerox 5